"The repackaging of classics is a tried and trusted winner, but Tim Coates has come up with something entirely original: the repackaging of history. His **uncovered editions** *collect papers from the archive of The Stationery Office into verbatim narratives, so, for instance, in* UFOs in the House of Lords *we get a hilarious recreation, directly from Hansard, of a nutty debate that took place in 1979 ... This is inspired publishing, not only archivally valuable but capable of bringing the past back to life without the usual filter of academic or biographer."* **Guardian**

"The Irish Uprising is a little treasure of a book and anyone with an interest in Irish history will really enjoy it. Its structure is extremely unusual as it is compiled from historic official reports published by the British government from 1914 to 1920 ... For anyone studying this period of history The Irish Uprising *is a must as the correspondence and accounts within it are extremely illuminating and the subtle nuances of meaning can be teased out of the terms and phrasing to be more revelatory than the actual words themselves."* **Irish Press, Belfast**

"Voyeurs of all ages will enjoy the original text of the Denning report on Profumo. It is infinitely superior to the film version of the scandal, containing such gems as: 'One night I was invited to a dinner party at the home of a very, very rich man. After I arrived, I discovered it was rather an unusual dinner party. All the guests had taken off their clothes ... The most intriguing person was a man with a black mask over his face. At first I thought this was a party gimmick. But the truth was that this man is so well known and holds such a responsible position that he did not want to be associated with anything improper.'" **Times Higher Education Supplement**

"Very good to read ... insight into important things ... inexorably moving ... If you want to read about the Titanic, *you won't read a better thing ... a revelation."* **Open Book, BBC Radio 4**

*"Congratulations to The Stationery Office for unearthing and reissuing such an enjoyable vignette" [*on *Wilfrid Blunt's Egyptian Garden]* **The Spectator**

uncovered editions
www.uncovered-editions.co.uk

Series editor: Tim Coates
Managing editor: Michele Staple

Other titles in the series

The Amritsar Massacre: General Dyer in the Punjab, 1919
Attack on Pearl Harbor, 1941
Bloody Sunday, 1972: Lord Widgery's Report
The Boer War: Ladysmith and Mafeking, 1900
British Battles of World War I, 1914–15
The British Invasion of Tibet: Colonel Younghusband, 1904
Defeat at Gallipoli: the Dardanelles Commission Part II, 1915–16
D Day to VE Day: General Eisenhower's Report, 1944–45
Escape from Germany, 1939–45
Florence Nightingale and the Crimea, 1854–55
The Irish Uprising, 1914–21
John Profumo and Christine Keeler, 1963
The Judgment of Nuremberg, 1946
King Guezo of Dahomey, 1850–52
Letters of Henry VIII, 1526–29
Lord Kitchener and Winston Churchill: the Dardanelles Commission Part I, 1914–15
The Loss of the Titanic, 1912
R.101: the Airship Disaster, 1930
Rillington Place, 1949
The Russian Revolution, 1917
The Siege of Kars, 1855
The Siege of the Peking Embassy, 1900
The Strange Story of Adolf Beck
Tragedy at Bethnal Green
Travels in Mongolia, 1902
UFOs in the House of Lords, 1979
War in the Falklands, 1982
War 1914: Punishing the Serbs
War 1939: Dealing with Adolf Hitler
Wilfrid Blunt's Egyptian Garden: Fox-hunting in Cairo

Other compendium titles in the *uncovered editions* series

The Siege Collection
The World War I Collection
The World War II Collection

Forthcoming titles

The Assassination of John F Kennedy, 1963
The Cuban Missile Crisis, 1962
The Great Train Robbery, 1963
Mr Hosie's Journey to Tibet, 1904
St Valentine's Day Massacre, 1929
Trials of Oscar Wilde
UFOs in the US, 1947

uncovered editions

TRAGIC JOURNEYS

∞⊗⊗∞

THE LOSS OF THE *TITANIC*, 1912

R.101: THE AIRSHIP DISASTER, 1930

THE MUNICH AIR CRASH, 1958

London: The Stationery Office

© The Stationery Office 2001

Applications for reproduction should be made in writing to
The Stationery Office Limited, St Crispins, Duke Street, Norwich NR3 1PD.

ISBN 0 11 702465 1

The Loss of the Titanic, 1912 was first published as Cd 6352, 1912; Cd 6738, 1913; and as
RMS "Titanic": Reappraisal of Evidence Relating to SS "Californian" (HMSO, 1992).
© Crown copyright
Also available separately, ISBN 0117024031, © The Stationery Office 1999.

R. 101: the Airship Disaster, 1930 was first published by HMSO as Cmd. 3825 (1931).
© Crown copyright
Also available separately, ISBN 0117024074, © The Stationery Office 1999.

The Munich Air Crash was first published by HMSO as CAP 153 (1959), CAP 167 (1960) and
CAP 318 (1969).
© Crown copyright

A CIP catalogue record for this book is available from the British Library.

Cover photograph © (top) Corbis; (middle) Nick le Neve Walmsley/Airship Heritage Trust;
(lower) Hulton/Archive.
Maps on page 246 produced by Sandra Lockwood of Artworks Design, Norwich.

Typeset by J&L Composition Ltd, Filey, North Yorkshire.
Printed in the United Kingdom by The Stationery Office, London.
TJ4396 C30 8/01 652829 19585

CONTENTS

About the series

Uncovered editions are historic official papers which have not previously been available in a popular form.
The series has been created directly from the archive of The Stationery Office in London, and the books have been chosen for the quality of their story-telling. Some subjects are familiar, but others are less well known.
Each is a moment in history.

About the series editor, Tim Coates

Tim Coates studied at University College, Oxford and at the University of Stirling. After working in the theatre for a number of years, he took up bookselling and became managing director, firstly of Sherratt and Hughes bookshops, and then of Waterstone's. He is known for his support for foreign literature, particularly from the Czech Republic. The idea for *uncovered editions* came while searching through the bookshelves of his late father-in-law, Air Commodore Patrick Cave OBE. He is married to Bridget Cave, has two sons, and lives in London.

Tim Coates welcomes views and ideas on the *uncovered editions* series. He can be e-mailed at tim.coates@theso.co.uk

THE LOSS OF THE TITANIC, *1912*

REPORT OF THE FORMAL INVESTIGATION AND A REAPPRAISAL OF THE EVIDENCE RELATING TO THE SS CALIFORNIAN

CONTENTS

SELECTED GLOSSARY OF NAUTICAL TERMS

abaft	towards the rear (stern) of the ship
aft	near or towards the stern of the ship
amidships	in or towards the middle of the ship
boat deck	upper deck on which lifeboats are stored
bow	front of the boat
bulkhead	vertical partition separating compartments in a ship
coaming	vertical piece around the edge of a hatch to prevent water on deck from running below
cofferdam	a watertight enclosure from which water is pumped to expose bottom
CQD	general distress signal in Morse code
davit	crane for hoisting/lowering boats
forecastle	short raised deck at the bow of the ship
freeboard	the minimum vertical distance from the surface of the water to the gunwale
gunwale	the upper edge of a boat's sides
MGY	*Titanic's* call letters, in Morse code
Orlop deck	lowest deck in the ship
poop	partial deck above the main stern deck
port	the left side of a boat when looking forward
starboard	the right side of a boat when looking forward
stern	the back of the boat
weather deck	deck having no overhead protection from the weather

On the 11th April 1912, the White Star liner SS Titanic set sail from Queenstown (now known as Cobh) in Ireland on her maiden voyage towards New York. Three days later, on 14th April, at about 11.40 pm ship's time, she collided with an iceberg. The ship sank less than two-and-three-quarter hours later, with the loss of 1,490 lives.

This is the report of the government inquiry into the loss of the SS Titanic, which was initiated immediately after the disaster. Lord Mersey, as Wreck Commissioner, headed the formal investigation, assisted by five assessors. Their findings, published in July 1912, were unanimous: "that the loss of the said ship was due to collision with an iceberg, brought about by the excessive speed at which the ship was being navigated."

Also accompanying this report is a return of the expenses incurred by the Board of Trade and other government departments at the time of the inquiry, which was held during May, June and July 1912. The list includes the surviving crew members and their respective positions on board the Titanic.

The book concludes with a reappraisal of the evidence relating to the SS Californian, which was instigated in 1990 by the Right Honourable Cecil Parkinson MP, following the discovery of the wreck of the Titanic in 1985.

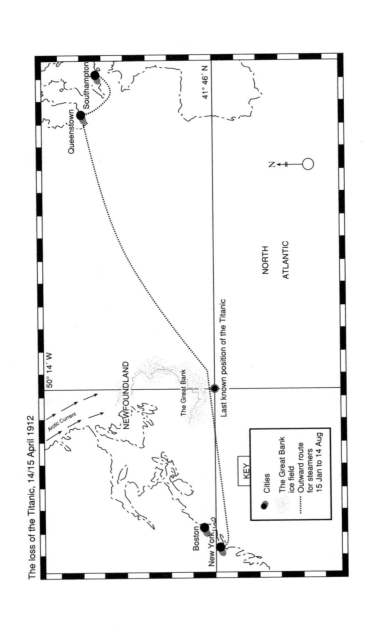

The loss of the Titanic, 14/15 April 1912

NORTH ATLANTIC

NEWFOUNDLAND

The Great Bank

Arctic Current

Southampton

Queenstown

Boston

New York

Last known position of the Titanic

41° 46' N

50° 14' W

N

KEY

● Cities

The Great Bank ice field

Outward route for steamers 15 Jan to 14 Aug

REPORT OF THE COURT
ON THE LOSS OF THE TITANIC

The Court, having carefully enquired into the circumstances of the above-mentioned shipping casualty, finds, for the reasons appearing in the following account, that the loss of the said ship was due to collision with an iceberg, brought about by the excessive speed at which the ship was being navigated.

Dated this 30th day of July, 1912.

MERSEY
Wreck Commissioner

We concur in the above report.
ARTHUR GOUGH-CALTHORPE
A W CLARKE
F C A LYON   } *Assessors*
J H BILES
EDWARD C CHASTON

INTRODUCTION

On the 23rd April, 1912, the Lord Chancellor appointed a Wreck Commissioner under the Merchant Shipping Acts, and on the 26th April the Home Secretary nominated five assessors. On the 30th April the Board of Trade requested that a Formal Investigation of the circumstances attending the loss of the Steamship *Titanic* should be held, and the Court accordingly commenced to sit on 2nd May. Since that date there have been 37 public sittings, at which 97 witnesses have been examined, while a large number of documents, charts and plans have been produced. The 26 questions formulated by the Board of Trade, which are set out in detail below, appear to cover all the circumstances to be enquired into. Briefly summarised, they deal with the history of the ship, her design, construction, size, speed, general equipment, life-saving apparatus, wireless installation, her orders and course, her passengers, her crew, their training, organisation, and discipline. They request an account of the casualty, its cause and effect, and of the means taken for saving those on board the ship, and they call for a report on the efficiency of the rules and regulations made by the Board of Trade under the Merchant Shipping Acts and on their administration, and, finally, for any recommendations to obviate similar disasters which may appear to the Court to be desirable. The 26 questions as subsequently amended are here attached:

1   When the *Titanic* left Queenstown on or about 11th April last:
    (a) What was the total number of persons employed in any capacity on board her, and what were their respective ratings?
    (b) What was the total number of her passengers, distinguishing sexes and classes, and discriminating between adults and children?
2   Before leaving Queenstown on or about 11th April last did the *Titanic* comply with the requirements of the Merchant Shipping Acts,

1894–1906, and the rules and regulations made thereunder with regard to the safety and otherwise of "passenger steamers" and "emigrant ships"?

3 In the actual design and construction of the *Titanic* what special provisions were made for the safety of the vessel and the lives of those on board in the event of collisions and other casualties?

4 Was the *Titanic* sufficiently and efficiently officered and manned? Were the watches of the officers and crew usual and proper? Was the *Titanic* supplied with proper charts?

5 What was the number of the boats of any kind on board the *Titanic*? Were the arrangements for manning and launching the boats on board the *Titanic* in case of emergency proper and sufficient? Had a boat drill been held on board, and, if so, when? What was the carrying capacity of the respective boats?

6 What installations for receiving and transmitting messages by wireless telegraphy were on board the *Titanic*? How many operators were employed on working such installations? Were the installations in good and effective working order, and were the number of operators sufficient to enable messages to be received and transmitted continuously by day and night?

7 At or prior to the sailing of the *Titanic* what, if any, instructions as to navigation were given to the Master or known by him to apply to her voyage? Were such instructions, if any, safe, proper and adequate, having regard to time of year and dangers likely to be encountered during the voyage?

8 What was in fact the track taken by the *Titanic* in crossing the Atlantic Ocean? Did she keep to the track usually followed by liners on voyages from the United Kingdom to New York in the month of April? Are such tracks safe tracks at that time of the year? Had the Master any and, if so, what discretion as regards the track to be taken?

9 After leaving Queenstown on or about the 11th April last did information reach the *Titanic* by wireless messages or otherwise by signals of the existence of ice in certain latitudes? If so, what were such messages or signals and when were they received, and in what position or positions was the ice reported to be, and was the ice reported in or near the track actually being followed by the *Titanic*? Was her course altered in consequence of receiving such information, and, if so, in what way? What replies to such messages or signals did the *Titanic* send, and at what times?

10 If at the times referred to in the last preceding question or later the *Titanic* was warned of or had reason to suppose she would encounter ice, at what time might she have reasonably expected to encounter it? Was a good and proper look-out for ice kept on board? Were any and, if so, what directions given to vary the speed — if so, were they carried out?

11 Were binoculars provided for and used by the look-out men? Is the use of them necessary or usual in such circumstances? Had the *Titanic* the means of throwing searchlights around her? If so, did she make use of

them to discover ice? Should searchlights have been provided and used?

12 What other precautions were taken by the *Titanic* in anticipation of meeting ice? Were they such as are usually adopted by vessels being navigated in waters where ice may be expected to be encountered?

13 Was ice seen and reported by anybody on board the *Titanic* before the casualty occurred? If so, what measures were taken by the officer on watch to avoid it? Were they proper measures and were they promptly taken?

14 What was the speed of the *Titanic* shortly before and at the moment of the casualty? Was such speed excessive under the circumstances?

15 What was the nature of the casualty which happened to the *Titanic* at or about 11.45 pm on the 14th April last? In what latitude and longitude did the casualty occur?

16 What steps were taken immediately on the happening of the casualty? How long after the casualty was its seriousness realised by those in charge of the vessel? What steps were then taken? What endeavours were made to save the lives of those on board and to prevent the vessel from sinking?

17 Was proper discipline maintained on board after the casualty occurred?

18 What messages for assistance were sent by the *Titanic* after the casualty and at what times respectively? What messages were received by her in response and at what times respectively? By what vessels were the messages that were sent by the *Titanic* received, and from what vessels did she receive answers? What vessels other than the *Titanic* sent or received messages at or shortly after the casualty in connection with such casualty? What were the vessels that sent or received such messages? Were any vessels prevented from going to the assistance of the *Titanic* or her boats owing to messages received from the *Titanic* or owing to any erroneous messages being sent or received? In regard to such erroneous messages, from what vessels were they sent, and by what vessels were they received and at what times respectively?

19 Was the apparatus for lowering the boats on the *Titanic* at the time of the casualty in good working order? Were the boats swung out, filled, lowered, or otherwise put into the water and got away under proper superintendence? Were the boats sent away in seaworthy condition and properly manned, equipped and provisioned? Did the boats, whether those under davits or otherwise, prove to be efficient and serviceable for the purpose of saving life?

20 What was the number of (a) passengers, (b) crew taken away in each boat on leaving the vessel? How was this number made up, having regard to:

1 Sex
2 Class
3 Rating

How many were children and how many adults? Did each boat carry its full load and, if not, why not?

21 How many persons on board the *Titanic* at the time of the casualty were ultimately rescued and by what means? How many lost their lives prior to the arrival of the SS *Carpathia* in New York? What was the number of passengers distinguishing between men and women and adults and children of the first, second, and third classes respectively who were saved? What was the number of the crew, discriminating their ratings and sex, that were saved? What is the proportion which each of these numbers bears to the corresponding total number on board immediately before the casualty? What reason is there for the disproportion, if any?

22 What happened to the vessel from the happening of the casualty until she foundered?

23 Where and at what time did the *Titanic* founder?

24 What was the cause of the loss of the *Titanic*, and of the loss of life which thereby ensued or occurred? What vessels had the opportunity of rendering assistance to the *Titanic*, and, if any, how was it that assistance did not reach the *Titanic* before the SS *Carpathia* arrived? Was the construction of the vessel and its arrangements such as to make it difficult for any class of passenger or any portion of the crew to take full advantage of any of the existing provisions for safety?

25 When the *Titanic* left Queenstown on or about 11th April last was she properly constructed and adequately equipped as a passenger steamer and emigrant ship for the Atlantic service?

26 The Court is invited to report upon the Rules and Regulations made under the Merchant Shipping Acts, 1894–1906, and the administration of those Acts and of such Rules and Regulations, so far as the consideration thereof is material to this casualty, and to make any recommendations or suggestions that it may think fit, having regard to the circumstances of the casualty, with a view to promoting the safety of vessels and persons at sea.

In framing this report it has seemed best to divide it into sections in the following manner:

1 A description of the ship as she left Southampton on the 10th of April and of her equipment, crew and passengers

2 An account of her journey across the Atlantic, of the messages she received and of the disaster

3 A description of the damage to the ship and of its gradual and final effect with observations thereon

4 An account of the saving and rescue of those who survived

5 The circumstances in connection with the SS *Californian*

6 An account of the Board of Trade's administration

7 The finding of the Court on the questions submitted, and

8 The recommendations held to be desirable.

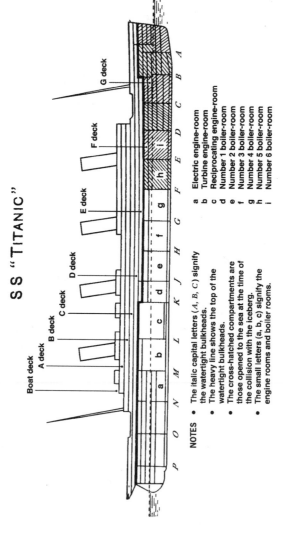

S S "TITANIC"

NOTES
- The italic capital letters (A, B, C) signify the watertight bulkheads.
- The heavy line shows the top of the watertight bulkheads.
- The cross-hatched compartments are those opened to the sea at the time of the collision with the iceberg.
- The small letters (a, b, c) signify the engine rooms and boiler rooms.

a   Electric engine-room
b   Turbine engine-room
c   Reciprocating engine-room
d   Number 1 boiler-room
e   Number 2 boiler-room
f   Number 3 boiler-room
g   Number 4 boiler-room
h   Number 5 boiler-room
i   Number 6 boiler-room

DESCRIPTION OF THE SHIP

THE WHITE STAR LINE

The *Titanic* was one of a fleet of 13 ships employed in the transport of passengers, mails, and cargo between Great Britain and the United States, the usual ports of call for the service in which she was engaged being Southampton, Cherbourg, Plymouth, Queenstown and New York.

The owners are the Oceanic Steam Navigation Company Limited, usually known as the White Star Line, a British registered company with a capital of £750,000, all paid up, the directors being Mr J Bruce Ismay (Chairman), the Right Hon. Lord Pirrie, and Mr H A Sanderson.

The Company are owners of 29 steamers and tenders; they have a large interest in 13 other steamers, and also own a training sailing ship for officers.

All the shares of the Company, with the exception of eight held by Messrs E C Grenfell, Vivian H Smith, W S M Burns, James Gray, J Bruce Ismay, H A Sanderson, A Kerr and the Right Hon. Lord Pirrie, have, since the year 1902, been held by the International Navigation Company Limited, of Liverpool, a British registered company with a capital of £700,000, of which all is paid up, the directors being Mr J Bruce Ismay (Chairman), and Messrs H A Sanderson, Charles F Torrey and H Concanon.

The debentures of the Company, £1,250,000, are held mainly, if not entirely, in the United Kingdom by the general public.

The International Navigation Company Limited, of Liverpool, in addition to holding the above-mentioned shares of the Oceanic Steam Navigation Company Limited, is also the owner of:

1 Practically the whole of the issued share capital of the British and North Atlantic Steam Navigation Company Limited, and the Mississippi and Dominion Steamship Company Limited (the Dominion Line)
2 Practically the whole of the issued share capital of the Atlantic Transport Company Limited (the Atlantic Transport Line)
3 Practically the whole of the issued ordinary share capital and about one-half of the preference share capital of Frederick Leyland and Company Limited (the Leyland Line).

As against the above-mentioned shares and other property, the International Navigation Company Limited have issued share lien certificates for £25,000,000.

Both the shares and share lien certificates of the International Navigation Company Limited are now held by the International Mercantile Marine Company of New Jersey, or by trustees for the holders of its debenture bonds.

THE STEAMSHIP *TITANIC*

The *Titanic* was a three-screw vessel of 46,328 tons gross and 21,831 net register tons, built by Messrs Harland and Wolff for the White Star Line service between Southampton and New York. She was registered as a British steamship at the port of Liverpool, her official number being 131,428. Her registered dimensions were:

Length	852.50 ft
Breadth	92.50 ft
Depth from top of keel to top of beam at lowest point of sheer of C deck, the highest deck, which extends continuously from bow to stern	64.75 ft
Depth of hold	59.58 ft
Height from B to C deck	9.00 ft
Height from A to B deck	9.00 ft
Height from Boat to A deck	9.50 ft
Height from Boat deck to waterline amidships at time of accident about	60.50 ft
Displacement at 34 ft 7 in	52,310 tons

The propelling machinery consisted of two sets of four-cylinder reciprocating engines, each driving a wing propeller, and a turbine driving the centre propeller. The registered horse-power of the propelling machinery was 50,000. The power which would probably have been developed was at least 55,000.

	Height to next deck above		Distance from 34 ft 7 in waterline amidships			
			Above		Below	
	ft	in	ft	in	ft	in
Boat deck, length about 500 ft	–		58	0	–	
A deck, length about 500 ft	9	6	48	6	–	
B deck, length about 550 ft with						
125 ft forecastle and 105 ft poop	9	0	39	6	–	
C deck, whole length of ship	9	0	30	6	–	
D deck, whole length of ship	10	6	20	0	–	
			(tapered down at ends)			
E deck, whole length of ship	9	0	11	0	–	
F deck, whole length of ship	8	6	2	6	–	
G deck, 190 ft forward of boilers,						
210 ft aft of machinery	8	0	–		5	6
Orlop deck, 190 ft forward of boilers,						
210 ft aft of machinery	8	0	–		13	6

C, D, E and F were continuous from end to end of the ship. The decks above these were continuous for the greater part of the ship, extending from amidships both forward and aft. The Boat deck and A deck each had two expansion joints, which broke the strength continuity. The decks below were continuous outside the boiler- and engine-rooms and extended to the ends of the ship. Except in small patches, none of these decks was watertight in the steel parts, except the weather deck and the Orlop deck aft.

Structural arrangements

The *Titanic* consisted primarily of:

1 *An outer shell* This was made of steel plating, giving form to the ship up to the top decks.
2 *Steel decks* These were enumerated according to the table above.
3 *Transverse vertical bulkheads* There were 15 of these, by which the ship was divided lengthwise into 16 separate compartments. These bulkheads are referred to as A to P, commencing forward.

Watertightness

The watertightness of the bulkheads extended up to one or other of the decks D or E; the bulkhead A extended to C, but was only watertight to D deck. The position of the D, E and F decks, which were the only ones to which the watertight bulkheads extended, was in relation to the waterline (34 ft 7 in draught) approximately as follows:

	Height above waterline (34 ft 7 in)		
	Lowest part amidships	At bow	At stern
	ft in	ft in	ft in
D	20 0	33 0	25 0
E	11 0	24 0	16 0
F	2 6	15 6	7 6

These were the three of the four decks which, as already stated, were continuous, all fore and aft. The other decks, G and Orlop, which extended only along a part of the ship, were spaced about 8 ft apart. The G deck forward was about 7 ft 6 in above the waterline at the bow and about level with the waterline at bulkhead D, which was at the fore end of boilers. The G deck aft and the Orlop deck at both ends of the vessel were below the waterline. The Orlop deck abaft of the turbine engine-room and forward of the collision bulkhead was watertight. Elsewhere, except in very small patches, the decks were not watertight. All the decks had large openings or hatchways in them in each compartment, so that water could rise freely through them.

There was also a watertight inner bottom, or tank top, about 5 ft above the top of the keel, which extended for the full breadth of the vessel from bulkhead A to 20 ft before bulkhead P — i.e. for the whole length of the vessel except a small distance at each end. The transverse watertight divisions of this double bottom practically coincided with the watertight transverse bulkheads; there was an additional watertight division under the middle of the reciprocating engine-room compartment (between bulkheads K and L). There were three longitudinal watertight divisions in the double bottom, one at the centre of the ship, extending for about 670 ft, and one on each side, extending for 447 ft.

All the transverse bulkheads were carried up watertight to at least the height of the E deck. Bulkheads A and B, and all bulkheads from K (90 ft abaft amidships) to P, both inclusive, further extended watertight up to the underside of D deck. A bulkhead further extended to C deck, but it was watertight only to D deck.

Bulkheads A and B forward, and P aft, had no openings in them. All the other bulkheads had openings in them, which were fitted with watertight doors. Bulkheads D to O, both inclusive, had each a vertical sliding watertight door at the level of the floor of the engine- and boiler-rooms for the use of the engineers and firemen. On the Orlop deck there was one door, on bulkhead N, for access to the refrigerator rooms. On G deck there were no watertight doors in the bulkheads. On both the F and E decks nearly all the bulkheads had watertight doors, mainly for giving communication between the different blocks of passenger accommodation. All the doors, except those in the engine-rooms and boiler-rooms, were horizontal sliding doors workable by hand both at the door and at the deck above.

There were twelve vertical sliding watertight doors which completed the watertightness of bulkheads D to O inclusive, in the boiler- and engine-rooms. These were capable of being simultaneously closed from the bridge. The operation of closing was intended to be preceded by the ringing from the bridge of a warning bell.

These doors were closed by the bringing into operation of an electric current and could not be opened until this current was cut off from the bridge. When this was done the doors could only be opened by a mechanical operation, manually worked separately at each door. They could, however, be individually lowered again by operating a lever at the door. In addition they would be automatically closed, if open, should water enter the compartment. This operation was done in each case by means of a float actuated by the water which was in either of the compartments which happened to be in the process of being flooded.

There were no sluice valves or means of letting water from one compartment to another.

DETAILED DESCRIPTION

The following is a more detailed description of the vessel, her passenger and crew accommodation, and her machinery.

Watertight compartments

The table below shows the decks to which the bulkheads extended, and the number of doors in them.

The table on p. 18 shows the actual contents of each separate watertight compartment. The compartments are shown in the left column, the contents of each compartment being read off horizontally. The contents of each watertight compartment are separately given in the deck space in which it is.

The vessel was constructed under survey of the British Board of Trade for a passenger certificate, and also to comply with the American Immigration Laws.

Steam was supplied from six entirely independent groups of boilers in six separate watertight compartments. The after boiler-room No 1 contained

Bulkhead letter	Extends up to under side of deck	Number of doors			
		Engine and boiler spaces (all controlled from bridge)	Orlop to G deck	F to E deck	E to D deck
A	C				
B	D				
C	E			1	
D	E	★1		1	
E	E	†1			
F	E	†1		2	
G	E	†1			
H	E	†1		2	
J	E	†1		2	
K	D	1			2
L	D	1			2
M	D	1		1	2
N	D	1	1	1	2
O	D	1			1
P	D				

★There was another watertight door at the after end of the watertight passage through the bunker immediately aft of "D" bulkhead. This door and the one on the "D" bulkhead formed a double protection to the forward boiler-room.
†The watertight doors for these bulkheads were not on them, but were at the end of a watertight passage (about 9 ft long), leading from the bulkhead through the bunker into the compartment.

Contents of each watertight compartment

Watertight (WT) compt	Length of each WT compt	Hold	Orlop to G deck	G to F deck	F to E deck	E to D deck
Bow to A	46 ft	Fore peak tank (not used excepting for trimming ship)	Fore peak store-room	Fore peak store-room	Fore peak store-room	Fore peak store-room
A–B	45 ft	Cargo	Cargo	Living spaces for firemen etc.	Living spaces for firemen	Living spaces for firemen
B–C	51 ft	Cargo	Cargo	3rd class passenger accommodation	3rd class passenger accommodation	3rd class passenger accommodation and seamen's spaces
C–D	51 ft	Alternatively coal and cargo	Luggage and mails	Baggage, squash rackets and 3rd class passengers	3rd class passenger accommodation	3rd class passenger accommodation
D–E	54 ft	No 6 boiler-room	No 6 boiler-room	Coal and boiler casing	3rd class passenger accommodation	1st class passenger accommodation
E–F	57 ft	No 5 boiler-room	No 5 boiler-room	Coal bunker and boiler casing and swimming bath	Linen rooms and swimming bath	1st class passenger accommodation
F–G	57 ft	No 4 boiler-room	No 4 boiler-room	Coal bunker and boiler casing	Stewards, Turkish baths etc.	1st class and stewards
G–H	57 ft	No 3 boiler-room	No 3 boiler-room	Coal bunker and boiler casing	3rd class saloon	1st and 2nd class and stewards
H–J	60 ft	No 2 boiler-room	No 2 boiler-room	Coal bunker and boiler casing	3rd class saloon	1st class
J–K	36 ft	No 1 boiler-room	No 1 boiler-room	Coal bunker and boiler casing	3rd class galley, stewards, etc.	1st class and stewards
K–L	69 ft	Reciprocating engine-room	Reciprocating engine-room	Reciprocating engine-room casing, work-shop and engineers' stores	Engineers' stores and reciprocating engine casing	1st class and engineers' mess etc.
L–M	57 ft	Turbine engine-room	Turbine engine-room	Turbine engine-room casing and small stewards' stores	2nd class and turbine engine-room casing	2nd class and stewards etc.
M–N	63 ft	Electric engine-room	Provisions and electric engine casing	Provisions	2nd class	2nd and 3rd class
N–O	54 ft	Tunnel	Refrigerated cargo	3rd class	2nd class	2nd and 3rd class
O–P	57 ft	Tunnel	Cargo	3rd class	3rd class	3rd class
P to Stern	36 ft	After peak tank for trimming ship	After peak tank for trimming ship	Stores	Stores	Stores

five single-ended boilers. Four other boiler-rooms, Nos 2, 3, 4 and 5, each contained five double-ended boilers. The forward boiler-room, No 6, contained four double-ended boilers. The reciprocating engines and most of the auxiliary machinery were in a seventh separate watertight compartment aft of the boilers; the low-pressure turbine, the main condensers and the thrust blocks of the reciprocating engine were in an eighth separate watertight compartment. The main electrical machinery was in a ninth separate watertight compartment immediately abaft the turbine engine-room. Two emergency steam-driven dynamos were placed on the D deck, 21 ft above the level of the load waterline. These dynamos were arranged to take their supply of steam from any of the three of the boiler-rooms Nos 2, 3 and 5, and were intended to be available in the event of the main dynamo room being flooded.

The ship was equipped with the following:

1   Wireless telegraphy.
2   Submarine signalling.
3   Electric lights and power systems.
4   Telephones for communication between the different working positions in the vessel. In addition to the telephones, the means of communication included engine and docking telegraphs, and duplicate or emergency engine-room telegraph, to be used in the event of any accident to the ordinary telegraph.
5   Three electric elevators for taking passengers in the first class up to A deck, immediately below the Boat deck, and one in the second class for taking passengers up to the Boat deck.
6   Four electrically driven boat winches on the Boat deck for hauling up the boats.
7   Life-saving appliances to the requirements of the Board of Trade, including boats and lifebelts.
8   Steam whistles on the two foremost funnels, worked on the Willett-Bruce system of automatic control.
9   Navigation appliances, including Kelvin's patent sounding machines for finding the depth of water under the ship without stopping, Walker's taffrail log for determining the speed of the ship, and flash signal lamps fitted above the shelters at each end of the navigating bridge for Morse signalling with other ships.

Decks and accommodation

Boat deck
The Boat deck was an uncovered deck on which the boats were placed. At its lowest point it was about 92 ft 6 in above the keel. The overall length of this deck was about 500 ft. The forward end of it was fitted to serve as the navigating bridge of the vessel and was 190 ft from the bow. On the after end of the bridge was a wheel house, containing the steering wheel and a steering compass. The chart room was immediately abaft this. On the starboard side of the wheel house and funnel casing were the navigating room, the captain's quarters, and some officers' quarters. On the port side were the remainder of the officers' quarters. At the middle line abaft the forward funnel casing were the wireless telegraphy rooms and the operators' quarters. The top of the officers' house formed a short deck. The connections from the Marconi aerials were made on this deck, and two of the collapsible boats were placed on it. Aft of the officers' house were the first-class passengers' entrance and stairways, and other adjuncts to the passengers' accommodation below. These stairways had a minimum effective width of 8 ft. They had

assembling landings at the level of each deck, and three elevators communicating from E to A decks, but not to the Boat deck, immediately on the fore side of the stairway.

All the boats except two Engelhardt liferafts were carried on this deck. There were seven lifeboats on each side, 30 ft long, 9 ft wide. There was an emergency cutter, 25 ft long, on each side at the fore end of the deck. Abreast of each cutter was an Engelhardt liferaft. One similar raft was carried on the top of the officers' house on each side. In all there were 14 lifeboats, 2 cutters, and 4 Engelhardt liferafts.

The forward group of four boats and one Engelhardt raft were placed on each side of the deck alongside the officers' quarters and the first-class entrance. Further aft at the middle line on this deck was the special platform for the standard compass. At the after end of this deck was an entrance house for second-class passengers, with a stairway and elevator leading directly down to F deck. There were two vertical iron ladders at the after end of this deck, leading to A deck, for the use of the crew. Alongside and immediately forward of the second-class entrance was the after group of lifeboats, four on each side of the ship.

In addition to the main stairways mentioned, there was a ladder on each side amidships, giving access from the A deck below. At the forward end of the Boat deck there was on each side a ladder leading up from A deck, with a landing there, from which, by a ladder, access to B deck could be obtained direct. Between the reciprocating engine casing and the third funnel casing there was a stewards' stairway, which communicated with all the decks below as far as E deck. Outside the deck houses was promenading space for first-class passengers.

A deck

The next deck below the Boat deck was A deck. It extended over a length of about 500 ft. On this deck was a long house, extending nearly the whole length of the deck. It was of irregular shape, varying in width from 24 ft to 72 ft. At the forward end it contained 34 state-rooms, and abaft these a number of public rooms etc. for first-class passengers, including two first-class entrances and stairway, reading-room, lounge and the smoke-room. Outside the deck house was a promenade for first-class passengers. The forward end of it on both sides of the ship, below the forward group of boats and for a short distance further aft, was protected against the weather by a steel screen, 192 ft long, with large windows in it. In addition to the stairway described on the Boat deck, there was near the after end of the A deck, and immediately forward of the first-class smoke-room, another first-class entrance, giving access as far down as C deck. The second-class stairway at the after end of this deck (already described under the Boat deck) had no exit on to the A deck. The stewards' staircase opened on to this deck.

B deck

The next lowest deck was B deck, which constituted the top deck of the strong structure of the vessel, the decks above and the side plating between them being light plating. This deck extended continuously for 550 ft. There were breaks or wells both forward and aft of it, each about 50 ft long. It was terminated by a poop and forecastle. On this deck were placed the principal state-rooms of the vessel, 97 in number, having berths for 198 passengers, and aft of these was the first-class stairway and reception-room, as well as the restaurant for first-class passengers and its pantry and galley. Immediately aft of this restaurant were the second-class stairway and smoke-room. At the forward end of the deck outside the house was an assembling area, giving access by the ladders, previously mentioned, leading directly to the Boat deck. From this same space a ladderway led to the forward third-class promenade on C deck. At the after end of it were two ladders giving access to the after third-class promenade on C deck. At the after end of this deck, at the middle line, was placed another second-class stairway, which gave access to C, D, E, F and G decks.

At the forward end of the vessel, on the level of the B deck, was situated the forecastle deck, which was 125 ft long. On it were placed the gear for working the anchors and cables and for warping (or moving) the ship in dock. At the after end, on the same level, was the poop deck, about 105 ft long, which carried the after-warping appliances and was a third-class promenading space. Arranged above the poop was a light docking bridge, with telephone, telegraphs etc., communicating to the main navigating bridge forward.

C deck

The next lowest deck was C deck. This was the highest deck which extended continuously from bow to stern. At the forward end of it, under the forecastle, was placed the machinery required for working the anchors and cables and for the warping of the ship referred to on B deck above. There were also the crew's galley and the seamen's and firemen's mess-room accommodation, where their meals were taken. At the after end of the forecastle, at each side of the ship, were the entrances to the third-class spaces below. On the port side, at the extreme after end and opening on to the deck, was the lamp-room. The break in B deck between the forecastle and the first-class passenger quarters formed a well about 50 ft in length, which enabled the space under it on C deck to be used as a third-class promenade. This space contained two hatchways, the No 2 hatch and the bunker hatch. The latter of these hatchways gave access to the space allotted to the first- and second-class baggage hold, the mails, specie and parcel room, and to the lower hold, which was used for cargo or coals.

Abaft of this well there was a house 450 ft long and extending for the full breadth of the ship. It contained 148 state-rooms for first class, besides service rooms of various kinds. On this deck, at the forward first-class entrance, were the purser's office and the inquiry office, where passengers' telegrams were received for sending by the Marconi apparatus. Exit doors through the ship's side were fitted abreast of this entrance. Abaft the after end of this long house was a promenade at the ship's side for second-class passengers, sheltered by bulwarks and bulkheads. In the middle of the promenade stood the second-class library. The two second-class stairways were at the ends of the library, so that from the promenade access was obtained at each end to a second-class main stairway. There was also access by a door from this space into each of the alleyways in the first-class accommodation on each side of the ship, and by two doors at the after end into the after-well. This after-well was about 50 ft in length and contained two hatchways called No 5 and No 6 hatches.

Abaft this well, under the poop, was the main third-class entrance for the after end of the vessel, leading directly down to G deck, with landings and access at each deck. The effective width of this stairway was 16 ft to E deck. From E to F it was 8 ft wide. Aft of this entrance on B deck were the third-class smoke-room and the general room. Between these rooms and the stern was the steam steering gear and the machinery for working the after-capstan gear, which was used for warping the after end of the vessel. The steam steering gear had three cylinders. The engines were in duplicate, to provide for the possibility of breakdown of one set.

D deck

The general height from D deck to C deck was 10 ft 6 in, this being reduced to 9 ft 6 in at the forward end, and 9 ft 6 in at the after end, the taper being obtained gradually by increasing the sheer of the D deck. The forward end of this deck provided accommodation for 108 firemen, who were in two separate watches. There was the necessary lavatory accommodation, abaft the firemen's quarters at the sides of the ship. On each side of the middle line immediately abaft the firemen's quarters there was a vertical spiral staircase leading to the forward end of a tunnel, immediately above the tank top, which extended from the foot of the staircase to the forward stokehole, so that the firemen could pass direct to their work without going through any passenger accommodation or over any passenger decks.

On D deck abaft of this staircase was the third-class promenade space which was covered in by C deck. From this promenade space there were four separate ladderways with two ladders, 4 ft wide, to each. One ladderway on each side forward led to C deck, and one, the starboard, led to E deck and continued to F deck as a double ladder and to G deck as a single ladder. The two ladderways at the after end led to E deck on both sides and to F deck on the port side.

Abaft this promenade space came a block of 50 first-class staterooms. This surrounded the forward funnel. The main first-class reception room and dining saloon were aft of these rooms and surrounded the No 2 funnel. The reception room and staircase occupied 83 ft of the length of the ship. The dining saloon occupied 112 ft, and was between the second and third funnels. Abaft this came the first-class pantry, which occupied 56 ft of the length of the ship. The reciprocating engine hatch came up through this pantry.

Aft of the first-class pantry, the galley, which provides for both first- and second-class passengers, occupied 45 ft of the length of the ship. Aft of this were the turbine engine hatch and the emergency dynamos. Abaft of and on the port side of this hatch were the second-class pantry and other spaces used for the saloon service of the passengers. On the starboard side abreast of these there was a series of rooms used for hospitals and their attendants. These spaces occupied about 54 ft of the length. Aft of these was the second-class saloon occupying 70 ft of the length. In the next 88 ft of length there were 38 second-class rooms and the necessary baths and lavatories. From here to the stern was accommodation for third-class passengers and the main third-class lavatories for the passengers in the after end of the ship. The watertight bulkheads come up to this deck throughout the length from the stern as far forward as the bulkhead dividing the after boiler-room from the reciprocating engine-room. The watertight bulkhead of the two compartments abaft the stern was carried up to this deck.

E deck

The watertight bulkheads, other than those mentioned as extending to D deck, all stopped at this deck. At the forward end was provided accommodation for three watches of trimmers, in three separate compartments, each holding 24 trimmers. Abaft this, on the port side, was accommodation for 44 seamen. Aft of this, and also on the starboard side of it, were the lavatories for crew and third-class passengers; further aft again came the forward third-class lavatories. Immediately aft of this was a passageway right across the ship communicating directly with the ladderways leading to the decks above and below and gangway doors in the ship's side. This passage was 9 ft wide at the sides and 15 ft at the centre of the ship.

From the after end of this cross-passage main alleyways on each side of the ship ran right through to the after end of the vessel. That on the port side was about $8\frac{1}{2}$ ft wide. It was the general communication passage for the crew and third-class passengers and was known as the "working passage". In this passage at the centre line in the middle of the length of the ship direct access was obtained to the third-class dining rooms on the deck below by means of a ladderway 20 ft wide. Between the working passage and the ship's side was the accommodation for the petty officers, most of the stewards, and the engineers' mess-room. This accommodation extended for 475 ft. From this passage access was obtained to both engine-rooms and the engineers' accommodation, some third-class lavatories and also some third-class accommodation at the after end. There was another cross-passage at the end of this accommodation about 9 ft wide, terminating in gangway doors on each side of the ship. The port side of it was for third-class passengers and the starboard for second class. A door divided the parts, but it could be opened for any useful purpose, or for an emergency. The second-class stairway leading to the Boat deck was in the cross-passage way.

The passage on the starboard side ran through the first- and then the second-class accommodation, and the forward main first-class stairway and elevators extended to this deck, whilst both the second-class main stairways were also in communication with this starboard passage. There were four first-class, eight first- or second- alternatively, and 19 second-class rooms leading off this starboard passage.

The remainder of the deck was appropriated to third-class accommodation. This contained the bulk of the third-class accommodation. At the forward end of it was the accommodation for 53 firemen constituting the third watch. Aft of this in three watertight compartments there was third-class accommodation extending to 147 ft. In the next watertight compartment were the swimming bath and linen rooms. In the next watertight compartments were stewards' accommodation on the port side, and the Turkish baths on the starboard side. The next two watertight compartments each contained a third-class dining-room.

The third-class stewards' accommodation, together with the third-class galley and pantries, filled the watertight compartment. The engineers' accommodation was in the next compartment directly alongside the casing of the reciprocating engine-room. The next three compartments were allotted to 64 second-class state-rooms. These communicated direct with the second-class main stairways. The after compartments contained third-class accommodation. All spaces on this deck had direct ladderway communication with the deck above, so that if it became necessary to close the watertight doors in the bulkheads an escape was available in all cases. On this deck in way of the boiler-rooms were placed the electrically driven fans which provided ventilation to the stokeholds.

G deck

The forward end of this deck had accommodation for 15 leading firemen and 30 greasers. The next watertight compartment contained third-class accommodation in 26 rooms for 106 people. The next watertight compartment contained the first-class baggage room, the post office accommodation, a racquet court, and seven third-class rooms for 34 passengers. From this point to the after end of the boiler-room the space was used for the 'tween deck bunkers. Alongside the reciprocating engine-room were the engineers' stores and workshop. Abreast of the turbine engine-room were some of the ship's stores. In the next watertight compartment abaft the turbine-room was the main body of the stores. The next two compartments were appropriated to 186 third-class passengers in 60 rooms; this deck was the lowest on which any passengers or crew were carried.

Orlop and Lower Orlop decks

Below G deck were two partial decks, the Orlop and Lower Orlop decks, the latter extending only through the fore peak and No 1 hold; on the former deck, abaft the turbine engine-room, were some store-rooms containing stores for ship's use.

Below these decks again came the inner bottom, extending fore and aft through about nine-tenths of the vessel's length, and on this were placed the boilers, main and auxiliary machinery and the electric light machines. In the remaining spaces below G deck were cargo holds or 'tween decks, seven in all, six forward and one aft. The firemen's passage, giving direct access from their accommodation to the forward boiler-room by stairs at the forward end, contained the various pipes and valves connected with the pumping arrangements at the forward end of the ship, and also the steam pipes conveying steam to the windlass gear forward and exhaust steam pipes leading from winches and other deck machinery. It was made thoroughly watertight throughout its length, and at its after end was closed by a watertight vertical sliding door of the same character as other doors on the inner bottom. Special arrangements were made for pumping this space out, if necessary. The pipes were placed in this tunnel to protect them from possible damage by coal or cargo, and also to facilitate access to them.

Accommodation

On the decks was provided generally, in the manner above described, accommodation for a maximum number of 1,034 first-class passengers, and at the same time 510 second-class passengers and 1,022 third-class passengers. Some of the accommodation was of an alternative character, and could be used for either of two classes of passengers. In the statement of figures the higher alternative class has been reckoned. This makes a total accommodation for 2,566 passengers.

Accommodation was provided for the crew as follows: about 75 of the deck department, including officers and doctors, 326 of the engine-room department, including engineers, and 544 of the victualling department, including pursers and leading stewards.

Access of passengers to the Boat deck

The following routes led directly from the various parts of the first-class passenger accommodation to the Boat deck. From the forward ends of A, B, C, D and E decks by the staircase in the forward first-class entrance direct to the Boat deck. The elevators led from the same decks as far as A deck, where further access was obtained by going up the top flight of the main staircase.

The same route was available for first-class passengers forward of midships on B, C and E decks.

First-class passengers abaft amidships on B and C decks could use the staircase in the after main entrance to A deck, and then could pass out on to the deck, and by the midships stairs besides the house ascend to the Boat deck. They could also use the stewards' staircase between the reciprocating engine casing and Nos 1 and 2 boiler casing, which led direct to the Boat deck. This last route was also available for passengers on E deck in the same divisions who could use the forward first-class main stairway and elevators.

Second-class passengers on D deck could use their own after stairway to B deck, and could then pass up their forward stairway to the Boat deck, or else could cross their saloon and use the same stairway throughout.

Of the second-class passengers on E deck, those abreast of the reciprocating engine casing, unless the watertight door immediately abaft them was closed, went aft and joined the other second-class passengers. If, however, the watertight door at the end of their compartment was closed, they passed through an emergency door into the engine-room, and directly up to the Boat deck, by the ladders and gratings in the engine-room casing.

The second-class passengers on E deck in the compartment abreast the turbine casing on the starboard side, and also those on F deck on both sides below, could pass through M watertight bulkhead to the forward second-class main stairway. If this door were closed, they could pass by the stairway up to the serving space at the forward end of the second-class saloon, and go into the saloon and thence up the forward second-class stairway.

Passengers between M and N bulkheads on both E and F decks could pass directly up to the forward second-class stairway to the Boat deck.

Passengers between N and O bulkheads on D, E, F and G decks could pass by the after second-class stairway to B deck, and then cross to the forward second-class stairway and go up to the Boat deck.

Third-class passengers at the fore end of the vessel could pass by the staircases to C deck in the forward well and by ladders on the port and starboard sides at the forward end of the deck-houses, thence direct to the Boat deck outside the officers' accommodation. They might also pass along the working passage on E deck and through the emergency door to the forward first-class main stairway, or through the door on the same deck at the forward end of the first-class alleyway and up the first-class stairway direct to the Boat deck.

The third-class passengers at the after end of the ship passed up their stairway way to E deck, and into the working passage, and through the emergency doors to the two second-class stairways, and so to the Boat deck, like second-class passengers. Or, alternatively, they could continue up their own stairs and entrance to C deck, thence by the two ladders at the after end of the bridge on to the B deck, and thence by the forward second-class stairway direct to the Boat deck.

Access of crew to the Boat deck
From each boiler-room an escape or emergency ladder was provided direct to the Boat deck by the fidleys, in the boiler casings, and also into the working passage on E deck, and thence by the stair immediately forward of the reciprocating engine casing, direct to the Boat deck.

From both the engine-rooms ladders and gratings gave direct access to the Boat deck.

From the electric engine-room, the after tunnels, and the forward pipe tunnels, escapes were provided direct to the working passage on E deck, and thence by one of the several routes already detailed from that space. From the crew's quarters they could go forward by their own staircases into the forward well, and thence, like the third-class passengers, to the Boat deck.

The stewards' accommodation being all connected to the working passage or the forward main first-class stairway, they could use one of the routes from thence.

The engineers' accommodation also communicated with the working passage, but, as it was possible for them to be shut between two watertight bulkheads, they had also a direct route by the gratings in the engine-room casing to the Boat deck.

On all the principal accommodation decks the alleyways and stairways provided a ready means of access to the Boat deck, and there were clear deck spaces in way of all first-, second- and third-class main entrances and stairways on Boat deck and all decks below.

Structure

The vessel was built throughout of steel and had a cellular double bottom of the usual type, with a floor at every frame, its depth at the centre line being 63 in, except in way of the reciprocating machinery, where it was 78 in. For about half of the length of the vessel this double bottom extended up the ship's side to a height of 7 ft above the keel. Forward and aft of the machinery space the protection of the inner bottom extended to a less height above the keel. It was so divided that there were four separate watertight compartments in the breadth of the vessel. Before and abaft the machinery space there was a watertight division at the centre line only, except in the foremost and aftermost tank. Above the double bottom the vessel was constructed on the usual transverse frame system, reinforced by web frames, which extended to the highest decks.

At the forward end the framing and plating was strengthened with a view to preventing panting and damage when meeting thin harbour ice.

Beams were fitted on every frame at all decks, from the Boat deck downwards. An external bilge keel, about 300 ft long and 25 in deep, was fitted along the bilge amidships.

The heavy ship's plating was carried right up to the Boat deck, and between the C and B decks was doubled. The stringer or edge plate of the B deck was also doubled. This double plating was hydraulic riveted.

All decks were steel plated throughout.

The transverse strength of the ship was in part dependent on the 15 transverse watertight bulkheads, which were specially stiffened and strengthened to enable them to stand the necessary pressure in the event of accident, and they were connected by double angles to decks, inner bottom, and shell plating.

The two decks above the B deck were of comparatively light scantling, but strong enough to ensure their proving satisfactory in these positions in rough weather.

Watertight sub-division

In the preparation of the design of this vessel it was arranged that the bulkheads and divisions should be so placed that the ship would remain afloat in the event of any two adjoining compartments being flooded, and that they should be so built and strengthened that the ship would remain afloat under this condition. The minimum freeboard that the vessel would have, in the event of any two compartments being flooded, was between 2 ft 6 in and 3 ft from the deck adjoining the top of the watertight bulkheads. With this object in view 15 watertight bulkheads were arranged in the vessel. The lower part of C bulkhead was doubled, and was in the form of a cofferdam. So far as possible, the bulkheads were carried up in one plane to their upper sides, but in cases where they had for any reason to be stepped forward or aft, the deck, in way of the step, was made into a watertight flat, thus completing the watertightness of the compartment. In addition to this, G deck in the after peak was made a watertight flat. The Orlop deck between bulkheads which formed the top of the tunnel was also watertight. The Orlop deck in the fore-peak tank was also a watertight flat. The electric machinery compartment was further protected by a structure some distance in from the ship's side, forming six separate watertight compartments, which were used for the storage of fresh water.

Where openings were required for the working of the ship in these watertight bulkheads, they were closed by watertight sliding doors, which could be worked from a position above the top of the watertight bulkhead, and those doors immediately above the inner bottom were of a special automatic closing pattern, as described below. By this sub-division there were in all 73 compartments, 29 of these being above the inner bottom.

Watertight doors

The doors (12 in number) immediately above the inner bottom were in the engine- and boiler-room spaces. They were of Messrs Harland and Wolff's latest type, working vertically. The doorplate was of cast iron of heavy section, strongly ribbed. It closed by gravity, and was held in the open position by a clutch which could be released by means of a powerful electro-magnet controlled from the captain's bridge. In the event of accident, or at any time when it might be considered desirable, the captain or officer on duty could, by simply moving an electric switch, immediately close all these doors. The time required for the doors to close was between 25 and 30 seconds. Each door could also be closed from below by operating a hand lever fitted alongside the door. As a further precaution floats were provided beneath the floor level, which, in the event of water accidentally entering any of the compartments, automatically lifted and thus released the clutches, thereby permitting the doors in that particular compartment to close if they had not already been dropped by any other means. These doors were fitted with cataracts which controlled the speed of closing. Due notice of closing from the bridge was given by a warning bell.

A ladder or escape was provided in each boiler-room, engine-room, and similar watertight compartment, in order that the closing of the doors at any time should not imprison the men working therein.

The watertight doors on E deck were of horizontal pattern, with wrought steel doorplates. Those on F deck and the one aft on the Orlop deck were of similar type, but had cast iron doorplates of heavy section, strongly ribbed. Each of the 'tween deck doors, and each of the vertical doors on the tank top level, could be operated by the ordinary hand gear from the deck above the top of the watertight bulkhead, as well as from a position on the next deck above, almost directly above the door. To facilitate the quick closing of the doors, plates were affixed in suitable positions on the sides of the alleyways indicating the positions of the deckplates, and a box spanner was provided for each door, hanging in suitable clips alongside the deckplate.

Ship's side doors
Large side doors were provided through the side plating, giving access to passengers' or crew's accommodation as follows:

On the saloon (D) deck on the starboard side in the forward third-class open space, one baggage door.
In way of the forward first-class entrance, two doors close together on each side.
On the upper (E) deck, one door each side at the forward end of the working passage.
On the port side abreast the engine-room, one door leading into the working passage. One door each side on the port and starboard sides aft into the forward second-class entrance.

All the doors on the upper deck were secured by lever handles, and were made watertight by means of rubber strips. Those on the saloon deck were closed by lever handles but had no rubber.

Accommodation ladder
One teak accommodation ladder was provided, and could be worked on either side of the ship in the gangway door opposite the second-class entrance on the upper deck (E). It had a folding platform and portable stanchions, hand rope, etc. The ladder extended to within 3 ft 6 in of the vessel's light draft, and was stowed overhead in the entrance abreast the forward

second-class main staircase. Its lower end was arranged so as to be raised and lowered from a davit immediately above.

Masts and rigging
The vessel was rigged with two masts, and fore and aft sails. The two pole masts were constructed of steel, and stiffened with angle irons. The poles at the top of the mast were made of teak.

A look-out cage, constructed of steel, was fitted on the foremast at a height of about 95 ft above the waterline. Access to the cage was obtained by an iron vertical ladder inside of the foremast, with an opening at C deck and one at the look-out cage. An iron ladder was fitted on the foremast from the hounds to the masthead light.

Life-saving appliances

Lifebuoys
Forty-eight, with beckets, were supplied, of pattern approved by the Board of Trade. They were placed about the ship.

Lifebelts
Some 3,560 lifebelts, of the latest improved overhead pattern approved by the Board of Trade, were supplied and placed on board the vessel, and there inspected by the Board of Trade. These were distributed throughout all the sleeping accommodation.

Lifeboats
Twenty boats in all were fitted on the vessel, and were of the following dimensions and capacities:

14 wood lifeboats, each 30 ft long by 9 ft 1 in broad by 4 ft deep, with a cubic capacity of 655.2 cubic ft, constructed to carry 65 persons each;

1 wood cutter, 25 ft 2 in long by 7 ft 2 in broad by 3 ft deep, with a cubic capacity of 326.6 cubic ft, constructed to carry 40 persons (emergency boat);

1 wood cutter, 25 ft 2 in long by 7 ft 1 in broad by 3 ft deep, with a cubic capacity of 322.1 cubic ft, constructed to carry 40 persons (emergency boat);

4 Engelhardt collapsible boats, 27 ft 5 in long by 8 ft broad by 3 ft deep, with a cubic capacity of 376.6 cubic ft, constructed to carry 47 persons each.

Or a total of 11,327.9 cubic ft for 1,178 persons.

The lifeboats and cutters were constructed as follows. The keels were of elm. The stems and stern posts were of oak. They were all clinker built of yellow pine, double fastened with copper nails, clinched over rooves. The timbers were of elm, spaced about 9 in apart, and the seats pitch pine secured with galvanized iron double knees. The buoyancy tanks in the lifeboats were of 18 oz copper, and of capacity to meet the Board of Trade requirements.

The lifeboats were fitted with Murray's disengaging gear with arrangements for simultaneously freeing both ends if required. The gear was fastened at a suitable distance from the forward and after ends of the boats, to suit the davits. Lifelines were fitted round the gunwales of the lifeboats. The davit blocks were treble for the lifeboats and double for the cutters. They were of elm, with lignum vitæ roller sheaves, were bound inside with iron, and had swivel eyes. There were manilla rope falls of sufficient length for lowering the boats to the vessel's light draft and, when the boats were lowered, to be able to reach to the boat winches on the Boat deck.

The lifeboats were stowed on hinged wood chocks on the Boat deck, by groups of three at the forward and four at the after ends. On each side of the Boat deck the cutters were arranged forward of the group of three, and fitted to lash outboard as emergency boats. They were immediately abaft the navigating bridge.

The Engelhardt collapsible lifeboats were stowed abreast of the cutters, one on each side of the ship, and the remaining two on top of the officers' house, immediately abaft the navigating bridge.

The boat equipment was in accordance with the Board of Trade requirements. Sails for each lifeboat and cutter were supplied and stowed in painted bags. Covers were supplied for the lifeboats and cutters, and a sea anchor for each boat. Every lifeboat was furnished with a special spirit boat compass and fitting for holding it; these compasses were carried in a locker on the Boat deck. A provision tank and water beaker were supplied to each boat.

Compasses
Compasses were supplied as follows:

> One Kelvin standard compass, with azimuth mirror on compass platform;
> One Kelvin steering compass inside of wheel house;
> One Kelvin steering compass on captain's bridge;
> One light card compass for docking bridge;
> Fourteen spirit compasses for lifeboats.

All the ships' compasses were lighted with oil and electric lamps. They were adjusted by Messrs C J Smith, of Southampton, on the passage from Belfast to Southampton and Southampton to Queenstown.

Charts
All the necessary charts were supplied.

Distress signals

These were supplied of number and pattern approved by Board of Trade, i.e. 36 socket signals in lieu of guns, 12 ordinary rockets, 2 Manwell Holmes deck flares, 12 blue lights, and 6 lifebuoy lights.

Pumping arrangements

The general arrangement of piping was designed so that it was possible to pump from any flooded compartment by two independent systems of 10 in mains having cross connections between them. These were controlled from above by rods; and wheels led to the level of the bulkhead deck. By these it was possible to isolate any flooded space, together with any suctions in it. If any of these should happen accidentally to be left open, and consequently out of reach, it could be shut off from the main by the wheel on the bulkhead deck. This arrangement was specially submitted to the Board of Trade and approved by them.

The double bottom of the vessel was divided by 17 transverse watertight divisions, including those bounding the fore and aft peaks, and again subdivided by a centre fore and aft bulkhead, and two longitudinal bulkheads, into 46 compartments. Fourteen of these compartments had 8 in suctions, 23 had 6 in suctions, and three had 5 in suctions connected to the 10 in ballast main suction; six compartments were used exclusively for fresh water.

The following bilge suctions were provided for dealing with water above the double bottom, namely, in No 1 hold two $3\frac{1}{2}$ in suctions, No 2 hold two $3\frac{1}{2}$ in and two 3 in suctions, bunker hold two $3\frac{1}{2}$ in and two 3 in suctions.

The valves in connection with the forward bilge and ballast suctions were placed in the firemen's passage, the watertight pipe tunnel extending from No 6 boiler-room to the after end of No 1 hold. In this tunnel, in addition to two 3 in bilge suctions, one at each end, there was a special $3\frac{1}{2}$ in suction with valve rod leading up to the lower deck above the load line, so as always to have been accessible should the tunnel be flooded accidentally. The remaining bilge suctions were as follows:

In No 6 boiler-room there were three $3\frac{1}{2}$ in, one $4\frac{1}{2}$ in, and two 3 in suctions.

In No 5 boiler-room there were three $3\frac{1}{2}$ in, one 5 in, and two 3 in suctions.
In No 4 boiler-room there were three $3\frac{1}{2}$ in, one $4\frac{1}{2}$ in, and two 3 in suctions.
In No 3 boiler-room there were three $3\frac{1}{2}$ in, one 5 in, and two 3 in suctions.
In No 2 boiler-room there were three $3\frac{1}{2}$ in, one 5 in, and two 3 in suctions.
In No 1 boiler-room there were two $3\frac{1}{2}$ in, one 5 in, and two 3 in suctions.
In the reciprocating engine-room there were two $3\frac{1}{2}$ in, six 3 in, two 18 in, and two 5 in suctions.
In the turbine engine-room there were two $3\frac{1}{2}$ in, three 3 in, two 18 in, two 5 in, and one 4 in suctions.
In the electric engine-room there were four $3\frac{1}{2}$ in suctions.

In the store-rooms above the electric engine-room there was one 3 in
  suction.
In the forward tunnel compartment there were two $3\frac{1}{2}$ in suctions.
In the watertight flat over the tunnel compartment there were two 3 in suc-
  tions.
In the tunnel after compartment there were two $3\frac{1}{2}$ in suctions.
In the watertight flat over the tunnel after compartment there were two
  3 in suctions.

Electrical installation

Main generating sets
There were four engines and dynamos, each having a capacity of 400 kilo-
watts at 100 volts, and consisting of a vertical three-crank compound-forced
lubrication enclosed engine, of sufficient power to drive the electrical plant.
The engines were direct-coupled to their respective dynamos.

These four main sets were situated in a separate watertight compartment
about 63 ft long by 24 ft high, adjoining the after end of the turbine-room
at the level of the inner bottom.

Steam to the electric engines was supplied from two separate lengths of
steam pipes, connecting on the port side to the five single-ended boilers in
compartment No 1 and two in compartment No 2, and on the starboard
side to the auxiliary steam pipe, which derived steam from the five single-
ended boilers in No 1 compartment, two in No 2, and two in No 4. By
connections at the engine-room forward bulkhead steam could be taken
from any boiler in the ship.

Auxiliary generating sets
In addition to the four main generating sets, there were two 30 kilowatt
engines and dynamos situated on a platform in the turbine engine-room
casing on saloon deck level, 20 ft above the water line. They were of the
same general type as the main sets.

These auxiliary emergency sets were connected to the boilers by means
of a separate steam pipe running along the working passage above E deck,
with branches from three boiler-rooms, Nos 2, 3 and 5, so that, should the
main sets be temporarily out of action, the auxiliary sets could provide current for such lights and power appliances as would be required in the event
of emergency.

Electric lighting
The total number of incandescent lights was 10,000, ranging from 16 to
100 candle power, the majority being of Tantallum type, except in the
cargo spaces and for the portable fittings, where carbon lamps were provided. Special dimming lamps of small amount of light were provided in
the first-class rooms.

Electric heating and power and mechanical ventilation
Altogether 562 electric heaters and 153 electric motors were installed throughout the vessel, including six 50-cwt and two 30-cwt cranes, four 3-ton cargo winches, and four 15-cwt boat winches.

There were also four electric passenger lifts, three forward of the first-class main entrance and one in the second-class forward entrance, each to carry 12 persons.

Telephones
Loud-speaking telephones of navy pattern were fitted for communication between the following:

Wheel house on the navigating bridge and the forecastle;
Wheel house on the navigating bridge and the look-out station on the crow's-nest;
Wheel house on the navigating bridge and the engine-room;
Wheel house on the navigating bridge and the poop;
Chief engineer's cabin and the engine-room;
Engine-room and Nos 1, 2, 3, 4, 5 and 6 stokeholds.

These were operated both from the ship's lighting circuit, through a motor generator, and alternatively by a stand-by battery, which by means of an automatic switch could be introduced in the circuit should the main supply fail.

There was also a separate telephone system for intercommunication between a number of the chief officials and service rooms, through a 50-line exchange switch-board. A number of the pantries and galleys were also in direct telephonic communication.

Wireless telegraphy
The wireless telegraphy system was worked by a Marconi 5 kilowatt motor generator. The house for the Marconi instruments was situated on the Boat deck close to the bridge. There were four parallel aerial wires extended between the masts, fastened to light booms. From the aerials the connecting wires were led to the instruments in the house. There were two complete sets of apparatus, one for the transmitting and one for receiving messages, the former being placed in a sound-proof chamber in one corner of the wireless house.

There was also an independent storage battery and coil, in event of the failure of the current supply, which came from the ship's dynamos.

Submarine signalling
The Submarine Signal Company's apparatus was provided for receiving signals from the submarine bells. Small tanks containing the microphones were placed on the inside of the hull of the vessel on the port and starboard sides

below the water level, and were connected by wires to receivers situated in the navigating room on the port side of the officer's deck-house.

Various

The whistles were electrically actuated on the Willett Bruce system. The boiler-room telegraphs, stoking indicators, rudder indicators, clocks and thermostats were also electrical. The watertight doors were released by electric magnets.

Emergency circuit

A separate and distinct installation was fitted in all parts of the vessel, deriving current from the two 30 kilowatt sets above-mentioned, so that in the event of the current from the main dynamos being unavailable an independent supply was obtainable. Connected to the emergency circuit were more than 500 incandescent lamps fitted throughout all passenger, crew and machinery compartments, at the end of passages, near stairways, and also on the Boat deck, to enable anyone to find their way from one part of the ship to the other.

The following were also connected to the emergency circuit by means of change-over switches: five arc lamps, seven cargo and gangway lanterns, Marconi apparatus, mast, side and stern lights, and all lights on the bridge, including those for captain's, navigating and chart rooms, wheel house, telegraphs and Morse signalling lanterns, and four electrically driven boat winches. These latter, situated on the Boat deck, were each capable of lifting a load of 15 cwt at a speed of 100 ft per minute.

Ventilating

There were 12 electrically driven fans for supplying air to the stokeholds, six electrically driven fans for engine- and turbine-room ventilation. There were fans for engine- and boiler-rooms.

Machinery

Description

The propelling machinery was of the combination type, having two sets of reciprocating engines driving the wing propellers, and a low-pressure turbine working the centre propeller. Steam was supplied by 24 double-ended boilers, and five single-ended boilers, arranged for a working pressure of 215 lb per square inch. The turbine was placed in a separate compartment aft of the reciprocating engine-room and divided from it by a watertight bulkhead. The main condensers, with their circulating pumps and air pumps, were placed in the turbine-room. The boilers were arranged in six watertight compartments, the single-ended boilers being placed in the one nearest the main engines, the whole being built under Board of Trade survey for passenger certificate.

Reciprocating engines

The reciprocating engines were of the four-crank triple expansion type. Each set had four inverted, direct-acting cylinders, the high-pressure having a diameter of 54 in, the intermediate pressure of 84 in, and each of the two low-pressure cylinders of 97 in, all with a stroke of 6 ft 3 in. The valves of the high-pressure and intermediate cylinders were of the piston type, and the low-pressure cylinder had double-ported slide valves, fitted with Stephenson link motion. Each engine was reversed by a Brown's type of direct-acting steam and hydraulic engine. There was also a separate steam-driven high-pressure pump fitted for operating either or both of the reversing engines. This alternative arrangement was a stand-by in case of breakdown of the steam pipes to these engines.

Turbine

The low-pressure turbine was of the Parson's reaction type, direct-coupled to the centre line of shafting and arranged for driving in the ahead direction only. It exhausted to the two condensers, placed one on each side of it. A shut-off valve was fitted in each of the eduction pipes leading to the condensers. An emergency governor was fitted and arranged to shut off steam to the turbine and simultaneously change over the exhaust from the reciprocating engines to the condensers, should the speed of the turbine become excessive through the breaking of a shaft or other accident.

Boilers

All the boilers were 15 ft 9 in in diameter, the 24 double-ended boilers being 20 ft long, and the single-ended 11 ft 9 in long. Each double-ended boiler had six, and each single-ended boiler three furnaces, with a total heating surface of 144,142 sq ft and a grate surface of 3,466 sq ft. The boilers were constructed, in accordance with the rules of the Board of Trade, for a working pressure of 215 lb per square inch. They were arranged for working under natural draught, assisted by fans, which blew air into the open stokehold.

Auxiliary steam pipes

The five single-ended boilers and those in boiler-rooms Nos 2 and 4 had separate steam connections to the pipe supplying steam for working the auxiliary machinery, and the five single-ended boilers and the two port boilers in boiler-room No 2 had separate steam connections to the pipe supplying steam for working the electric light engines. A cross connection was also made between the main and auxiliary pipes in the reciprocating engine-room, so that the auxiliaries could be worked from any boiler in the ship. Steam pipes also were led separately from three of the boiler-rooms (Nos 2, 3, 5) above the watertight bulkheads and along the working passage to the emergency electric light engines placed above the load-line in the turbine-room. Pipes were also led from this steam supply to the pumps in the engine-room, which were connected to the bilges throughout the ship.

Main steam pipes

There were two main lines of steam pipes leading to the engine-room, with shut-off valves at three of the bulkheads. Besides the shut-off valves at the engine-room bulkhead, a quick-acting emergency valve was fitted on each main steam pipe, so that the steam could at once be shut off in case of rupture of the main pipe.

Condensing plant and pumps

There were two main condensers, having a combined cooling surface of 50,550 sq ft, designed to work under a vacuum of 28 in with cooling water at 60 deg F. The condensers were pear-shaped in section, and built of mild steel plates. Four gunmetal centrifugal pumps were fitted for circulating water through the condensers. Each pump had suction and discharge pipes of 29 in bore, and was driven by a compound engine. Besides the main sea suctions, two of the pumps had direct bilge suctions from the turbine-room and the other two from the reciprocating engine-room. The bilge suctions were 18 in diameter. Four of Weir's "Dual" air pumps were fitted, two to each condenser, and discharged to two feed-tanks in the turbine engine-room.

Bilge and ballast pumps

The ship was also fitted with the following pumps: five ballast and bilge pumps, each capable of discharging 250 tons of water per hour, and three bilge pumps, each of 150 tons per hour capacity.

One ash ejector was placed in each of the large boiler compartments to work the ash ejectors, and to circulate or feed the boilers as required. This pump was also connected to the bilges, except in the case of three of the boiler-rooms, where three of the ballast and bilge pumps were placed. The pumps in each case had direct bilge suctions as well as a connection to the main bilge pipe, so that each boiler-room might be independent. The remainder of the auxiliary pumps were placed in the reciprocating and turbine engine-rooms. Two ballast pumps were placed in the reciprocating engine-room, with large suctions from the bilges direct and from the bilge main. Two bilge pumps were also arranged to draw from bilges. One bilge pump was placed in the turbine-room and one of the hot salt-water pumps had a connection from the bilge main pipe for use in emergency. A 10 in main ballast pipe was carried fore and aft through the ship with separate connections to each tank, and with filling pipes from the sea connected at intervals for trimming purposes. The five ballast pumps were arranged to draw from this pipe. A double line of bilge main pipe was fitted forward of No 5 boiler room and aft of No 1.

General

There were four elliptical-shaped funnels, the three forward ones took the waste gases from the boiler furnaces, and the after one was placed over the turbine hatch and was used as a ventilator. The galley funnels were led up this funnel. The uptakes by which the waste gases were conveyed to the funnels were united immediately above the watertight bulkhead which separated the boiler-rooms.

All overhead discharge from the circulating pumps, ballast pumps, bilge pumps etc. were below the deep load-line, but above the light line.

The boilers were supported in built steel cradles, and were stayed to the ship's side and to each other across the ship by strong steel stays. Built steel chocks were also fitted to prevent movement fore and aft.

Silent blow-offs from the main steam pipes were connected direct to both condensers.

CREW AND PASSENGERS

When the *Titanic* left Queenstown on 11th April the total number of persons employed on board in any capacity was 885.

The respective ratings of these persons were as follows:

Deck Department	66
Engine Department	325
Victualling Department	494
	885

Eight bandsmen were included in the second-class passenger list.

In the Deck Department the following qualifications were held:

Master, Edward Charles Smith, held an Extra Master's Certificate.
Chief Officer H F Wilde held an Ordinary Master's Certificate.
1st Officer W M Murdoch held an Ordinary Master's Certificate.
2nd Officer C H Lightoller held an Extra Master's Certificate.
3rd Officer H J Pitman held an Ordinary Master's Certificate.
4th Officer J G Boxall held an Extra Master's Certificate.
5th Officer H G Lowe held an Ordinary Master's Certificate.
6th Officer J P Moody held an Ordinary Master's Certificate.

In the Engine Department were included the Chief Engineer and 7 senior and 17 assistant engineers.

In the Victualling Department there were 23 women employed.

The total number of passengers on board was 1,316. Of these:

	Male	Female	Total
1st class	180	145	325
2nd class	179	106	285
3rd class	510	196	706
Total			1,316

Of the above number of passengers, six children were in the 1st class, 24 were in 2nd class, and 79 were in 3rd class, or 109 in all.

About 410 of the 3rd-class passengers were foreigners, and these, with the foreigners in the 1st and 2nd class and in the Victualling Department, would make a total of nearly 500 persons on board who were presumably not English-speaking, so far as it is possible to ascertain. The disposition of the different classes of passengers and of the crew in the ship has already been described. In all 2,201 persons were on board.

ACCOUNT OF THE SHIP'S JOURNEY ACROSS THE ATLANTIC, THE MESSAGES SHE RECEIVED AND THE DISASTER

THE SAILING ORDERS

The masters of vessels belonging to the White Star Line are not given any special "sailing order" before the commencement of any particular voyage. It is understood, however, that the "tracks" or "lane routes" proper to the particular time of the year, and agreed upon by the great steamship companies, are to be generally adhered to. Should any master see fit during this passage to deviate from his route he has to report on and explain this deviation at the end of his voyage. When such deviation has been in the interests of safety, and not merely to shorten his passage, his action has always been approved of by the Company.

A book of "General Ship's Rules and Uniform Regulations" is also issued by the Company as a guide. There are in this book no special instructions in regard to ice, but there is a general instruction that the safety of the lives of the passengers and ship are to be the first consideration.

Besides the book of Ship's Rules, every master, when first appointed to command a ship, is addressed by special letter from the Company, of which the following passage is an extract:

> You are to dismiss all idea of competitive passages with other vessels and to concentrate your attention upon a cautious, prudent and ever watchful system of navigation, which shall lose time or suffer any other temporary inconvenience rather than incur the slightest risk which can be avoided.

Mr Sanderson, one of the directors, in his evidence says with reference to the above letter:

We never fail to tell them in handing them these letters that we do not wish them to take it as a mere matter of form, that we wish them to read these letters, and to write an acknowledgment to us that they have read them, and that they will be influenced by what we have said in those letters.

THE ROUTE FOLLOWED

The *Titanic* left Southampton on Wednesday, 10th April, and, after calling at Cherbourg, proceeded to Queenstown, from which port she sailed on the afternoon of Thursday, 11th April, following what was at that time the accepted outward-bound route for mail steamers from the Fastnet Light, off the south-west coast of Ireland, to the Nantucket Shoal light vessel, off the coast of the United States.

It is desirable here to explain that it has been, since 1899, the practice, by common agreement between the great North Atlantic steamship companies, to follow lane routes, to be used by their ships at the different seasons of the year. Speaking generally, it may be said that the selection of these routes has hitherto been based on the importance of avoiding as much as possible the areas where fog and ice are prevalent at certain seasons, without thereby unduly lengthening the passage across the Atlantic, and also with the view of keeping the tracks of "outward" and "homeward" bound mail steamers well clear of one another. A further advantage is that, in case of a breakdown, vessels are likely to receive timely assistance from other vessels following the same route. The decisions arrived at by the steamship companies referred to above have, from time to time, been communicated to the Hydrographic Office, and the routes have there been marked on the North Atlantic route charts printed and published by the Admiralty, and they have also been embodied in the Sailing Directions.

Before the *Titanic* disaster the accepted mail steamers' outward track between January 15th and August 14th followed the arc of a great circle between the Fastnet Light and a point in latitude 42° N and 47° W (sometimes termed the "turning point"), and from thence by Rhumb Line so as to pass just south of the Nantucket Shoal light vessel, and from this point on to New York. This track, usually called the Outward Southern Track, was that followed by the *Titanic* on her journey.

An examination of the North Atlantic route chart shows that this track passes about 25 miles south (that is outside) of the edge of the area marked "field ice between March and July", but from 100 to 300 miles to the northward (that is inside) of the dotted line on the chart marked: "Icebergs have been seen within this line in April, May and June."

That is to say, assuming the areas indicated to be based on the experience of many years, this track might be taken as passing clear of field ice under the usual conditions of that time of year, but well inside the area in which icebergs might be seen.

It is instructive here to remark that had the "turning point" been in long. 45° W and lat. 38° N, that is some 240 miles to the south-eastward, the total distance of the passage would only have been increased by about 220 miles, or some 10 hours' steaming for a 22-knot ship. This is the route which was provisionally decided on by the great Transatlantic companies subsequent to the *Titanic* disaster.

It must not be supposed that the lane routes referred to had never been changed before. Owing to the presence of ice in 1903, 1904 and 1905 from about early in April to mid-June or early in July, westward-bound vessels crossed the meridian of 47° W in lat. 41° N, that is 60 miles further south than the then accepted track.

The publications known as "Sailing Directions", compiled by the Hydrographic Office at the Admiralty, indicate the caution which it is necessary to use in regions where ice is likely to be found.

The following is an extract from one of these books, named "United States Pilot (East Coast)", part I (second edition, 1909, page 34), referring to the ocean passages of the large Transatlantic mail and passenger steamers:

To these vessels, one of the chief dangers in crossing the Atlantic lies in the probability of encountering masses of ice, both in the form of bergs and of extensive fields of solid compact ice, released at the breaking up of winter in the Arctic regions, and drifted down by the Labrador Current across their direct route. Ice is more likely to be encountered in this route between April and August, both months inclusive, than at other times, although icebergs have been seen at all seasons northward of the parallel of 43° N, but not often so far south after August.

These icebergs are sometimes over 200 ft in height and of considerable extent. They have been seen as far south as lat. 39° N, to obtain which position they must have crossed the Gulf Stream impelled by the cold Arctic current underrunning the warm waters of the Gulf Stream. That this should happen is not to be wondered at when it is considered that the specific gravity of fresh-water ice, of which these bergs are composed, is about seven-eighths that of sea water, so that, however vast the berg may appear to the eye of the observer, he can in reality see one-eighth of its bulk, the remaining seven-eighths being submerged and subject to the deep-water currents of the ocean. The track of an iceberg is indeed directed mainly by current, so small a portion of its surface being exposed to the action of the winds that its course is but slightly retarded or deflected by moderate breezes. On the Great Bank of Newfoundland bergs are often observed to be moving south or south-east; those that drift westward of Cape Race usually pass between Green and St Pierre Banks.

The route chart of the North Atlantic, No 2058, shows the limits within which both field ice and icebergs may be met with, and where it should be carefully looked out for at all times, but especially during the spring and summer seasons. From this chart it would appear that whilst the southern and eastern limits of field ice are about lat. 42° N and long. 45° W, icebergs may be met with much farther from Newfoundland; in April, May and June they have been seen as far south as lat. 39° N, and as far east as long. 38° 30′ W.

And again on page 35:

> It is, in fact, impossible to give, within the outer limits named, any distinct idea of where ice may be expected, and no rule can be laid down to ensure safe navigation, as its position and the quantity met with differs so greatly in different seasons. Everything must depend upon the vigilance, caution and skill with which a vessel is navigated when crossing the dangerous ice-bearing regions of the Atlantic Ocean.

Similar warnings as to ice are also given in the "Nova Scotia (South-East Coast) and Bay of Fundy Pilot" (sixth edition, 1911) which is also published by the Hydrographic Office. Both the above-quoted books were supplied to the master of the *Titanic* (together with other necessary charts and books) before that ship left Southampton.

The above extracts show that it is quite incorrect to assume that icebergs had never before been encountered or field ice observed so far south at the particular time of year when the *Titanic* disaster occurred, but it is true to say that the field ice was certainly at that time further south than it has been seen for many years.

It may be useful here to give some definitions of the various forms of ice to be met with in these latitudes, although there is frequently some confusion in their use.

An iceberg may be defined as a detached portion of a Polar glacier carried out to sea. The ice of an iceberg formed from a glacier is of quite fresh water; only about an eighth of its mass floats above the surface of sea water.

A growler is a colloquial term applied to icebergs of small mass, which therefore only show a small portion above the surface. It is not infrequently a berg which has turned over, and is therefore showing what has been termed "black ice", or more correctly, dark blue ice.

Pack ice is the floating ice which covers wide areas of the Polar seas, broken into large pieces which are driven ("packed") together by wind and current, so as to form a practically continuous sheet. Such ice is generally frozen from sea water and not derived from glaciers.

Field ice is a term usually applied to frozen sea water floating in much looser form than pack ice.

An icefloe is the term generally applied to the same ice (i.e. field ice) in a smaller quantity.

A floe berg is a stratified mass of floe ice (i.e. sea-water ice).

ICE MESSAGES RECEIVED

The *Titanic* followed the Outward Southern Track until Sunday, the 14th April, in the usual way. At 11.40 pm on that day she struck an iceberg and at 2.20 am on the next day she foundered.

At 9 am (*Titanic* time) on that day [14th April] a wireless message from the SS *Caronia* was received by Captain Smith. It was as follows:

> Captain, *Titanic* — West-bound steamers report bergs growlers and field ice in 42° N from 49° to 51° W, 12th April. Compliments — Barr

It will be noticed that this message referred to bergs, growlers and field ice sighted on the 12th April — at least 48 hours before the time of the collision. At the time this message was received the *Titanic's* position was about lat. 43° 35′ N and long. 43° 50′ W. Captain Smith acknowledged the receipt of this message.

At 1.42 pm a wireless message from the SS *Baltic* was received by Captain Smith. It was as follows:

> Captain Smith, *Titanic* — Have had moderate, variable winds and clear, fine weather since leaving. Greek steamer *Athenai* reports passing icebergs and large quantities of field ice to-day in lat. 41° 51′ N, long. 49° 52′ W. Last night we spoke German oiltank steamer *Deutschland*, Stettin to Philadelphia, not under control, short of coal, lat. 40° 42′ N, long. 55° 11′ W. Wishes to be reported to New York and other steamers. Wish you and *Titanic* all success — Commander

At the time this message was received the *Titanic* position was about 42° 35′ N, 45° 50′ W. Captain Smith acknowledged the receipt of this message also.

Mr Ismay, the Managing Director of the White Star Line, was on board the *Titanic*, and it appears that the Master handed the *Baltic's* message to Mr Ismay almost immediately after it was received. This no doubt was in order that Mr Ismay might know that ice was to be expected. Mr Ismay states that he understood from the message that they would get up to the ice "that night". Mr Ismay showed this message to two ladies, and it is therefore probable that many persons on board became aware of its contents. This message ought in my opinion to have been put on the board in the chart-room as soon as it was received. It remained, however, in Mr Ismay's possession until 7.15 pm, when the Master asked Mr Ismay to return it. It was then that it was first posted in the chart-room.

This was considerably before the time at which the vessel reached the position recorded in the message. Nevertheless, I think it was irregular for the Master to part with the document, and improper for Mr Ismay to retain it, but the incident had, in my opinion, no connection with or influence upon the manner in which the vessel was navigated by the Master.

It appears that about 1.45 pm (*Titanic* time) on the 14th a message was sent from the German steamer *Amerika* to the Hydrographic Office in Washington, which was in the following terms:

Amerika passed two large icebergs in 41° 27′ N, 50° 8′ W, on the 14th April.

This was a position south of the point of the *Titanic's* disaster. The message does not mention at what hour the bergs had been observed. It was a private message for the hydrographer at Washington, but it passed to the *Titanic* because she was nearest to Cape Race, to which station it had to be sent in order to reach Washington. Being a message affecting navigation, it should in the ordinary course have been taken to the bridge. So far as can be ascertained, it was never heard of by anyone on board the *Titanic* outside the Marconi room. There were two Marconi operators in the Marconi room, namely, Phillips, who perished, and Bride, who survived and gave evidence. Bride did not receive the *Amerika* message, nor did Phillips mention it to him, though the two had much conversation together after it had been received. I am of opinion that when this message reached the Marconi room it was put aside by Phillips to wait until the *Titanic* would be within call of Cape Race (at about 8 or 8.30 pm), and that it was never handed to any officer of the *Titanic*.

At 5.50 pm the *Titanic's* course (which had been S 62° W) was changed to bring her on a westerly course for New York. In ordinary circumstances this change in her course should have been made about half an hour earlier, but she seems on this occasion to have continued for about ten miles longer on her south-westerly course before turning, with the result that she found herself, after altering course at 5.50 pm about four or five miles south of the customary route on a course S 86° W true. Her course, as thus set, would bring her at the time of the collision to a point about two miles to the southward of the customary route and four miles south and considerably to the westward of the indicated position of the *Baltic's* ice. Her position at the time of the collision would also be well to the southward of the indicated position of the ice mentioned in the *Caronia* message. This change of course was so insignificant that in my opinion it cannot have been made in consequence of information as to ice.

In this state of things, at 7.30 pm a fourth message was received, and is said by the Marconi operator Bride to have been delivered to the bridge. This message was from the SS *Californian* to the SS *Antillian*, but was picked up by the *Titanic*. It was as follows:

To Captain, *Antillian* — 6.30 pm apparent ship's time, lat. 42° 3′ N, long. 49° 9′ W. Three large bergs five miles to southward of us — Regards Lord.

Bride does not remember to what officer he delivered this message. By the time the *Titanic* reached the position of the collision (11.40 pm) she had gone about 50 miles to the westward of the indicated position of the ice mentioned in this fourth message. Thus it would appear that before the collision she had gone clear of the indicated positions of ice contained in the messages from the *Baltic* and *Californian*. As to the ice advised by the *Caronia* message, so far as it consisted of small bergs and field ice, it had before the time of the collision possibly drifted with the Gulf Stream to the eastward, and so far as it consisted of large bergs (which would be deep enough in the water to reach the Labrador current) it had probably gone to the southward. It was urged by Sir Robert Finley, who appeared for the owners, that this is strong evidence that the *Titanic* had been carefully and successfully navigated so as to avoid the ice of which she had received warning. Mr Ismay, however, stated that he understood from the *Baltic* message that "we would get up to the ice that night".

There was a fifth message received in the Marconi room of the *Titanic* at 9.40 pm. This was from a steamer called the *Mesaba*:

From *Mesaba* to *Titanic* and all east-bound ships. Ice report in lat. 42° N to 41° 25′ N, long. 49° to long. 50° 30′ W. Saw much heavy pack ice and great number large icebergs. Also field ice. Weather good, clear.

This message clearly indicated the presence of ice in the immediate vicinity of the *Titanic*, and if it had reached the bridge would perhaps have affected the navigation of the vessel. Unfortunately, it does not appear to have been delivered to the Master or to any of the officers. The Marconi operator was very busy from 8 o'clock onward transmitting messages via Cape Race for passengers on board the *Titanic*, and the probability is that he failed to grasp the significance and importance of the message, and put it aside until he should be less busy. It was never acknowledged by Captain Smith, and I am satisfied that it was not received by him. But, assuming Sir Robert Finlay's contentions to be well founded that the *Titanic* had been navigated so as to avoid the *Baltic* and the *Californian* ice, and that the *Caronia* ice had drifted to the eastward and to the southward, still there can be no doubt, if the evidence of Mr Lightoller, the second officer, is to be believed, that both he and the Master knew that the danger of meeting ice still existed.

Mr Lightoller says that the Master showed him the *Caronia* message at about 12.45 pm on the 14th April when he was on the bridge. He was about to go off watch, and he says he made a rough calculation in his head which satisfied him that the *Titanic* would not reach the position mentioned in the message until he came on watch again at 6 pm. At 6 pm Mr Lightoller came on the bridge again to take over the ship from Mr Wilde, the chief officer (dead). He does not remember being told anything about the *Baltic* message, which had been received at 1.42 pm. Mr Lightoller then requested Mr Moody, the sixth officer (dead), to let him know "at what time we should reach the vicinity of ice", and says that he thinks Mr Moody reported "about 11 o'clock".

Mr Lightoller says that 11 o'clock did not agree with a mental calculation he himself had made and which showed 9.30 as the time. This mental calculation he at first said he had made before Mr Moody gave him 11 o'clock as the time, but later on he corrected this, and said his mental calculation was made between 7 and 8 o'clock, and after Mr Moody had mentioned 11. He did not point out the difference to him, and thought that perhaps Mr Moody had made his calculations on the basis of some "other" message. Mr Lightoller excuses himself for not pointing out the difference by saying that Mr Moody was busy at the time, probably with stellar observations. It is, however, an odd circumstance that Mr Lightoller, who believed that the vicinity of ice would be reached before his watch ended at 10 pm, should not have mentioned the fact to Mr Moody, and it is also odd that, if he thought that Mr Moody was working on the basis of some "other" message, he did not ask what the other message was or where it came from. The point, however, of Mr Lightoller's evidence is that they both thought that the vicinity of ice would be reached before midnight.

When he was examined as to whether he did not fear that on entering the indicated ice region he might run foul of a growler (a low-lying berg) he answers: "No, I judged I should see it with sufficient distinctness" and at a distance of a "mile and a half, more probably two miles". He then adds: "In the event of meeting ice there are many things we look for. In the first place, a slight breeze. Of course, the stronger the breeze the more visible will the ice be or, rather, the breakers on the ice." He is then asked whether there was any breeze on this night, and he answers: "When I left the deck at 10 o'clock there was a slight breeze Oh, pardon me, no, I take that back. No, it was calm, perfectly calm." And almost immediately afterwards he describes the sea as "absolutely flat". It appeared, according to this witness, that at about 9 o'clock the Master came on the bridge and that Mr Lightoller had a conversation with him which lasted half an hour. This conversation, so far as it is material, is described by Mr Lightoller in the following words:

> We commenced to speak about the weather. He said, "There is not much
> wind." I said, "No, it is a flat calm as a matter of fact." He repeated it. He said,
> "A flat calm." I said, "Quite flat, there is no wind." I said something about it was
> rather a pity the breeze had not kept up whilst we were going through the ice
> region. Of course, my reason was obvious, he knew I meant the water ripples
> breaking on the base of the berg ... We then discussed the indications of ice. I
> remember saying: "In any case, there will be a certain amount of reflected light
> from the bergs." He said, "Oh, yes, there will be a certain amount of reflected
> light." I said or he said — blue was said between us — that even though the
> blue side of the berg was towards us, probably the outline, the white outline,
> would give us sufficient warning, that we should be able to see it at a good
> distance, and as far as we could see, we should be able to see it. Of course, it was
> just with regard to that possibility of the blue side being towards us, and that if

it did happen to be turned with the purely blue side towards us, there would still be the white outline.

Further on Mr Lightoller says that he told the Master nothing about his own calculation as to coming up with the ice at 9.30 or about Mr Moody's calculation as to coming up with it at 11.

The conversation with the Master ended with the Master saying, "If it becomes at all doubtful let me know at once, I will be just inside." This remark, Mr Lightoller says, undoubtedly referred to ice.

At 9.30 the Master went to his room, and the first thing that Mr Lightoller did afterwards was to send a message to the crow's-nest "to keep a sharp look-out for ice, particularly small ice and growlers", until daylight. There seems to be no doubt that this message was in fact sent, and that it was passed on to the next look-outs when they came on watch. Hitchins, the quartermaster, says he heard Mr Lightoller give the message to Mr Moody, and both the men in the crow's-nest at the time (Jewell and Symons) speak to having received it. From 9.30 to 10 o'clock, when his watch ended, Mr Lightoller remained on the bridge "looking out for ice". He also said that the night order book for the 14th had a footnote about keeping a sharp look-out for ice, and that this note was "initialled by every officer". At 10 o'clock Mr Lightoller handed over the watch to Mr Murdoch, the first officer (dead), telling him that "we might be up around the ice any time now". That Mr Murdoch knew of the danger of meeting ice appears from the evidence of Hemming, a lamp trimmer, who says that at about 7.15 pm Mr Murdoch told him to go forward and see the forescuttle hatch closed, "as we are in the vicinity of ice and there is a glow coming from that, and I want everything dark before the bridge".

The foregoing evidence establishes quite clearly that Captain Smith, the Master, Mr Murdoch, the first officer, Mr Lightoller, the second officer, and Mr Moody, the sixth officer, all knew on the Sunday evening that the vessel was entering a region where ice might be expected, and this being so, it seems to me to be of little importance to consider whether the Master had by design or otherwise succeeded in avoiding the particular ice indicated in the three messages received by him.

SPEED OF THE SHIP

The entire passage had been made at high speed, though not at the ship's maximum, and this speed was never reduced until the collision was unavoidable. At 10 pm the ship was registering 45 knots every two hours by the Cherub log.

The quartermaster on watch aft, when the *Titanic* struck, states that the log, reset at noon, then registered 260 knots, and the fourth officer, when working up the position from 7.30 pm to the time of the collision, states he estimated the *Titanic's* speed as 22 knots, and this is also borne out by evidence that the engines were running continuously at 75 revolutions.

THE WEATHER CONDITIONS

From 6 pm onwards to the time of the collision the weather was perfectly clear and fine. There was no moon, the stars were out, and there was not a cloud in the sky. There was, however, a drop in temperature of 10 deg. in slightly less than two hours, and by about 7.30 pm the temperature was 33 deg. F, and it eventually fell to 32 deg. F. That this was not necessarily an indication of ice is borne out by the Sailing Directions. The Nova Scotia (SE Coast) and Bay of Fundy Pilot (6th edition, 1911, page 16) says:

> No reliance can be placed on any warning being conveyed to a mariner by a fall of temperature either of the air or sea, on approaching ice. Some decrease in temperature has occasionally been recorded, but more often none has been observed.

Sir Ernest Shackleton was, however, of the opinion that:

> if there was no wind and the temperature fell abnormally for the time of the year, I would consider that I was approaching an area which might have ice in it.

ACTION THAT SHOULD HAVE BEEN TAKEN

The question is what ought the Master to have done. I am advised that, with the knowledge of the proximity of ice which the Master had, two courses were open to him. The one was to stand well to the southward instead of turning up to a westerly course; the other was to reduce speed materially as night approached. He did neither. The alteration of the course at 5.50 pm was so insignificant that it cannot be attributed to any intention to avoid ice. This deviation brought the vessel back to within about two miles of the customary route before 11.30 pm and there was certainly no reduction of speed. Why, then, did the Master persevere his course and maintain his speed?

The answer is to be found in the evidence. It was shown that for many years past, indeed, for a quarter of a century or more, the practice of liners using this track when in the vicinity of ice at night had been in clear weather to keep the course, to maintain the speed and to trust to a look-out to enable them to avoid the danger. This practice, it was said, had been justified by experience, no casualties having resulted from it. I accept the evidence as to the practice and as to the immunity from casualties which is said to have accompanied it. But the event has proved the practice to be bad. Its root is probably to be found in competition and in the desire of the public for passages rather than in the judgement of navigators. But unfortunately experience appeared to justify it.

In these circumstances I am not able to blame Captain Smith. He had not the experience which his own misfortune has afforded to those whom he has left behind, and he was doing only that which other skilled men would have done in the same position. It was suggested at the bar that he was open to influences which ought not to have affected him: that the presence of Mr Ismay on board and the knowledge which he perhaps had of a conversation between Mr Ismay and the Chief Engineer at Queenstown about the speed of the ship and the consumption of coal probably induced him to neglect precautions which he would otherwise have taken. But I do not believe this. The evidence shows that he was not trying to make any record passage or indeed any exceptionally quick passage. He was not trying to please anybody, but was exercising his own discretion in the way he thought best. He made a mistake, a very grievous mistake, but one in which, in face of the practice and of past experience, negligence cannot be said to have any part, and in the absence of negligence it is, in my opinion, impossible to fix Captain Smith with blame. It is, however, to be hoped that the last has been heard of the practice and that for the future it will be abandoned for what we now know to be more prudent and wiser measures. What was a mistake in the case of the *Titanic* would without doubt be negligence in any similar case in the future.

THE COLLISION

Mr Lightoller turned over the ship to Mr Murdoch, the first officer, at 10 o'clock, telling him that the ship was within the region where ice had been reported. He also told him of the message he had sent to the crow's-nest, and his conversation with the Master, and of the latter's orders.

The ship appears to have run on the same course, until, at a little before 11.40 pm, one of the look-outs in the crow's-nest struck three blows on the gong, which was the accepted warning for something ahead, following this immediately afterwards by a telephone message to the bridge: "Iceberg right ahead". Almost simultaneously with the three gong signal, Mr Murdoch, the officer of the watch, gave the order "Hard-a-starboard", and immediately telegraphed down to the engine-room "Stop. Full speed astern". The helm was already "hard over", and the ship's head had fallen off about two points to port when she collided with an iceberg well forward on her starboard side.

Mr Murdoch at the same time pulled the lever over, which closed the watertight doors in the engine- and boiler-rooms.

The Master "rushed out" on to the bridge and asked Mr Murdoch what the ship had struck.

Mr Murdoch replied: "An iceberg, Sir; I hard-a-starboarded and reversed the engines, and I was going to hard-a-port round it but she was too close. I could not do any more. I have closed the watertight doors."

From the evidence given it appears that the *Titanic* had turned about two points to port before the collision occurred. From various experiments subsequently made with the SS *Olympic*, a sister ship to the *Titanic*, it was found that, travelling at the same rate as the *Titanic*, about 37 seconds would be required for the ship to change her course to this extent after the helm had been put hard-a-starboard. In this time the ship would travel about 466 yards, and allowing for the few seconds that would be necessary for the order to be given, it may be assumed that 500 yards was about the distance at which the iceberg was sighted either from the bridge or crow's-nest.

That it was quite possible on this night, even with a sharp look-out at the stemhead, crow's-nest and on the bridge, not to see an iceberg at this distance is shown by the evidence of Captain Rostron of the *Carpathia*.

The injuries to the ship, which are described in the next section, were of such a kind that she foundered in two hours and forty minutes.

DESCRIPTION OF THE DAMAGE TO THE SHIP AND OF ITS GRADUAL AND FINAL EFFECT, WITH OBSERVATIONS THEREON

EXTENT OF THE DAMAGE

The collision with the iceberg, which took place at 11.40 pm, caused damage to the bottom of the starboard side of the vessel at about 10 ft above the level of the keel, but there was no damage above this height. There was damage in the fore peak, No 1 hold, No 2 hold, No 3 hold, No 6 boiler-room, and No 5 boiler-room.

The damage extended over a length of about 300 ft.

TIME IN WHICH DAMAGE WAS DONE

As the ship was moving at over 20 knots, she would have passed through 300 ft in less than 10 seconds, so that the damage was done in about this time.

THE FLOODING IN THE FIRST TEN MINUTES

At first it is desirable to consider what happened in the first ten minutes.

The forepeak was not flooded above the Orlop deck — i.e. the peak tank top — from the hole in the bottom of the peak tank.

In No 1 hold there was 7 ft of water.

In No 2 hold, five minutes after the collision, water was seen rushing in at the bottom of the firemen's passage on the starboard side, so that the ship's side was damaged abaft of bulkhead B sufficiently to open the side of the firemen's passage, which was $3\frac{1}{2}$ ft from the outer skin of the ship, thereby flooding both the hold and the passage.

In No 3 hold the mail-room was filled soon after the collision. The floor of the mail-room is 24 ft above the keel.

In No 6 boiler-room, when the collision took place, water at once poured in at about 2 ft above the stokehold plates, on the starboard side, at the after end of the boiler-room. Some of the firemen immediately went through the watertight door opening to No 5 boiler-room because the water was flooding the place. The watertight doors in the engine-rooms were shut from the bridge almost immediately after the collision. Ten minutes later it was found that there was water to the height of 8 ft above the double bottom in No 6 boiler-room.

No 5 boiler-room was damaged at the ship's side in the starboard forward bunker at a distance of 2 ft above the stokehold plates, at 2 ft from the watertight bulkhead between Nos 5 and 6 boiler-rooms. Water poured in at that place as it would from an ordinary fire hose. At the time of the collision this bunker had no coal in it. The bunker door was closed when water was seen to be entering the ship.

In No 4 boiler-room there was no indication of any damage at the early stages of the sinking.

GRADUAL EFFECT OF THE DAMAGE

It will thus be seen that all the six compartments forward of No 4 boiler-room were open to the sea by damage which existed at about 10 ft above the keel. At ten minutes after the collision the water seems to have risen to about 14 ft above the keel in all these compartments except No 5 boiler-room. After the first ten minutes, the water rose steadily in all these six compartments. The fore peak above the peak tank was not filled until an hour after the collision, when the vessel's bow was submerged to above C deck. The water then flowed in from the top through the deck scuttle forward of the collision bulkhead. It was by this scuttle that access was obtained to all the decks below C down to the peak tank top on the Orlop deck.

At 12 o'clock water was coming up in No 1 hatch. It was getting into the firemen's quarters and driving the firemen out. It was rushing round No 1 hatch on G deck and coming mostly from the starboard side, so that in 20 minutes the water had risen above G deck in No 1 hold.

In No 2 hold, about 40 minutes after the collision, the water was coming into the seamen's quarters on E deck through a burst fore and aft wooden bulkhead of a third-class cabin opposite the seamen's wash place. Thus, the water had risen in No 2 hold to about 3 ft above E deck in 40 minutes.

In No 3 hold the mail-room was afloat about 20 minutes after the collision. The bottom of the mailroom, which is on the Orlop deck, is 24 ft above the keel.

The watertight doors on F deck at the fore and after ends of No 3 compartment were not closed then.

The mail-room was filling and water was within 2 ft of G deck, rising fast, when the order was given to clear the boats.

There was then no water on F deck.

There is a stairway on the port side on G deck which leads down to the first-class baggage-room on the Orlop deck immediately below. There was water in this baggage room 25 minutes after the collision. Half an hour after the collision water was up to G deck in the mail-room.

Thus the water had risen in this compartment to within 2 ft of G deck in 20 minutes, and above G deck in 25 to 30 minutes.

No 6 boiler-room was abandoned by the men almost immediately after the collision. Ten minutes later the water had risen to 8 ft above the top of the double bottom, and probably reached the top of the bulkhead at the after end of the compartment, at the level of E deck, in about one hour after the collision.

In No 5 boiler-room there was no water above the stokehold plates, until a rush of water came through the pass between the boilers from the forward end, and drove the leading stoker out.

It has already been shown in the description of what happened in the first ten minutes that water was coming into No 5 boiler-room in the forward starboard bunker at 2 ft above the plates in a stream about the size of a deck hose. The door in this bunker had been dropped, probably when water was first discovered, which was a few minutes after the collision. This would cause the water to be retained in the bunker until it rose high enough to burst the door, which was weaker than the bunker bulkhead. This happened about an hour after the collision.

One hour and 40 minutes after collision, water was coming in forward in small quantities, in No 4 boiler-room, from underneath the floor in the forward part. The men remained in that stokehold till ordered on deck.

When the men left No 4, some of them went through Nos 3, 2 and 1 boiler-rooms into the reciprocating engine-room, and from there on deck. There was no water in the boiler-rooms abaft No 4 1 hour 40 minutes after the collision (1.20 am), and there was then none in the reciprocating and turbine engine-rooms.

There was no damage to the electrical engine-room and tunnels.

From the foregoing it follows that there was no damage abaft No 4 boiler-room.

All the watertight doors aft of the main engine-room were opened after the collision.

Half an hour after the collision the watertight doors from the engine-room to the stokehold were opened as far forward as they could be to No 4 boiler-room.

FINAL EFFECT OF THE DAMAGE

The later stages of the sinking cannot be stated with any precision owing to a confusion of the times, which was natural under the circumstances.

The forecastle deck was not under water at 1.35 am. Distress signals were fired until two hours after the collision (1.45 am). At this time the foredeck was under water. The forecastle head was not then submerged, though it was getting close down to the water about half an hour before she disappeared (1.50 am).

When the last boat, lowered from davits (D), left the ship, A deck was under water, and water came up the stairway under the Boat deck almost immediately afterwards. After this the other port collapsible (B), which had been stowed on the officers' house, was uncovered, the lashings cut adrift, and she was swung round over the edge of the coamings of the deckhouse on to the Boat deck.

Very shortly afterwards the vessel, according to Mr Lightoller's account, seemed to take a dive, and he just walked into the water. When he came to the surface all the funnels were above the water.

Her stern was gradually rising out of the water, and the propellers were clear of the water. The ship did not break in two and she did eventually attain the perpendicular, when the second funnel from aft about reached the water. There were no lights burning then, though they kept alight practically until the last.

Before reaching the perpendicular, when at an angle of 50 or 60 degrees, there was a rumbling sound which may be attributed to the boilers leaving their beds and crashing down on to or through the bulkheads. She became more perpendicular and finally absolutely perpendicular, when she went slowly down.

After sinking as far as the after part of the Boat deck she went down more quickly. The ship disappeared at 2.20 am.

OBSERVATIONS

I am advised that the *Titanic* as constructed could not have remained afloat long with such damage as she received. Her bulkheads were spaced to enable her to remain afloat with any two compartments in communication with the sea. She had a sufficient margin of safety with any two of the compartments flooded which were actually damaged.

In fact any three of the four forward compartments could have been flooded by the damage received without sinking the ship to the top of her bulkheads.

Even if the four forward compartments had been flooded, the water would not have got into any of the compartments abaft of them, though it would have been above the top of some of the forward bulkheads. But the ship, even with these found compartments flooded would have remained afloat. But she could not remain afloat with the four forward compartments and the forward boiler-room (No 6) also flooded.

The flooding of these five compartments alone would have sunk the ship sufficiently deeply to have caused the water to rise above the bulkhead at the after end of the forward boiler-room (No 6) and to flow over into the next boiler-room (No 5), and to fill it up until in turn its after bulkhead would be overwhelmed and the water would thereby flow over and fill No 4 boiler-room, and so on in succession to the other boiler-rooms, till the ship would ultimately fill and sink.

It has been shown that water came into the five forward compartments to a height of about 14 ft above the keel in the first ten minutes. This was at a rate of inflow with which the ship's pumps could not possibly have coped, so that the damage done to these five compartments alone inevitably sealed the doom of the ship.

The damage done in the boiler-rooms Nos 5 and 4 was too slight to have hastened appreciably the sinking of the ship, for it was given in evidence that no considerable amount of water was in either of these compartments for an hour after the collision. The rate at which water came into No 6 boiler-room makes it highly probable that the compartment was filled in not more than an hour, after which the flow over the top of the bulkhead between 5 and 6 began and continued till No 5 was filled.

It was shown that the leak in No 5 boiler-room was only about equal to the flow of a deck hose pipe about 3 inches in diameter.

The leak in No 4, supposing that there was one, was only enough to admit about 3 ft of water in that compartment in 1 hour 40 minutes.

Hence the leaks in Nos 4 and 5 boiler-rooms did not appreciably hasten the sinking of the vessel.

The evidence is very doubtful as to No 4 being damaged. The pumps were being worked in No 5 soon after the collision. The 10 inch leather special suction pipe which was carried from aft is more likely to have been carried for use in No 5 than No 4, because the doors were probably ordered to be opened soon after the collision, when water was known to be coming into No 5. There is no evidence that the pumps were being worked in No 4.

The only evidence possibly favourable to the view that the pipe was required for No 4, and not for No 5, is that Scott, a greaser, says that he saw engineers dragging the suction pipe along 1 hour after the collision. But even as late as this it may have been wanted for No 5 only.

The importance of the question of the damage to No 5 is small, because the ship as actually constructed was doomed as soon as the water in No 6 boiler-room and all compartments forward of it entered in the quantities it actually did. It is only of importance in dealing with the question of what would have happened to the ship had she been more completely subdivided.

It was stated in evidence that if No 4 had not been damaged or had only been damaged to an extent within the powers of the pumps to keep under, then, if the bulkheads had been carried to C deck, the ship might have been saved. Further methods of increased sub-division and their effect upon the fate of the ship are discussed later.

Evidence was given showing that after the watertight doors in the engine- and boiler-rooms had been all closed, except those forward of No 4 groups of boilers, they were opened again, and there is no evidence to show that they were again closed. Though it is probable that the engineers who remained below would have closed these doors as the water rose in the compartments, it was not necessary for them to do this as each door had an automatic closing arrangement which would have come into operation immediately a small amount of water came through the door.

It is probable, however, that the life of the ship would have been lengthened somewhat if these doors had been left open, for the water would have flowed through them to the after part of the ship, and the rate of flow of the water into the ship would have been for a time reduced, as the bow might have been kept up a little by the water which flowed aft.

It is thus seen that the efficiency of the automatic arrangements for the closing of the watertight doors, which was questioned during the inquiry, had no important bearing on the question of hastening the sinking of the ship, except that, in the case of the doors not having been closed by the engineers, it might have retarded the sinking of the ship if they had not acted. The engineers would not have prevented the doors from closing unless they had been convinced that the ship was doomed. There is no evidence that they did prevent the doors from closing.

The engineers were applying the pumps when Barrett, leading stoker, left No 5 boiler-room, but even if they had succeeded in getting all the pumps in the ship to work they could not have saved the ship or prolonged her life to any appreciable extent.

Effect of additional sub-division upon flotation

Watertight decks
It is in evidence that advantage might be obtained from the point of view of greater safety in having a watertight deck.

Without entering into the general question of the advantage of watertight decks for all ships, it is desirable to form an opinion in the case of the *Titanic* as to whether making the bulkhead deck watertight would have been an advantage in the circumstances of the accident, or in case of accident to ships of this class.

I am advised that it is found that with all the compartments certainly known to have been flooded, viz., those forward of No 4 boiler-room, the ship would have remained afloat if the bulkhead deck had been a watertight deck. If, however, No 4 boiler-room had also been flooded, the ship would not have remained afloat unless, in addition to making the bulkhead deck watertight, the transverse bulkhead abaft of No 4 boiler-room had been carried up to D deck.

To make the bulkhead deck effectively watertight for this purpose it would have been necessary to carry watertight trunks round all the openings in the bulkhead deck up to C deck.

It has been shown that with the bulkhead abaft No 5 boiler-room carried to C deck the ship would have remained afloat if the compartments certainly known to have been damaged had been flooded.

I do not desire to express an opinion upon the question whether it would have conduced to safety in the case of the *Titanic* if a watertight deck had been fitted below the water line, as there may be some objections to such a deck. There are many considerations involved, and I think that the matter should be dealt with by the Bulkhead Committee for ships in general.

Longitudinal sub-division

The advantages and disadvantages of longitudinal sub-division by means of watertight bunker bulkheads were pointed out in evidence.

While not attempting to deal with this question generally for ships, I am advised that if the *Titanic* had been divided in the longitudinal method, instead of in the transverse method only, she would have been able, if damaged as supposed, to remain afloat, though with a list which could have been corrected by putting water ballast into suitable places.

This subject is one, however, which again involves many considerations, and I think that for ships generally the matter should be referred to the Bulkhead Committee for their consideration and report.

Extending double bottom up the sides

It was shown in evidence that there would be increased protection in carrying the double bottom higher up the side than was done in the *Titanic*, and that some of the boiler-rooms would probably not then have been flooded, as water could not have entered the ship except in the double bottom.

In the case of the *Titanic* I am advised that this would have been an advantage, but it was pointed out in evidence that there are certain disadvantages which in some ships may outweigh the advantages.

In view of what has already been said about the possible advantages of longitudinal sub-division, it is unnecessary further to discuss the question of carrying up the double bottom in ships generally. This matter should also be dealt with by the Bulkhead Committee.

Watertight doors

With reference to the question of the watertight doors of the ship, there does not appear to have been any appreciable effect upon the sinking of the ship caused by either shutting or not shutting the doors. There does not appear to have been any difficulty in working the watertight doors. They appear to have been shut in good time after the collision.

But in other cases of damage in ships constructed like the *Titanic*, it is probable that the efficiency of the closing arrangement of the watertight door may exert a vital influence on the safety of the ship. It has been represented that, in future, consideration should be given to the question "as to how far bulkheads should be solid bulkheads, and how far there should be watertight doors, and, if there should be watertight doors, how far they may or may not be automatically operated". This again is a question on which it is not necessary here to express any general opinion, for there are conflicting considerations which vary in individual cases. The matter, however, should come under the effective supervision of the Board of Trade much more than it seems to come at present, and should be referred to the Bulkhead Committee for their consideration, with a view to their suggesting in detail where doors should or should not be allowed, and the type of door which should be adopted in the different parts of ships.

ACCOUNT OF THE SAVING AND RESCUE OF THOSE WHO SURVIVED

THE BOATS

The *Titanic* was provided with 20 boats. They were all on the Boat deck. Fourteen were lifeboats. These were hung inboard in davits, seven on the starboard side and seven on the port side, and were designed to carry 65 persons each. Two were emergency boats. These were also in davits, but were hung outboard, one on the starboard side and one on the port side, and were designed to carry 40 persons each. The remaining four boats were Engelhardt or collapsible boats. Two of these were stowed on the Boat deck and two on the roof of the officers' quarters, and they were designed to carry 47 persons each. Thus the total boat accommodation was for 1,178 persons. The boats in davits were numbered, the odd numbers being on the starboard side and the even numbers on the port side. The numbering began with the emergency boats which were forward, and ran aft. Thus the boats on the starboard side were numbered 1 (an emergency boat) 3, 5, 7, 9, 11, 13 and 15 (lifeboats), and those on the port side, 2 (an emergency boat), 4, 6, 8, 10, 12, 14 and 16 (lifeboats). The collapsible boats were lettered, A and B being on the roof of the officers' quarters, and C and D being on the Boat deck; C was abreast of No 1 (emergency boat) and D abreast of No 2 (emergency boat). Further particulars as to the boats are provided earlier in this report.

In ordinary circumstances all these boats (with the exception of 1 and 2) were kept covered up, and contained only a portion of their equipment, such as oars, masts and sails, and water, some of the remaining portion, such as lamps, compasses and biscuits being stowed in the ship in some convenient place, ready for use when required. Much examination was directed at the hearing to showing that some boats left the ship without a lamp and others without a compass and so on, but in the circumstances of confusion and excitement which existed at the time of the disaster this seems to me to be excusable.

Each member of the crew had a boat assigned to him in printed lists, which were posted up in convenient places for the men to see, but it appeared that in some cases the men had not looked at these lists and did not know their respective boats.

There had been no proper boat drill nor a boat muster. It was explained that great difficulty frequently exists in getting firemen to take part in a boat drill. They regard it as no part of their work. There seem to be no statutory requirements as to boat drills or musters, although there is a provision (Section 9 of the Merchant Shipping Act of 1906) that when a boat drill does take place the master of the vessel is, under a penalty, to record the fact in his log. I think it is desirable that the Board of Trade should make rules requiring boat drills and boat musters to be held of such a kind and at such times as may be suitable to the ship and to the voyage on which she is engaged. Boat drill, regulated according to the opportunities of the service, should always be held.

It is perhaps worth recording that there was an inspection of the boats themselves at Southampton by Mr Clarke, the emigration officer, and that, as a result, Mr Clarke gave his certificate that the boats were satisfactory. For the purpose of this inspection two of the boats were lowered to the water and crews exercised in them.

The collision took place at 11.40 pm (ship's time). About midnight it was realised that the vessel could not live, and at about 12.05 the order was given to uncover the 14 boats under davits. The work began on both sides of the ship under the superintendence of five officers. It did not proceed quickly at first; the crew arrived on the Boat deck only gradually, and there was an average of not more than three deck hands to each boat. At 12.20 the order was given to swing out the boats, and this work was at once commenced. There were a few passengers on the deck at this time. Mr Lightoller, who was one of the officers directing operations, says that the noise of the steam blowing off was so great that his voice could not be heard, and that he had to give directions with his hands.

Before this work had been begun, the stewards were rousing the passengers in their different quarters, helping them to put on lifebelts and getting them up to the Boat deck. At about 12.30 the order was given to place women and children in the boats. This was proceeded with at once, and at about 12.45 Mr Murdoch gave the order to lower No 7 boat (on the starboard side) to the water. The work of uncovering, filling and lowering the boats was done under the following supervision: Mr Lowe, the fifth officer, saw to Nos 1, 3, 5 and 7. Mr Murdoch (lost) saw also to 1 and 7 and to A and C. Mr Moody (lost) looked after Nos 9, 11, 13 and 15. Mr Murdoch also saw to 9 and 11. Mr

Lightoller saw to Nos 4, 6, 8, B and D. Mr Wilde (lost) also saw to 8 and D. Mr Lightoller and Mr Moody saw to 10 and 16, and Mr Lowe to 12 and 14. Mr Wilde also assisted at No 14, Mr Boxall helping generally.

The evidence satisfies me that the officers did their work very well and without any thought of themselves. Captain Smith, the Master, Mr Wilde, the chief officer, Mr Murdoch, the first officer, and Mr Moody, the sixth officer, all went down with the ship while performing their duties. The others, with the exception of Mr Lightoller, took charge of boats and thus were saved. Mr Lightoller was swept off deck as the vessel went down and was subsequently picked up.

So far as can be ascertained the boats left the ship at the times given in the table, but I think it is necessary to say that these, and, indeed, all the times subsequent to the collision which are mentioned by the witnesses, are unreliable.

Times at which the boats left the ship

No	Starboard side	No	Port side
7	12.45 am	6	12.55 am
5	12.55 am	8	1.10 am
3	1.00 am	10	1.20 am
1	1.10 am	12	1.25 am
9	1.20 am	14	1.30 am
11	1.25 am	16	1.35 am
13	1.35 am	2	1.45 am
15	1.35 am	4	1.55 am
C	1.40 am	D	2.05 am
A	Floated off when the ship sank and was utilised as a raft	B	Floated off when the ship sank and was utilised as a raft

As regards the collapsible boats, C and D were properly lowered; as to A and B, which were on the roof of the officers' house, they were left until the last. There was difficulty in getting these boats down to the deck, and the ship had at this time a list. Very few of the deck hands were left in the ship, as they had nearly all gone to man the lifeboats, and the stewards and firemen were unaccustomed to work the collapsible boats. Work appears to have been going on in connection with these two boats at the time that the ship sank. The boats seem to have floated from the deck and to have served in the water as rafts.

The table on the following page shows the numbers of male crew, male passengers, and women and children who, according to the evidence, left the ship in each boat. In three or four instances the numbers of women and

Reported numbers of people leaving Titanic *in boats*

Starboard side boat No	Men of crew	Men passengers	Women and children	Total	Port side boat No	Men of crew	Men	Women and children	Total
7	3	4	20	27	6	2	2	24	28
5	5	6	30	41	8	4	–	35	39
8	15	10	25	50	10	5	–	50	55
1	7	3	2	12	2	4	1	21	26
9	8	6	42	56	12	2	–	40	42
11	9	1	60	70	14	8	2	53	63
18	5	–	59	64	16	6	–	50	56
15	13	4	53	70	4	4	–	36	40
C	5	2	64	71	D	2	2	40	44
A utilized after the ship sank					B utilized after the ship sank				
Total	70	36	355	461		37	7	349	393

General total: 107 men of the crew; 43 men passengers; 704 women and children

children are only arrived at by subtracting the numbers of crew and male passengers from the total said to be in the boat (these are in italics). In each case the lowest figures given are taken.

The table shows that, in all, 107 men of the crew, 43 male passengers and 704 women and children, or a total of 854 people were in 18 boats. In addition, about 60 persons, two of whom were women, were said to have been transferred, subsequently, from A and B collapsible boats to other boats or rescued from the water, making a total of 914 who escaped with their lives. It is obvious that these figures are quite unreliable, for only 712 were, in fact, saved by the *Carpathia*, the steamer which came to the rescue at about 4 am, and all the boats were accounted for. Another remarkable discrepancy is that, of the 712 saved, 189 were, in fact, men of the crew, 129 were male passengers and 394 were women and children. In other words, the real proportion of women to men saved was much less than the proportion appearing in the evidence from the boats. Allowing for those subsequently picked up, of the 712 persons saved only 652 can have left the *Titanic* in boats, or an average of about 36 per boat. There was a tendency in the evidence to exaggerate the numbers in each boat, to exaggerate the proportion of women to men and to diminish the number of crew. I do not attribute this to any wish on the part of the witnesses to mislead the Court, but to a natural desire to make the best case for themselves and their ship. The seamen who gave evidence were too frequently encouraged, when under examination in the witness-box, to understate the number of crew in the boats. The number of crew actually saved was 189, giving an average of ten per boat, and if from this figure the 58 men of the 60 persons above-mentioned be deducted, the average number of crew leaving the ship in the boats must still have been at least 7. The probability, however, is that many of the 60 picked up were passengers.

The discipline both among passengers and crew during the lowering of the boats was good, but the organisation should have been better, and if it had been it is possible that more lives would have been saved.

The real difficulty in dealing with the question of the boats is to find the explanation of so many of them leaving the ship with comparatively few persons in them. No 1 certainly left with only 12; this was an emergency boat with a carrying capacity of 40. No 7 left with only 27, and No 6 with only 28; these were lifeboats with a carrying capacity of 65 each, and several of the others, according to the evidence and certainly according to the truth, must have left only partly filled. Many explanations are forthcoming, one being that the passengers were unwilling to leave the ship. When the earlier boats left, and before the *Titanic* had begun materially to settle down, there was a drop of 65 ft from the Boat deck to the water, and the women feared to get into the boats. Many people thought that the risk in the ship was less than the risk in the boats. This explanation is supported by the evidence of Captain Rostron of the *Carpathia*. He says that after those who were saved got on board his ship, he was told by some of them that when the boats first left the *Titanic* the people "really would not be put in the boats, they did not want to go in". There was a large body of evidence from the *Titanic* to the same effect, and I have no doubt that many people, particularly women, refused to leave the deck for the boats. At one time the Master appears to have had the intention of putting the people into the boats from the gang-way doors in the side of the ship. This was possibly with a view to allay the fears of the passengers, for from these doors the water could be reached by means of ladders, and the lowering of some of the earlier boats when only partly filled may be accounted for in this way. There is no doubt that the Master did order some of the partly filled boats to row to a position under one of the doors with the object of taking in passengers at that point. It appears, however, that these doors were never opened. Another explanation is that some women refused to leave their husbands. It is said further that the officers engaged in putting the people into the boats feared that the boats might buckle if they were filled, but this proved to be an unfounded appre-hension, for one or more boats were completely filled and then successfully lowered to the water.

At 12.35 the message from the *Carpathia* was received announcing that she was making for the *Titanic*. This probably became known and may have tended to make the passengers still more unwilling to leave the ship, and the lights of a ship (the *Californian*) which were seen by many people may have encour-aged the passengers to hope that assistance was at hand. These explanations are perhaps sufficient to account for so many of the lifeboats leaving without a full boat load; but I think, nevertheless, that if the boats had been kept a little longer before being lowered, or if the after gangway doors had been opened, more pas-sengers might have been induced to enter the boats. And if women could not be induced to enter the boats, the boats ought then to have been filled up with men. It is difficult to account for so many of the lifeboats being sent from the sinking ship, in a smooth sea, far from full. These boats left behind them many hundreds of lives to perish. I do not, however, desire these observations to be read as casting any reflection on the officers of the ship or on the crew who were working on the Boat deck. They all worked admirably, but I think that if there had been better organisation the results would have been more satisfactory.

I heard much evidence as to the conduct of the boats after the *Titanic* sank and when there must have been many struggling people in the water, and I regret to say that in my opinion some, at all events, of the boats failed to attempt to save lives when they might have done so, and might have done so successfully. This was particularly the case with boat No 1. It may reason-ably have been thought that the risk of making the attempt was too great, but it seems to me that if the attempt had been made by some of these boats it might have been the means of saving a few more lives. Subject to these few adverse comments, I have nothing but praise for both passengers and crew. All the witnesses speak well of their behaviour. It is to be remembered that the night was dark, the noise of the escaping steam was terrifying, the peril, though perhaps not generally recognised, was imminent and great, and many passengers who were unable to speak or to understand English were being collected together and hurried into the boats.

CONDUCT OF SIR DUFF GORDON AND MR ISMAY

An attack was made in the course of the Inquiry on the moral conduct of two of the passengers, namely, Sir Cosmo Duff Gordon and Mr Bruce Ismay. It is no part of the business of the Court to enquire into such matters, and I should pass them by in silence if I did not fear that my silence might be misunderstood. The very gross charge against Sir Cosmo Duff Gordon that, having got into No 1 boat, he bribed the men in it to row away from drowning people is unfounded. I have said that the members of the crew in that boat might have made some attempt to save the people in the water, and that such an attempt would probably have been successful, but I do not believe that the men were deterred from making the attempt by any act of Sir Cosmo Duff Gordon's. At the same time I think that if he had encouraged the men to return to the position where the *Titanic* had foundered, they would probably have made an effort to do so and could have saved some lives.

As to the attack on Mr Bruce Ismay, it resolved itself into the suggestion that, occupying the position of Managing Director of the Steamship Company, some moral duty was imposed upon him to wait on board until the vessel foundered. I do not agree. Mr Ismay, after rendering assistance to many passengers, found "C" collapsible, the last boat on the starboard side, actually being lowered. No other people were there at the time. There was room for him and he jumped in. Had he not jumped in he would merely have added one more life, namely his own, to the number of those lost.

THE THIRD-CLASS PASSENGERS

It had been suggested before the Inquiry that the third-class passengers had been unfairly treated, that their access to the Boat deck had been impeded, and that when at last they reached that deck the first- and second-class passengers were given precedence in getting places in the boats. There appears to have been no truth in these suggestions. It is no doubt true that the proportion of third-class passengers saved falls far short of the proportion of the first- and second-class, but this is accounted for by the greater reluctance of the third-class passengers to leave the ship, by their unwillingness to part with their baggage, by the difficulty in getting them up from their quarters, which were at the extreme ends of the ship, and by other similar causes. The interests of the relatives of some of the third-class passengers who had perished were in the hands of Mr Harbinson, who attended the Inquiry on their behalf. He said at the end of his address to the Court:

> I wish to say distinctly that no evidence has been given in the course of this
> case which would substantiate a charge that any attempt was made to keep back

the third-class passengers. I desire further to say that there is no evidence that when they did reach the Boat deck there was any discrimination practised either by the officers or the sailors in putting them into the boats.

I am satisfied that the explanation of the excessive proportion of third-class passengers lost is not to be found in the suggestion that the third-class passengers were in any way unfairly treated. They were not unfairly treated.

MEANS TAKEN TO PROCURE ASSISTANCE

As soon as the dangerous condition of the ship was realised, messages were sent by the Master's orders to all steamers within reach. At 12.15 am the distress signal CQD was sent. This was heard by several steamships and by Cape Race. By 12.25, Mr Boxall, the fourth officer, had worked out the correct position of the *Titanic*, and then another message was sent: "Come at once, we have struck a berg." This was heard by the Cunard steamer *Carpathia*, which was at this time bound from New York to Liverpool and 58 miles away. The *Carpathia* answered, saying that she was coming to the assistance of the *Titanic*. This was reported to Captain Smith on the Boat deck. At 12.26 a message was sent out: "Sinking, cannot hear for noise of steam." Many other messages were also sent, but as they were only heard by steamers which were too far away to render help it is not necessary to refer to them. At 1.45 a message was heard by the *Carpathia*: "Engine room full up to boilers." The last message sent out was "CQ", which was faintly heard by the steamer *Virginian*. This message was sent at 2.17. It thus appears that the Marconi apparatus was at work until within a few minutes of the foundering of the *Titanic*.

Meanwhile Mr Boxall was sending up distress signals from the deck. These signals (rockets) were sent off at intervals from a socket by No 1 emergency boat on the Boat deck. They were the ordinary distress signals, exploding in the air and throwing off white stars. The firing of these signals began about the time that No 7 boat was lowered (12.45 am), and it continued until Mr Boxall left the ship at about 1.45.

Mr Boxall was also using a Morse light from the bridge in the direction of a ship whose lights he saw about half a point on the port bow of the *Titanic*, at a distance, as he thought, of about five or six miles. He got no answer. In all, Mr Boxall fired about eight rockets. There appears to be no doubt that the vessel whose lights he saw was the *Californian*. The evidence from the *Californian* speaks of eight rockets having been seen between 12.30 and 1.40. The *Californian* heard none of the *Titanic's* messages; she had only one Marconi operator on board and he was asleep.

THE RESCUE BY THE SS *CARPATHIA*

On the 15th of April the SS *Carpathia*, 13,600 tons gross, of the Cunard Line (Mr Arthur Henry Rostron, Master) was on her passage to Liverpool from New York. She carried some 740 passengers and 325 crew.

On receipt of the *Titanic's* first distress message the Captain immediately ordered the ship to be turned round and driven at her highest speed (17½ knots) in the direction of the *Titanic*. He also informed the *Titanic* by wireless that he was coming to her assistance, and he subsequently received various messages from her. At about 2.40 am he saw a green flare which, as the evidence shows, was being sent up by Mr Boxall in No 2 boat. From this time until 4 am Captain Rostron was altering his course continually in order to avoid icebergs. He fired rockets in answer to the signals he saw from Boxall's boat. At 4 o'clock he considered he was practically up to the position given and he stopped his ship at 4.05. He sighted the first boat (No 2) and picked her up at 4.10. There was then a large number of icebergs round him, and it was just daylight. Eventually he picked up in all 13 lifeboats, two emergency boats and two collapsible boats, all of which were taken on board the *Carpathia*, the other boats being abandoned as damaged or useless. From these boats he took on board 712 persons, one of whom died shortly afterwards. The boats were scattered over an area of four to five miles, and it was 8 am before they had all been picked up. He saw very little wreckage when he got near to the scene of the disaster: only a few deck chairs, cork lifebelts, etc. and only one body. The position was then 41° 46′ N, 50° 14′ W.

The *Carpathia* subsequently returned to New York with the passengers and crew she had rescued.

The Court desires to record its great admiration of Captain Rostron's conduct. He did the very best that could be done.

Numbers saved

		1st class
Adult males	57	out of 175 or 32.57 per cent
Adult females	140	out of 144 or 97.22 per cent
Male children	5	All saved
Female children	1	All saved
	203	out of 325 or 62.46 per cent

		2nd class
Adult males	14	out of 168 or 8.33 per cent
Adult females	80	out of 93 or 86.02 per cent
Male children	11	All saved
Female children	13	All saved
	118	out of 285 or 41.40 per cent

		3rd class
Adult males	75	out of 462 or 16.23 per cent
Adult females	76	out of 165 or 46.06 per cent
Male children	13	out of 48 or 27.08 per cent
Female children	14	out of 31 or 45.16 per cent
	178	out of 706 or 25.21 per cent
Total	499	out of 1,316 or 37.94 per cent

		Crew
Deck Department	43	out of 66 or 65.15 per cent
Engine-room Department	72	out of 325 or 22.15 per cent
Victualling Department (including 20 women out of 23)	97	out of 494 or 19.63 per cent
Total	212	out of 885 or 23.95 per cent

		Passengers and crew
Adult males	338	out of 1,667 or 20.27 per cent
Adult females	316	out of 425 or 74.35 per cent
Children	57	out of 109 or 52.29 per cent
Total	711	out of 2,201 or 32.30 per cent

THE CIRCUMSTANCES IN CONNECTION WITH
THE SS CALIFORNIAN

It is here necessary to consider the circumstances relating to the SS *Californian*.

On the 14th of April, the SS *Californian* of the Leyland Line (Mr Stanley Lord, Master) was on her passage from London, which port she left on April 5th, to Boston, US, where she subsequently arrived on April 19th. She was a vessel of 6,223 tons gross and 4,038 net. Her full speed was 12½ to 13 knots. She had a passenger certificate, but was not carrying any passengers at the time. She belonged to the International Mercantile Marine Company, the owners of the *Titanic*.

At 7.30 pm, ship's time, on 14th April, a wireless message was sent from this ship to the *Antillian*:

> To Captain, *Antillian*, 6.30 pm, apparent ship's time, lat. 42° 3' N, long. 49° 9' W. Three large bergs, 5 miles to southward of us. Regards Lord.

The message was intercepted by the *Titanic*, and when the Marconi operator (Evans) of the *Californian* offered this ice report to the Marconi operator of the *Titanic*, shortly after 7.30 pm, the latter replied:

> It is all right; I heard you sending it to the *Antillian*, and I have got it.

The *Californian* proceeded on her course S 89° W true until 10.20 pm, ship's time, when she was obliged to stop and reverse engines because she was running into field ice, which stretched as far as could then be seen to the northward and southward.

The Master told the Court that he made her position at that time to be 42° 5′ N, 57° 7′ W.★ This position is recorded in the log book, which was written up from the scrap log book by the chief officer. The scrap log is destroyed. It is a position about 19 miles N by E of the position of the *Titanic* when she foundered, and is said to have been fixed by dead reckoning and verified by observations. I am satisfied that this position is not accurate. The Master "twisted her head" to E N E by the compass and she remained approximately stationary until 5.15 am on the following morning. The ship was slowly swinging round to starboard during the night.

At about 11 pm a steamer's light was seen approaching from the eastward. The Master went to Evans' room and asked what ships he had. The latter replied: "I think the *Titanic* is near us. I have got her." The Master said: "You had better advise the *Titanic* we are stopped and surrounded with ice." This Evans did, calling up the *Titanic* and sending: "We are stopped and surrounded by ice." The *Titanic* replied: "Keep out." The *Titanic* was in communication with Cape Race, which station was then sending messages to her. The reason why the *Titanic* answered "Keep out" was that her Marconi operator could not hear what Cape Race was saying, as, from her proximity, the message from the *Californian* was much stronger than any message being taken in by the *Titanic* from Cape Race, which was much further off. Evans heard the *Titanic* continuing to communicate with Cape Race up to the time he turned in at 11.30 pm.

The Master of the *Californian* states that, when observing the approaching steamer as she got nearer, he saw more lights, a few deck lights, and also her green side light. He considered that at 11 o'clock she was approximately six or seven miles away, and at some time between 11 and 11.30 he first saw her green light; she was then about 5 miles off. He noticed that at about 11.30 she stopped. In his opinion this steamer was of about the same size as the *Californian*, a medium-sized steamer, "something like ourselves".

From the evidence of Mr Groves, third officer of the *Californian*, who was the officer of the first watch, it would appear that the Master was not actually on the bridge when the steamer was sighted.

Mr Groves made out two masthead lights; the steamer was changing her bearing slowly as she got closer, and as she approached he went to the chartroom and reported this to the Master. He added: "She is evidently a passenger steamer." In fact, Mr Groves never appears to have had any doubt on this subject. In answer to a question during his examination: "Had she much light?", he said: "Yes, a lot of light. There was absolutely no doubt of her being a passenger steamer, at least in my mind."

Gill, the assistant donkey-man of the *Californian*, who was on deck at midnight, said referring to this steamer: "It could not have been anything but a passenger boat, she was too large."

★ According to a later report, RMS *Titanic*: Reappraisal of Evidence Relating to SS *Californian* (HMSO, 1992), 57° was a misprint for 50°.

By the evidence of Mr Groves, the Master, in reply to his report, said: "Call her up on the Morse lamp, and see if you can get any answer." This he proceeded to do. The Master came up and joined him on the bridge and remarked: "That does not look like a passenger steamer." Mr Groves replied: "It is, Sir. When she stopped, her lights seemed to go out, and I suppose they have been put out for the night." Mr Groves states that these lights went out at 11.40, and remembers that time because "one bell was struck to call the middle watch". The Master did not join him on the bridge until shortly afterwards, and consequently after the steamer had stopped.

In his examination Mr Groves admitted that if this steamer's head was turning to port after she stopped, it might account for the diminution of lights, by many of them being shut out. Her steaming lights were still visible and also her port side light.

The Captain only remained upon the bridge for a few minutes. In his evidence he stated that Mr Groves had made no observations to him about the steamer's deck lights going out. Mr Groves' Morse signalling appears to have been ineffectual (although at one moment he thought he was being answered), and he gave it up. He remained on the bridge until relieved by Mr Stone, the second officer, just after midnight. In turning the *Californian* over to him, he pointed out the steamer and said: "She has been stopped since 11.40, she is a passenger steamer. At about the moment she stopped she put her lights out."

When Mr Groves was in the witness-box the following questions were put to him by me:

> *Wreck Commissioner.* Speaking as an experienced seaman and knowing what you do know now, do you think that steamer that you know was throwing up rockets, and that you say was a passenger steamer, was the *Titanic*?
>
> *Groves*: Do I think it?
>
> *Wreck Commissioner.* Yes.
>
> *Groves*: From what I have heard subsequently?
>
> *Wreck Commissioner.* Yes.
>
> *Groves*: Most decidedly I do, but I do not put myself as being an experienced man.
>
> *Wreck Commissioner.* But that is your opinion as far as your experience goes?
>
> *Groves*: Yes, it is, my Lord.

Mr Stone states that the Master, who was also up (but apparently not on the bridge), pointed out the steamer to him with instructions to tell him if her bearings altered or if she got any closer. He also stated that Mr Groves had called her up on the Morse lamp and had received no reply.

Mr Stone had with him during the middle watch an apprentice named Gibson, whose attention was first drawn to the steamer's lights at about 12.20 am. He could see a masthead light, her red light (with glasses) and a "glare of white lights on her after deck". He first thought her masthead light was flickering and next thought it was a Morse light, "calling us up". He replied, but could not get into communication, and finally came to the conclusion that it was, as he had first supposed, the masthead light flickering.

Some time after 12.30 am, Gill, the donkey-man, states that he saw two rockets fired from the ship which he had been observing, and about 1.10 am, Mr Stone reported to the Captain by voice pipe that he had seen five white rockets from the direction of the steamer. He states that the Master answered, "Are they Company's signals?" and that he replied, "I do not know, but they appear to me to be white rockets." The Master told him to "go on Morsing", and, when he received any information, to send the apprentice down to him with it. Gibson states that Mr Stone informed him that he had reported to the Master, and that the Master had said the steamer was to be called up by Morse light. This witness thinks the time was 12.55. He at once proceeded again to call the steamer up by Morse. He got no reply, but the vessel fired three more white rockets. These rockets were also seen by Mr Stone.

Both Mr Stone and the apprentice kept the steamer under observation, looking at her from time to time with their glasses. Between 1 o'clock and 1.40 am some conversation passed between them. Mr Stone remarked to Gibson: "Look at her now, she looks very queer out of water, her lights look queer." He also is said by Gibson to have remarked, "A ship is not going to fire rockets at sea for nothing", and admits himself that he may possibly have used that expression.

Mr Stone states that he saw the last of the rockets fired at about 1.40, and after watching the steamer for some 20 minutes more he sent Gibson down to the Master:

> I told Gibson to go down to the Master, and be sure and wake him, and tell him that altogether we had seen eight of these white lights like white rockets in the direction of this other steamer, that this steamer was disappearing in the south-west, that we had called her up repeatedly on the Morse lamp and received no information whatsoever.

Gibson states that he went down to the chartroom and told the Master, that the Master asked him if all the rockets were white, and also asked him the time. Gibson stated that at this time the Master was awake. It was five minutes past two, and Gibson returned to the bridge to Mr Stone and reported. They both continued to keep the ship under observation until she disappeared. Mr Stone describes this as "a gradual disappearing of all her lights, which would be perfectly natural with a ship steaming away from us".

At about 2.40 am Mr Stone again called up the Master by voice pipe and told him that the ship from which he had seen the rockets come had disappeared bearing S W $\frac{1}{2}$W, the last he had seen of the light, and the Master again asked him if he was certain there was no colour in the lights. "I again assured him they were all white, just white rockets."

There is considerable discrepancy between the evidence of Mr Stone and that of the Master. The latter states that he went to the voice pipe at about 1.15, but was told then of a white rocket (not five white rockets). Moreover, between 1.30 and 4.30, when he was called by the chief officer (Mr Stewart), he had no recollection of anything being reported to him at all, although he remembered Gibson opening and closing the chart-room door.

Mr Stewart relieved Mr Stone at 4 am. The latter told him he had seen a ship four or five miles off when he went on deck at 12 o'clock, and at 1 o'clock he had seen some white rockets, and that the moment the ship started firing them she started to steam away. Just at this time (about 4 am) a steamer came in sight with two white masthead lights and a few lights amidships. He asked Mr Stone whether he thought this was the steamer which had fired rockets, and Mr Stone said he did not think it was. At 4.30 he called the Master and informed him that Mr Stone had told him he had seen rockets in the middle watch. The Master said, "Yes, I know, he has been telling me." The Master came at once on to the bridge, and apparently took the fresh steamer for the one which had fired rockets, and said: "She looks all right, she is not making any signals now." This mistake was not corrected. He, however, had the wireless operator called.

At about 6 am Captain Lord heard from the *Virginian* that "the *Titanic* had struck a berg, passengers in boats, ship sinking", and he at once started through the field ice at full speed for the position given.

Captain Lord stated that at about 7.30 am he passed the *Mount Temple* stopped, and that she was in the vicinity of the position given him as where the *Titanic* had collided (lat. 41° 46′ N, long. 50° 14′ W). He saw no wreckage there, but did later on near the *Carpathia*, which ship he closed soon afterwards, and he stated that the position where he subsequently left this wreckage was 41° 33′ N, 50° 1′ W. It is said in the evidence of Mr Stewart that the position of the *Californian* was verified by stellar observations at 7.30 pm on the Sunday evening, and that he verified the Captain's position given when the ship stopped (42° 5′ N, 50° 7′ W) as accurate on the next day. The position in which the wreckage was said to have been seen on the Monday morning was verified by sights taken on that morning.

All the officers are stated to have taken sights, and Mr Stewart in his evidence remarks that they all agreed. If it is admitted that these positions were correct, then it follows that the *Titanic's* position as given by that ship when making the CQD signal was approximately S 16° W (true), 19 miles from the *Californian*, and further that the position in which the *Californian* was stopped during the night was 30 miles away from where the wreckage was seen by her in the morning, or that the wreckage had drifted eleven miles in a little more than five hours.

There are contradictions and inconsistencies in the story as told by the different witnesses. But the truth of the matter is plain. The *Titanic* collided with the berg at 11.40 pm. The vessel seen by the *Californian* stopped at this time. The rockets sent up from the *Titanic* were distress signals. The *Californian* saw distress signals. The number sent up by the *Titanic* was about eight. The *Californian* saw eight. The time over which the rockets from the *Titanic* were sent up was from about 12.45 to 1.45 am. It was about this time that the *Californian* saw the rockets. At 2.40 am Mr Stone called to the Master that the ship from which he had seen the rockets had disappeared. At 2.20 am the *Titanic* had foundered. It was suggested that the rockets seen by the *Californian* were from some other ship, not the *Titanic*. But no other ship to fit this theory has ever been heard of.

These circumstances convince me that the ship seen by the *Californian* was the *Titanic*, and if so, according to Captain Lord, the two vessels were about five miles apart at the time of the disaster. The evidence from the *Titanic* corroborates this estimate, but I am advised that the distance was probably greater, though not more than eight to ten miles. The ice by which the *Californian* was surrounded was loose ice extending for a distance of not more than two or three miles in the direction of the *Titanic*. The night was clear and the sea was smooth. When she first saw the rockets the *Californian* could have pushed through the ice to the open water without any serious risk and so have come to the assistance of the *Titanic*. Had she done so she might have saved many if not all of the lives that were lost.

THE BOARD OF TRADE'S ADMINISTRATION

The Court was invited by the Board of Trade "to report upon the Rules and Regulations made under the Merchant Shipping Acts 1894–1906, and the administration of those Acts and of such Rules and Regulations, so far as the consideration thereof is material to this casualty" (No 26 of the questions submitted to the Court by the Board of Trade). Charges were made against the Board of Trade during the progress of the Inquiry of a twofold kind. First it was said that the Board had been negligent in that they had failed to keep up to date their Rules and Regulations relating generally to the provision of lifesaving appliances at sea, and secondly it was said that their officials had in the particular instance of the *Titanic* failed to exercise due care in the supervision of the vessel's plans and the inspection of the work done upon her.

With reference to the first of these charges, it was reduced in the course of the Inquiry to a charge of neglect to keep the Board's scale for the provision of lifeboat accommodation up to date. The circumstances are these. In March 1886, the Board appointed a Departmental Committee consisting of three of their principal officers to enquire into the question of boats, rafts and life-saving apparatus carried by sea-going merchant ships. In their report this Committee pointed out that as regards boats for ocean-going steamers carrying large numbers of passengers, the boats would be of little use in saving life (although they might for a time prolong its existence) unless succour were at hand from other ships, or from proximity to shore, and speaking with special reference to passenger steam vessels carrying emigrants across the Atlantic to ports on the east coast of North America, they said as follows:

> Considering the number of vessels employed in this trade, and the large number
> of passengers they carry, and also taking into consideration the stormy character of
> the ocean they have to cross, and the thick and foggy weather encountered, we

think this class is the most important of any, and we cannot pass over the fact that of late years this traffic has been carried on with remarkable immunity from loss of life.

The boat accommodation these vessels are forced to carry when sailing with emigrants is regulated by the scale in the Passengers Act, 1855, which provides for boat accommodation for 216 people as a maximum, so that supposing a vessel leaves with 1,000 passengers and 200 crew under the present statutory requirements, she need only carry sufficient boat accommodation for 216 of these people. Thus it will be seen that the boats carried by this class of vessel are also quite inadequate as an effectual means of saving life should a disaster happen to a ship with her full complement of passengers on board. We are glad to be able to say that there are many liberal and careful shipowners who do all in their power to provide for the safety of their passengers by equipping their vessels with boats far in excess of the number required by statute. But, at the same time, there are others carrying large numbers of emigrants who do no more than they are required to do by law.

We have gone into this question with reference to this class of vessel very fully, and have visited many of them, and we think that the boats required by Act should be increased 100 per cent, and in addition to them that the owners should be induced to carry sufficient collapsible boats and approved rafts, so that each ship shall have sufficient life-saving gear for all on board at any one time, provided, as said before, that no ship need carry more boat accommodation than is sufficient for all on board at that time.

In 1887 a Select Committee of the House of Commons, of which Lord Charles Beresford was the Chairman, was appointed to report on Saving Life at Sea, and they found in their report:

that many passenger ships could not, without great inconvenience, carry so many of the ordinary wooden boats as would suffice to carry the whole of the passengers and crew with safety in bad weather. Under such circumstances the crew would not be sufficient to man so many boats; nor could they all be got into the water in sufficient time in the event of very rapid foundering. Having regard, however, to the fact that accidents occur probably as often in moderate weather as in bad, and having regard also to the fact that the very cause of the accident frequently incapacitates many of the boats, and to the further fact that an insufficiency of boats undoubtedly tends to cause panic, we are of opinion that all sea-going passenger ships should be compelled by law to carry such boats, and other life-saving apparatus, as would in the aggregate best provide for the safety of all on board in moderate weather.

As a result of these reports, the Merchant Shipping (Life-Saving Appliances) Act, 1888, appears to have been passed, under which rules were made by the Board of Trade at different dates. The Merchant Shipping Act, 1894, repealed the Act of 1888, and substituted therefor sections 427 to 431 and the seventeenth schedule of the new Act. Under this Act (1894), a table showing the minimum number of boats to be placed under davits, and their minimum cubic contents, was issued by the Board. It was dated 9th March, 1894, and came into operation on the 1st June of that year. This table was based on the gross tonnage of the vessels to which it was to apply, and not upon the numbers carried, and it provided that the number of boats and their capacity should increase as the tonnage increased. The table, however, stopped short at the point where the gross tonnage of the vessels reached "10,000 and upwards". As to all such vessels, whatever their size might be, the minimum number of boats under davits was fixed by the table at 16, with a total minimum capacity of 5,500 cubic feet.

But as regarded emigrant steamships there was a rule which provided that if the boats under davits required by the table did not furnish sufficient accommodation for all on board, then additional boats of approved description (whether under davits or not) or approved liferafts should be carried, and that these additional boats or rafts should be of at least such carrying capacity that they and the boats required by the table should provide together in vessels of 5,000 tons and upwards three-fourths more than the minimum cubic contents required by the table, so that in the case of an emigrant ship such as the *Titanic* the requirements under the rules and table together exacted a provision of 9,625 cubic feet of lifeboat and raft accommodation (5,500 feet in boats under davits with three-fourths, namely, 4,125, added). Taken at 10 cubic feet per person, this would be equivalent to a provision for 962 persons. No doubt at the time these rules were made and this table was drawn up it was thought that, having regard to the size of vessels then built and building, it was unnecessary to carry the table further. The largest emigrant steamer then afloat was the *Lucania*, of 12,952 tons.

In the report of the Select Committee of the House of Commons a reference to watertight bulkheads had been made, which was in the following terms:

> Though the question of construction was clearly not included in the reference to the Committee, still they think it only right to state, after having heard the evidence, that the proper placing of bulkheads, so as to enable a ship to keep afloat for some length of time after an accident has occurred, is most important for saving life at sea, and a thing upon which the full efficiency of life-saving appliances largely depends.

This passage probably explains the insertion in the Board of Trade's Rules for Life-Saving Appliances of Rule No 12, which is as follows:

> *Watertight compartments* When ships of any class are divided into efficient watertight compartments to the satisfaction of the Board of Trade, they shall only be required to carry additional boats, rafts and buoyant apparatus of one-half of the capacity required by these Rules, but the exemption shall not extend

to life-jackets or similar approved articles of equal buoyancy suitable to be worn on the person.

If this rule had become applicable to the *Titanic*, then the total cubical lifeboat or raft accommodation which she would have been required to carry would not have been more than 7,562 (equivalent to accommodation for 756 persons). It did not, however, become applicable, for the owners never required the Board of Trade to express any opinion under the rule as to the efficiency of the watertight compartments. The *Titanic*, in fact, carried boat accommodation for 1,178 persons, a number far in excess of the requirements of the table and rules, and therefore no concession under Rule 12 was needed. Speaking generally, recourse to this Rule (12) by shipowners has been so insignificant that the rule itself may be regarded as of no practical account.

The foregoing rules with the table were laid before Parliament in the usual way, and so received the required statutory sanction.

After 1894 steamers were built of a much larger tonnage than 10,000, the increase culminating in the *Titanic*, with a gross tonnage of 46,328. As the vessels built increased in size, so one would have thought the necessity for increased lifeboat accommodation would grow, but the rules and table remained stationary, and nothing was done to them by way of change. The explanation of this long delay (from 1894 to 1912) was given before me by Sir Alfred Chalmers, who had served under the Board of Trade as Nautical Advisor from 1896 to August 1911. He is now retired. I think it will be well if I give his explanation in his own words. He says:

I considered the matter very closely from time to time. I first of all considered the record of the trade — that is to say, the record of the casualties — and to see what immunity from loss there was. I found it was the safest mode of travel in the world, and I thought it was neither right nor the duty of a State Department to impose regulations upon that mode of travel as long as the record was a clean one. Secondly, I found that, as ships grew bigger, there were such improvements made in their construction that they were stronger and better ships, both from the point of view of watertight compartments and also absolute strength, and I considered that that was the road along which the shipowners were going to travel, and that they should not be interfered with. I then went to the maximum that is down in the table — 16 boats and upwards, together with the supplementary boats — and I considered from my experience that that was the maximum number that could be rapidly dealt with at sea and that could be safely housed without encumbering the vessel's decks unduly. In the next place, I considered that the traffic was very safe on account of the routes — the definite routes being agreed upon by the different companies, which tended to lessen the risk of collision, and to avoid ice and fog. Then, again, there was the question of wireless telegraphy, which had already come into force on board of these passenger ships. I was seized of the fact that in July, 1901, the *Lucania* had been fitted with wireless telegraphy, and the Cunard Line, generally, fitted it during that year to all their ships. The Allan Line fitted it in 1902, and I am not sure that in 1904 it had not become quite general on the trans-Atlantic ships. That, of course, entered into my consideration as well. Then another point was the manning. It was quite evident to me that if you went on crowding the ships with boats you would require a crew which were not required otherwise for the safe navigation of the ship, or for the proper upkeep of the ship, but you are providing a crew which would be carried uselessly across the ocean, that never would be required to man the boats. Then the last point, and not the least, was this, that the voluntary action of the owners was carrying them beyond the requirements of our scale, and when voluntary action on the part of shipowners is doing that, I think that any State Department should hold its hand before it steps in to make a hard-and-fast scale for that particular type of shipping. I considered that that scale fitted all sizes of ships that were then afloat, and I did not consider it necessary to increase it, and that was my advice to Sir Walter Howell.

I appreciate this explanation, and I think there is much force in it. At the same time, it seems to me that it does not justify the delay. Even taking all these matters into consideration, it cannot be that the provision for boat accommodation made in 1894 for vessels of 10,000 tons and upwards remained sufficient to 1910, when vessels of 45,000 tons were being built. Two considerations demonstrate this. The first is that some shipowners recognised the insufficiency of the requirements of the Board of Trade, and voluntarily exceeded those requirements by providing larger boat accommodation than the old rules and table exacted. The second is that shortly before Sir Alfred Chalmers left the Board of Trade, the Board had begun to direct attention to the amending of their rules in this connection.

It appears that in November, 1910, a question was asked in the House of Commons as to whether the attention of the President of the Board of Trade had been called to the fact that the *Olympic*, a sister ship of the *Titanic*, was provided with 14 lifeboats only. The answer given was that the *Olympic* (which was then in course of construction) would carry 14 lifeboats and two ordinary boats of an aggregate capacity of 9,752 cubic feet, which was in excess of the requirements of the statutory rules. On the 15th February, 1911, a further question was asked as to the date of the last regulations, and whether, having regard to the increased tonnage of modern ships the desirability of revising the regulations would be considered by the Board of Trade. The President's answer was:

Those regulations were last revised in 1894. The question of their further revision is engaging the serious attention of the Board of Trade, and I have decided to refer the matter to the Merchant Shipping Advisory Committee for consideration and advice.

Three days afterwards, namely on the 18th of February, 1911, a circular letter was sent out by the Board of Trade to the Board's principal officers at Liverpool, London and Glasgow, asking each of those gentlemen to draft such an extension of the existing boat scale as he might think satisfactory and reasonable for the conditions of large passenger steamers. This circular letter was answered by the principal officer in Glasgow (Mr Harris) on the 24th February, 1911, by the principal officer in London (Mr Park) on the 27th February, 1911, and by the principal officer in Liverpool (Mr Young) on the 3rd March, 1911. It is sufficient to say of these answers that they all suggested a large extension of the statutory requirements.

Meanwhile, namely, on the 28th February, 1911, Mr Archer, the Board of Trade's principal ship surveyor, had also drawn up a scale. This was a more exacting scale than that of any of the three principal officers. By his scale a vessel of the tonnage of the *Titanic* would have had to carry boat accommodation equivalent to at least 24,937 cubic feet, which would have been sufficient to hold all, and more than all, the persons who were on board at the time of the disaster (2,201). It would not, however, have been nearly sufficient to have held all that the vessel might lawfully have carried, viz. 3,547, and it is to be observed with reference to Mr Archer's scale that in it he suggests an extension of Rule 12, by which (if the vessel were divided into efficient watertight compartments) the total boat accommodation might be reduced much more than Rule 12 as it stands would permit. If this reduction be taken into account, the boat accommodation would fall so that it would be sufficient only for 1,750 persons.

Mr Archer's view was that shipowners should be encouraged to increase the flotability of the ships they built, and that the way to encourage them to do this was to relax the legal requirements as to boats as their plans advanced in that direction. The great object was so to build the ship that in the event of a disaster she would be her own lifeboat. (It may be mentioned that Mr Archer stated in the witness-box that since the disaster to the *Titanic* he had modified his views and thought that Rule 12 should be discontinued.)

Having obtained these four reports, the Board of Trade, on the 4th April, 1911, submitted the matter to their Advisory Committee, and obtained the Committee's report on the 4th July, 1911. The following are copies (with omissions of immaterial passages) of the Board of Trade's letter of the 4th April, 1911, and of the Advisory Committee's report of the 4th July, 1911:

Board of Trade, Marine Department to Merchant Shipping Advisory Committee
7 Whitehall Gardens, London S W
4th April, 1911

Sir,

I am directed by the Board of Trade to enclose herewith, for the information of the Merchant Shipping Advisory Committee, a copy of a question asked in the House of Commons on the 15th February and of the answer given by the President of the Board of Trade with reference to the Life-Saving Appliances Rules made under section 427 of the Merchant Shipping Act, 1894.

The Board are of opinion that the Table in the Appendix to the Rules should be extended upwards in the form indicated in the accompanying scale, so as to provide for vessels of tonnage up to 50,000 tons gross and upwards.

It appears to the Board that the number of boats and the boat capacity need not necessarily increase in a regular proportion according to the increase in tonnage, and that due regard should be paid to what is reasonable and practicable in passenger steamers exceeding 10,000 tons.

I am to state that the Board would be obliged if the Merchant Shipping Advisory Committee would be so good as to suggest in what manner the scale (see accompanying copy) should be continued upwards, having due regard to the considerations indicated above.

I am further to state that the Board would be glad to learn whether the Advisory Committee are of the opinion that Rule 12 should or should not be revised so as to exempt altogether from the requirement of additional boats and/or rafts those vessels which are divided into efficient watertight compartments to the satisfaction of the Board of Trade . . .

WALTER J HOWELL

Merchant Shipping Advisory Committee to Sir Walter J Howell, Marine Department, Board of Trade

4th July, 1911

Sir,

We have the honour to report that your letter of the 4th April with reference to the minimum number of lifeboats to be carried on vessels of 10,000 tons gross tonnage and upwards, and your letter of the 17th May on the subject of the depth of lifeboats, have been very carefully considered by the Merchant Shipping Advisory Committee, and that it was unanimously decided at a meeting held on the 29th ultimo to adopt the report of a Sub-Committee which was specially appointed to inquire into these questions.

A copy of the report is accordingly forwarded herewith, and the Committee desire us to suggest for the consideration of the Board of Trade, that effect should be given to the recommendations contained in it.

NORMAN HILL
Chairman
R W MATTHEW
Secretary

REPORT OF THE LIFE-SAVING APPLIANCES SUB-COMMITTEE TO THE MERCHANT SHIPPING ADVISORY COMMITTEE

In accordance with the decision of the Merchant Shipping Advisory Committee at their meeting on Friday, the 28th April, we have given careful consideration to the letter of the 4th April from the Board of Trade, in which the Committee were asked to advise:

1 as to the manner in which the table in the Appendix to the Life-Saving Appliances Rules should be extended so as to provide for vessels of tonnage up to 50,000 tons gross and upwards, and

2 as to whether Rule 12 should, or should not, be revised so as to exempt altogether from the requirement of additional boats and/or rafts those vessels which are divided into efficient watertight compartments to the satisfaction of the Board of Trade.

In considering these questions, we have had specially in mind the fact that the number of passengers carried does not necessarily increase in proportion to the increase in the tonnage of the vessel. This is particularly true in the case of vessels exceeding 10,000 tons, a type of vessel which is practically only built to provide special accommodation for large numbers of first- and second-class passengers.

Similarly, there is no fixed relation between the tonnage of vessels and the deck space available for the carrying of lifeboats under davits. Increase in the length of a vessel is only one of the factors, and often not the most material factor, contributing to the increase in its tonnage, and it should also be remembered, in estimating the space available for the launching of lifeboats, that it is impossible to place davits forward of the bridge, and very undesirable to have them on the quarters of the vessel.

We are strongly of the opinion that every encouragement should be given to secure the provision of vessels which by their construction have been rendered as unsinkable as possible, and which are provided with efficient means for communicating with the shore or with other vessels in case of disaster.

In view of these considerations, we have agreed upon the following recommendations:

1 That it is questionable whether it is practicable to increase the number of davits.

2 That any increase in the number of lifeboats to be carried can probably be best effected by providing for the launching of further boats from the existing davits.

3 That the table should be extended in the manner indicated. It is further recommended that all passenger vessels of 10,000 tons gross tonnage and upwards should be required to be fitted with wireless telegraphy apparatus.

4 That the Rules should be amended so as to admit of decked lifeboats of an approved type being stowed on top of one another or under an open lifeboat, subject to suitable arrangements being made for launching promptly the boats so stowed.

5 That the additional boats and rafts required under the provisions of Division A, Class 1(d) of the Life-Saving Appliances Rules shall be of at least such carrying capacity that they, and the boats required by columns 2 and 3 of the table supplied, provide together three-fourths more than the minimum cubic contents required by column 4 of that table.

Life-saving appliances for vessels of tonnage up to 50,000 tons and upwards

Gross tonnage	Minimum number of boats to be placed under davits	Minimum number of additional boats to be readily available for attachment to davits	Total minimum cubic contents of boats required by columns 2 and 3
(1)	(2)	(3)	(4)
			Cubic ft
10,000 and under 12,000	16	–	5,500
12,000 and under 20,000	16	2	6,200
20,000 and under 35,000	16	4	6,900
35,000 and under 45,000	16	6	7,600
45,000 and upwards	16	8	8,300

6 That vessels divided into efficient watertight compartments to the satisfaction of the Board of Trade should (provided they are fitted with wireless telegraphy apparatus) be exempt from the requirement of additional boats and/or rafts. The Committee suggest, in this connection, that the Board of Trade should review the requirements designed to attain the standards as to watertight compartments at present enforced by them under Rule 12, having regard to the developments of shipbuilding since the report of the Committee on the spacing and construction of watertight bulkheads.

We have also had before us the Board's further letter of the 17th May enquiring whether, in the opinion of the Advisory Committee, it would be advisable to prescribe a maximum depth for lifeboats as compared with their breadth, and, if so, what that proportion should be.

In connection with this letter, we have been supplied by the Board of Trade with reports from their principal officers in Great Britain, giving the dimensions and cubic capacities of the various kinds of boats on five typical ships in each of eight ports.

We recommend that the Board should be advised to alter the Life-Saving Appliances Rules so as to provide that, in future, the depth of lifeboats supplied to a British merchant vessel shall not exceed 44 per cent of their breadth.

ROBERT A OGILVIE	NORMAN HILL
T ROYDEN	A M CARLISLE
T ROME	S CROSS
THOMAS SPENCER	W M THEODORE DOXFORD
J HAVELOCK WILSON	GEO N HAMPSON

It will be observed that if effect had been given by the Board of Trade to the Report of the Advisory Committee the requirements for a vessel of the size of the *Titanic* would have reached 14,525 cubic feet (8,300 plus three-fourths of 8,300, namely 6,225), with, however, this qualification: that if the vessel were divided into efficient watertight compartments (as she probably was) and fitted with wireless telegraphy (as she certainly was) a provision of a boat capacity of 8,300 cubic feet, equivalent to space for 830 persons, would have been legally sufficient. This would have been much less than the accommodation with which the *Titanic* when she put to sea was, in fact, provided (namely for 1,178 persons).

Effect, however, was not given to the report. A question arose with reference to the dimensions of lifeboats, and it was thought better to get that question settled before proceeding to revise the rules. The examination of this question involved making several experiments which caused delay, and it was not until the 16th April, 1912, that a reply was sent by the Board of Trade to the Advisory Committee. It will be noticed that the date of this reply is just after the disaster to the *Titanic* became known. I am, however, quite satisfied that instructions for the preparation of this letter had been

given in the offices of the Board of Trade some days before the 16th, and that
the letter was not sent in consequence of the disaster. It is desirable to set it
out:

Board of Trade, Marine Department to Merchant Shipping Advisory Committee
7 Whitehall Gardens, London S W
16th April, 1912

Sir,

With reference to your letter of the 4th July last respecting certain questions
raised in connection with the proposed revision of the Life-Saving Appliances
Rules, I am directed by the Board of Trade to state, for the information of the
Advisory Committee, that they have given very careful consideration to the
report of the Life-Saving Appliances Sub-Committee which was forwarded with
your letter.

As regards the recommendations with reference to the proposed extension of
the table (Appendix to the Life-Saving Appliances Rules) showing the minimum
number of boats to be placed under davits, the Board are glad to observe that the
Committee agree that alterations and additions are now necessary to meet the
changed conditions due to recent developments in the size of passenger
steamships and in the number of persons which these vessels can accommodate.

The Board of Trade note that the gradations of tonnage in the extension of
the scale suggested by the Advisory Committee are not the same as those in the
form of scale submitted to them by the Board, while the increase in the number
of boats is not in the number to be placed under davits, but in the number of
additional boats required to be readily available for attachment to davits. It is
observed that the Committee hold the view that "it is questionable whether it is
practicable to increase the number of davits", and "that any increase in the
number of lifeboats to be carried can probably be best effected by providing for
the launching of further boats from the existing davits".

The Board presume that, in arriving at these conclusions, the Committee
have had regard to ships already built rather than to new ships, as they see no
reason why there would be any difficulty in having more than eight pairs of
davits on each side of the ship, provided that the requirements of Life-Saving
Appliances Rules were known before the plans were prepared.

The Board are of the opinion that a very careful and thorough revision of the
table should now be made, and I am to transmit herewith a copy of a
memorandum and tables prepared by the Professional Adviser to the Marine
Department, containing a full and considered opinion on the subject of the
extension of the boat scale and cognate questions [not included here].

As regards the proposed amendment of the rules, so as to admit of decked
lifeboats of an approved type being stowed one above another, or under an open
lifeboat, I am to state that this question is now under consideration, and a
communication will be addressed to you shortly on the subject.

With reference to the Advisory Committee's recommendation regarding the
amendment of Rule 12 of the General Rules, the Board desire me to state that

the questions raised in the recommendation are of wide application, and of such importance that the Board do not think that they can be adequately considered except by a Committee of equal standing to the Committee which reported in 1891 on the Spacing and Construction of Watertight Bulkheads in the Mercantile Marine. The Board have the question of the appointment of a Committee under consideration.

In connection with the Advisory Committee's recommendation that the depth of lifeboats shall not exceed 44 per cent of their breadth, I am to transmit herewith, a draft amendment of Rules Nos 1, 2, and 3 of the General Rules with reference to the construction of ships' boats [not included here].

The Board have made full inquiry into the question of the construction of ships' boats, and obtained some useful information as to the average depth of boat which is deemed desirable for safety and utility, and the ratio of that depth to the breadth, and they attach so much importance to this element of boat construction that they think it should receive the careful attention of the Committee. The Board think that the Committee, in the light of this additional information, may reconsider the opinions expressed on this point in their letter of the 4th July.

I am therefore to transmit herewith copies of memoranda by the Professional Adviser to the Marine Department and the acting Principal Ship Surveyor [not included here].

The Board desire me to state that they would be glad to be furnished with the Advisory Committee's views as to the application of the proposed new rules and boat scale, e.g., whether they should apply to ships already built, and, if so, to what extent. They regard it as of great importance, on the one hand, that all British vessels should be provided with a proper and sufficient equipment of life-saving appliances, and, on the other, that regulations should not be enforced without notice which would necessitate important structural alterations and consequent heavy expense in vessels already built.

I am to add that in order to make the constitution of the Committee, when considering this question, agree with that of the Statutory Life-Saving Appliances Committee indicated in the Seventeenth Schedule to the Merchant Shipping Act, 1894, the Board have followed the course adopted on previous occasions, and have invited Lloyd's Register of British and Foreign Shipping and the Institute of London Underwriters to select a representative who will be available to sit on the Advisory Committee when the question is under consideration.

WALTER J HOWELL

Subsequently Sir Walter Howell wrote and sent three letters to the Advisory Committee which were as follows:

Board of Trade, Marine Department to Merchant Shipping Advisory Committee
7 Whitehall Gardens, London SW

Immediate   20th April, 1912

Sir,

With reference to previous correspondence between the Department and your Committee respecting the revision of the statutory rules for Life-Saving Appliances on British ships, and particularly to the letter from this Department of the 16th April, I am directed by the Board of Trade to state that as an entirely new situation has been created by the recent disaster to the SS *Titanic* they assume that the Committee, in reconsidering the matter in connection with the suggestions already put before them by the Board, will have full regard to this new situation, and the facts of the disaster so far as ascertained.

As you are doubtless aware, suggestions have been made in the House of Commons and elsewhere to the effect that, in view of the loss of the *Titanic*, action should be taken by the Board of Trade in regard to certain questions other than those expressly dealt with in the Life-Saving Appliance Rules, e.g., in regard to (1) steamship routes in the North Atlantic, (2) the speed of steamers where there may be dangers to navigation, and (3) the provision and use of searchlights on large passenger steamers, and the Board would be glad to know the Committee's views in regard to these and any other suggestions which may have come to their knowledge, intended to diminish the risk or to mitigate the effects of accidents to passenger vessels at sea.

WALTER J HOWELL

Board of Trade, Marine Department to Merchant Shipping Advisory Committee
7 Whitehall Gardens, London SW
24th April, 1912

Sir,

With reference to previous correspondence between this Department and your Committee respecting the revision of the statutory rules for life-saving appliances on British ships, and particularly to the letter from this Department of the 16th April, in which you were informed that the question of the proposed amendment of the rules, so as to admit of decked lifeboats being stowed one above another or one under an open lifeboat, was under consideration, I am directed by the Board of Trade to state, for the information of your Committee, that the Board of Trade will be glad if the Committee will consider whether any, and if so what, amendments of the rules, and in particular of the rule of the 19th April, 1910, and the rule of the 14th June, 1911, are in their opinion desirable with the object of supplementing the boats immediately under davits by as much additional boat accommodation as is practicable, having regard to the new situation which has been created by the recent disaster to the SS *Titanic*.

A plan illustrating the principle is being prepared so as to be in readiness for your Committee by Friday.

WALTER J HOWELL

Board of Trade, Marine Department to Merchant Shipping Advisory Committee
7 Whitehall Gardens, London SW
25th April, 1912

Sir,

With reference to previous correspondence respecting the proposed revision of the statutory regulations as to boats and life-saving appliances on ships, I am directed by the Board of Trade to state, for the information of the Merchant Shipping Advisory Committee, that, apart from the questions which have been raised regarding the boat accommodation on vessels over 10,000 tons, it seems desirable to consider whether the provision of boats and other life-saving appliances required by the rules in the case of vessels under 10,000 tons is satisfactory, or whether the rules or the boat scale should be altered in respect of their application to such vessels, and the Board would be glad to be favoured with the observations of the Committee on this point in addition to those that have already been referred to them.

WALTER J HOWELL

To these letters the Advisory Committee sent the following answer:

Merchant Shipping Advisory Committee to Sir Walter Howell, Marine Department, Board of Trade
7 Whitehall Gardens, London SW
27th April, 1912

Sir,

We are desired by the Merchant Shipping Advisory Committee to inform you that your letters of the 16th, 20th, 24th and 25th instant were brought before the Committee at a meeting held yesterday.

The Committee fully recognise that the proved impossibility of keeping such a vessel as the *Titanic* afloat after a collision with ice, until the arrival of outside succour, has created an entirely new situation which was neither in the contemplation of the Board of Trade nor of the Committee in the consideration of the extension of the existing boat scale in regard to vessels of 10,000 tons and upwards.

In advising on such extension in July last, the Committee aimed at providing ample boat accommodation on large passenger vessels in accordance with the principles that were adopted by the original Life-Saving Appliances Committee, and which principles had apparently been fully justified by many years of experience. It is with satisfaction that the Committee note that the Board of Trade, apart from the new possibilities demonstrated by the loss of the *Titanic*, agreed in the essentials with the recommendation of the Committee.

In face of the new facts, the Committee at their meeting yesterday re-opened entirely the question of the revision of the boat scale for large passenger vessels with a view of providing the maximum of protection for the passengers and crew in the event of an overwhelming disaster, whilst, at the same time, maintaining the principles in regard to the stability and sea-going qualities of the ship itself, and to the prompt and efficient handling of the boats carried under the existing scale, which hitherto have proved not only essential to safety, but also adequate for all ordinary emergencies. The questions involved are not free from difficulty, but they will receive the immediate attention of the Committee. Pending their consideration, the Committee note that assurances have been received by the Board of Trade from representatives of most of the large passenger lines to the effect that every effort will be made to equip their vessels, at the earliest possible moment, with boats and rafts sufficient to accommodate all persons on board.

In regard to the recommendation forwarded with the Committee's letter of the 4th July last, that the Board of Trade should, having regard to the developments in shipbuilding since the Report of the Committee of 1891 on Spacing and Construction of Watertight Bulkheads, review the requirements designed to attain the standards at present enforced under Rule 12, the Advisory Committee note that the Board of Trade have under consideration the appointment of a Committee of equal standing to that of the Committee of 1891. In view of the great importance of this question the Advisory Committee desire us respectfully to urge that such a Committee be appointed at as early a date as possible.

The subject of the general revision of the statutory regulations as to boats and life-saving appliances on all ships, which, apart from the questions regarding the boat accommodation on vessels over 10,000 tons, is for the first time referred to the Advisory Committee by the letter of the 25th instant, together with the particular questions raised in the letters of the 16th, 20th, and 24th instant, are also receiving the immediate attention of the Committee.

At yesterday's meeting sub-committees were appointed to give immediate consideration to the subjects requiring detailed examination. These sub-committees will pursue their enquiries concurrently, and we are desired by the Advisory Committee to inform you that their investigation into the revision of the Life-Saving Appliances Rules will be proceeded with as expeditiously as possible.

Norman Hill
Chairman
R W Matthew
Secretary

This letter was acknowledged by the Board of Trade on the 10th May, 1912, as follows:

Board of Trade, Marine Department to Merchant Shipping Advisory Committee

7 Whitehall Gardens, London SW
10th May, 1912

Sir,

I am directed by the Board of Trade to acknowledge the receipt of, and to thank you for, your letter of the 27th April, stating that their letters of the 16th, 20th,

24th, and 25th April, have been considered by the Merchant Shipping Advisory Committee.

The Board observe with satisfaction that, in view of the entirely new situation which has arisen, the Advisory Committee have decided to re-open the question of the revision of the table in the Life-Saving Appliances Rules in so far as it governs the boat accommodation in vessels over 10,000 tons gross. The Board are further glad to observe that the question of a general revision of the Life-Saving Appliances Rules is also under consideration by the Committee, and in this connection they presume that, in considering the question of a general revision of the rules including the table, the Committee will consider the principles on which the requirements as to boat accommodation should be based, including, *inter alia*, whether the table should continue to be based on tonnage. Any conclusion reached by the Committee on this question would naturally affect the revision of the present table as applying to vessels of more than 10,000 tons, upon which the Committee has already been engaged.

The Board agree with the view expressed by the Advisory Committee that the appointment of another Committee on the Spacing and Construction of Watertight Bulkheads is desirable. Steps have already been taken by the President to form such a Committee, and he hopes to be able to announce the names within a few days. A further communication on this point will be addressed to the Committee in the course of a few days.

The Board are glad to note that Sub-Committees have been appointed to deal concurrently with the subjects requiring detailed consideration in connection with the revision of the Life-Saving Appliances Rules.

The Board desire me to add that they assume that the Committee, in considering the matters referred to them, will have regard to all important aspects of the question of Life-Saving Appliances, whether expressly dealt with in the Statutory Rules or not, and in particular to the essential question of the adequacy of the provision for lowering and manning the boats and rafts carried by vessels.

WALTER J HOWELL

This finishes the history of the action of the Board of Trade in relation to the provision of boat accommodation on emigrant ships. The outstanding circumstance in it is the omission, during so many years, to revise the rules of 1894 and this, I think, was blameable, notwithstanding the excuse or explanation put forward by Sir Alfred Chalmers. I am, however, doubtful whether, even if the rules had been revised, the change would have been such as to have required boat accommodation which would have increased the number of lives saved. Having regard to the recommendations of the Advisory Committee, the Board of Trade would probably not have felt justified in making rules which would have required more boat accommodation than that with which the *Titanic* was actually provided, and it is not to be forgotten that the *Titanic* boat accommodation was utilized to less than two-thirds of its capacity. These considerations, however, afford no excuse for the delay of the Board of Trade.

The gross tonnage of a vessel is not, in my opinion, a satisfactory basis on which to calculate the provision of boat accommodation. Hitherto, I believe, it has been accepted as the best basis by all nations. But there seems much more to be said in favour of making the number of lives carried the basis, and for providing boat or raft accommodation for all on board. Rule 12 of the Life-Saving Appliances Rules of 1902, which deals with watertight compartments and boat accommodation, ought to be abolished. The provision of such compartments is of supreme importance, but it is clear that it should not be sought at the expense of a decrease in boat accommodation. When naval architects have devised practical means for rendering ships unsinkable, the question of boat accommodation may have to be reconsidered, but until that time arrives boat accommodation should, where practicable, be carried for all on board. This suggestion may be thought by some to be extravagant. It has never been enforced in the mercantile marine of Great Britain, nor as far as I know in that of any foreign nation. But it appears, nevertheless, to be admitted by all that it is possible, without undue inconvenience or undue interference with commerce, to increase considerably in many cases the accommodation hitherto carried, and it seems, therefore, reasonable that the law should require an increase to be made. As far as foreign-going passenger and emigrant steamships are concerned, I am of opinion that, unless justification be shown for deviating from this course, such ships should carry boats or rafts for all on board.

With reference to the second branch of the complaint against the Board of Trade, namely that their officials had failed to exercise due care in the supervision of the vessel's plans and in the inspection of the work done upon her, the charges broke down. Suggestions were made that the Board's requirements fell short of those of Lloyd's Registry; but no evidence was forthcoming to support the suggestions. The investigation of the charges took much time, but it only served to show that the officials had discharged their duties carefully and well.

POWERS OF THE BOARD OF TRADE AS REGARDS THE SUPERVISION OF DESIGNS OF VESSELS

The *Titanic* was efficiently designed and constructed to meet the contingencies which she was intended to meet.

The bulkheads were of ample strength. They were sufficiently closely spaced and were carried up in the vessel to a height greater than sufficient to meet the requirements of the 1891 Bulkheads Committee.

But I am advised that the ship could have been further sub-divided so that she would probably have remained afloat longer than she did. The Board of Trade have, however, apparently no power to exercise any real supervision in the matter of sub-division. All they have express power to insist upon in this connection with respect to any steam vessel is that there shall be four watertight bulkheads — a provision quite inadequate for safety in a collision damaging the vessel abaft the collision bulkhead. They can also, if invited by the shipowner (but not otherwise), exercise supervision under Rule 12. This supervision I am told they have been invited to exercise in only 103 cases over a period of 18 years. In 69 of these cases the Board have expressed their satisfaction with the sub-division provided. It seems to me that the Board should be empowered to require the production of the designs of all passenger steamers at an early period of their construction, and to direct such alterations as may appear to them to be necessary and practicable for the purpose of securing proper watertight sub-division.

FINDING OF THE COURT

It is now convenient to answer the 26 questions submitted by the Board of Trade.

1 When the *Titanic* left Queenstown on or about 11th April last:
   (a) What was the total number of persons employed in any capacity on board her, and what were their respective ratings?
   (b) What was the total number of her passengers, distinguishing sexes and classes, and discriminating between adults and children?

   Answer

   (a) The total number of persons employed in any capacity on board the *Titanic* was 885. Their respective ratings were as follows:

Deck Department	66
Engine Department	325
Victualling Department	494
	885

   NB: The eight bandsmen are not included in this number as their names appear in the 2nd-class passenger list.

   (b) The total number of passengers was 1,316. Of these:

	Male	Female	Total
1st class	180	145	325
2nd class	179	106	285
3rd class	510	196	706
			1,316

   Of the above, 6 children were in the 1st class, 24 in the 2nd class and 79 in the 3rd class. Total 109.

2 Before leaving Queenstown on or about 11th April last, did the *Titanic* comply with the requirements of the Merchant Shipping Acts, 1894–1906, and the rules and regulations made thereunder with regard to the safety and otherwise of "passenger steamers" and "emigrant ships"?
Answer
Yes.

3 In the actual design and construction of the *Titanic* what special provisions were made for the safety of the vessel and the lives of those on board in the event of collisions and other casualties?
Answer
These have been already described.

4 (a) Was the *Titanic* sufficiently and efficiently officered and manned?
(b) Were the watches of the officers and crew usual and proper?
(c) Was the *Titanic* supplied with proper charts?
Answer
(a) Yes.
(b) Yes.
(c) Yes.

5 (a) What was the number of the boats of any kind on board the *Titanic*?
(b) Were the arrangements for manning and launching the boats on board the *Titanic* in case of emergency proper and sufficient?
(c) Had a boat drill been held on board and, if so, when?
(d) What was the carrying capacity of the respective boats?
Answer
(a) 2 emergency boats; 14 lifeboats; 4 Engelhardt boats.
(b) No, but see comments in the report.
(c) No.
(d) The carrying capacity of the respective boats was:

2 emergency boats	80 persons
14 lifeboats	910 persons
4 Engelhardt boats	188 persons
or a total of	1,178 persons

6 (a) What installations for receiving and transmitting messages by wireless telegraphy were on board the *Titanic*?
(b) How many operators were employed on working such installations?
(c) Were the installations in good and effective working order, and were the number of operators sufficient to enable messages to be received and transmitted continuously by day and night?
Answer
(a) A Marconi 5-kilowatt motor generator with two complete sets of apparatus supplied from the ship's dynamos, with an independent

storage battery and coil for emergency, was fitted in a house on the Boat deck.

(b) Two.

(c) Yes.

7 (a) At or prior to the sailing of the *Titanic* what, if any, instructions as to navigation were given to the Master or known by him to apply to her voyage?

(b) Were such instructions, if any, safe, proper and adequate, having regard to the time of year and dangers likely to be encountered during the voyage?

Answer

(a) No special instructions were given, but he had general instructions contained in the book of Rules and Regulations supplied by the Company.

(b) Yes, but having regard to subsequent events they would have been better if a reference had been made to the course to be adopted in the event of reaching the region of ice.

8 (a) What was in fact the track taken by the *Titanic* in crossing the Atlantic Ocean?

(b) Did she keep to the track usually followed by liners on voyages from the United Kingdom to New York in the month of April?

(c) Are such tracks safe tracks at that time of the year?

(d) Had the Master any and, if so, what discretion as regards the track to be taken?

Answer

(a) The Outward Southern Track from Queens-town to New York, usually followed in April by large steam vessels.

(b) Yes, with the exception that instead of altering her course on approaching the position 42° N 47° W she stood on on her previous course for some 10 miles further south-west, turning to S 86° W true at 5.50 pm.

(c) The Outward and Homeward bound Southern Tracks were decided on as the outcome of many years' experience of the normal movement of ice. They were reasonably safe tracks for the time of year, provided, of course, that great caution and vigilance when crossing the ice region were observed.

(d) Yes. Captain Smith was not fettered by any orders to remain on the track should information as to the position of ice make it in his opinion undesirable to adhere to it. The fact, however, of lane routes having been laid down for the common safety of all would necessarily influence him to keep on (or very near) the accepted route, unless circumstances as indicated above should induce him to deviate largely from it.

9 (a) After leaving Queenstown on or about the 11th April last did information reach the *Titanic* by wireless messages or otherwise by signals of the existence of ice in certain latitudes?

(b) If so, what were such messages or signals and when were they received, and in what position or positions was the ice reported to be, and was the ice reported in or near the track actually being followed by the *Titanic*?

(c) Was her course altered in consequence of receiving such information, and, if so, in what way?

(d) What replies to such messages or signals did the *Titanic* send, and at what times?

Answer

(a) Yes.

(b) See particulars of ice messages already set out earlier in the report.

(c) No. Her course was altered as hereinbefore described, but not in consequence of the information received as to ice.

(d) The material answers were:

At 12.55 pm SS *Titanic*:

To Commander, *Baltic*. Thanks for your message and good wishes. Had fine weather since leaving. Smith.

At 1.26 pm SS *Titanic*:

To Captain, *Caronia*. Thanks for message and information. Have had variable weather throughout. Smith.

10 (a) If at the times referred to in the last preceding question or later the *Titanic* was warned of or had reason to suppose she would encounter ice, at what time might she have reasonably expected to encounter it?

(b) Was a good and proper look-out for ice kept on board?

(c) Were any and, if so, what directions given to vary the speed — if so, were they carried out?

Answer

(a) At, or even before, 9.30 pm ship's time, on the night of the disaster.

(b) No. The men in the crow's-nest were warned at 9.30 pm to keep a sharp look-out for ice. The officer of the watch was then aware that he had reached the reported ice region, and so also was the officer who relieved him at 10 pm. Without implying that those actually on duty were not keeping a good look-out, in view of the night being moonless, there being no wind and perhaps very little swell, and especially in view of the high speed at which the vessel was running, it is not considered that the look-out was sufficient. An extra look-out should, under the circumstances, have been placed at the stemhead, and a sharp look-out should have been kept from both sides of the bridge by an officer.

(c) No directions were given to reduce speed.

11 (a) Were binoculars provided for and used by the look-out men?

(b) Is the use of them necessary or usual in such circumstances?

(c) Had the *Titanic* the means of throwing searchlights around her?

(d) If so, did she make use of them to discover ice?

(e) Should searchlights have been provided and used?

Answer

(a) No.

(b) No.

(c) No.

(d) No.

(e) No, but searchlights may at times be of service. The evidence before the Court does not allow of a more precise answer.

12 (a) What other precautions were taken by the *Titanic* in anticipation of meeting ice?

(b) Were they such as are usually adopted by vessels being navigated in waters where ice may be expected to be encountered?

Answer

(a) Special orders were given to the men in the crow's-nest to keep a sharp look-out for ice, particularly small ice and growlers. The fore scuttle hatch was closed to keep everything dark before the bridge.

(b) Yes, though there is evidence to show that some masters would have placed a look-out at the stemhead of the ship.

13 (a) Was ice seen and reported by anybody on board the *Titanic* before the casualty occurred?

(b) If so, what measures were taken by the officer on watch to avoid it?

(c) Were they proper measures and were they promptly taken?

Answer

(a) Yes, immediately before the collision.

(b) The helm was put hard-a-starboard and the engines were stopped and put full-speed astern.

(c) Yes.

14 (a) What was the speed of the *Titanic* shortly before and at the moment of the casualty?

(b) Was such speed excessive under the circumstances?

Answer

(a) About 22 knots.

(b) Yes.

15 (a) What was the nature of the casualty which happened to the *Titanic* at or about 11.45 pm on the 14th April last?

   (b) In what latitude and longitude did the casualty occur?

Answer

   (a) A collision with an iceberg which pierced the starboard side of the vessel in several places below the waterline between the fore peak tank and No 4 boiler-room.

   (b) In latitude 41° 46' N, longitude 50° 14' W.

16 (a) What steps were taken immediately on the happening of the casualty?

   (b) How long after the casualty was its seriousness realised by those in charge of the vessel?

   (c) What steps were then taken?

   (d) What endeavours were made to save the lives of those on board and to prevent the vessel from sinking?

Answer

   (a) The 12 watertight doors in the engine- and boiler-rooms were closed from the bridge, some of the boiler fires were drawn, and the bilge pumps abaft No 6 boiler-room were started.

   (b) About 15–20 minutes.

   (c) and (d) The boats were ordered to be cleared away. The passengers were roused and orders given to get them on deck, and lifebelts were served out. Some of the watertight doors, other than those in the boiler- and engine-rooms, were closed. Marconigrams were sent out asking for help. Distress signals (rockets) were fired, and attempts were made to call up by Morse a ship whose lights were seen. Eighteen of the boats were swung out and lowered, and the remaining two floated off the ship and were subsequently utilized as rafts.

17 Was proper discipline maintained on board after the casualty occurred?

Answer

Yes.

18 (a) What messages for assistance were sent by the *Titanic* after the casualty and at what times respectively?

   (b) What messages were received by her in response and at what times respectively?

   (c) By what vessels were the messages that were sent by the *Titanic* received, and from what vessels did she receive answers?

   (d) What vessels other than the *Titanic* sent or received messages at or shortly after the casualty in connection with such casualty?

   (e) What were the vessels that sent or received such messages?

   (f) Were any vessels prevented from going to the assistance of the *Titanic* or her boats owing to messages received from the *Titanic* or owing to any erroneous messages being sent or received?

(g) In regard to such erroneous messages, from what vessels were they sent and by what vessels were they received and at what times respectively?

Answer

(a) (b) (c) (d) and (e) are answered together (see below).

(f) Several vessels did not go owing to their distance.

(g) There were no erroneous messages.

Messages sent and received by Titanic after the casualty

New York time	Titanic time (approx.)	Communications
10.25 pm	12.15 am	*La Provence* receives *Titanic* distress signals.
10.25 pm	12.15 am	*Mount Temple* heard *Titanic* sending CQD. Says require assistance. Gives position. Cannot hear me. Advise my Captain his position 41.46 N 50.24 W.
10.25 pm	12.15 am	Cape Race hears *Titanic* giving position on CQD 41.44 N, 50.24 W.
10.28 pm	12.18 am	*Ypiranga* hears CQD from *Titanic*. *Titanic* gives CQD here. Position 41.44 N, 50.24 W. Require assistance (calls about 10 times).
10.35 pm	12.25 am	CQD call received from *Titanic* by *Carpathia*. *Titanic* said: "Come at once. We have struck a berg. It's a CQD OM. Position 41.46 N, 50.14 W."
10.35 pm	12.25 am	Cape Race hears MGY (*Titanic*) give corrected position 41.46 N, 50.14 W. Calling him, no answer.
10.36 pm	12.26 am	MGY (*Titanic*) says CQD. "Here corrected position 41.46 N, 50.14 W. Require immediate assistance. We have collision with iceberg. Sinking. Can nothing hear for noise of steam." Sent about 15 to 20 times to *Ypiranga*.
10.37 pm	12.27 am	*Titanic* sends following: "I require assistance immediately. Struck by iceberg in 41.46 N, 50.14 W."
10.40 pm	12.30 am	*Titanic* gives his position to *Frankfurt*, and says: "Tell your Captain to come to our help. We are on the ice."
10.40 pm	12.30 am	*Caronia* sent CQ message to MBC *Baltic* and CQD: "MGY (*Titanic*) struck iceberg, require immediate assistance."
10.40 pm	12.30 am	*Mount Temple* hears MGY (*Titanic*) still calling CQD. Our Captain reverses ship. We are about 50 miles off.
10.46 pm	12.26 am	DKF (*Prinz Friedrich Wilhelm*) calls MGY (*Titanic*) and gives position at 12 am 39.47 N, 50.10 W. MGY (*Titanic*) says: "Are you coming to our?" DFT (*Frankfurt*) says: "What is the matter with u?" MGY (*Titanic*): "We have collision with iceberg. Sinking. Please tell Captain to come." DFT (*Frankfurt*) says: "OK will tell?"

10.48 pm	12.38 am	*Mount Temple* hears *Frankfurt* give MGY (*Titanic*) his position 39.47 N, 52.10 W.
10.55 pm	12.45 am	*Titanic* calls *Olympic* SOS.
11.00 pm	12.50 am	*Titanic* calls CQD and says: "I require immediate assistance. Position 41.46 N, 50.14 W." Received by *Celtic*.
11.03 pm	12.53 am	*Caronia* to MBC (*Baltic*) and SOS: "MGY (*Titanic*) CQD in 41.46 N, 50.14 W. Wants immediate assistance."
11.10 pm	1.00 am	MGY gives distress signal. DDC replies. MGY's position 41.46 N, 50.14 W. Assistance from DDC not necessary as MKC shortly afterwards answers distress call.
11.10 pm	1.00 am	*Titanic* replies to *Olympic* and gives his position as 41.46 N, 50.14 W, and says: "We have struck an iceberg."
11.12 pm	1.02 am	*Titanic* calls *Asian* and said: "Want immediate assistance." *Asian* answered at once and received *Titanic's* position as 41.46 N, 50.14 W, which he immediately takes to the bridge. Captain instructs operator to have *Titanic's* position repeated.
11.12 pm	1.02 am	*Virginian* calls *Titanic* but gets no response. Cape Race tells *Virginian* to report to his Captain the *Titanic* has struck iceberg and requires immediate assistance.
11.20 pm	1.10 am	*Titanic* to MKC (*Olympic*): "We are in collision with berg. Sinking head down. 41.46 N, 50.14 W. Come soon as possible."
11.20 pm	1.10 am	*Titanic* to MKC (*Olympic*). Captain says: "Get your boats ready. What is your position?"
11.25 pm	1.15 am	*Baltic* to *Caronia*: "Please tell *Titanic* we are making towards her."
11.30 pm	1.20 am	*Virginian* hears MCE (Cape Race) inform MGY (*Titanic*) "that we are going to his assistance. Our position 170 miles N of *Titanic*."
11.35 pm	1.25 am	*Caronia* tells *Titanic*: *Baltic* coming to your assistance."
11.35 pm	1.25 am	*Olympic* sends position to *Titanic* 4.24 am GMT 40.52 N, 61.18 W. "Are you steering southerly to meet us?" *Titanic* replies: "We are putting the women off in the boats."
11.35 pm	1.25 am	*Titanic* and *Olympic* work together.
11.37 pm	1.27 am	MGY (*Titanic*) says: "We are putting the women off in the boats."
11.40 pm	1.30 am	*Titanic* tells *Olympic*: "We are putting passengers off in small boats."
11.45 pm	1.35 am	*Olympic* asks *Titanic* what weather he had. *Titanic* replies: "Clear and calm."
11.45 pm	1.35 am	*Baltic* hears *Titanic* say "engine-room getting flooded".
11.45 pm	1.35 am	*Mount Temple* hears DFT (*Frankfurt*) ask: "Are there any boats around you already?" No reply.
11.47 pm	1.37 am	*Baltic* tells *Titanic*: "We are rushing to you."
11.50 pm	1.40 am	*Olympic* to *Titanic*: "Am lighting up all possible boilers as fast as can."
11.50 pm	1.40 am	Cape Race says to *Virginian*: "Please tell your Captain this: The *Olympic* is making all speed for *Titanic*, but his (*Olympic's*) position is 40.32 N, 61.18 W. You are much nearer to *Titanic*. The *Titanic* is already putting women off in the boats, and he says the weather

there is calm and clear. The *Olympic* is the only ship we have heard say: 'Going to the assistance of the *Titanic*.' The others must be a long way from the *Titanic*."

11.55 pm	1.45 am	Last signals heard from *Titanic* by *Carpathia*: "Engine-room full up to boilers."
11.55 pm	1.45 am	*Mount Temple* hears DFT (*Frankfurt*) calling MGY (*Titanic*). No reply.
11.57 pm	1.47 am	*Caronia* hears MGY (*Titanic*) though signals unreadable still.
11.58 pm	1.48 am	*Asian* heard *Titanic* call SOS. *Asian* answers *Titanic* but receives no answer.
Midnight	1.50 am	*Caronia* hears *Frankfurt* working to *Titanic*. *Frankfurt* according to position 172 miles from MGY (*Titanic*) at time first SOS sent out.
12.05 am	1.55 am	Cape Race says to *Virginian*: "We have not heard *Titanic* for about half an hour. His power may be gone."
12.10 am	2.00 am	*Virginian* hears *Titanic* calling very faintly, his power being greatly reduced.
12.20 am	2.10 am	*Virginian* hears 2 v's signalled faintly in spark similar to *Titanic's*; probably adjusting spark.
12.27 am	2.17 am	*Virginian* hears *Titanic* call CQ, but unable to read him. *Titanic's* signals end very abruptly as power suddenly switched off. His spark rather blurred or ragged. Called MGY (*Titanic*) and suggested he should try emergency set, but heard no response.
12.30 am	2.20 am	*Olympic*, his sigs. strong, asked him if he had heard anything about MGY (*Titanic*) he says, No. Keeping strict watch, but hear nothing more from MGY (*Titanic*). No reply from him.
12.52 am		This was the official time the *Titanic* foundered in 41.46 N, 50.14 W as given by the *Carpathia* in message to the *Olympic*; about 2.20 am.
1.15 am		*Virginian* exchanges signals *Baltic*. He tries send us MSG for MGY (*Titanic*), but his signals died utterly away.
1.25 am		*Mount Temple* hears MPA (*Carpathia*) send: "If you are there we are firing rockets."
1.35 am		*Baltic* sent 1 MSG to *Virginian* for *Titanic*.
1.40 am		MPA (*Carpathia*) calling MGY (*Titanic*).
1.58 am		SBA (*Birma*) thinks he hears *Titanic* so sends: "Steaming full speed for you. Shall arrive you 6.00 in morning. Hope you are safe. We are only 50 miles now."
2.00 am		MPA (*Carpathia*) calling MGY (*Titanic*).
2.00 am		Have not heard *Titanic* since 11.50 pm. Received from *Ypiranga*.
2.28 am		*La Provence* to *Celtic*, "Nobody has heard the *Titanic* for about 2 hours."
3.24 am		SBA (*Birma*) says we are 30 miles SW off *Titanic*.
3.35 am		*Celtic* sends message to *Caronia*, for the *Titanic*. *Caronia* after trying for two hours to get through to the *Titanic* tells the *Celtic* impossible to clear his message to *Titanic*. *Celtic* then cancels message.

3.45 am	*Californian* exchanges signals with MLQ (*Mount Temple*). He gave position of *Titanic*.
4.10 am	*Californian* receives MSG from MGN (*Virginian*).
5.05 am	*Baltic* signals MPA (*Carpathia*).
5.40 am	*Parisian* hears weak signals from MPA (*Carpathia*) or some station saying *Titanic* struck iceberg. *Carpathia* has passengers from lifeboats.
5.40 am	*Olympic TR Asian*, with German oil tank in tow for *Halifax* asked what news of MGY (*Titanic*). Sends service later saying heard MGY (*Titanic*) v. faint wkg. C. Race up to 10.0 pm, local time. Finished calling SOS midnight.
6.05 am	*Parisian* exchanges TRs *Virginian*. OK nil. Informed Captain Haines what I heard passing between ships regarding *Titanic*, and he decided not to return as MPA (*Carpathia*) was there, and *Californian* was 50 miles astern of us but requested me to stand by in case required.
6.45 am	*Mount Temple* hears MPA (*Carpathia*) report rescued 20 boat loads.
7.07 am	*Baltic* sends following to *Carpathia*: "Can I be of any assistance to you as regards taking some of the passengers from you? Will be in position about 4.30. Let me know if you alter your position."
7.10 am	*Baltic* in communication with MPA (*Carpathia*). Exchanged traffic re passengers, and get instructions to proceed to Liverpool.
7.15 am	*Baltic* turns round for Liverpool, having steamed 134 miles W towards *Titanic*.
7.40 am	*Mount Temple* hears MPA (*Carpathia*) call CQ and say: "No need to std. bi him." Advise my Captain, who has been cruising round the icefield with no result. Ship reversed.
7.45 am	*Olympic* sent MSG to owners, New York via Sable Island, saying: "Have not communicated with *Titanic* since midnight."
7.55 am	*Carpathia* replies to *Baltic*: "Am proceeding to Halifax or New York full speed. You had better proceed to Liverpool. Have about 800 passengers on board."
8.00 am	*Carpathia* to *Virginian*: "We are leaving here with all on board about 800 passengers. Please return to your northern course."

19 (a) Was the apparatus for lowering the boats on the *Titanic* at the time of the casualty in good working order?

   (b) Were the boats swung out, filled, lowered, or otherwise put into the water and got away under proper superintendence?

   (c) Were the boats sent away in seaworthy condition and properly manned, equipped and provisioned?

   (d) Did the boats, whether those under davits or otherwise, prove to be efficient and serviceable for the purpose of saving life?

Answer

   (a) Yes.

   (b) Yes.

(c) The 14 lifeboats, two emergency boats, and C and D collapsible boats were sent away in a seaworthy condition, but some of them were possibly undermanned. The evidence on this point was unsatisfactory. The total number of crew taken on board the *Carpathia* exceeded the number which would be required for manning the boats. The collapsible boats A and B appear to have floated off the ship at the time she foundered. The necessary equipment and provisions for the boats were carried in the ship, but some of the boats, nevertheless, left without having their full equipment in them.

(d) Yes.

20 (a) What was the number of (1) passengers, (2) crew taken away in each boat on leaving the vessel?

(b) How was this number made up, having regard to: (1) Sex, (2) Class, (3) Rating?

(c) How many were children and how many adults?

(d) Did each boat carry its full load and, if not, why not?

Answer

(a) (b) (c) It is impossible exactly to say how many persons were carried in each boat or what was their sex, class and rating, as the totals given in evidence do not correspond with the numbers taken on board the *Carpathia*. The boats eventually contained in all 712 persons* made up as shown in the answer to Question 21.

(d) No. At least 8 boats did not carry their full loads for the following reasons:

1 Many people did not realise the danger or care to leave the ship at first.

2 Some boats were ordered to be lowered with an idea of then coming round to the gangway doors to complete loading.

3 The officers were not certain of the strength and capacity of the boats in all cases (and see other reasons in this report).

21 (a) How many persons on board the *Titanic* at the time of the casualty were ultimately rescued and by what means?

(b) How many lost their lives prior to the arrival of the SS *Carpathia* in New York?

(c) What was the number of passengers, distinguishing between men and women and adults and children of the 1st, 2nd, and 3rd classes respectively who were saved?

(d) What was the number of the crew, discriminating their ratings and sex, that were saved?

(e) What is the proportion which each of these numbers bears to the corresponding total number on board immediately before the casualty?

* One person died shortly after being picked up by the *Carpathia*.

(f) What reason is there for the disproportion, if any?

Answer

(a) 712, rescued by *Carpathia* from the boats.

(b) One.

(c) (d) and (e) are answered together. The following is a list of the saved:

1st Class

Adult males	57	out of 175, or 32.57 per cent
Adult females	140	out of 144, or 97.22 per cent
Male children	5	All saved
Female children	1	All saved
	203	out of 325, or 62.46 per cent

2nd Class

Adult males	14	out of 168, or 8.33 per cent
Adult females	80	out of 93, or 86.02 per cent
Male children	11	All saved
Female children	13	All saved
	118	out of 285, or 41.40 per cent

3rd Class

Adult males	75	out of 462, or 16.23 per cent
Adult females	76	out of 165, or 46.06 per cent
Male children	13	out of 48, or 27.08 per cent
Female children	14	out of 31, or 45.16 per cent
	178	out of 706, or 25.21 per cent

Total passengers	499	out of 1,316, or 37.94 per cent

Crew

Deck Department	43	out of 66, or 65.15 per cent
Engine-room Department	72	out of 325, or 22.15 per cent
Victualling Department	97	out of 494, or 19.63 per cent
including women	20	out of 23, or 86.95 per cent
	212	out of 885, or 23.95 per cent

Total on board saved	711	out of 2,201, or 32.30 per cent

(f) The disproportion between the numbers of the passengers saved in the first, second, and third-classes is due to various causes, among which the difference in the position of their quarters and the fact that many of the third-class passengers were foreigners are perhaps the most important. Of the Irish emigrants in the third class a large proportion was saved. The disproportion was certainly not due to any discrimination by the officers or crew in assisting the passengers to the boats. The disproportion between the numbers of the passengers and crew saved is due to the fact that the crew, for the most part, all attended to their duties to the last, and until all the boats were gone.

22 What happened to the vessel from the happening of the casualty until she foundered?
Answer
A detailed description has already been given.

23 Where and at what time did the *Titanic* founder?
Answer
2.20 am (ship's time) 15th April, 1912. Latitude 41° 46′ N, longitude 50° 14′ W.

24 (a) What was the cause of the loss of the *Titanic*, and of the loss of life which thereby ensued or occurred?
   (b) What vessels had the opportunity of rendering assistance to the *Titanic*, and, if any, how was it that assistance did not reach the *Titanic* before the SS *Carpathia* arrived?
   (c) Was the construction of the vessel and its arrangements such as to make it difficult for any class of passenger or any portion of the crew to take full advantage of any of the existing provisions for safety?
   Answer
   (a) Collision with an iceberg and the subsequent foundering of the ship.
   (b) The *Californian*. She could have reached the *Titanic* if she had made the attempt when she saw the first rocket. She made no attempt.
   (c) No.

25 When the *Titanic* left Queenstown on or about April 11th last was she properly constructed and adequately equipped as a passenger steamer and emigrant ship for the Atlantic service?
Answer
Yes.

26 The Court is invited to report upon the Rules and Regulations made under the Merchant Shipping Acts, 1894–1906, and the administration of those Acts and of such Rules and Regulations, so far as the consideration thereof is material to this casualty, and to make any recommendations or suggestions that it may think fit, having regard to the circumstances of the casualty, with a view to promoting the safety of vessels and persons at sea.
Answer
An account of the Board of Trade's Administration has already been given and certain recommendations are subsequently made.

RECOMMENDATIONS

The following recommendations are made. They refer to foreign-going passenger and emigrant steamships.

WATERTIGHT SUB-DIVISION

1   That the newly appointed Bulkhead Committee should enquire and report, among other matters, on the desirability and practicability of providing ships with (a) a double skin carried up above the waterline; or, as an alternative, with (b) a longitudinal, vertical, watertight bulkhead on each side of the ship, extending as far forward and aft as convenient; or (c) with a combination of (a) and (b). Any one of the three (a), (b) and (c) to be in addition to watertight transverse bulkheads.
2   That the Committee should also enquire and report as to the desirability and practicability of fitting ships with (a) a deck or decks at a convenient distance or distances above the waterline which shall be watertight throughout a part or the whole of the ship's length; and should in this connection report upon (b) the means by which the necessary openings in such deck or decks should be made watertight, whether by watertight doors or watertight trunks or by any other and what means.
3   That the Committee should consider and report generally on the practicability of increasing the protection given by sub-division, the object being to secure that the ship shall remain afloat with the greatest practicable proportion of her length in free communication with the sea.
4   That when the Committee has reported upon the matters before mentioned, the Board of Trade should take the report into their consideration, and to the extent to which they approve of it should seek

Statutory powers to enforce it in all newly built ships, but with a discretion to relax the requirements in special cases where it may seem right to them to do so.

5 That the Board of Trade should be empowered by the Legislature to require the production of the designs and specifications of all ships in their early stages of construction and to direct such amendments of the same as may be thought necessary and practicable for the safety of life at sea in ships. (This should apply to all passenger-carrying ships.)

LIFEBOATS AND RAFTS

6 That the provision of lifeboat and raft accommodation on board such ships should be based on the number of persons intended to be carried in the ship and not upon tonnage.

7 That the question of such accommodation should be treated independently of the question of the sub-division of the ship into watertight compartments. (This involves the abolition of Rule 12 of the Life-Saving Appliances Rules of 1902.)

8 That the accommodation should be sufficient for all persons on board, with, however, the qualification that in special cases where, in the opinion of the Board of Trade, such provision is impracticable, the requirements may be modified as the Board may think right. (In order to give effect to this recommendation changes may be necessary in the sizes and types of boats to be carried and in the method of stowing and floating them. It may also be necessary to set apart one or more of the boat decks exclusively for carrying boats and drilling the crew, and to consider the distribution of decks in relation to the passengers' quarters. These, however, are matters of detail to be settled with reference to the particular circumstance affecting the ship.)

9 That all boats should be fitted with a protective, continuous fender, to lessen the risk of damage when being lowered in a seaway.

10 That the Board of Trade should be empowered to direct that one or more of the boats be fitted with some form of mechanical propulsion.

11 That there should be a Board of Trade regulation requiring all boat equipment (under Sections 5 and 6, page 15 of the Rules, dated February, 1902, made by the Board of Trade under Section 427 Merchant Shipping Act, 1894) to be in the boats as soon as the ship leaves harbour. The sections quoted above should be amended so as to provide also that all boats and rafts should carry lamps and pyrotechnic lights for purposes of signalling. All boats should be provided with compasses and provisions, and should be very distinctly marked in such a way as to indicate plainly the number of adult persons each boat can carry when being lowered.

12 That the Board of Trade inspection of boats and life-saving appliances should be of a more searching character than hitherto.

MANNING THE BOATS AND BOAT DRILLS

13 That in cases where the deck hands are not sufficient to man the boats, enough other members of the crew should be men trained in boat work to make up the deficiency. These men should be required to pass a test in boat work.

14 That in view of the necessity of having on board men trained in boat work, steps should be taken to encourage the training of boys for the Merchant Service.

15 That the operation of Section 115 and Section 134(a) of the Merchant Shipping Act, 1894, should be examined, with a view to amending the same so as to secure greater continuity of service than hitherto.

16 That the men who are to man the boats should have more frequent drills than hitherto. That in all ships a boat drill, a fire drill and a water-tight door drill should be held as soon as possible after leaving the original port of departure and at convenient intervals of not less than once a week during the voyage. Such drills to be recorded in the official log.

17 That the Board of Trade should be satisfied in each case before the ship leaves port that a scheme has been devised and communicated to each officer of the ship for securing an efficient working of the boats.

GENERAL

18 That every man taking a look-out in such ships should undergo a sight test at reasonable intervals.

19 That in all such ships a police system should be organised so as to secure obedience to orders, and proper control and guidance of all on board in times of emergency.

20 That in all such ships there should be an installation of wireless telegraphy, and that such installation should be worked with a sufficient number of trained operators to secure a continuous service by night and day. In this connection regard should be had to the resolutions of the International Conference on Wireless Telegraphy recently held under the presidency of Sir H Babington Smith. That where practicable a silent chamber for "receiving" messages should form part of the installation.

21 That instruction should be given in all Steamship Companies' Regulations that when ice is reported in or near the track the ship should proceed in the dark hours at a moderate speed or alter her course so as to go well clear of the danger zone.

22 That the attention of Masters of vessels should be drawn by the Board of Trade to the effect that under the Maritime Conventions Act, 1911, it is a misdemeanour not to go to the relief of a vessel in distress when possible to do so.

23 That the same protection as to the safety of life in the event of casualty
which is afforded to emigrant ships by means of supervision and inspection should be extended to all foreign-going passenger ships.

24 That (unless already done) steps should be taken to call an International
Conference to consider and as far as possible to agree upon a common
line of conduct in respect of (a) the sub-division of ships, (b) the provision and working of life-saving appliances, (c) the installation of wireless
telegraphy and the method of working the same, (d) the reduction of
speed or the alteration of course in the vicinity of ice, and (e) the use of
searchlights.

MERSEY
Wreck Commissioner

We concur.

ARTHUR GOUGH-CALTHORPE
A W CLARKE
F C A LYON   } *Assessors*
J H BILES
EDWARD C CHASTON
30*th July*, 1912

RETURN OF THE EXPENSES OF THE TITANIC INQUIRY

EXPENSES PAID BY THE BOARD OF TRADE

	£	s.	d.
Counsel for the Board of Trade:			
Sir Rufus Isaacs, MP	2,458	2	0
Sir J A Simon, MP	2,425	4	0
Mr Aspinall	2,345	12	0
Mr Rowlatt	1,249	3	6
Mr R Asquith	864	0	0
Counsel and Solicitors representing			
other interests:			
Mr A Smith	250	0	0
who instructed			
Mr Thos Scanlan, MP, as Counsel on behalf of the National Sailors' and Firemen's Union	500	0	0
Messrs Helder, Roberts & Co.	250	0	0
who instructed			
Mr A C Edwards, MP, as Counsel on behalf of the Dock, Wharf, Riverside and General Workers' Union	500	0	0
Mr C G P Farrell	230	0	0
who instructed			
Mr H D Harbinson as Counsel on behalf of the 3rd-class passengers	400	0	0

	£	s.	d.
Messrs C G Bradshaw and Waterson who instructed Mr Adair Roche as Counsel on behalf of the Marine Engineers' Association	212	10	7
Messrs Miller, Taylor and Holmes, Solicitors, who appeared by their Mr L S Holmes on behalf of the Imperial Merchant Service Guild	250	0	0
Mr Lewis who appeared on behalf of the British Seafarers' Union	72	0	6
Mr Cotter who appeared on behalf of the National Union of Stewards	68	2	0

Witnesses (allowances for travelling and subsistence):

	£	s.	d.
Sir A J G Chalmers, ex-Professional Officer to the Board of Trade	9	0	0

Officers of the Titanic:

	£	s.	d.
C H Lightoller, 2nd Officer	26	2	6
H J Pitman, 3rd Officer	20	2	6
J G Boxall, 4th Officer	20	15	0
H G Lowe, 5th Officer	20	7	6

Officers of other vessels:

	£	s.	d.
R S Friend, Surgeon, *Oceanic*	3	5	0
C Evans, 3rd Officer, *Californian*	4	3	0
D Dow, Master, *Carmania*		15	0
C V Groves, 2nd Officer, *Californian*	5	8	0
J B Ranson, Master, *Baltic*		15	0
J H Frodsham, 1st Officer, *Tunisian*		12	6
J C Ban, Master, *Caronia*	5	8	0
R O Jones, Master, *Canada*		15	0
H Stone, 1st Officer, *Californian*	4	13	6
G F Stewart, 1st Officer, *Californian*	5	3	0
G T Gambell, Master, *Virginian*		15	0
S Lord, Master, *Californian*	7	0	6
J A Murray, Master, *Empress of Britain*		15	0
J Gibson, Apprentice (acting 4th Officer) *Californian*	4	13	0
J H Moore, Master, *Mount Temple*	3	14	9

	£	s.	d.
Crew of Titanic:			
S Humphreys, Quartermaster	9	7	6
W Wynn, Quartermaster	11	8	0
G T Rowe, Quartermaster	6	11	6
A J Bright, Quartermaster	6	5	6
R Hitchens, Quartermaster	3	4	0
A J Olliver, Quartermaster	6	5	6
W J Perkis, Quartermaster	6	5	6
H Mailey, Master-at-Arms	9	7	6
J Foley, Storekeeper	9	7	6
F Prentice, Storekeeper	11	17	6
A Harris, Boatswain's Mate	5	9	6
A E Jewell, Look-out	5	12	6
F Fleet, Look-out	8	7	6
G A Hagg, Look-out	5	18	0
R R Lee, Look-out	6	6	6
G Symons, Look-out	6	10	10
S Hemmings, Lamp Trimmer	6	5	6
J Anderson, AB	8	12	6
F Evans, AB	8	12	6
J Forward, AB	8	12	6
W Lucas, AB	5	18	0
W McCarthy AB	8	12	6
G McGough, AB	10	6	0
C H Pascoe, AB	8	12	6
W C Peters, AB		15	0
J Scarrott, AB	5	5	0
W Weller, AB	8	12	6
A E J Horswell, AB	12	4	0
J Poingdestre, AB	6	7	6
P Vigott, AB	8	12	6
E Archer, AB	7	18	6
E J Buley, AB	7	13	0
W Brice, AB	5	1	0
F Clinch, AB	5	1	0
F O Evans, AB	5	1	0
T Jones, AB	6	13	0
G Moore, AB	6	4	6
F Osman, AB	5	1	0
F Barrett, Leading Fireman	6	6	0
C Hendrikson, Leading Fireman	13	11	0
T Threlfall, Leading Fireman	11	6	6
G Beauchamp, Fireman	5	4	6
G Combes, Fireman	7	16	6

	£	s.	d.
W Clarke, Fireman	7	16	6
R Couper, Fireman	7	16	6
S Collins, Fireman	11	4	0
J Dilley, Fireman	7	19	8
F Doel, Fireman	7	16	6
F Dymond, Fireman	13	16	6
J Draper, Fireman	10	3	0
E Flarty, Fireman	7	16	6
G Goldley, Fireman	7	16	6
T Graham, Fireman	7	15	0
W Hurst, Fireman	9	7	0
J Haggan, Fireman	8	1	0
F Harris, Fireman	7	18	0
C Judd, Fireman	12	13	0
J Kemish, Fireman	7	16	6
F T Kasper, Fireman	7	16	6
W Lindsay, Fireman	9	0	6
F Knowles, Fireman	8	10	0
F Mason, Fireman	7	16	6
J Moore, Fireman	9	0	6
T Mayzes, Fireman	7	16	6
W Major, Fireman	9	8	6
W Murdock, Fireman	8	1	0
H Noss, Fireman	10	4	6
W Nuttbeam, Fireman	7	16	6
C Othen, Fireman	7	16	6
H Oliver, Fireman	7	16	6
F O'Connor, Fireman	10	4	6
J Pearce, Fireman	7	16	6
J Priest, Fireman	7	16	6
J Podesta, Fireman	7	16	6
R Pusey, Fireman	9	18	6
C Rice, Fireman	7	16	6
H Spackman, Fireman	11	10	0
A Spiers, Fireman	5	6	0
A Strur, Fireman	7	16	6
E Self, Fireman	7	16	6
H Senior, Fireman	7	18	0
G Thresher, Fireman	7	16	6
R Triggs, Fireman	7	16	6
J Taylor, Fireman	10	1	6
W H Taylor, Fireman	4	11	6
J Thompson, Trimmer	3	16	6
J Avery, Trimmer	7	16	6

	£	s.	d.
E Allen, Trimmer	7	16	6
W Binstead, Trimmer	7	16	6
P Blake, Trimmer	9	7	0
G Cavell, Trimmer	11	0	6
A Dore, Trimmer	7	16	6
W Fredericks, Trimmer	7	16	6
A Fryer, Trimmer	7	16	6
A Hunt, Trimmer	7	16	6
A Hebb, Trimmer	7	16	6
J McGann, Trimmer	8	17	0
E Perry, Trimmer	7	16	6
G Petham, Trimmer	8	19	0
F Sheath, Trimmer	9	18	6
E Snow, Trimmer	9	7	0
W White, Trimmer	9	7	0
T P Dillon, Trimmer	5	16	0
W McIntyre, Trimmer	4	11	6
G Pregnell, Greaser	9	7	6
F Scott, Greaser	11	15	6
A White, Greaser	9	7	6
T Ranger, Greaser	7	0	6
W S Halford, Steward		13	0
E Brown, Steward	15	2	6
A Baggott, Steward	11	17	6
F Crafter, Steward	14	15	6
F Hartnell, Steward	14	15	6
A Harrison, Steward	11	17	6
C Cullen, Steward	11	15	0
R Pfropper, Steward	9	9	0
W C Foley, Steward	10	4	6
J W Gibbons, Steward	10	7	0
J Hart, Steward	9	13	0
L Heyland, Steward	7	18	0
J Johnston, Steward	7	10	6
G Knight, Steward	11	17	6
P Keene, Steward	11	17	6
W Lucas, Steward	12	4	0
A Littlejohn, Steward	11	12	6
A Lewis, Steward	7	18	0
W S Faulkner, Steward	11	15	0
S Daniels, Steward	9	10	6
C Mackay, Steward	15	5	0
A McMicken, Steward	11	17	6
F Morris, Steward	10	11	6

	£	s.	d.
W H Nichols, Steward	9	9	0
F Port, Steward	7	18	0
W J Prior, Steward	7	19	6
A Pugh, Steward	10	4	6
S Rule, Steward	12	13	6
W E Ryerson, Steward	9	10	6
O Savage, Steward	7	18	0
A Thessinger, Steward	9	9	0
F Terrell, Steward	9	9	0
J Wheat, Steward	16	2	6
W William, Steward	9	9	0
J Witter, Steward	9	9	0
W Wright, Steward	7	13	0
H Yearsley, Steward	11	17	6
H Phillamore, Steward	9	9	0
C W Fitzpatrick, Steward	9	9	0
F Toms, Steward	11	17	6
B Thomas, Steward	11	17	6
A C Thomas, Steward	11	17	6
A Burrage, Steward	7	18	0
J Chapman, Steward	12	2	6
A Pearcey, Steward	8	12	6
J Stewart, Steward	15	0	6
W Seward, Steward	10	8	0
C E Andrews, Steward	5	14	0
W Burke, Steward	7	2	6
G F Crowe, Steward	6	17	6
A Cunningham, Steward	6	17	6
A Crawford, Steward	14	2	0
H Etchis, Steward	6	17	6
J Hardy, Steward	6	17	6
F P Ray, Steward	7	2	6
E Wheelton, Steward	6	17	6
W Ward, Steward	6	17	6
J G Widgery, Bath Room Steward	5	12	6
V C Jessop, Stewardess	7	1	0
B Lavington, Stewardess		13	0
Mrs Bennett, Stewardess	7	7	0
Mrs Gold, Stewardess	7	7	0
Miss Gregson, Stewardess	7	4	0
Mrs Leather, Stewardess	12	15	0
Mrs A Martin, Stewardess	7	1	0
Miss Marsden, Stewardess	8	12	6
Mrs McLann, Stewardess	7	7	0

	£	s.	d.
Mrs Pritchard, Stewardess	7	6	0
Mrs Roberts, Stewardess	8	12	6
Mrs Robinson, Stewardess	11	0	0
Miss Stap, Stewardess	7	2	6
Miss Sloan, Stewardess	8	12	6
Miss Smith, Stewardess	7	7	0
Mrs Bliss, Stewardess	7	9	6
Miss Caton, Turkish Bath Attendant	6	1	0
Miss Slocombe, Turkish Bath Attendant	6	1	0
Miss R Bowker, Cashier	9	0	0
Miss Martin, Assistant Cashier	7	4	0
J Ellis, Cook	9	9	0
J Collins, Cook	5	8	0
J Windebank, Assistant Cook	9	9	0
I Maynard, Entree Cook	9	9	0
C Jonghim, Chief Baker	14	19	0
C Burgess, Baker	9	9	0
C Mills, Assistant Baker	7	18	0
H Neal, Assistant Baker	9	9	0
J Colgan, Scullion	7	18	0
F Martin, Scullion	6	8	6
H Ross, Scullion	7	18	6
A Simmons, Scullion	10	6	0
P Ball, Plate Washer	6	7	0
R Hardwick, Kitchen Porter	7	18	0
J Guy, Assistant Boots	9	9	0
W Harder, Window Cleaner	7	16	6
P Mauge, Secretary to Chief		15	0
H S Bride, Marconi Wireless Operator	4	5	0
Tram fares of 28 of crew paid by Receiver of Wreck, Southampton		4	8
Cab fares of injured members of crew paid by Receiver of Wreck, Southampton		2	6
Crew of other vessels:			
E Gill, Donkey-man, *Californian*	9	18	0
W Ross, AB, *Californian*	3	2	6
G Glenn, Fireman, *Californian*	3	7	6
W Thomas, Greaser, *Californian*	6	14	0
Mr H Wolferstan, Solicitor's Agent at Plymouth, expenses incurred in taking depositions at Plymouth	205	15	10

	£	s.	d.
Marconi Wireless company for charts, particulars of telegrams, and work of, and attendance at Inquiry of, their Deputy Manager	173	13	9
Messrs Harland and Wolff for plans, models, and attendance at Inquiry of Mr Wilding and three others in their service	574	11	0
Messrs Malby and Sons for enlarging and mounting charts	10	0	0
Messrs J D Potter for charts	1	4	0
Service of Summonses:			
Customs Officers at Plymouth		1	6
Customs Officers at Southampton	3	4	6
Customs Officers at Liverpool		19	6
Customs Officers at London, Dock Street, E		3	0
Affidavits:			
Various Commissioners at Liverpool		13	6
Various Commissioners at Southampton	3	8	6
Consular Expenses			
HM Consul-General at Havre	5	13	0
HM Consul at Philadelphia	5	16	2
HM Consul-General at New York:			
Cables	6	15	8
Travelling and expenses of Vice-Consul	29	7	8
Charles Fox, Esq. (legal)	154	6	5
Stenographer for notes of evidence of certain witnesses	48	4	4
Shorthand notes of proceedings of United States Committee	308	3	0
Fees for taking depositions	9	0	0
J Swan, packing cases for evidence	7	3	6
Cost of reproduction of evidence taken by United States Senate Committee	201	9	4
Cunard Steamship Company, expenses in securing attendance of Captain Rostron, of SS *Carpathia*	77	14	7
Remuneration for the staff of the Board of Trade Solicitor for additional work:			
Mr G C Vaux	126	0	0
Mr L J Block	63	0	0

	£	s.	d.
Mr R A Macaskill	52	10	0
Mr F Studley	42	0	0
Mr W H Biggs	31	10	0
Telegrams and cablegrams	15	12	9
Copying and typing	175	0	0
Incidentals (including cabs, etc.)	15	0	0
	£16,331	16	6

EXPENSES PAID BY THE TREASURY FROM THE VOTE FOR MISCELLANEOUS LEGAL EXPENSES

	£	s.	d.
Wreck Commissioner (Right Hon. Lord Mersey)	1,050	0	0
Wreck Commissioner's Secretary (The Hon. Clive Bigham)	125	0	0
Wreck Commissioner's Clerk (Mr A Dones)	75	0	0
Assessors (remuneration and travelling and subsistence allowances):			
Professor J H Biles, DSc, LLD	500	0	0
Rear-Admiral Hon. A Gough-Calthorpe, CVO, RN	139	2	0
Mr E C Chaston, RNR	156	17	8
Captain A W Clarke	80	19	6
Commander FCA Lyon, RNR	73	18	0
Shorthand writing	622	15	6
Clerical assistance, indexing, etc.	78	12	11
Travelling and incidental expenses	39	3	8
Hire of Hall and Offices (including cost of fitting up Hall as Court)	341	7	1
	£3,282	16	4

CHARGES FOR STATIONERY AND PRINTING

	£	s.	d.
Cost of printing Report and Evidence	1,147	3	0
Cost of Miscellaneous Stationery	67	10	0
	1,214	13	0
Less proceeds from sale of copies of Report and Evidence (estimate)	280	0	0
	£934	13	0

TOTAL EXPENSES INCURRED

	£	s.	d.
TOTAL PAID BY THE BOARD OF TRADE	16,331	16	6
TOTAL PAID BY THE TREASURY FROM THE MISCELLANEOUS LEGAL EXPENSES VOTE	3,282	16	4
TOTAL STATIONERY AND PRINTING	934	13	0
GRAND TOTAL	£20,549	5	10

REAPPRAISAL OF EVIDENCE RELATING TO
SS CALIFORNIAN

On 14th April 1912 at about 11.40 pm ship's time the White Star liner *Titanic*, on her maiden voyage from Southampton towards New York, struck an iceberg and was severely damaged. She foundered less than two-and-three quarter hours later, with the loss of 1,490 lives. In response to her wireless distress signals various ships attempted to come to her aid but the first to reach the scene, the Cunard liner *Carpathia*, did not arrive until about 4.00 am, well after *Titanic* had sunk.

There is no doubt that other vessels were nearer to hand than *Carpathia*, but in 1912 many ships did not have wireless and those that did, did not necessarily keep continuous watch with their apparatus. One such ship was the British cargo/passenger vessel *Californian* whose single wireless operator had gone off duty shortly before the first distress call was sent. At the Formal Investigation (FI) held in London between 2nd May and 3rd July 1912, evidence was heard from *Californian's* Master and some of her officers and crew. It was put to the Court that although they had not heard *Titanic's* wireless messages, they had seen distress signals which she had fired; and that had they responded to those signals they might have saved many of the lives lost. The Court was asked the specific question (which was added to the original list of questions during the hearing):

> What vessels had the opportunity of rendering assistance to the *Titanic* and, if any, how was it that assistance did not reach the *Titanic* before the SS *Carpathia* arrived?

The Court's answer was:

The *Californian*. She could have reached the *Titanic* if she had made the attempt when she saw the first rocket. She made no attempt.

Californian's Master was Captain Stanley Lord and it was upon him that the great weight of the extremely grave accusation implied by the Court's finding fell. Captain Lord always disputed the justice of the finding and he requested a re-hearing of that part of the Inquiry which concerned his ship; the request was rejected, and as no formal charge had been laid against him, and no action had been taken against his Certificate, he had no right of appeal.

For many years the matter rested, but in the mid-1950s the book *A Night to Remember* written by Walter Lord (no relation to Captain Lord) appeared; it was widely read and a successful film based upon it was made. The allegations against the *Californian* were repeated and this led Captain Lord, by then over 80 years old, to renew his plea for the matter to be re-examined. His case was taken up by others, including especially Mr W L S Harrison who was at that time General Secretary of the Mercantile Marine Service Association, the body representing British shipmasters. In particular, two petitions were made to the Board of Trade asking for the Inquiry to be re-opened; both were rejected.

In 1985 an expedition led by Dr Robert Ballard of the Woods Hole Oceanographic Institute, Massachusetts, discovered the wreck of *Titanic*, in a position some 13 miles from that accepted by the 1912 Inquiry as being the position of the casualty. This "new evidence" led to further pressure for the Inquiry to be re-opened, and although initially the Department of Transport (which by now had taken responsibility for shipping matters) refused, in 1990 the Secretary of State for Transport, The Right Honourable Cecil Parkinson MP, determined that the Marine Accident Investigation Branch (MAIB) should make a reappraisal of the relevant evidence.

In order to prepare this report, MAIB appointed an experienced inspector from outside the branch. The Deputy Chief Inspector of Marine Accidents, whose report this is, did not agree with all of the Inspector's findings.

TERMS OF REFERENCE AND SUMMARY OF CONCLUSIONS

The terms of reference of the reappraisal were as follows:

Taking into account the discovery of the wreckage of *Titanic* and other evidence which has become available since the Formal Investigation was held, together with recorded evidence given at the Investigation:

(a) To establish so far as is now possible the positions of *Titanic* when she struck an iceberg on 14 April 1912 and when she subsequently foundered; to estimate the positions of *Californian* at the same times; and to deduce the distance apart of the two vessels during the period between those times.

(b) To consider whether *Titanic* was seen by *Californian* during that period, and if so, when and by whom.

(c) To consider whether distress signals from *Titanic* were seen by *Californian* and if so, whether proper action was taken.

(d) To assess the action taken by Captain Stanley Lord, Master of *Californian*, between about 10.00 pm ship's time on 14th April and the time on 15th April when passage was resumed.

The conclusions reached are:

(a) *Titanic* was in approximate position 41°47'N 49°55'W when she struck the iceberg at 11.45 pm on 14th April, and in position 41°43'.6N 49°56'.9W when she foundered. The position of *Californian* cannot be deduced so accurately; the Inspector considers she may have been in about 41°50'N 50°07'W at the time *Titanic* struck the iceberg, but was probably further east and only 5 to 7 miles off. In my opinion, *Californian* was in about 42°00'N 50°09'W or a little north of that position, and between 17 and 20 miles from *Titanic* — most likely about 18 miles. A current was setting southerly but is likely to have affected both vessels similarly until *Titanic* sank, so their distance apart will not have appreciably changed during the period in question. These conclusions are discussed below.

(b) The Inspector considers that *Titanic* was seen by *Californian*, by her Master and others. I think it possible that she was seen, due to abnormal refraction permitting sight beyond the ordinary visible horizon; but more likely that she was not seen (see below).

(c) The Inspector considers that *Titanic's* distress signals were seen, and that proper action was not taken. I agree on both accounts (see below).

(d) See "Assessment of the Action taken by Captain Lord".

BACKGROUND

Californian was a steam ship of 6,223 gross tons, owned by the Leyland Line. (It is perhaps slightly ironic that both the Leyland and White Star Lines were ultimately controlled by the same conglomerate, the International Mercantile Marine Company; but the two lines operated independently it is believed so far as the direct management of their ships was concerned.) *Californian* left London bound for Boston on 5th April; her subsequent voyage is the subject of a good deal of what follows in this report and need not be further described now. She was primarily a cargo ship and though she had some accommodation for passengers, none were carried on the voyage in question. Her Master, Captain Lord, held an Extra Master Certificate, and she carried three qualified deck officers: Mr Stewart, chief officer; Mr Stone, second officer; and Mr Groves, third officer. Evidence was given to the Formal Investigation by all these officers as well as by Captain Lord, and also by Mr Evans, her wireless operator, a donkey-man (Ernest Gill) and an apprentice (James Gibson). The evidence made it clear that a ship was seen to approach the ice field and to stop at about the same time as *Titanic* struck the iceberg. Later, rockets were seen apparently coming from this ship, but no action was taken except to try, unsuccessfully, to call her up by morse lamp. No evidence was called from any rating apart from Mr Gill which, in retrospect, is a pity, for an account by the seamen on watch during the night of 14th/15th April might well have been valuable.

It has been mentioned briefly that a number of other ships were in the general area and three of these will be referred to later.

Carpathia, a Cunard liner of 13,600 gross tons commanded by Captain A H Rostron, had sailed from New York for Mediterranean ports on 11th April. She was the first vessel to reach the scene in response to *Titanic's* wireless signals and picked up all those who survived. *Mount Temple*, owned by the Canadian Pacific Railway Company was westbound from London. She also responded to the distress calls but did not reach the position of foundering. She was a ship of 6,661 tons and on the voyage in question had a complement of some 1,600 including over 1,400 passengers. A rather different type of vessel was the Norwegian sealer *Samson*, a large motorised barque with a crew of 45. Nothing was known of this ship at the time of the Formal Investigation, but many years later her chief officer, Henrik Naess, said that she had been some 10 miles from *Titanic* and had seen the distress rockets. Why she did not assist is explained briefly later.

THE RELATIVE POSITIONS OF *TITANIC* AND *CALIFORNIAN*

As is briefly stated above, the Inspector has found that the two ships were between 5 and 10 miles apart whilst they lay stopped, and probably nearer five; whereas in my opinion the distance was substantially greater, probably about 18 miles. I summarise below the evidence available and our respective interpretations.

The position of *Titanic*

This is the one almost fully substantiated piece of new evidence since the 1912 Inquiry. Dr Robert Ballard, leader of the expedition which found the wreckage, gives the position of the boilers and stern section, and the Inspector supports his view that these very heavy items will have sunk almost straight to the seabed: their position must therefore be very close indeed to the position of sinking. I agree. The position is 41°43'.6N 49°56'.9W. This will not of course be the position of the collision, as the ship must have drifted some distance before she foundered; how far and in what direction will have depended entirely upon the current, for the night was calm with virtually no wind. The current is discussed below, for it is an important feature in this reappraisal: there is strong evidence that it was setting a little west of south at rather more than 1 knot. Allowing such a current, and working back from the position of sinking, the position yielded for collision with the berg is approximately 41°47′N 49°55′W. This position is substantially different from that given by *Titanic* in her wireless distress messages and accepted by the Court of Formal Investigation, namely 41°46′N 50°14′W.

The position of *Californian*

There is no really new concrete evidence as to *Californian's* position. A number of documents have been produced over the years since the accident, and during the present reappraisal, with the aim of assisting its establishment, but the evidence they call upon is either speculative or was available at the time of the FI. The Investigation was not specifically required to establish *Californian's* position in absolute terms, and the report found simply that the ships were "not more than eight to ten miles apart". It is clear from the report that the Court based this finding on the two facts — which were not contested — that during the time *Titanic* was sinking those on board her saw a ship, and so did those on *Californian*. They decided that the ship seen by *Titanic* was *Californian* and vice versa. For the present appraisal, however, it is obviously desirable to assess *Californian's* actual position so far as is possible, especially now that that of *Titanic* is known.

The evidence on which such an assessment can be based is principally that of Captain Lord and his officers. *Californian* was bound from London towards Boston. On 14th April, her noon position by observation was recorded as 42°05′N 47°25′W. Her passage plan was not examined in detail at the FI but it appears clear that, as was and indeed still is common, the intention was to follow a Great Circle course to a position south-east of the Grand Banks and then to steer a Rhumb Line to her destination — much the same as *Titanic*. Accordingly, the course being steered from noon was due west. At 6.30 pm three large icebergs were seen five miles to the south and an estimated position was worked up, and at 7.30 pm a warning signal was sent to another Leyland liner:

> To Captain, *Antillian*—6.30 pm apparent ship's time, lat. 42.3N, long. 49.9W. Three large bergs five miles to southward of us—Regards Lord.

Although addressed to *Antillian*, the message was broadcast for any ship within wireless range to hear, and shortly after 7.30 pm *Titanic* called up *Californian* to say that she had picked it up. Also at about 7.30 pm, Mr Stewart, *Californian's* chief officer, took a Pole Star sight which gave a latitude of 42°05′N.

At 8.00 pm the third officer, Mr Groves, took over the bridge watch from Mr Stewart and very soon afterwards Captain Lord joined him on the bridge. At about 11.15 pm ice was seen ahead and *Californian* was stopped; the time of stopping was noted as 10.21 pm and Captain Lord estimated the position as 42°05′N 50°07′W. Some time after this, a ship was seen to approach and then to stop (it was assumed because of the ice) at a distance estimated as five miles.

The crucial position is that in which the *Californian* stopped. The Wreck Commissioner was "satisfied that this position was not accurate". Captain Lord's case was not improved by the fact that the only log records he could produce were written up after the event; the scrap log kept by the officers had been destroyed. There is evidence that this was normal practice in Leyland Line ships, but it is certainly unfortunate that an exception to the normal rule was not made: this, coupled with the Court's rejection of Captain Lord's position, has led to a common assumption by those commenting on the case that the Court considered deliberately false evidence to have been given. I am, however, not sure that that was indeed the Court's opinion. It is interesting and perhaps instructive to read Lord Mersey's final comments again:

> These circumstances convince me that the ship seen by the *Californian* was the *Titanic*, and if so, according to Captain Lord, the two vessels were about five miles apart at the time of the disaster. The evidence from the *Titanic* corroborates this estimate, but I am advised that the distance was probably greater, though not more than eight to ten miles.

The "advice" presumably came from the assessors. No reason for it is given, but the most reasonable inference to draw seems to be that they agreed that the two ships were in sight of one another but they accepted Captain Lord's position as his genuine estimate; the discrepancy was due to error in reckoning, not deliberate deception, and they did not consider the error likely to be great enough to bring the ships so close to each other as five miles. On the other hand, they would not see each other even on a very clear night at a distance greater than 8 to 10 miles.

The Inspector in his assessment has followed an approach broadly along the same lines and has explained how he thinks the error arose. He considers that the current had set southerly since noon on 14th April; no allowance for this current was made, with the result that at the time of the casualty *Californian* would indeed be some 8 to 10 miles from *Titanic*. It is here that I differ from the Inspector, for reasons set out below; and as the current is an important factor (though not the only one), it is convenient at this point to discuss it more fully.

For the month of April the prevailing current in the region of the casualty sets east or ENE; the region is roughly where the Gulf Stream develops into the North Atlantic Drift. However, not far to the north-west the south-going Labrador current prevails, and the exact course of these two conflict-ing streams varies from year to year. There is no doubt that in 1912 the Labrador current extended further south and east than is usual in April: the principal evidence for this is the presence of ice and, particularly, the ice field. That this was exceptional is clear from evidence given at the FI, espe-cially that of Captain Moore of *Mount Temple* who told the Court that in 27 years of regular trading across the North Atlantic he had never known the ice to be so far south. The position of the flotsam as given by the *Californian*, when compared with the position of sinking as now established, is further evidence of a southerly set and — assuming the position to be cor-rect — allows it to be quantified: the direction of set was about 196° True and the rate about 1.3 knots.

There is still further suggestive evidence in support of these figures in that, when run back to give the likely position of collision, the position arrived at, though different from that sent by *Titanic* in her distress calls, does lie practically on the line of her course through that position. Perhaps the error in the position as transmitted was caused by the wrong distance being allowed along the course line from the last known position — a simple mis-take to make under stress.

Thus far I am entirely with the Inspector. I think there can be no rea-sonable doubt that a current setting about south by west at something like 1¼ knots existed in the area of the accident. But for his assessment of *Californian's* position when the accident occurred to be correct he has found it necessary to assume that this current had affected her since at least noon on 14th April; indeed he suggests that it had been felt since noon on 13th. I have to say that I think this most unlikely, for several reasons:

(a) It has already been shown that the presence of a southerly current in the region of the accident was unusual. For it to have been present much fur-ther east, in the region normally associated with the North Atlantic Drift, would clearly be even more unusual, progressively so the further east one goes.

(b) The Pole Star sight taken by the chief officer at 7.30 pm (and confirmed by him in Court) gave the same latitude — 42°05'N — as that observed at noon on the same day, showing a course made good of west, which is that stated as having been steered. It follows that the net effect of set was nil, at least until 7.30 pm, unless either the observations were in error or false evidence was given.

(c) The one piece of evidence on *Californian's* track which cannot have been fabricated is the signal sent to *Antillian* concerning the sighting of ice-bergs. This in isolation gives no proof of the track followed but — unless all the other evidence was doctored — it adds weight to the statement that the *Californian* was steering westerly and thus, coupled with the Pole Star sight, to the evidence against a southerly set. (In fact, the latitude sent to *Antillian* of 42°03'N, which was based on dead reckoning, suggests that the course steered was slightly south of west which, given the subsequent sight, argues a slight *northerly* set. This is not impossible given the current to be expected; but Captain Lord later recalled the latitude which he wrote out for the wireless operator as 42°05′N, and it may well be that the figure 5 was misread for 3. But neither figure offers any grounds for deducing a set to the south.)

(d) The evidence given by Captain Rostron of *Carpathia* is significant. On receiving *Titanic's* distress call he steered for the position given which was some 58 miles distant, bearing N 52 W (308°T). After about two hours he sighted a flare from one of the liner's boats about half a point on the port bow. From *Carpathia's* starting-out position, the position transmitted by *Titanic* towards which *Carpathia* was steering, and *Titanic's* sinking position, it will be seen that at the time the flare was seen (2.40 am) the boat which it came from must have been to the north of *Carpathia's* course line and it follows that during the two hours the ship must have been set to the north: otherwise the boat would have been seen on the *starboard* bow. Bearing in mind that at the time *Carpathia* was eastbound (from New York) it will be appreciated that this argument essentially holds good even if there was some error in her position by dead-reckoning when she received the distress call: the rate of current would be affected but not the fact that its net effect was to the north.

(e) Finally, there is the ice and particularly the ice field which lay in a roughly north/south direction close to the 50th meridian. It seems clearly reasonable to associate this field with a southerly current; but if such a current was to be found much further east, why was no ice there? There appear to be no reports even of isolated bergs east of 49°W. It is suggested that the limits of the ice field probably indicate the axis of the southerly drift, and these are fairly clear from the evidence. It cannot have extended much further south than the region of the accident, for Captain Moore, westbound in *Mount Temple* before he received *Titanic's* distress call and turned back, had crossed the 50th meridian in latitude 41°20′N and seen no ice; its western edge must have been near to the distress position sent by *Titanic* as *Mount Temple* encountered it in that vicinity; and its eastern edge was somewhere to the west of *Titanic's* actual position, for she at no time seems to have sighted the field, while *Carpathia*, when she was picking up survivors, was among icebergs but still east of field ice.

In order to bring this part of my report to a sensible conclusion it is necessary to anticipate the next section: for clearly none of the arguments are significant if it is the case, as the FI believed, that the *Californian* was the ship seen by *Titanic* and was no more than, at the most, 8 to 10 miles away. If that was so, then whether the discrepancy with Captain Lord's statement of her position was due to abnormal current, simple error, or deliberate falsification of evidence is (at least for the present purpose) academic. It will be seen from the next section that on the matter of the two ships seeing each other I unfortunately again cannot fully agree with the Inspector; and our respective opinions on *Californian's* position are undoubtedly coloured by this difference.

In the Inspector's view the FI finding is right and indeed his personal opinion, based upon his assessment of the evidence of what was seen by both ships, is that their distance apart was between 5 and 7 miles. In my opinion, *Titanic* was not seen by *Californian* nor vice versa, except possibly at a range much greater than the ordinarily visible horizon owing to abnormal refraction. This being so, then unlike the Court and the Inspector, I have no need nor cause to discount *Californian's* evidence, and the only adjustment to her position as tendered to the FI which is required is that which follows from what we can now deduce as to the current.

For all the reasons set out previously I do not believe that *Californian* will have been affected by the southerly set for more than at the most a few hours before she reached the ice field and stopped. She may have met it before the chief officer took his Pole Star sight, its effect up to that point being cancelled by a northerly set earlier in the afternoon; but even given that, her southerly set between 7.30 pm and stopping will have been some 3½ miles at most. While stopped she would have drifted further, for some 2 miles up to the time *Titanic* hit the berg.

Applying this maximum drift and the direction as deduced previously, the position of the *Californian* at the time of collision becomes 42°00'N 50°09'W. More likely, especially taking into account the implication of *Carpathia's* evidence, the full strength of current was only felt when close to the ice field. I therefore consider that the *Californian* was between 17 and 20 miles from *Titanic* at the time of her collision with the iceberg, bearing about NW by N from her.

Between the collision and sinking, both ships will in all probability have drifted similarly so that their position relative to each other would not appreciably change.

WAS *TITANIC* SEEN BY *CALIFORNIAN*?

The Inspector considers that *Titanic* was seen by *Californian* and indeed kept under observation from 11.00 pm or soon after on 14th April until she sank. He bases this view on the evidence from Captain Lord and the two watch officers, Mr Groves and Mr Stone, and on the extent of coincidence between what they saw and what is known of *Titanic's* movements. As the Inspector points out, there is a good deal of evidence as to what was seen by *Californian* which does not coincide with what is known of *Titanic*; but his opinion — which if review were to be confined to what was seen by *Californian* I would not dissent from — is that the balance is strongly in favour of *Titanic* having been the ship seen.

However, I do not propose in this report to discuss the evidence from *Californian* in detail, because to my mind the question posed is answered, conclusively, by the evidence of what was seen — and by what was not seen — from *Titanic*. It is absolutely clear, unless there is conspiracy involving not only Captain Lord and his officers but also the donkey-man, Mr Gill (whose independent statement made in America precipitated the case against his ship), that the ship thought by the Court to be *Titanic* was in view continuously from *Californian* from 11.00 pm or thereabouts. *Titanic's* speed, maintained until collision at 11.40 pm, suggests that if at that time she was 5 miles from the *Californian*, then at 11.00 pm she will have been nearly 20 miles away, which is a very long way off for her to be seen, but given the possible difference in the two ships' clocks and the imprecision of times, this point is perhaps not very important. What is significant, however, is that no ship was seen by *Titanic* until well after the collision; the exact time is not recorded but seems to have been about 00.30 am and certainly substantially past midnight. During all this time, although many of the crew were preparing boats or attending to the passengers, watch was maintained with officers on the bridge and seamen in the crow's-nest, and with their ship in grave danger the lookout for another vessel which could come to their help must have been most anxious and keen. It is in my view inconceivable that *Californian* or any other ship was within the visible horizon of *Titanic* during that period; it equally follows that *Titanic* cannot have been within *Californian's* horizon. It is no argument to say that *Titanic* was much the more conspicuous vessel of the two: the ship seen by the *Californian* was readily noticed, not only from the bridge but also from the deck, by the casual observation of Mr Gill coming up from the lighted engine-room; and the watch officers easily distinguished her individual navigation lights. It is clear therefore that sighting did not depend upon particular conspicuity; and this must equally have been the case in the reverse direction.

In his closing speech at the Formal Investigation, Mr Robertson Dunlop (on behalf of *Californian*) clearly drew attention to the marked inconsistency between what was seen by the two ships. It is no part of this reappraisal to criticise the Court, but it must be remarked as surprising that no consideration of what he said appears in their report.

There are two possible explanations for what the *Californian* saw. The first and most obvious is that a third ship was present which approached from the east, stopped on meeting the field ice, and then after a period steamed away to seek a break in the ice. This is very far from unlikely; the North Atlantic trade was busy in 1912 and a number of other ships are known to have been in the area. A good deal of print has been expended on consideration of the identity of such a ship but the question is not within the remit of the present reappraisal and I do not consider that an attempt to answer it with certainty would be likely to be successful or would be a proper expenditure of public resources.

The second explanation, which was first advanced some years ago in an unpublished document, is that the *Californian* did actually see *Titanic* but at a very much greater range than her horizon because of abnormal ("super-") refraction. In favour of this theory, the phenomenon is variable in its effect and this might explain the apparent movement of each ship as seen by the other when both were in fact stopped. In addition, the rockets seen by *Californian* were described as low-lying (quoted as rising to less than mast-head height) and this could be because they actually rose to a height above the refracting layer and were seen directly. Against the theory, it requires a long period during which the *Californian* could see *Titanic* but not vice versa. This is not impossible: the phenomenon does lead to curious results, and further it is possible that the *Californian's* lights (though they were electric and could certainly be seen on a night such as this at 5 miles or more range) could not be seen even with super-refraction at 17 to 20 miles.

There are two further objections to the super-refraction theory, both of which are, equally, objections to the general theory that *Titanic* was seen. The first is that, although when he first saw the other ship Captain Lord recalls seeing a green (starboard) sidelight as one would expect with a ship to the south and approaching on a westerly course, later her red (port) light came into view, arguing that after stopping she swung markedly to starboard. Evidence of *Titanic's* change of heading after collision is not absolutely conclusive, but it is known that initially she went to port and the balance of evidence seems to be that afterwards her heading did not much change. Her port sidelight would therefore not be seen. The second is that Mr Stone, *Californian's* officer on watch from midnight till 4.00 am, noticed a change of bearing before the other ship disappeared. I do not place great weight on this, for Mr Stone had no particular reason to take accurate compass bearings of the other ship, and the explanation may have been that his own ship was swinging, leading to a change in *relative* bearing; but clearly if the compass bearing did change appreciably the vessel cannot have been *Titanic* for she remained stopped; super-refraction could not explain a substantial change in bearing.

In sum, I do not consider that a definite answer to the question "Was *Titanic* seen?" can be given; but if she was, then it was only because of the phenomenon of super-refraction for she was well beyond the ordinary visible horizon. More probably, in my view, the ship seen by the *Californian* was another, unidentified, vessel. Whether the ship seen during the later stages of the tragedy by *Titanic* was this third ship, becoming visible to her and then disappearing as she sought a break in the ice field, or a fourth vessel is a matter of speculation outside the scope of this reappraisal.

WERE *TITANIC'S* ROCKETS SEEN?

The Inspector's answer is "Yes", and I entirely agree with him. There is no doubt that some rockets were seen and while it has been suggested that these were Company signals from the other ship seen by the *Californian*, I think this possibility is quite unrealistic. Quite apart from the extreme coincidence required, the argument which I advanced in the previous section against *Titanic* and *Californian* being in sight of each other equally rules out any vessel other than *Titanic* having fired rockets in the area. It is, if anything, even more certain that rockets would have been seen by *Titanic* than lights. My opinion that *Titanic* was much further from the *Californian* than the FI found or the Inspector considers does not of course rule out her rockets being seen, but it would explain their apparent low altitude. It has been objected that the timings of *Titanic* firing her distress signals do not precisely accord with the times the rockets were seen by the *Californian*, but none of the times were recorded precisely and I place no value on that point.

Linking the question with the previous one, it will be realised that if the ship seen by the *Californian* was a third vessel, she must have been for a considerable period on just the same bearing as *Titanic* for the latter's rockets to be seen apparently coming from her. This may at first glance seem to be stretching credibility, but in fact it is far from impossible. The third ship must have encountered the ice field and, like the *Californian*, will have stopped as indeed she was seen to do. Her position will have depended upon the exact configuration of the field which — unlike its general outline — cannot be known, but it is perfectly feasible that it lay on *Titanic's* line of bearing. With all three ships stopped, their only movement will have been with the current and their bearings from each other will not have changed.

This does, manifestly, beg the question of why the third vessel — who must also have seen the rockets — did not respond. One possibility is that she was the Norwegian sealer *Samson*; the then mate of that vessel, many years after the events, did indeed state publicly that his ship had been near the scene of the accident and that rockets had been seen. According to his statement, *Samson* had been sealing illegally and, fearing that the rockets were from a US Coastguard vessel, she dowsed her lights and made off. There are fairly obvious weaknesses in this account if it is put forward as fully explaining the third ship theory; but one thing it does do is remind us that in those days, before wireless was common at sea, rockets were much more used than is now the case for reasons other than indicating distress. The most likely explanation for the *Californian* not responding to the rockets is put forward later in this report, and perhaps some similar reason applied to any other ship which saw them. Given the amount of shipping in the area, it must be very probable that the *Californian* was not the only ship to see the signals, irrespective of whether the "third ship" between her and *Titanic* existed.

ASSESSMENT OF THE ACTION TAKEN BY CAPTAIN LORD

Although the terms of reference of this reappraisal relate specifically to Captain Lord, the Inspector rightly points out that the Court did not single him out personally for criticism but simply referred to the *Californian*. While, as Master, Captain Lord was of course responsible for his ship's action (and inaction), it is impossible to avoid some consideration of others on board, at least Mr Stone who was the middle watch officer and therefore in immediate charge of the ship between midnight and 4.00 am.

In broad terms, there is indeed little contention as to what happened on board. There are differences in detail between the accounts given by various witnesses but nobody experienced in accident investigation will find this odd: even the most honest witnesses allow their recollection of events to be coloured to some extent, perhaps unconsciously, by what they would like to recall.

There is no dispute that the *Californian* encountered field ice and very properly stopped; nor that she then sent a wireless message reporting this; nor that she remained stopped throughout the night. There is no dispute that another ship was seen to approach and to stop some few miles off. There is no reason to doubt that an attempt was made to call up that ship by Morse lamp and there can be no reason to suggest that at that stage any further attempt to communicate should have been made even though the other ship failed to respond.

Nor is there any dispute that during the middle watch rockets were seen which were thought to come from this other ship; that Captain Lord was told that rockets had been seen; and that no action was taken save to make further attempts to raise her with the Morse lamp.

Finally, there is no doubt that when wireless messages were received in the morning reporting *Titanic's* distress, the *Californian* went to the position given and, finding no sign of the liner, then steamed through the ice field to join *Carpathia*.

Given the degree of correspondence on these salient points, I see neither profit from nor need for a detailed examination of the evidence of each witness so as to attempt to reconcile such differences as exist, except so far as is required to answer the crucial questions. These are: should the *Californian* have taken further action when the rockets were seen; and if so, what action, and why was it not taken?

The Inspector considers that further action should have been taken, and I agree. Although as has been pointed out the use of rockets was much more common 80 years ago than it is today, it was certainly not so ordinary an event that their sighting, especially in an area where ice was about, required anything less than all practicable positive measures to establish the reason for them being fired. Merely attempting to call by Morse lamp fell far short of what was needed. The action which should have been taken by Mr Stone as soon as he was sure that he was indeed seeing rockets was:

(a) The Master should have been called and if he did not immediately respond Mr Stone should have reported to him in person;

(b) Engine-room should have been placed on immediate readiness by ringing "Stand By Engines";

(c) The wireless operator should have been called; and

(d) Captain Lord on being called should have at once gone to the bridge,
verified that the engine-room was at readiness and the wireless operator
at his post, and then got under way towards the apparent source of the
rockets.

It is only possible to speculate why this action was not taken. None of the
more picturesque or indeed scurrilous suggestions which have been
advanced from time to time — that Captain Lord lay drunk in his cabin, that
he was entirely callous or that he was frightened to attempt to manoeuvre
in the ice — stand up to even the most cursory examination. On the first,
Captain Lord was in fact almost tee-total; and it requires not just that he was
incapable but the entire watch on deck as well. That this was not so is patent
from the very evidence which leads to criticism of them, namely their
admitted sighting of rockets and the degree of correspondence between
what they saw and the evidence from *Titanic*.

On the second, even if (which I do not for a moment believe) Captain
Lord had been devoid of all normal human feelings of compassion, he would
still have done his utmost to assist for reasons of personal glory; and of course
again it assumes equal callousness or at least extreme pusillanimity on the
part of Mr Stone and his watch. As to the third, Captain Lord in fact took
his ship through the ice twice once he learnt of *Titanic's* distress: first to head
for the reported position, which was west of the ice field, and second to join
Carpathia in her search. The second passage was made after he had gone to
the reported position and found *Mount Temple* there, and it ought to be
noted that the latter ship did not attempt to traverse the field to assist
Carpathia. This is not mentioned in critical spirit; one can well understand
the caution of *Mount Temple's* Master with his very large complement of passengers, and he no doubt realised that it was too late for his ship to be of any
practical help: but the fact remains that Captain Lord made the effort and he
did not. Captain Lord's action may very well have been that of a man who
realised that his ship had failed to do what should have been done earlier,
and was desperate to make amends; but it is certainly not the action of a
coward. Moreover, clearly all these "explanations" require a high degree of
conspiracy in totally fabricating evidence by the witnesses from the
Californian and, quite apart from the inherent improbability of this, the dis-
crepancies which do exist in their evidence argues against it.

I have little doubt that the true explanation is more prosaic. There are
appreciable differences between the evidence given by Mr Stone, by the
apprentice, Mr Gibson, who was on watch with him, and by Captain Lord
himself as to the exact information passed from the bridge to Captain Lord.
There is, however, no doubt that Mr Stone spoke directly to Captain Lord by
voice-pipe and that, separately, he sent Mr Gibson down to call the Master.

Captain Lord's recollection of what he was told by Mr Stone is some-what at variance with what that officer recalled; and he had only the vaguest memory, according to his evidence, of Mr Gibson's call. This seems to me entirely consistent with a common condition when a man is called while he is sleeping heavily: there is a state of somnambulism quite often experienced in which the subject appears to respond to a call but the message given does not break the barrier between sleep and consciousness. Commonly, when the subject does wake he has no recollection of the call until he is told of it, when there is some memory but only in a very hazy sense. In plain language, I think the message from the bridge simply did not get through.

This inevitably points to weakness on the part of Mr Stone. Again, I think we need look no further than human fallibility for the cause. There is a natural tendency to reject the signals of disaster and to hope that all is well despite the evidence of one's own eyes and senses. Of course, Mr Stone should have gone down himself to the Master when there was no proper response from him, but the impression one gets of Captain Lord, is that, far from being slack as has sometimes been suggested, he was in fact something of a martinet, and the young officer may have feared to leave the bridge (normally a grave dereliction of duty) even though under the circumstances it would have been safe and right to do so. One can readily imagine Mr Stone on the bridge, knowing in his heart what ought to be done (he is recorded as saying to Mr Gibson that "a ship doesn't fire rockets for noth-ing") but trying to persuade himself that there was no real cause for alarm — and desperately wishing it was four o'clock and the mate was there. I sympathise with Mr Stone, but it must be said that he was seriously at fault.

CONCLUDING COMMENTS

A few further points require some mention.

Although it is not specifically within the terms of reference of the reap-praisal, this report would be incomplete without some consideration of whether the action which the *Californian* should have taken would have led to the saving of the lives of those who were lost.

The first rocket appears to have been fired at about 00.45 am (*Titanic* time). The ship sank at about 2.20 am. If the *Californian* saw the first rocket and took immediate action to head straight for it, and had quickly worked up to full speed (which would have taken several minutes) she would probably, given my minimum distance off of 17 miles, have reached the scene at just about the time of sinking. This, however, is unrealistic. No officer would take such action on seeing a single distant flash which might be a shooting star or even a visual aberration: such sights are quite common. More practically, if proper action had been taken as set out above, Captain Lord would have been on the bridge at perhaps 0.55 am and begun head-ing towards the rockets, but cautiously at first because of the ice for at that stage the urgency of the situation would not be known and it would be right for him to have regard for the safety of his own ship. Meanwhile, the wireless operator would have been called and would shortly receive *Titanic's* SOS with its incorrect position. This would have put Captain Lord in something of a quandary: probably he would have called *Titanic* by wireless giving *Californian's* position, saying what had been seen, and asking *Titanic* to check her position. This would very likely have led to the error in dead reckoning being discovered, after which full speed would be made towards the correct position; but with the time lost *Californian* would arrive well after the sinking. It therefore seems clear that — if I am right as to the distance apart — the effect of *Californian* taking proper action would have been no more than to place on her the task actually carried out by *Carpathia*, that is the rescue of those who escaped. I do not think any reasonably probable action by Captain Lord could have led to a different outcome of the tragedy. This of course does not alter the fact that the attempt should have been made.

There is one rather curious point about the distress signals which is worth mentioning. In 1912, under the International Regulations then in force, such signals could be of any colour (*Titanic's* were in fact white) and there was therefore nothing immediately to distinguish them from other rockets. The *Titanic* disaster led to a number of changes improving provisions for emergency at sea, but it was not until 1948 that the rules for distress signals were amended to make the (present) requirement that they be *red*. Had that rule been in force in 1912, when it was much more needed than now, Mr Stone would surely not have remained passive.

A final word seems called for on the aftermath of the FI and its finding so far as Captain Lord is concerned. He lost his post with the Leyland Line, but soon gained employment with another British company, Lawther Latta, quickly regaining command: he remained at sea throughout the Great War and into the 1920s with that Company. He died in 1962. No formal action was ever taken against him, even though the conduct of his ship, as found by the Court, seems clearly to call for inquiry into his fitness to continue to hold a Certificate of Competency. Examination of contemporary records shows that proceedings were considered but does not make it entirely clear why they were not pursued. Part of the reason may have been that, with the weight of a recent FI headed by a very senior and distinguished judge, it was seen as difficult for there to be a completely unprejudiced Inquiry. Be that as it may, it is difficult not to believe that some at least of those responsible at the Board of Trade felt a substantial measure of doubt as to the justice of the findings. It is not surprising if this were so: the case has continued to divide opinion to this day, and has been argued strenuously both on Captain Lord's behalf and against him. Some of the arguments have been well-reasoned but some — on both sides — have been absurd and scurrilous.

Neither party will be entirely satisfied with this report, but while it does not purport to answer all the questions which have been raised it does attempt to distinguish the essential circumstances and set out reasoned and

realistic interpretations. It is for others if they wish to go further into speculation; it is to be hoped that they will do so rationally and with some regard
to the simple fact that there are no villains in this story: just human beings with
human characteristics.

R.101: THE AIRSHIP DISASTER, 1930

REPORT OF THE R.101 INQUIRY PRESENTED TO PARLIAMENT IN MARCH 1931

CONTENTS

Acknowledgements

All the photographs relating to the R.101 in the plate section have been reproduced with the permission of Nick le Neve Walmsley of the Airship Heritage Trust. These photographs were previously published in *R.101: A Pictorial History* (Sutton Publishing, 2000). The map of the final journey on p. 210 is also reproduced from that publication with permission.

Abbreviations

AID	Aeronautical Inspection Directorate
DAD	Director of Airship Development
DAI	Director of Aeronautical Inspection
RAW	Royal Airship Works

The R.101, the largest airship in the world, was built at Cardington near Bedford in England, and was the product of more than four years' work in design and construction. On October 4th, 1930, at 6.30 p.m., she set out on her maiden voyage to India, carrying 54 passengers and crew. Seven-and-a-half hours later, the R.101 had crashed into a hillside at Beauvais in France. All but eight of the people perished instantly in the resulting inferno.

This uncovered edition *is the report of the inquiry called to investigate the cause and circumstances of this tragic accident.*

∞◦◁▷◦∞

To The Right Honourable The Lord Amulree, GBE, Secretary of State for Air, from Sir John Allsebrook Simon

27th March, 1931

My Lord,

I was appointed, under the Order of October 22nd, 1930, made by you under the Air Navigation (Investigation of Accidents) Regulations, to hold an investigation into the causes and circumstances of the accident which occurred on October 5th, 1930, near Beauvais in France, to the Airship R.101, and to make a Report on the matter. Lieut.-Colonel J. T. C. Moore-Brabazon, MC, and Professor C. E. Inglis, FRS, OBE, were appointed to act as Assessors for the purposes of the said investigation.

I now have the honour to transmit the Report.

The Inquiry, over which I presided, was held in public at the Institution of Civil Engineers. It was opened on October 28th, 1930, and lasted in all for 13 days. The Attorney-General (Sir William Jowitt, KC), the Solicitor-General (Sir Stafford Cripps, KC), and Mr Wilfred Lewis, appeared at the Inquiry on behalf of the Crown, and Mr P. L. Teed appeared on behalf of the widow of Flight-Lieutenant Irwin, Captain of the R.101.

The sittings of the public Inquiry were divided into two periods, the first occupying ten days' hearing and ending on November 10th, 1930. The Court then adjourned till Wednesday, December 3rd, when three more sittings were held, ending on December 5th. In the interval, Professor Bairstow undertook, at the request of the Court, a special investigation for the purpose of supplying further calculations which would help in analysing the cause of the accident. In order to assist these further calculations, an exact model of the R.101 as she was finally shaped, was constructed, at the National Physical Laboratory, and a number of valuable experiments were

145

made by the staff there, which have been of great assistance. I desire to express my deep obligation to the authorities at the National Physical Laboratory for the help they thus rendered, and also for further investigations specially made at the request of the Court after the Inquiry had concluded, which are referred to in the Report.

In the course of the Inquiry 42 witnesses were examined. The authorities at the Air Ministry and the Staff at Cardington throughout rendered the fullest assistance to the Inquiry, and a full disclosure was made of official records. It may be confidently asserted that all available information of any material value was placed before the Court and everything possible has been done by officials, experts, and private persons to make the Inquiry complete. The Court desires to put on record its special obligations to Professor Bairstow, who has devoted himself with constant assiduity and skill to assisting the investigation. Without his conclusions and explanations it would have been impossible to appreciate the scientific and theoretic aspect of the questions raised by the disaster.

It is a matter of great satisfaction to me, as it will also be to yourself and to the public, that my two Assessors, Lieut.-Colonel Moore-Brabazon and Professor Inglis, find themselves in agreement with me on all points in the Report which I am presenting. I may be permitted to express my deep sense of obligation to them both for assistance and guidance without which the Report could not have been written. The document may therefore be taken as our joint work and opinion.

Lastly, my Assessors join with me in putting on record our deep appreciation of the constant devotion and exceptional skill exhibited throughout the Inquiry by the Registrar of the Court, Mr L. F. C. Darby, and the Assistant-Registrar, Squadron-Leader A. H. Wann. The mass of documents to be digested and arranged was very large, and the evidence to be analysed and brought together was extremely voluminous. Whatever of clearness or completeness the following Report may possess is largely due to their efforts.

JOHN SIMON

INTRODUCTION

At six thirty-six on the evening of October 4th, 1930, the R.101, the biggest airship in the world, on the design and construction of which so much care had been lavished for several years past, left her base at Cardington, near Bedford, and set out on a maiden voyage to India via Ismailia. She carried, besides officers and crew, her designer Colonel Richmond, the Director of Airship Development Wing-Commander Colmore, the Director of Civil Aviation Sir Sefton Brancker, the Secretary of State for Air Lord Thomson, and other officials specially associated with airship construction and navigation.

About seven and a half hours later, shortly after two o'clock in the morning of October 5th, she came to earth 216 miles away, in undulating country south of the town of Beauvais in France, and immediately became a blazing wreck. Of the 54 people on board, all but eight perished instantly in the flames; two of these eight died of their injuries shortly after the disaster. The six survivors—five engineers and the electrician—were called as witnesses at the Inquiry.

It is the cause and circumstances of this tragedy that the Court is required to investigate.

EARLIER HISTORY OF BRITISH AIRSHIPS

In order to appreciate the technical evidence and to form a just conclusion on matters immediately relating to the accident, it is necessary to provide a sketch of the course of airship development before the construction of the R.101 was undertaken. Down to the outbreak of the War, the airship as a means of transport had made more advance than the aeroplane. Between 1910 and 1914, five German airships had carried 42,000 passengers in 2,000 flights without mishap to any passenger. On the other hand, the first successful aeroplane flight from London to Manchester was not performed until 1910, and this was without carrying any passengers.

By the end of the War, the relative position of aeroplane and airship was reversed. The technical progress of the aeroplane was definitely in advance of that of the airship. The vital part played in the War by aeroplanes as military instruments and the constant increase in the number of purposes to which they were applied, produced a service in which the heavier-than-air machine became more and more important. Rapid development on the technical and engineering side kept step with a numerous and highly skilled personnel engaged in aeroplane flying, while airships fell into the background. The theoretic problems connected with flight are, no doubt, to a considerable extent, common to both types of aircraft. But the intensive research organised and carried on by the Advisory Committee for Aeronautics, and the aeronautical investigations carried out at the National Physical Laboratory and at various experimental stations, were inevitably directed, for the most part, to securing improvements in aeroplanes. The experience of German Zeppelins seemed to show that the large rigid airship could not successfully operate in the face of organised aeroplane attack and anti-aircraft defence, though airships of the Zeppelin type carried out during the War many noteworthy operations, including a continuous flight by the German L.57 in

1917 to East Africa and back, covering a distance of 4,200 miles in 96 hours. The rigid airships built in England during the War—e.g. R.33 and R.34—were practically copies of Zeppelin airships, and though later designs were evolved from earlier ones, no complete examination of aerodynamical problems was adequately made in connection with airship construction and behaviour until a later date.

In June, 1919, the British airship R.34, on returning from a reconnaissance flight over the North Sea, encountered a gale of such severity that although flying through the air (with her after-engine entirely out of action) at 40 knots, she was actually going astern over the sea for eight hours. Nevertheless, she returned to her base successfully after 57 hours of continuous flight.

In the following month the R.34 flew to America in 108 hours; remained moored there for four days; and then flew back to England in 75 hours, thus covering a total distance of 6,400 miles in 183 hours.

Among the performances of foreign airships in the years following the war may be noted that of the German *Bodensee* in the latter half of 1919 (103 flights covering 32,000 miles and carrying 2,450 passengers); the *Los Angeles*, which flew in October, 1924 from Friedrichshafen to Lakehurst in the United States in $80\frac{3}{4}$ hours; and the Italian *Norge*, which in the summer of 1926 flew with Amundsen over the North Pole between Spitzbergen and Alaska.

PREVIOUS AIRSHIP ACCIDENTS

In connection with this record of post-war achievement in various parts of the world three serious airship accidents must be borne in mind.

The French *Dixmude* met with destruction in the air in 1923; the facts of the accident are exceedingly obscure, and the French Court of Inquiry attributed the disaster to lightning.

The United States *Shenandoah* (inflated with helium gas), which had successfully fulfilled a programme of American flights between places as far apart as Texas, California, Illinois, and New York, was carried up to a great height and broke up in the air on September 2nd, 1925. The ship came to the ground in several portions and of its complement of 43 persons 14 were killed outright, 2 were hurt, and 27 escaped uninjured. The American Court of Inquiry found that her destruction "was due primarily to large unbalanced external aerodynamic forces arising from high-velocity wind currents".

Earlier in point of date than either of these disasters was the misfortune which overtook the British R.38 on August 24th, 1921. British rigid airships up to and including R.37 were little more than copies of Zeppelins, and the later Zeppelins had been evolved from earlier types by a process of slight but continuous variation without resorting to the fundamental research work which has since been pursued. The R.38 represented a departure from the older types, but in this case also the design was based rather on empirical knowledge than on fundamental research. She broke in two when at a great height in the air during a trial flight, and the two halves of her came to earth separately, the fore-end catching fire and descending into the Humber. A Report made by the Aeronautical Research Sub-Committee established that the accident was due to structural weakness, and the Committee found that the calculations which had been made about the strength of the R.38 were confined to statical conditions, qualified by a factor of safety which was thought to be adequate, and had not paid regard to the aerodynamic forces to which the airship would be subjected in motion through the air. The factor of safety was 4, i.e. it was assumed that if the strength of the R.38 was sufficient to withstand four times the static strain, this would be sufficient to cover adequately the additional stresses due to dynamic action.

STATIC AND AERODYNAMIC FORCES

This distinction between static and aerodynamic forces is so important in itself, and has led to so valuable an enlargement of theoretical investigation, that it is desirable to explain the matter in simple terms at this point before going further.

The first sort of calculation, which is purely statical, is made by imagining the ship to be constructed according to its design and to be poised in the air motionless, with no wind operating upon it, and exposed to no strains or stresses except those which are due to the distribution of weights in the structure, and to the amount and distribution of the lift of the gasbags. On this assumption, the lift of the gas must necessarily be equal to the weight of the ship, and the object of this first set of calculations is to ascertain whether the distribution of weights and the strength of different parts of the structure are such as to make it quite certain that in this condition of rest no part of the airship would buckle or break. A factor of safety was chosen which was believed to be suitable in connection with each calculation, and the assumption was that if the design was found to satisfy those conditions the airship might be regarded as sufficiently strong for the work it had to do in the air. It will be observed, however, that if reliance is placed upon statical calculations alone, no attempt will have been made to measure the wholly different strains and stresses to which the machine will be exposed when it is propelled by its engine-power through the medium in which it floats. All that will have been done is to provide empirically against these further forces, known as aerodynamical forces, which necessarily exert themselves only when the ship is in flight or is no longer free to float in and with the medium like a jellyfish floats in and with the tide.

These aerodynamical forces require to be most elaborately calculated; they depend, amongst other things, upon the rate at which the ship is passing through the air and, indeed, increase with the square of the speed. Not only so, but on passing from the hypothesis that the airship is at rest to the assumption that she is travelling under engine power, bending moments in some of the ship's members may be actually reduced, though in other cases pressure of the resisting wind will cause them to be greatly increased. The resultant effect will, in many cases, vary according to the angle which the ship takes up with reference to the air stream, and very great changes will be brought about by different positions of the elevator or the rudder. Aerodynamical factors, therefore, have to be considered as well as purely statical factors, though it is necessary here to emphasise that neither of these sets of calculations do anything more than provide a guide for securing that the airship and every part of it will have sufficient structural strength. The question of how she will *behave* in the air in various assumed conditions, in what circumstances she will retain her stability, and at what point she may become unstable, is a yet further enquiry which must be distinguished from both the statical and aerodynamical calculations to which reference has been made.

In view of the disaster to the R.38 in 1921, the Aerodynamical Research Sub-Committee which investigated the accident reported that research by both model and full-scale experiment was essential to determine and verify the aerodynamical forces to which a given airship would be subjected and that

> in the construction of such an airship, reference to first principles of design is necessary; and for progressive development of airships in size and speed, it is not sufficient to place exclusive reliance on a comparison with existing ships, using the routine methods adopted for R.38.

THE TWO PANELS

Hence arose two bodies, upon whose Reports and Memoranda the more scientific construction of later airships in this country largely depends. Each of these bodies was appointed by the Aeronautical Research Committee, of which Sir Richard Glazebrook has been Chairman throughout. The first of them was known as the "Airship Stressing Panel", and over it Professor R.V. Southwell presided. The main work of this Panel was to consider methods of calculating the strains and stresses which would arise in various parts of the structure of an airship from aerodynamic forces. Its Report, dated August, 1922, contains a mass of highly technical information on this subject and urges the importance of model experiments as a check on the theoretical results which had been reached.

The other body, known as the "Airworthiness of Airships Panel", was presided over by Professor L. Bairstow, who gave most valuable evidence at the Inquiry.

The Report of the Airworthiness of Airships Panel was published in October, 1924, and recommended a number of factors of safety which the Panel considered appropriate for various conditions—that is to say, it fixed how many times stronger the airship must be than would be theoretically just sufficient to bear the strain put upon it under different circumstances. In constructions which have not to sustain their own weight by lifting power, a generous factor of safety is often consistent with good design, but, as is pointed out in the Report of the Airworthiness of Airships Panel:

> it would be easy to stipulate figures which would hamper design without approaching the factors of safety used in engineering practice: however, the standpoint has been taken that such factors are inadmissible and that success in airship design requires a more thorough knowledge of principles and data than the older engineering applications: full use must, therefore, be made of this new knowledge by designers and a high standard of workmanship is required.

In other words, the condition that airships must not be too heavy to fly makes it impossible to provide so wide a margin for uncertainties as might be possible in the case of a bridge. The importance of the results of theoretic conclusions proving correct in practice is thereby greatly increased. The factors of safety laid down by Professor Bairstow's Committee were, as will be seen later, taken as the basis for certifying the airworthiness of the R.101. The Report added that the factors of safety which it laid down:

> necessitate consideration of the stability of the ship, and of the amount of available control through the elevators and rudders. Information on the effect of gusts is so scanty as to be valueless for calculations, and the Panel has followed the lead given by the Accidents Investigation Sub-Committee in assuming that the worst conditions in a natural wind will not be more severe than those contemplated in certain extreme cases set out in the schedule.

THE 1924 PROGRAMME

In the meantime, however, the reduction of expenditure which was called for in 1920 had compelled the Air Ministry to close down the Airship Branch of the Royal Air Force. By the end of 1921 there was a possibility that airship operations in this country would be stopped and the airships and stations disposed of. In 1922 and 1923 much consideration was given to a scheme of airship development urged by Commander Burney (now Sir Dennistoun Burney), and in 1924 the former Government of Mr Ramsay MacDonald appointed a Cabinet Committee to reconsider the position. This Inquiry went to show that if airship development was to proceed upon a sound technical basis, it was inevitable that the Government should undertake the research and experiment which the disaster to R.38 had shown to be necessary, and His Majesty's Government, therefore, decided to adopt the experimental programme of airship development which was in the course of being carried out when the loss of the R.101 occurred. This experimental programme was to extend over three years, and was at first calculated to cost £1,350,000. Events were to prove that both the period and the cost were underestimated. The programme was designed to test the capacity of modern rigid airships as a standard means of long distance transport, and to this end it was resolved to set on foot a thorough scheme of research and investigation in preparation for two practical operations:

(a) The construction of two airships with such improved speed, range, and load-carrying capacity as would enable them to make long voyages overseas with a substantial margin of lifting power; and

(b) The carrying out of flights to and from an overseas' terminal in order to test whether the airships were suitable for the work for which they were designed.

The Memorandum prepared by Sir Samuel Hoare as Secretary of State for Air, and laid before the Imperial Conference in 1926, in explaining the nature of this experimental programme, went on to say:

> It was held that once this programme had been successfully carried out the further developments of airships would be assured, and it was recognised that the practical progress of the experimental programme might well prove to be of decisive importance in the history of airship development. It was, therefore, decided to develop the programme in a spirit of scientific caution, holding considerations of prudence and safety to be of paramount importance. Two airships were to be built, one by the Air Ministry (R.101) and one by the Airship Guarantee Company (R.100). This ensured competition in design and provided that a purely accidental failure of one ship should not terminate the whole programme. Elaborate researches and experiments were to be made; new sheds and masts were to be erected in England, Egypt, and India; and the weather conditions of the route were to be carefully investigated in their application to airship navigation. During the last two years work has been proceeding under this programme.

Model and full-scale experiments

The course of research contemplated by the 1924 programme was carried out with great thoroughness and care. Reference has already been made to the recommendation that both model and full-scale experiment was essential, and accordingly a series of model experiments was carried out in the wind tunnels of the National Physical Laboratory to determine, or to assist in determining, the best shape for the two new airships. These experiments eventually led, in 1926, to the selection of a shape of hull which differed substantially from that of the older airships, and which was found to give for a given volume a much lower resistance. Whereas the R.33 was 645 feet long and 78 feet in diameter, the R.101, as originally designed, was 732 feet long with a diameter of 132 feet. The ratio of diameter to length is described as the "fineness" of an airship, and both the R.100 and the R.101 had a

Name of ship	Length in feet	Diameter in feet	L over D	Capacity cubic feet
R.38	694.5	85.5	8.1 to 1	2,724,000
Graf Zeppelin	776.9	100	7.7 to 1	3,708,000
R.100	709.2	133	5.3 to 1	5,000,000
R.101 (as originally designed)	732	132	5.5 to 1	5,000,000
The R.101 (as altered)	777	132	5.9 to 1	5,508,800

lower fineness ratio—i.e. are "thicker" in comparison with their length—than either the Zeppelin type or the earlier British airships. The table above illustrates this contrast.

In addition to the model experiments in the wind tunnels of the National Physical Laboratory, full-scale experiments were made in accordance with the policy laid down in 1924. R.33 was re-conditioned and carried out a series of full-scale flights to accumulate data for the acquisition of which full-scale facilities had not previously been available. Further, a full-scale section of the future R.101 was constructed for strength tests before the construction of the airship itself was put in hand.

After the R.33 had been re-conditioned, and while she was moored to the mast at Pulham in April, 1925, before the full-scale experiments could be carried out, a gale, which reached 45 miles an hour, tore her from the mast and carried her out over the North Sea. Although she had a severely damaged bow with two gasbags in her nose partially deflated, she withstood the storm for 30 hours and returned safely to Pulham, showing that a well-built airship with a good Commander and crew could withstand the most severe conditions without having to make a forced landing. This incident also proved the practical value of meteorological information. The R.33 throughout her flight was sent forecasts as to the probable course and duration of the gale, and her Commander was, therefore, able to gauge his capacity to weather the storm and to return to his base on its cessation.

Conditions to be fulfilled by R.100 and R.101

The above account of the course of British airship development down to the time when the building of the R.100 and the R.101 was contemplated and taken in hand will show how important was the new stage which was to be represented by these two air vessels. The next part of this Report will contain a more detailed account of the design and construction of the

The RMS Titanic *leaves the Belfast yard of Harland and Wolff for sea trials, 1912. The luxury liner was thought to be unsinkable. Archive: Corbis.*

The promenade deck of the ill-fated White Star liner Titanic. *Archive: Corbis.*

Chief Officer Henry Wilde of the Titanic in his British Admiralty uniform. Wilde went down with the Titanic on 15 April 1912. *Archive: Corbis.*

Captain Edward C. Smith (right), captain of the Titanic, and another officer on board the luxury liner during the run from Southampton to Queenstown. *Archive: Corbis.*

Titanic *survivors on board the* Carpathia. *Underwood & Underwood, Corbis.*

A pin-sharp image of the R.101 riding at the mast head in Cardington, near Bedford.
Nick le Neve Walmsley / Airship Heritage Trust.

The men behind the British Airship Programme of 1924–30, photographed before boarding the R.101 on 4 October 1930. In the centre is Lord Thomson, the Secretary of State for Air; to the right, Lt.-Col. Vincent Richmond, the chief designer, and Sir Sefton Brancker, Director of Civil Aviation, with his trademark rimless monocle. Nick le Neve Walmsley / Airship Heritage Trust.

A fully inflated gasbag of 500,000 cubic feet, seen from the rear. Each bag took three days to fill with hydrogen.
Nick le Neve Walmsley / Airship Heritage Trust.

Sir Sefton Brancker (with monocle), Director of Civil Aviation, with some of the crew of the R.101 shortly before they ascended the mast for the last time on 4 October 1930. The monocle was the key to the identification of Brancker's remains after the fire.
Nick le Neve Walmsley / Airship Heritage Trust.

Passengers boarding the R.101 for a test flight. Note the crewman in the bow keeping an eye on the flexible pipes used for gassing, fuelling and watering the airship.
Nick le Neve Walmsley / Airship Heritage Trust.

Below *A view of the saloon of the R.101, fully fitted out for the visit by the Members of Parliament in November 1929. The furnishings included curtains, potted plants and even deckchairs on the promenade decks.*
Nick le Neve Walmsley / Airship Heritage Trust.

The skeleton of the R.101 near Beauvais in France. The picture shows that the framework remained fairly intact, even after the fabric had burnt away. Nick le Neve Walmsley / Airship Heritage Trust.

The players of the Manchester United football team line up on the pitch at Belgrade before their European Cup quarter final match against Red Star Belgrade. The match resulted in a 3-3 draw that qualified United for the semi-finals. The journey home, however, proved ill-fated. Hulton Archive.

The BEA aircraft on the apron at Munich-Riem airport a few minutes before taxi-ing out for the third (attempted) take-off (i.e. the fatal attempt). The photograph was taken from a window fairly high up in the terminal building. HMSO.

The scene of the accident on 6 February 1958 at Munich airport. HMSO.

Left side of the fuselage and the port engine mounting of the BEA aircraft, after the crash in February 1958. HMSO.

Back to health: on 19 February 1958 the Manchester United football player, Bobby Charlton, survivor of the Munich air crash, gets back into gentle training with some young fans in his home town of Ashington, Northumberland. Hulton Archive.

R.101, but before entering upon technical matters it will be well to summarise the main features aimed at as the new objective. Not only were the
R.100 and the R.101 to embody designs and methods of construction
which were based on a far more thorough programme of experiment and
research than had hitherto been undertaken, but the ships themselves were
to be much larger in size than any previously existing airship, and the
intention was that each of them should satisfy the following general
requirements:

(i) *Capacity* To be 5 million cubic feet, giving with hydrogen gas about 150
tons gross lift, i.e. nearly twice that of any airship previously constructed
in this country, and more than a third as much again as the largest existing Zeppelin.

(ii) *Strength* To afford certain definite factors of safety (particularly with
regard to aerodynamic forces) laid down by the Aeronautical Research
Committee in 1924—a condition never before imposed on any airship
in this country.

(iii) *Speed* The full speed to be not less than 70 miles an hour and the cruising speed 63 miles an hour.

(iv) *Accommodation* Passenger accommodation, including both sleeping and
eating accommodation, to be provided for 100 people.

(v) *Weights and useful lift* The structure weight, including power plant, but
excluding fuel, not to be more than 90 tons, giving a useful lift of 60 tons,
or 40 per cent of the gross lift of the airship.

(vi) *Power plant* To be operated on fuel which could safely be carried and
used in sub-tropical or tropical climates.

Modification in original conditions

As will be seen hereafter, some of these projected requirements were not
persisted in or finally secured. The final requirement really meant that both
the R.100 and the R.101 were to be fitted with heavy-oil engines instead
of petrol engines, but in the end the R.100 was propelled by Rolls-Royce
petrol-burning engines of the "Condor" type, and accomplished its journey
to Canada and back★ by means of this motive power. If, therefore, the condition implied in (vi) is insisted upon, the type of engine used in the R.100
makes that ship inappropriate for a journey to India. The R.101, on the
other hand, was fitted with a specially designed heavy-oil engine built by
Messrs Beardmore.

Another serious departure from what was originally contemplated
arose, in the case of the R.101, at any rate, in connection with requirement

★ The R.100 left Cardington for Canada on 28th July, 1930, and reached Montreal in 79 hours; she
returned to Cardington from Montreal on 16th August after a flight of 57 hours.

(v). For when this vessel as originally designed and constructed was inflated, it was found that instead of 90 tons out of her gross lift of 150 being needed to carry fixed weights so as to give a useful lift of 60 tons (40 per cent of the gross lift), the fixed weights amounted to 113.6 tons out of a gross lift of 148.6 tons, thus giving a useful lift of only 35 tons, about 24 per cent of the gross lift. It is out of this so-called "useful lift" that provision has to be made, not only for crew, passengers, stores and water, but for the weight of fuel with which the vessel starts. As will be seen hereafter, this was so serious a diminution in the original lift which had been prescribed and estimated, that the R.101 could not contemplate attempting a voyage to India without undergoing changes which would increase its balance of lifting power, and hence arose two alterations of which much was heard at the Inquiry—the insertion of an additional "bay" or section in the middle of the ship, and the re-arrangement of the gasbag-wiring so as to increase the capacity of the gasbags. In addition, some reduction in weight was secured by cutting out certain conveniences and other details which could be dispensed with.

Bigger mooring towers

One other matter needs mention before entering upon a description of the nature of the design and the course of the construction of the R.101. Airships of the size contemplated could not undertake distant journeys without the previous provision of a system of mast-mooring suitable for vessels of such large dimensions. Such mooring towers must be established at both ends of the journey and at any necessary intermediate points. The system of mast-mooring which had been evolved at Pulham, in 1921, was suitable for airships of two million cubic feet capacity or less, but it was now necessary to provide mooring-masts on a scale and of a size which would be suitable for airships of five million cubic feet and upwards. One was erected at Cardington. The Canadian Government erected a suitable mooring tower at Montreal, which was successfully used for the R.100 on her Canadian flight. For the R.101, mooring towers were prepared at Karachi and also at the intermediate station of Ismailia, on the Suez Canal. The question was considered by the authorities whether it would not really be necessary, or at any rate highly advantageous, to have intermediate towers at other points, but the decision was reached that this, which would involve further expense and delay, could not be authorised in advance of the first attempt to reach India, while matters were still so largely in an experimental stage.

Unhappily, the disaster to the R.101 while crossing France has meant that the mooring towers at Ismailia and Karachi, which between them have cost £105,000, have never been used at all.

DESIGN AND CONSTRUCTION
OF R.101

In the construction of the R.101, the designers broke away almost completely from conventional methods and in every direction an attempt was made to improve upon standard Zeppelin practice. Some of these inventions were a natural consequence of the great size of the airship, while others aimed at securing interchangeability of component parts. These novelties in design, however, were not confined to the general anatomy of the hull, but extended to many important details such as gasbag-wiring, relief valves, steering mechanism, and even included the adoption of a novel design of heavy-oil engine.

Originality and courage in design are not to be deprecated, but there is an obvious danger in giving too many separate hostages to fortune at one time. Indeed, the only effective security against the risk of trying many new experiments in design simultaneously is a prolonged series of trials designed to test out the airworthiness of each new feature in turn. During the construction, and in the early trial flights of the R.101, this policy of cautious experiment at each step was admirably fulfilled; but in the later stages, when it became important to avoid further postponement and the flight to India thus became urgent, there was a tendency to rely on limited experiment instead of tests under all conditions. The programme of trials as at first submitted to Major Scott by the Captain of the R.101 was far from being completed as originally intended (see below), and, as will appear in a later part of this Report, the R.101 started for India before she could be regarded as having emerged successfully from all the exhaustive tests proper to an experimental stage.

SHAPE ADOPTED FOR THE HULL

As stated before, an extensive series of aerodynamic experiments, more complete than anything previously attempted in connection with airship design, were initiated in 1924, and carried out at the National Physical Laboratory during the following two years. Two hull forms were tested for drag, lateral forces, yawing moments, and damping coefficients.

These forms, designated by A.M.3a and A.M.3b, are shown in the diagram opposite. A.M.3a was of circular section throughout. A.M.3b was identical with A.M.3a so far as the part forward of the maximum diameter was concerned, but its tail was fish-shaped and non-circular in section.

On the completion of these tests, the results were forwarded to the Royal Airship Works and, at a meeting between representatives of that establishment and of the National Physical Laboratory, it was decided to adopt form A.M.3a, and a further set of experiments was planned for determining the most efficient shape and size of the fins. After two preliminary experiments, a type of fin and control surface was found to be highly satisfactory that combined adequate stability with a remarkably low drag coefficient.

The general shape of the R.101 is one of lower fineness ratio (5.5) than had been employed in previous rigid airships, i.e. the R.101, like the R.100, was "fatter" in proportion to length. This formation had the great advantage of giving a very low resistance or drag to longitudinal movement through the air, this resistance being little more than 2 per cent of the resistance of a circular plate of the same diameter as the maximum diameter of the hull.

No length of the hull as originally designed was of uniform section, and the longitudinal members between the frames were shaped to give continuity of curvature, decreasing progressively from bow to stern.

As originally designed the hull was 732 feet long, with a maximum diameter of 132 feet, and its gas capacity was expected to give it a lift of approximately 150 tons gross. At a later stage its length was increased to 777 feet by the addition of a bay in the region of maximum girth and the extra gasbag accommodation thus provided, together with other alterations, brought the gross lift up to about 167 tons.

GENERAL STRUCTURE OF HULL

The general anatomical structure of the hull before it was lengthened consisted of a number of ring-shaped transverse frames joined together by 15 continuous main longitudinal girders. In order to prevent the gasbags which were situated between the frames being too unequal in size, the frames were not spaced equally apart but in the regions of large girth were brought somewhat more closely together.

Frames 3 to 13 were of novel design, in that the rings were devoid of spokes or radial bracing. This construction is illustrated in the diagram on p. 161. The inner perimeter of the ring was a single member; the outer

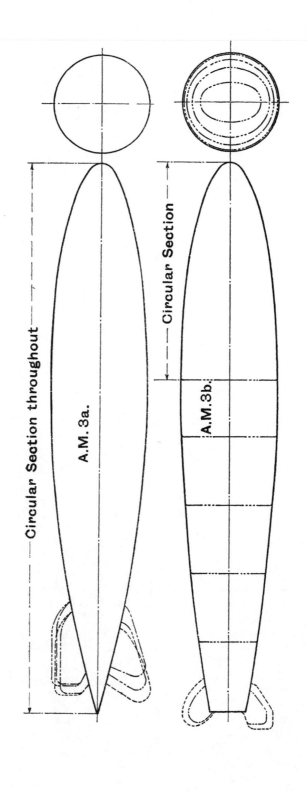

Two possible hull forms for the R.101

The general shape of the R.101 as originally planned

Leading Edge
Girder

16A 16 15B 15A 15 14 13 12 11 10 9 8 7 6 5 4 3 2 1 0 0A

Structure of the ring-shaped transverse frames

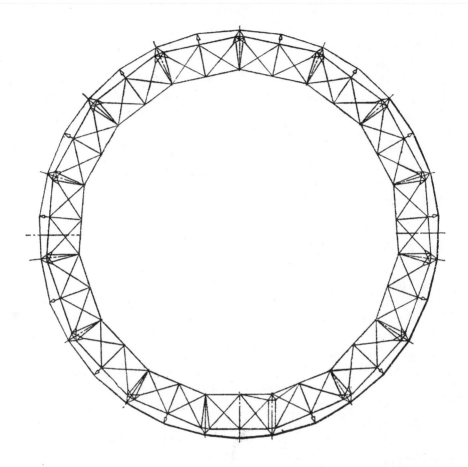

consisted of two parallel members about 10 feet apart, so that the cross-section of the ring was triangular.

The main longitudinal members, also triangular in section, were attached to the outside of the transverse frames.

The outer cover was stretched over the main longitudinal girders, but to reduce the tension in the fabric, 15 intermediate longitudinals known as "reefing girders" were provided, and in consequence the external surface of the ship became thirty-sided.

These reefing girders in no way contributed to the stiffness of the structure as a whole. Reefing girders running between adjacent frames were provided with intermediate flexible joints which shielded these girders from indeterminate bending moments and also from longitudinal stress arising from slight relative displacements of adjacent frames.

The attachment of the reefing girders to the transverse frames was effected by telescopic "kingposts" which were designed so that they could be jacked out radially and thereby produce any desired degree of tension in the outer cover.

Bending moments in the hull structure were resisted by the main longitudinal girders. Resistance to shear was provided for by a system of diagonal wires, these wires joining up the corners of the rectangular panels formed by adjacent frames and longitudinals. For the transverse frames and longitudinal girders, high tensile stainless-steel tubes were employed, while considerable use was made of duralumin for joints and attachments. For additional protection against corrosion, the stainless steel was coated with lacquer and all duralumin was given anodic treatment.

The light reefing girders were of a type usual in Zeppelin construction, being built up of duralumin members having a trough section.

METHOD OF ERECTION

Apart from the fact that the unprecedented size of the R.101 made it possible and even desirable to depart from conventional methods of construction, the novelty of the design was mainly dictated by considerations of ease of erection and the possibility of subsequent repair or replacement of members. The various component members were delivered at the erecting shed at Cardington fully machined and complete with every necessary attachment. All that had to be done on the site was the linking together of these component parts with accurately fitting bolts. The work of assembly was in consequence reduced to a minimum.

This policy, of course, entailed a vast amount of preliminary work in computing the dimensions of the various parts to a very high degree of accuracy. It also involved an extensive use of jigs, and the machining had to be carried out to tolerances ranging from 0.015 of an inch in girders 11 feet long, to 0.030 of an inch in girders 30 feet long. That this high degree of accuracy was attained reflects great credit on the makers.

The R.101 may be said to have been machine-made, in contradistinction to having been constructed by hand, and those responsible for the policy doubtless had in view the saving of time and cost which would be effected in the event of repeat orders being placed. For a single ship, the time occupied in the vast amount of preliminary work which had to be performed more than counterbalanced the time saved in erection, and this largely accounts for the striking fact that some four years were spent in connection with the design and construction of the R.101.

In connection with the evolution of the various types of girders, where exaggerated factors of safety could not (from considerations of weight) be permitted, an immense amount of mechanical testing was carried out to verify the validity of stress calculations, both in connection with component parts and in connection with completed girders. In addition, a complete full-sized bay was set up with a gasbag in position, and the strains in the various members were measured by recording strain-gauges.

The care taken in this preliminary experimental work is beyond all praise, and its comprehensive character can be estimated by the fact that approximately a hundred separate girders were tested to destruction. It is probably no exaggeration to say that never before in the history of structural engineering has so much care been taken to explore the strength of a structure before it was used, and to check the stress calculations by actual measurement.

The main credit for the general character of the design and methods of construction of the R.101 must be given to the late Lieutenant-Colonel V. C. Richmond. His powers were almost autocratic. He kept the work of design centralised in his own hands, though he was always open to receive and adopt suggestions which seemed to him helpful, and in doing so, he never omitted to acknowledge the help he had received. Although the general design, stress calculations and geometrical computations were carried out under Colonel Richmond's supervision at Cardington, there remained the formidable task of designing and manufacturing the innumerable structural details of the hull, in order to carry into effect the general plan laid down. This work was wholly entrusted to the firm of Messrs Boulton & Paul, and Colonel Richmond was unsparing in the praise he bestowed upon this firm and the Chief Engineer, Mr J. D. North, for the admirable way in which this very difficult and responsible task was performed.

GASBAGS

It will be understood that an airship of the type to which the R.101 belonged, derives its lift from a row of gasbags of suitably graduated dimensions which are attached to its structure and enclosed within its outer envelope.

Though the gasbags of the R.101 were of unprecedented size, their construction was in close accordance with standard Zeppelin practice.

In the lengthened ship there were seventeen such gasbags, and the largest of these, which was situated in the new bay, had a capacity of no less than 510,300 cubic feet and gave a gross lift of about $15\frac{1}{2}$ tons. The total gasbag capacity was 5,508,800 cubic feet, corresponding to a gross lift of 167.2 tons.

The gasbags, which completely filled the spaces between longitudinal girders and adjacent cross frames, were made of cotton fabric lined with gold-beater-skin, these two components being united by a special kind of glue.

Although constant experimental work has been carried out in the hope of finding a satisfactory substitute, gold-beater-skin has up to the present remained the best material for rendering fabric bags gas-tight. The skin is a fine membrane forming the outer coat of part of an ox's intestine known as the cæcum.

Lengths of 25 to 30 inches are freed from fat by washing in warm water and scraping with a blunt knife. In gasbag manufacture, the first process is to assemble skins so as to form large continuous sheets ready for glueing to the cotton fabric. A double layer of skins in their wet state is laid out on smoothly stretched canvas, which merely serves as a background on which the skins are assembled. As the skins dry out they adhere together and can then be readily peeled off from the canvas in one continuous sheet resembling thin transparent parchment. No adhesive of any kind is employed to make the individual skins unite in a continuous sheet, though, in order to keep the membrane pliable, glycerine is added to the water in which the skins are soaked before assembly.

After a sheet of gold-beater-skin has been thus prepared, it is ready to be glued to the inner side of the cotton fabric, which in its turn is built up by glueing together strips of the fabric with an overlap of about one inch.

In all bags (except the one in the additional bay) these panel seams were taped with cotton fabric $1\frac{1}{4}$ inch wide. This was done to guard against the danger of a seam lifting, but experience showed that this precaution was unnecessary.

All fabric seams in a finished gasbag, both longitudinal and circumferential, were overlapping glued connections as above described, while gold-beater-skin formed one continuous membrane on the inside of each bag. To improve its waterproof qualities the bag was given a coating of oil-varnish on its inner skin face, and on the outer cotton face the same varnish was used with the addition of some beeswax and aluminium powder.

Tests on glued seams were carried out on pieces 3 inches wide and 8 inches long, and the specification required that these test pieces should stand a load of 20 lb per inch run of seam. These tests were applied under various conditions of humidity. These requirements of strength would appear to have been ample to meet the stresses which were developed in the gasbags under normal conditions. Such stresses were relatively small, being of the order of 1 lb per inch run. But in this connection it should be observed that if a tear of any considerable length is started, the concentration of stress at its two ends is so great that it must almost inevitably extend, like a tear in the sail of a ship. This danger could be guarded against by using a fabric with additional diagonal fibres, and it is understood that in some at any rate of the Zeppelin airships, fabric of this variety has been employed.

At every stage, the materials and workmanship of the R.101 gasbags were under the closest possible scrutiny both by the Works Inspectors at Cardington, and by the Inspectors of the Aeronautical Inspection Department of the Air Ministry. The gasbags when incorporated in the airship were doubtless as perfect and free from defects as it was humanly possible to make them. But after the ship had been through some of its preliminary trials, and particularly after an increase in the size of the gasbags had caused serious chafing against the frames of the ship, leakage of gas through holes in the bags developed to an abnormal and indeed alarming extent. But although holes in gasbags are very far from being desirable, it must be borne in mind that the escape of gas from a small hole even at the top of a bag is relatively small in comparison with the whole contents of the bag. The gas pressure is only of the order of one ounce per square inch, and, unless small holes are very numerous, the resulting loss of gas is not a matter of serious consequence.

It is further to be remembered that if a rent occurs in a gasbag, the gas which escapes through the rent is that which is below the orifice: the rest of the gas, which is higher than the rent, remains in the bag. Consequently, to get anything approximating to the sudden deflation of a whole gasbag, the opening which lets the gas escape out of it must not only be of considerable size, but must be at the top of the bag.

As an indication of the rate of discharge of pure hydrogen from a gasbag, it may be mentioned that under a pressure difference of one ounce per square inch, the velocity of discharge is 327 feet per second, and assuming a coefficient of discharge of 0.6, the volume which will escape through a circular orifice 1 foot in diameter is 9,250 cubic feet per minute.

GASBAG-WIRING

The gasbag-wiring for the R.101 was of entirely novel, and extremely elaborate, construction. It formed the subject of a patent taken out in December, 1927, conjointly by Lieut.-Colonel V. C. Richmond and Squadron Leader F. M. Rope, both of whom perished in the disaster.

Some system of wiring is essential for the double purpose of reinforcing the gasbags to resist gas pressure, and for transmitting the upward lift to definite points on the framework of the airship. The wiring in this case consisted of two independent systems intersecting at right angles. One system formed circumferential girdles round the bags in planes at right angles to the axis of the ship, and the other system ran longitudinally around the curved side of the bags and terminated in rings at the centres of the flat ends as shown in the first gas-bag diagram on p. 166.

About 50 per cent of a gasbag lift was tapped off from the circumferential wires, this lift being transmitted to suitable points on the transverse frames by means of "bridles".

The longitudinal wires, running right and left across the circumferential surface of the bag, start from a sort of chain of wire (called in the Specification a "catenary chain") held midway between adjacent frames by means of "bridles" leading to the main joints as shown in the second gasbag diagram. This system of wires may accordingly be likened to a pair of parachutes, their crowns being the rings to which the wires converge, and their edges being the chain. One duty of this longitudinal system of wires was to control the axial displacement of the bag arising from pitching or from its

Termination of the longitudinal system of wires at the flat end of the gasbag

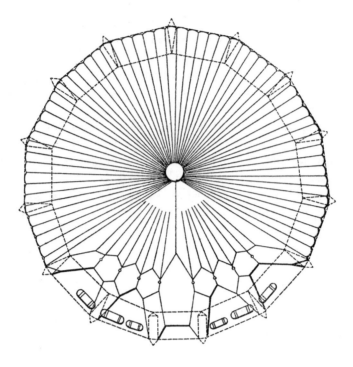

Gasbag wiring system showing "bridle" between two transverse frames

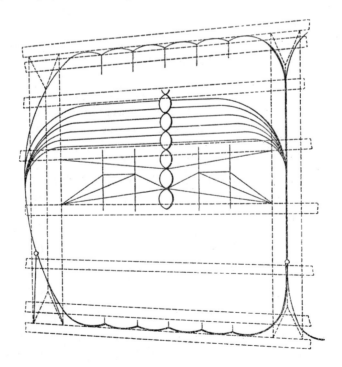

neighbour becoming deflated. If adjacent bags are equally inflated, the inter-vening bulkhead of radiating wires remains flat, but, in the event of the bag on one side becoming deflated, pressure on the wire bulkhead becomes unequal and it curves.

Another duty of the longitudinal wires was to transmit the remaining 50 per cent of the upward lift of the gasbag to the frame of the ship. This was done by means of tapping wires, which connected some of the bulkhead wires to points on the lower portion of the corresponding transverse ring. In the Patent Specification one of the advantages claimed for this system of gasbag wiring was that the gasbag was "kept from touching the longitudinal girders". However, in the later stages of the evolution of the R.101, in view of the urgent demand for increased lift, the wiring system was let out to such an extent that the gasbags in some places came into contact with the longi-tudinal girders and projecting corners of the transverse frames. The danger of attrition and of consequent holing was sought to be minimised, as will be seen hereafter, by the padding of numerous points.

The above description in necessarily technical, and it may assist in com-prehending it and in understanding the diagrams on p. 166 if a rough analogy is suggested. Imagine 17 immense regimental drums of the ordinary shape set up on their rims in a row. The drums are of graduated size, the biggest in the middle. Round the circumference of each drum will be wound a large number of wires each forming a circle at right angles to the axis of the drum. These wires correspond to the first of the two systems referred to. Now imagine that just outside the centre of each of the parch-ment ends of each drum there is a circular ring of metal, and that an immense number of strands of wire radiate out from each ring and pass over the barrel of the drum where they meet corresponding wires from the other side by being connected to a wire chain running round the barrel. If either end were looked at from the side, it would present an appearance corre-sponding to the first gasbag diagram. This series of radiating wires would obviously cross the circumferential wires at right angles in their passage from one side of the drum to the other, and it is this series of wires which con-stitute the second system of wiring referred to above. The analogy would be more complete if each drum were imagined to have one end somewhat smaller than the other, for each gasbag in the series was designed so as to fit into its place in the ship with due regard to the taper of the envelope.

Each drum-shaped gasbag was therefore contained within a complicated network involving many hundreds of wires and points of junction, planned so that the strain upon each wire at every point should be suitably distrib-uted and transmitted. The radial wires running from each ring towards the circumference were, as to the first portion of their length, common to the contiguous surfaces of each pair of adjoining gasbags, but before these radial wires reached the circumference they forked into two, so that one wire would run round the end of one gasbag towards its other side, and the other followed a corresponding course to enwrap the neighbouring bag. In other words, the system of radial wires spreading from each ring as a centre formed a sort of reticulated bulkhead which separated each gasbag from the next. And the whole construction constituted a cage within which each inflated gasbag was confined and was prevented from expanding further. It will be appreciated, therefore, that if the vessel when in flight pitched or rose suddenly, the tendency of the gasbags to surge or sway fore and aft was resisted (though it was not entirely prevented) by the system of wiring.

It only remains to bring home to the reader some appreciation of the size of the gasbags which were thus confined within the meshes of this wiring system. The largest of them, when fully inflated, measured from the crown to the bottom 126 feet, i.e. it would extend from the floor of Westminster Hall well above the roof. The whole row of them could not be accommodated within the extreme length of Westminster Abbey.

GAS VALVES OF R.101

Like the gasbag-wiring, the gas valves of the R.101 were of entirely novel design. In order to make clear in what the novelty consisted and how delicate a mechanism was involved, it is first necessary to appreciate the functions which gas valves have to discharge and the methods hitherto ordinarily adopted for fulfilling those functions.

As an airship ascends, the fall in atmospheric pressure causes the gas in the bags to expand. To prevent avoidable loss of gas, the bags, when the ship is at its mooring mast, are not usually inflated to their full extent and it is only after the airship has risen to, say, 1,000 feet, that the expanded gas fills the bags completely. To permit the ship to rise above this "pressure height", provision must be made for an escape of gas, and this provision takes the form of relief valves which blow off when the gas pressure in the bags slightly exceeds the normal. Change of gas volume may likewise be brought about by changes of temperature, but expansion due to this cause is not likely to be rapid, and relief valves of large capacity are mainly needed to deal with the possibility of the ship being caught up in a rapidly ascending current of air and thereby elevated several thousand feet in a very short space of time. The American airship *Shenandoah* experienced a phenomenon of this character, for she was caught in an up-current of air which was estimated to have attained the extreme velocity of 50 miles per hour. The destruction of the *Shenandoah* was attributed primarily to external aerodynamic forces, but in any case her experience illustrates the reason why relief valves should have sufficient capacity to deal with sudden changes of altitude.

With the care which characterised the specifications for the R.101, gas valves were called for which could deal with a vertical rise of 4,000 feet per minute (45.5 miles per hour). Though even more violent upward currents may occasionally be found in the heart of a severe thunderstorm, they are very rare, and meteorological reports would probably enable an airship to steer clear of any such extreme disturbance. In any case, weather conditions at the time and place of the R.101 disaster entirely rule out an explanation of it based on this class of consideration.

In former airships the usual practice was to fit a spring-loaded automatic relief valve at the bottom of each gasbag, so that the gas would "spill" out of the bottom of the bag as soon as the pressure within overcame the pressure of the spring. These automatic valves rested on cages when the bags were full, but moved upwards with the bottom of the bag when it became deflated. In addition to an automatic relief valve of this character, former practice usually prescribed the use of "manœuvring valves" which were fitted on the top of each gasbag. These latter valves are in no sense automatic, but are worked by controls from the control car if it is desired to discharge gas in order to decrease buoyancy.

Both types of valves—the automatic relief valve at the bottom and the manœuvring valve at the top—were in fact used in the R.100.

In the R.101, however, an entirely new and very ingenious arrangement was employed by which the functions of the automatic and the manœuvring valves were combined in the same piece of apparatus. On either side of a gasbag, at its midway height, a valve of this new pattern was fixed in position, so designed that its opening or closing did not depend upon any spring mechanism. Two sizes of valves were employed, of 30 inches and 40 inches diameter respectively, the smaller valves being used for the smaller bags. The rate of discharge, under normal pressure, if a bag had both of its 40-inch valves open, was calculated to be 72,000 cubic feet per minute.

It will be observed from this description that the valves installed in the R.101 are extremely sensitive. They are more easy to inspect than manœuvring valves placed at the top of a gasbag would be, though, as they are half-way up the side of the gasbag, they can only be approached by climbing. So long as they operate as designed, though they open under very small extra pressure, they close again automatically as soon as that pressure falls to normal. On the other hand, if by the intervention of some unexpected cause a valve sticks open, it would be necessary after discovering the defect, for a rigger to climb up to rectify it, since there is no quick alternative method of bringing the valve back again on to its seating. The loss of gas in these circumstances from the lower half of the gasbag might be very serious.

In the trial flights, these valves appear to have given general satisfaction, though it cannot be claimed that the weather conditions encountered, or the changes of altitude attempted, were at any time sufficiently severe to constitute an exhaustive or conclusive test. Owing to the very small force with which the valve face is pressed against its seating, the valves have a tendency to open slightly when the ship rolls through an angle of 5° or somewhat more, and if the ship were to roll from side to side through a larger angle it would seem that there might be a temporary opening of valves on the port and starboard side alternately with an intermittent loss of gas resulting. A further reference to this subject will be found below.

OTHER FEATURES OF CONSTRUCTION

The special features of construction already mentioned are far from exhaust-ing all the novelties introduced into the R.101 by the ingenuity of its designers. But it does not seem necessary, having regard to the purpose of this Report, to describe other matters in equal detail.

As regards the outer cover, the experiment was tried of doping the fabric before it was placed in position. By this means, some reduction of weight might have been achieved and, by the employment of tensioning devices in which the pull applied to the fabric was recorded on spring gauges, it was hoped that a definite state of tension could be assured. Owing, however, to subsequent absorption of moisture, this pre-doped fabric was apt to shrink and to develop long tears, and in consequence it was decided to discard the original pre-doped cover and to replace it with fabric which was doped after it had been stretched in position.

To maintain equality of air pressure between the inside of an airship and the surrounding atmosphere, inlets and outlets for air must be provided in the outer cover. For example, when the ship is rising rapidly, air inside the cover must be allowed to escape freely, and conversely, when the ship is descending, unless air is given sufficient opportunity to enter, a partial vac-uum will be developed in the interior. If the R.101 was to be able to rise with safety at a rate of 4,000 feet per minute, very full provision of outlets was necessary. She was provided with an ingenious arrangement of inlet and outlet holes for this purpose, supplemented by a series of slots arranged on a circumferential ring in the region of the maximum diameter. There is no need to describe these arrangements in detail, but it should be stated that they appear to have been excellently designed to serve the purpose already mentioned, as well as for the ventilation of the ship and for permitting the escaping of gas which might accumulate between the gasbags and the outer cover.

CONTROL MECHANISM

A most important part of the design, which also contained features of nov-elty, was the mechanism for controlling the flaps hinged to the vertical and horizontal tail fins which constituted the rudders and elevators of the vessel. These four control surfaces were identical in shape and area; each flap had a span of about 44 feet. They were operated by a very ingenious yet simple mechanism invented by Squadron Leader F. M. Rope.

The control car was placed amidships below the main body of the air-ship, and in the control car two men on duty would operate the rudder and elevator respectively. At the side of the elevator-coxswain were an altimeter and an inclinometer, and variations in height were secured, so far as the movement of the elevator was concerned, by turning a spoked wheel. The cable actuated by this wheel ran round a drum and thence to pulleys connected with the mechanism located in the lower vertical fin, and at first the movement of the controls was assisted by a "servo" gear actuated by oil pressure which helped to rotate the drums. Later on this "servo" mechanism was removed in connection with arrangements which were made to reduce the weight of the ship. But it would seem that this auxiliary power was found to be unnecessary and that man-power was quite adequate for the operation of steering and elevator controls. For small angles of movement no great effort was required, but to put the elevators hard over through their extreme range of 25° up to 25° down called for a considerable expenditure of energy. To move the elevator from the middle to its extreme position would require many turns of the wheel and the time occupied would be about half a minute. It may be noted here that the number of turns of wire on the drum was an indication of the position of the elevators, and consequently, after the disaster occurred, it was possible to infer with certainty that the elevators were hard up at the instant when the ship struck the ground.

MOTIVE POWER

In view of the fact that the organisation of an airship service to India was from the first an essential feature in the Government's programme of airship development, it was considered desirable to use some fuel less volatile than petrol, in order to minimise the risk of fire in sub-tropical regions. With this end in view, it was decided that the R.101 should be equipped with engines burning heavy oil on the compression ignition system, thus obtaining the advantages of a comparatively cheap and safe fuel, and furthermore reducing the risk of fire by the avoidance of electrical ignition. As might have been expected, the production of a new type of engine to satisfy the required conditions proved to be a matter of considerable difficulty and, both in respect to weight and horse-power developed, the power units fell short of the standard it was hoped to reach. It was originally hoped that each engine would be able to maintain 700 brake horse power (b.h.p.) at 1,000 revolutions per minute, whereas the result eventually achieved was a continuous full power of 585 b.h.p. with a possible maximum of 650 for a brief period.

The weight based upon the continuous full power worked out at 8 lb per b.h.p., and, though this figure was a great improvement on previous engines of a somewhat similar type, it was considerably in excess of the figure anticipated.

Each of the five engines consisted of eight cylinders of $8\frac{1}{4}$ inches diameter with a 12-inch stroke, arranged vertically in line. Oil was injected into each cylinder shortly before the position of maximum compression, when the temperature and density of the compressed air were sufficient to produce rapid burning, approximating to an explosion. The length of time during which fuel was pumped in could be varied, and this constituted the only means for controlling the power of the engine. The type was known as the Beardmore Tornado Engine, and they were designed and manufactured by

Messrs Beardmore, though in their evolution and development Wing Commander Cave-Browne-Cave played a prominent part.

The design necessitated a long crankshaft and, in the engine as first constructed, the torsional flexibility of this long shaft, associated with the periodic impulses due to eight cylinders, developed such violent torsional oscillations in the crankshaft at a critical resonance speed of about 950 revolutions per minute, that continuous running in the neighbourhood of this critical speed was a practical impossibility. This resonance phenomenon was the greatest stumbling block encountered in the evolution of this new type of engine.

Without a complete redesign of the engine it was not possible to keep clear of all critical resonance speeds, but by an increase of certain dimensions of the crankshaft, which could be effected without a drastic reconstruction of the whole engine, the major critical speed was raised well above the normal speed of running. The excess in actual weight over what had been anticipated was in part due to the necessity for this more robust and stiffer crankshaft, but it was mainly caused by the very substantial character of the crank-chamber, which in the absence of torsional oscillations could have been lightened to a very considerable extent. With the experience gained, there is reason to believe that in the future a similar engine could be designed which would weigh only 4 lb per brake-horse-power, thus making the weight comparable with airship engines of the petrol variety, though how far such an engine would be comparable in length of life and durability is a question which only prolonged experience could answer.

As installed, the total weight of the power installation of R.101 (including auxiliaries) amounted to 17 tons, in comparison with under 9 tons for R.100 and 7 tons for the Graf Zeppelin. But the comparatively heavy weight of the R.101 power installation is, for long voyages, largely compensated for by the reduction in fuel which has to be carried. Thus for a range of 2,500 miles, under still air conditions, R.101 required only about 17 tons of fuel oil at a cost of about £5 per ton as against a consumption of 23 tons of petrol, costing about £23 per ton, in the case of R.100.

The five engine units were carried in separate power cars attached to the outside of the hull, the propellor thrust in each case being transmitted to the frame of the ship by a thrust-wire leading from a bearing carried on the outer face of the airscrew hub.

Two of the power cars were near the bottom of the hull on either side of frame 4, in the forward part of the ship. Two others, somewhat higher up, were attached on either side of frame 9, and the fifth was placed centrally under frame 11 towards the stern of the ship, where it would give a good flow of air to the rudder, even when the ship was approaching its mooring mast at low speed.

Each engine was directly coupled to its airscrew, 16 feet in diameter, without any reduction gearing. Originally it was intended to use a form of hub by which the pitch of the propellors could be altered while in motion, and thereby enable them to give either ahead or astern thrust. These hubs, however, failed under a test in which they were exposed to excessive torsional oscillations, and it was considered advisable to substitute ordinary wooden propellors with fixed hubs. As originally engined, the vessel had four engines which propelled her only ahead, and the remaining engine worked only astern. Later, all five worked ahead, but since astern thrust is necessary to check the forward way of the airship as she approaches the mooring tower, the two forward engines were provided with a valve gear mechanism whereby they could be restarted to run in a reverse direction.

The main engines were started by auxiliary engines which developed 40 h.p. at 2,000 revs per minute and transmitted rotation to the main engines by a 20 to 1 reduction gear. These starting engines used petrol, though it was hoped in the future to replace them with engines of the heavy oil compression-ignition type, and in fact one of them had been so replaced when the R.101 started on her final flight. These auxiliary engines, in addition to starting the main engines, were available for driving electrical generators and air compressors. Two power cars carried electrical generators and, as an alternative to the petrol engines, power for these auxiliaries could be provided by constant speed windmills, which came into operation for airspeeds in excess of 40 m.p.h. and developed 10 to 15 horse-power.

During a flight, each power car was manned by a mechanic, who received his orders from the control car by means of an engine room telegraph dial. The main engines were water-cooled by an evaporative system, by which the steam which accumulated in the head of the separator was condensed in honeycomb radiators.

FUEL AND BALLAST

Most of the fuel storage tanks were of 224 gallons capacity each, though in certain positions it was more convenient to provide two tanks of half this capacity which were used as a single unit. From the storage tanks, fuel was led by gravity to transfer tanks from which it was pumped to feed tanks above each engine car. The storage tanks could accommodate about 29 tons of oil, which left a reasonable margin on the fuel requirements for a voyage to India, with a halt at Ismailia for refuelling, assuming that the weather conditions were not too unfavourable.

Certain of the storage tanks were fitted with jettison valves, by which their contents could be released very rapidly in cases of emergency. The stream of oil thus released quickly broke up into fine drops and, if released from a height of 1,000 feet or thereabouts, it eventually assumed the form of a very fine rain whose presence on the ground could hardly be detected.

The discharge of jettison tanks was in most cases operated from the control car, and the time taken to complete the process of emptying a tank was only three seconds.

Disposable water ballast to the amount of eight tons was carried in half-ton bags or tanks which could be released, in some cases, instantaneously from the control car, and in other cases locally by the execution of orders given from the control car to members of the crew. In addition, provision was made for another seven tons of water ballast in storage tanks similar to those used for fuel.

The above account of the main features in the design and construction of the R.101 has been for the most part compiled for the Court by Professor Inglis. It is based partly on verbal evidence directly supplied to the Court, partly on descriptions published in the technical press, and to a considerable extent on papers which have appeared in the *Journal of the Royal Aeronautical Society*, particularly two communications from Wing Commander Cave-Browne-Cave and Lieut.-Colonel V. C. Richmond, published in March, 1929, and August, 1929, respectively.

PRELIMINARY TRIALS AND RECONSTRUCTION

More than two years were spent on the elaborate investigations and calculations on which the design of the R.101 was based, and in 1927 actual erection began in the huge shed at Cardington prepared for the purpose.

The process of erection occupied two more years, and by the end of September, 1929, her construction, according to the design and dimensions originally intended, was complete. Before she left the shed, a "lift and trim" test had to be undertaken. As regards lift, when the gasbags were fully inflated it was found that instead of having a "useful lift" of 60 tons, as had originally been intended, her fixed weights amounted to as much as 113.6 tons which, when subtracted from her gross lift only gave a useful lift of about 35 tons. It had, of course, been appreciated, as the process of construction proceeded, that the sum total of fixed weights which she would have to lift would be greater than what had originally been hoped for, viz. 90 tons. In particular, her engines when delivered and installed in the five engine cars were heavier than estimated, though it was not the extra weight of the engines which chiefly explained the excess. So serious a reduction in useful lift was mainly due to additional weights in the main structure. It was soon realised that an airship with a useful lift of only 35 tons could not undertake the voyage to India, and hence arose the changes which were made in the R.101 at a later date by rearranging the gasbag-wiring so as to increase the capacity of the gasbags, and ultimately by inserting an additional "bay" .

LAUNCH AND FIRST TWO TRIALS

These alterations, however, were not at once resolved upon or undertaken. The next stage in the story is the bringing of the R.101 out of her shed for the first time and the mooring of her to the tower at Cardington (October

12th, 1929), followed by two preliminary trials (October 14th and 18th respectively). The first trial flight lasted for $5\frac{1}{2}$ hours, and the second for $9\frac{1}{2}$ hours. On the first occasion only two engines were working for a great part of the time. On the second occasion four engines were used—the fifth at this stage was a reversing engine only. These two trials took place in daylight and in calm weather; no written reports were made of them; but Colonel Richmond's diary records that he was well satisfied with the stability of the vessel and her response to control. No speed tests had as yet been attempted.

The late Lord Thomson was a passenger on this second flight. The Court was informed by an official from the Air Ministry that at the conclusion of this flight the Secretary of State was interviewed by press representatives, and announced his hope that he might be able to travel to India in the ship at Christmas of that year. But it is important to add that he emphasised that his policy was "safety first", and that as long as he was in charge no pressure would be brought to bear on the technical staff to undertake any flight until they were ready and satisfied that all was in order.

FOUR MORE TRIALS

The next incident was a warning from the Meteorological Department that a storm was approaching Cardington which threatened to cover a large area, and it was thought prudent to put the ship back in her shed (October 21st), where she remained until she was brought out again on November 1st. The third trial flight, lasting for $7\frac{1}{2}$ hours, took place on this date. On the next day the R.101 for the first time attempted night flying. This fourth flight lasted from 8 p.m. on November 2nd until 10 a.m. on November 3rd; the ship cruised in the direction of the Isle of Wight, returning safely to her tower at Cardington. An attempt was made to carry out a speed trial with the four engines that worked ahead, but one of them gave out before the course was completed. The fifth and sixth trials were short flights of three hours each in the early afternoon of November 8th and November 14th. A further flight was projected for November 16th, when it was proposed to take as passengers a large number of Members of Parliament who assembled at Cardington for the purpose. Weather conditions were, however, unfavourable, and this flight did not take place.

The Court had before it written reports made at the time as to the behaviour of the vessel on some of the flights referred to in this paragraph. Wing Commander Colmore had drawn up an elaborate schedule of Functioning Tests, covering details of engine working, the fuel and ballast systems, gas valves and gasbags, controls, instruments, and many other matters. The duty of making reports on these various matters was assigned to different officers of the ship according to the Department in which they were specially expert, and at a later date reports dealing with the behaviour of the vessel were collected and submitted to Major Scott, who was in charge of flying operations.

It is well to say at once that these documents evinced the greatest thoroughness and care in every department. Naturally, many minor defects or difficulties were noted for the purpose of subsequent correction, and one or two matters of greater importance must be referred to hereafter; but there can be no doubt that, in general, the behaviour of the vessel in these early trials gave general satisfaction, and thoroughly justified the confidence which those responsible for her design and navigation undoubtedly felt in her.

THE R.101 RIDES OUT A GALE

More impressive, perhaps, than the satisfactory performance of the R.101 in these calm weather trials, was the fact that on November 11th, 1929, she rode out a severe gale while attached to the tower. It was well known beforehand that strong winds might be expected, and the decision to leave the ship where she was indicates the confidence felt in her ability to withstand them. There were frequent gusts of over 70 miles per hour; the average wind speed during the afternoon was 55 m.p.h. and a maximum gust of 83 m.p.h. was recorded. Wing Commander Colmore's Report to the Air Ministry points out that the load on the nose-coupling, which at one time amounted to $15\frac{1}{2}$ tons, was successfully withstood, and that even with this maximum load the ship had an ample margin of strength. The observed results corresponded closely with theoretical calculations previously made. He added:

> throughout the period, the ship rode comfortably at the tower and without violent movement. There was, however, a slow rolling motion at the higher wind speeds, reaching a maximum of 6°. The ship was at all times well under control . . . Beyond the entry of rain and a certain amount of chafing of the gasbags due to the roll, no damage whatever was sustained.

Another report, made by Mr G. W. Hunt (who was Chief Coxswain on the voyage to India) must be quoted in full:

11th and 12th November, 1929

1st Officer R.101

During Storm Routine of the above dates whilst looking round it was observed that in the case of Nos. 3 to 14 bags inclusive, a very considerable movement from side to side was taking place on each flat end, as much as 3" to 4", and at times the surge of the bags in a forward and after direction was considerably more.

Owing to the combined two movements, where the bags were touching or nearly touching the radial struts round main frames, especially at C and D longitudinals, the plates on top of the radial struts rubbed and chafed the bags, and in places such as No. 8 starboard fore end tore the bag 9" in a jagged tear. No. 8 thus became deflated to 60% and on inspection taking place it was noticed that on every roll the valves opened to the extent of $\frac{1}{4}''$ to $\frac{1}{2}''$. The valves were lightly stopped back until the bag was gassed to 95%.

The holes on top of No. 14 bag were caused by the bag bearing hard on O girder, where several nuts project and combined with the movements of the bag caused punctures.

G. W. HUNT

The "O" girder is the topmost girder in the structure; girder C is just above and girder D just below the centre line of the ship.

It is noteworthy that, whatever repairs had to be effected, the vessel undertook further trials after this exacting experience, without first being taken back to its shed.

ENDURANCE FLIGHT

Next came a much longer trial flight, the seventh in the series (November 17th and 18th). This was an "endurance flight". The flight instructions issued by Wing Commander Colmore indicated that the duration of the flight was to be 36 hours, with the possibility of an extension to 48 hours. In fact the flight lasted for 30 hours and 41 minutes, from half-past-ten in the morning to about five o'clock on the following day, and in the course of it the vessel travelled over 1,000 miles, passing over much of Scotland and Ireland as well as making an extensive tour over English towns, usually at a height of 1,000 to 1,500 feet.

This is much the longest continuous flight which the R.101 ever accomplished. The performance gave much satisfaction to Major Scott and to the Captain, Flight-Lieutenant Irwin. In the course of this flight the vessel executed various "turning trials" with success; she encountered bumpy conditions without serious discomfort and, after flying for the last hour or more above fog, made a good descent to the mast as darkness was closing in. Just prior to landing one of the "bridles", by which the lift of a gasbag is transmitted to the frame, broke; but this seems to have been due to the small size of the pulley round which the bridle worked: at a later stage larger pulleys were substituted, and chain bridles were used instead of wire.

The R.101 remained at the Cardington tower until the end of the month, but on November 30th she was taken in and stayed continuously in her shed until June 23rd of the following year. She had thus, in the course of the seven weeks which had elapsed since she was first launched, flown for over 70 hours; and though these flights were in good weather and did not include any long trial at full speed, she had behaved well and had given officers and crew valuable experience of her capabilities. Moreover, in the storm of November 11th, she had proved her ability to withstand a severe buffeting, while attention had been directed to the risk of chafing of the gasbags when she rolled. A report made on December 23rd dealt with this last matter in the following terms:

There appeared to be a good deal of movement of the gasbags and gasbag wiring when the ship was rolling at the tower, the hull appearing to roll round them. This caused a fair amount of chafing on the bag all round the inner ridge, and a lot of padding will be necessary here. There is a clear mark on each bag where this has taken place, and it may be worthy of consideration as to whether the bag should not be slightly reinforced at this point . . . The gasbags held gas remarkably well and maintained a steady purity. The success of the new valve and its position on the bag largely contributed to this.

NEED TO INCREASE USEFUL LIFT

The time had now arrived when it was urgently necessary to reach a decision for surmounting the outstanding difficulty that the R.101, as at present designed and constructed, had too small a "useful lift" to make it possible for her to undertake a voyage to India. For such an enterprise she would need to carry some 25 tons of fuel oil, and this would not leave sufficient margin unless her lift was increased. Thus, alterations for the purpose of reducing her fixed weight or increasing her lift were inevitable.

This problem was the subject of the fullest and most careful consideration during the winter of 1929–30. The Air Ministry at the Inquiry produced to the Court all the minutes that passed on the subject, including elaborate memoranda by Wing Commander Colmore, and Sir John Higgins, who was at the time Air Member for Supply and Research. Two possible courses were suggested:

(1) To remove from the ship various fittings which could be dispensed with, such as the "Servo" gear which supplemented steering by hand, the look-out position on the top of the ship, the heavy glass in the windows of the promenade, certain unnecessary tanks, and a number of passenger sleeping cabins and other conveniences. By such means as these it was estimated that the fixed weights might be reduced by nearly three tons. At the same time it was proposed to enlarge the gasbag wiring so as to enable the inflated gasbags to fill more space and thus to increase the lift by over three tons. The total improvement in the "useful lift" which would be secured by these alterations would thus amount to about six tons.

(2) To increase the total length of the airship by inserting an additional middle section or "bay", thus providing space for an additional gasbag which it was at first estimated would add another nine tons to the useful lift. This, of course, would require a re-calculation of the strains, both static and aerodynamic, which the reconstructed ship would have to sustain. Moreover, this second change necessarily involved a further delay before the R.101 could attempt its Indian voyage.

It was proposed to put in hand the first group of changes as soon as the R.101 was put back into its shed at the end of November, 1929, and the Secretary of State was informed that this work might be completed by the following February, and that the ship might be ready for what was called "the demonstration flight to India" by the second week in March. On the other hand, it was realised that the adoption of this first set of changes alone might not be sufficient to secure that the vessel could get further than Egypt and that if regular operations on the Indian route were desired, the extra bay was also necessary. During the hot months of the summer, conditions for such a flight were more adverse, and the choice, therefore, was between making the first set of alterations alone and attempting a flight along the Indian route in the spring, or delaying the first attempt to the late autumn of 1930, by which time the additional bay could also be inserted.

These alternatives were put before the Secretary of State, Lord Thomson, in a full and careful minute by Sir John Higgins on November 21st, 1929, and a week later the Secretary of State replied as follows:

> Air Member for Supply and Research
> I am of opinion that no good, and quite possibly some harm, might be done by a flight to India in the early months of 1930. The best course would I think be:
>
> (a) To make the various alterations you suggest in para. 3 of your minute.
> (b) To insert the extra bay.
> (c) To make every effort for a flight with 55 tons disposable load to India and back at the end of Sept., 1930.
> 28.11.1929   T.

(The alterations referred to by Lord Thomson in (a) were those described above.)

LORD THOMSON'S DECISION

Lord Thomson thus determined to adopt the course of prudence even at the expense of further delay. The first set of changes were taken in hand during the spring of 1930, but it was decided not to cut the ship in two and insert the extra bay until after she had been again brought out of the shed and submitted to further tests in the course of the summer. In a letter to the Treasury dated December 12th, 1929, the Air Council announced that they had had under consideration the question whether the R.101 should carry out a flight to India and back in the following March with the minor improvements already referred to, or whether it would be better to delay the flight in order to increase the lift of the airship further. The letter went on to state that the Air Council believed that with these minor modifications the R.101 could fly to India without difficulty in March or April, but that the return flight would be less easy owing to the fact that conditions on the flight from Karachi to Ismailia were more adverse, and to the further fact that the lift of an airship is necessarily lower at Karachi than in this country, and that this loss of lift is heaviest during the summer months. The Air Council stated that they had therefore decided that:

> in order to avoid running any unnecessary risks it is better to postpone the
> flight to India until the lift of R.101 has been increased, by the addition of a
> section in the middle of the airship. No mechanical or aerodynamic
> difficulty is anticipated as the result of this alteration in the airship; but the
> Council propose to have the calculations and drawings examined by
> Professor Bairstow and Professor Sutton Pippard, as was done with the
> design of the main structure.

The total cost of both sets of alterations was estimated at £21,000 for direct labour and material, together with approximately £2,500 for the gas-bag, and £1,000 for the additional outer cover. The letter added:

> The Council contemplate that R.101's flight to India should now take place
> in September next, and, to enable this to be done the additional bay should
> be inserted by the end of July. If, however, the work is to be completed by
> this date, the preliminary design work and the ordering of material must be
> put in hand as soon as possible.

Treasury sanction was duly obtained for the carrying out of this scheme, and the Indian authorities were informed of the change of timetable. It is to be noted that the Air Ministry at this time undoubtedly contemplated that further flying trials would be necessary after the new bay was inserted, for Sir John Higgins' letter of December 27th, 1929, to Sir Geoffrey Salmond who was commanding the Air Force in India concluded by saying:

> Accordingly, in order to increase the lift of the airship still further we are
> proposing to put in another bay during the summer and then to carry out
> the first flight along the Indian route *after the airship has done some further
> flying trials with the new bay fitted.*

Indeed, a minute prepared for the Secretary of State by Sir John Higgins on December 6th, while setting out the good results already attained by the R.101 in previous trials, added:

> Before she gets a full Certificate of Airworthiness, R.101 has yet to do a 48
> hours' endurance flight. There has hitherto been no suitable opportunity for
> this, as we cannot run the risk of an endurance flight finishing in a gale.

DAMAGE TO OUTER COVER

The minor alterations having been completed, including the very important change of enlarging the gasbag-wiring so that the gasbags had more
room to expand, the R.101 was again brought out of its shed early on the
morning of June 23rd, 1930, and was moored to the tower. The wind was
light but there was much humidity in the atmosphere, and almost immediately a disturbing incident occurred. The outer cover, between panels A and
B on the starboard side of the ship, developed a split which extended to a
length of about 140 feet. As meteorological conditions indicated that the
wind was likely to rise, in which case the ship could not be got back into
her shed, it was decided to mend the tear in place, and by working all day,
in spite of gusts and heavy rain, a weather-tight repair was completed by
5.30 p.m. A second but shorter split occurred next day on the topmost part
of the cover, but this was similarly repaired in a few hours. Such ripping of
the outer cover would of course be extremely dangerous if the vessel was
in flight, and much consideration was given to the best way of preventing
its recurrence. It was decided to abandon the idea of using a "pre-doped"
cover, i.e. one which was made of fabric which had been treated before
being stretched round the structure, and to substitute, when the vessel next
returned to the shed, a new cover which would be doped after being fixed
to the ship. This latter method was the practice previously followed in other
airships, and the new system had been adopted as an experiment in order to
gain the advantage of some reduction in weight. In the meantime, it was
decided that by reinforcing the repaired cover with some strengthening bands,
it would still be possible for the ship to fly at the RAF Display on Saturday,
June 28th, which was the immediate reason for bringing her out of the shed
at this time.

RAF DISPLAY FLIGHTS IN JUNE 1930

Accordingly, three more flights took place on successive days—the eighth on
June 26th (undertaken for testing the repaired cover and lasting for $4\frac{1}{2}$
hours), the ninth on June 27th (undertaken as a rehearsal for the next day's
display and lasting $12\frac{1}{2}$ hours), and the tenth, again for some $12\frac{1}{2}$ hours when
the vessel successfully performed her part of the programme at Hendon.
Apart from the Report on these flights made by Flight-Lieutenant Irwin, to
which reference is made below, evidence was given at the Inquiry by several
witnesses who, either as officials from Cardington or as members of the crew
of the R.100, flew in the R.101 on one or other of these occasions. The
most important of these was Squadron Leader Booth, Captain of the R.100.
This officer, when asked his impression of the flight on the 27th of June, said:

> On the 27th of June we left the mooring tower at 8 o'clock in the morning,
> and landed again in the evening. The conditions during the day were rather

bumpy, and there was a clear sky with cumulus clouds and intermittent sunshine. We were only flying at reduced speed, 40 and 42 knots, and she appeared to be bumping rather a lot, which I attributed to the slow speed of flying. Also during the day I noticed that she was getting heavier than seemed to be consistent with the temperature and the height at which we were flying. During the day we had to let go some ballast, in the afternoon, as the height coxswain reported that she was difficult to keep at the flying height of 1,000 or 1,200 feet, and I think for the whole day we expended nine tons of ballast, and, assuming that we used about two tons of fuel, that makes up 11 tons of ballast that we expended. At the time, I remarked on this to Flight-Lieutenant Irwin, and he, I think, was under the impression that the gas valves were giving trouble owing to the slackness of the outer cover.

Flying "light" and "heavy"

Squadron Leader Booth's reference in the above quotation to the R.101 "getting heavier" makes this a convenient place to explain what is meant by saying that, in navigating an airship, she may be either "flown heavy" or "flown light". If a body is going to float in a medium without either falling or rising, it is obvious that its weight must be exactly equal to the weight of the medium it displaces. Sea-water, for example, is about 800 times heavier than air, and this is, of course, the reason why a vessel which displaces sea-water will float, though it is 800 times heavier than a vessel of the same size which floats in the air.

Yet an airship is seldom in an exactly neutral condition, i.e. of such a weight that when at rest in the air it will neither rise nor fall. But an airship which when at rest would not float without rising or falling can, by the use of its engine power combined with its elevators (within limits), be caused when in motion to travel so that it neither rises nor falls. If it is "heavy", i.e. if the condition and quantity of the gas it contains as compared with the outside atmosphere are such as would not sustain it in the air at rest so that it would fall towards the ground, its propellors will, nevertheless, keep it travelling level if its nose is somewhat turned up and the elevators are used so as to counteract its tendency to rise under engine power. An airship travelling under these conditions is described as flying "heavy". If it loses more lift and becomes heavier, its nose may be raised to a slightly larger angle and thus level flight still secured. This consideration will become of great importance when the cause of the disaster to the R.101 is considered hereafter.

On the other hand, it is also possible to fly an airship "light", i.e. to secure by the use of engine power and elevator that an airship which is lighter than the air surrounding her will, none the less, progress level with the ground instead of mounting higher. When the airship is flown "light" her nose must be turned slightly downwards, and here again if she becomes still lighter, her nose can be turned down through a somewhat larger angle in order to maintain a horizontal flight-path.

Squadron Leader Booth's observation, therefore, above quoted, really indicates that the R.101 on the flight in question was found to be losing gas, and was thus getting "heavier"—a condition of things which would be appreciated in the control car, as it would be counteracted by movement of the elevator so as to raise the nose of the vessel slightly higher.

OBSERVATIONS ON JUNE TRIALS

Colonel Richmond, when dealing with these June trials in his private diary, recorded that on the occasion of the flight on June 27th the ship had taken a steep dive. Squadron Leader Booth, however, when giving evidence at the Inquiry dealt with this point and explained what happened. He said that the dive actually happened over the Aerodrome at Hendon when the R.101 was intentionally brought down to a low altitude. She was, in fact, brought steeply down to 500 feet from the ground (which was lower than was intended), and the height-coxswain then pulled her rapidly up on the other side of the Aerodrome. At that moment the bridle just abaft the passenger coach, at frame 8, broke, causing a jerk which was distinctly felt in the control car, a hundred feet further forward.★

Captain Meager gave evidence that he was a watch-keeper on the RAF Display Flight of June 28th, and that he was on duty from 4 to 6 p.m., when he noticed that the ship seemed heavy, and the height-coxswain had difficulty in keeping height. This heaviness he considered was due to a loss of gas, caused either by the chafing of the gasbags or by the gas valves "chattering". During the morning he had noticed considerable bumpiness over the land, but over the sea the ship flew very steadily on an even keel with very little movement of the elevator. Over the land while going to the Display the ship again experienced bumpiness, and he observed that the height-coxswain, a man called Oughton (who lost his life in the ultimate disaster), experienced difficulty in keeping the ship at her flying height. In consequence of this difficulty Captain Meager dropped half a ton of ballast from No. 8 frame at about 5 p.m., and this made things easier. He reported, however, to Flight-Lieutenant Irwin, the Captain of the ship, that he considered the ship heavy, and as the ship was not far from Cardington he suggested landing immediately, but Irwin considered the weather too bumpy to make it advisable to land, and a landing was effected two hours later.

Wing Commander Cave-Browne-Cave, who was on the short flight which took place on June 26th, spoke of the dropping of the contents of two separate one-ton tanks of fuel-oil from about 1,000 feet as the ship came in to the mooring tower on that occasion. The oil was dropped in

★ After the return of the R.101 to the shed, all these bridles were examined, and it was decided to replace these wire bridles by chains.

order to lighten the R.101. The necessity for dropping this fuel oil was largely brought about by atmospheric conditions. When the R.101 left Cardington at 4 p.m., on June 26th, it was a hot sunny afternoon and the gas in the gasbags was considerably super-heated (that is, the gas was at a very much higher temperature than the surrounding air) and thus gave an increased lift; in the evening, when the ship landed at 9 p.m., the gas had cooled to approximately the same temperature as the surrounding air, thus causing a great loss of lifting power. It was in consequence of this loss of lift that the Captain considered it advisable to discharge two tons of oil from emergency tanks.

Some twelve hours later the Wing Commander went to the place where the oil had been dropped. Traces of it were found on the ground which was dry, but he formed the conclusion that if the ground had been wet it would have been very difficult to find any traces of the oil. This observation is of special interest in considering the probable course of events just before the R.101 crashed in France.

INVESTIGATION OF GAS LEAKAGE

It is of particular importance to study the incidents of these three flights in June and to consider how far they afforded evidence that the ship was air-worthy in various conditions of weather, since, after the Hendon Display was over, the R.101 was taken back (on June 29th) for the last time into her shed in order to have the extra bay inserted. She did not emerge again until October 1st, and after one more trial flight of 16 hours, which immediately followed, she started for India on the evening of October 4th.

Though there was little wind during the June flights, the weather could not be described as ideal for flying. On each of the three days there was a hot sun with detached cumulus cloud, and these constitute conditions which produce a very bumpy atmosphere when flying over the land. Apart from the indications that she was losing gas at an undesirable rate, to which further reference is made in the following paragraph, the R.101's flying in June may fairly be regarded as confirming the confidence, as well as increasing the experience, of those who navigated her. She had now flown for over 102 hours, over land and sea, and though she had never had to face really severe conditions in actual flight, the belief that she was capable of doing so was confirmed by the way in which she withstood the fierce gale while moored to the mast in the previous November.

But the flights in June must also be considered as affording some experience of how the vessel would behave with her gasbags enlarged till they rubbed at various points against surface projections in her main structure. This tendency to chafe had already been observed when the vessel rolled at the mast before the gasbag wiring had been altered. When she was brought into the shed at the end of November, 1929, a most careful gasbag inspection was made. Each bag was taken out of the ship in turn and examined for holes in the fabric; every gasbag except one was found to be holed, and in some of them the number of holes was considerable. For example, bag No. 11 had 103 holes in the fabric; bag No. 5 had 57, while some other bags were in much better condition. The holes were repaired and, before the vessel came out again for further trials in June, points in projections which were thought to be likely to press against the bags were carefully padded. It was, of course, obvious that the enlargement of the gasbags, by reducing the clearance between them and the surrounding structure, increased the danger of chafing, and no fewer than 4,000 pads were manufactured for the purpose of protection. It must be remembered, however, that many of these holes would be microscopic in size, and that owing to the small pressure of the gas inside the gasbag, the presence of a certain number of small holes would not necessarily produce a serious loss of gas.

CHAFING OF GASBAG FABRIC

Nevertheless, immediately after the June flights were over, there can be no question that a serious view was taken for a time of the danger which might be caused by the creation of holes due to chafing of the gasbag fabric and, in view of the amount of gas which the R.101 lost during the flights of June 27th and 28th, the question was raised whether this might be explained by imperfect functioning of the gas valves.

On July 1st, Flight-Lieutenant Irwin made a written report to Major Scott on the three flights which had just taken place, and a portion of this report is reproduced below:

> It was noticed during flight that the Outer Cover, E to F panel just for'd of Frame 13, was flapping considerably more than on previous trials. It should be worth while inflating this panel.
>
> The cover was also flapping all along between C and D and it is considered possible that gas valves may have been affected, as even allowing for the numerous holes which are now being found in gasbags where they have rubbed on protruding nuts of Main Longitudinals, the loss of gas would not have accounted for the heaviness of the ship during flight on Friday and Saturday.
>
> A report on gasbags will be rendered later on. The non-padding of girders before inflation and flying has resulted in an abundance of holes in gasbags.
>
> H. CARMICHAEL IRWIN,
> Capt. R.101

As regards the gas valves, it is stated in the minutes of a Conference held in Wing Commander Colmore's room at Cardington, when Flight-Lieutenant Irwin's report was considered, that the tests on gas valves had not been completed before the ship left the shed for the previous flights. This presumably refers to the testing of gas valves after they had been attached to the gasbags, and it was decided that these tests should be completed in the shed before the R.101 undertook another flight. The gas valves had, of course, been most carefully tested before they were placed in position in the ship. This work had been carried out by the Inspector-in-Charge, Mr McWade, and his staff.

Mr McWade in his evidence at the Inquiry told the Court that his instructions from the Design Department were to tilt each valve, under suitable conditions of pressure, to see that it did not open when placed at an angle of 3° from the vertical. But in fact, by increasing the tilt, he had ascertained and recorded at what angle the valve would begin to open. This limiting angle he found to be 5° or in some cases 4°. If, therefore, the valves retained this degree of sensitiveness, and the vessel at any time experienced weather which caused her to roll through a larger angle, the danger of gas beginning to escape was manifest.

As regards the loss of gas through holes worn in gasbags, Colonel Richmond also placed his own views on record. In the course of the Inquiry an "unregistered minute" dated July 2nd and bearing his initials was found. It was addressed to Major Scott and ran as follows:

> In connection with the reported loss of lift of R.101 during flight I have been investigating the effect of holes in the gasbags. I find that, if it be assumed that the average height of the holes is equal to three-quarters of the height of the ship, then, the rate of loss of lift is about 1 ton per square inch of opening in 12 hours. This calculation assumes quite a pessimistic coefficient of discharge such as would be applicable to a triangular hole. In my opinion, this result is somewhat startling and emphasises the great importance of guarding against holes in these present ships. Even if the holes are in the form of slits which have comparatively little effective area of discharge, it seems to me quite conceivable that we may have had leaks in both ships amounting to 4 or 5 square inches of area.
>
> In order to enable me and my staff to determine what should be done to check holes in the present ships and also to guard against their occurrence in future ships, I should be glad if you could arrange to let me have full particulars of the positions, approximate sizes, etc. of the holes found by the crew, from time to time.
>
> 2.7.1930   V. C. R.

A copy of the above minute was at the same time sent to Wing Commander Colmore, and another minute from the latter's Department, also of July 2nd, records that Colonel Richmond had discussed this matter with Wing Commander Colmore and "naturally regards it as very serious". It was decided, therefore, that the Captain of the R.101 should carry out a very minute inspection of the bags immediately; and that when a hole was found the exact position should be recorded, and the necessary padding applied to any projection that was the cause of the trouble.

REPORT TO AIR MINISTRY ON GASBAG DEFECTS

It will be appreciated that the minutes above quoted passed between the Officers concerned at Cardington, and at the Inquiry the Court endeavoured to ascertain whether the serious view then taken of gasbag leakage by the Cardington Officers came before the notice of the Air Ministry in London. It was ascertained that on the following day Mr McWade, the Inspector-in-Charge at Cardington, had written a letter addressed to the Secretary of the Air Ministry at Adastral House which he had specially marked "For the attention of the Director of Aeronautical Inspection", viz. Colonel Outram, whose office was at the Air Ministry. It will be observed that Mr McWade was taking the unusual course of addressing the Head of his Department instead of merely minuting his observations to his immediate superior. Mr McWade explained to the Court that his anxiety in part arose from the fact that it would be his duty at a later stage to hand over to the R.101, on behalf of the Air Ministry, a further "Permit to Fly". Mr McWade's letter was as follows:

Aeronautical Inspection Directorate,
At Royal Airship Works,
Cardington, Bedford
3rd July, 1930

The Secretary,
Air Ministry,
Adastral House,
Kingsway, WC2

For the attention of DAI (AID)
Subject: Confidential

HMA *R.101*

Airworthiness of the above ship
On the 26.6.30 I handed over the "Permit to Fly" dated 20.6.30—valid until 19.7.30 to DAD.

Owing to the modifications which have recently been carried out on the Wiring System, the gasbags are now hard up against the main longitudinals and rubbing very hard on the nuts of the bolts positioning the stirrup into which the tie rods are screwed. Further, the gasbags foul very badly the heads of the taper pins at the joints of the main and intermediate struts at the inner ridge girder ends. This matter, in my opinion, has become very serious, as the points of fouling occur throughout the ship and amount to thousands.

Padding has been resorted to by wrapping fabric over the parts mentioned above and this is the usual recognised method used in isolated cases. Padding to the extent now necessary is, in my opinion, very unsatisfactory, because the bags move when the ship is in flight and the padding becomes loose and the projection complained of is again exposed.

Although the gasbags have recently been reconditioned and were in good order when placed in the ship a few weeks ago, there are now many holes in them.

The next point is that where the fabric is wrapped round a joint it may be difficult to know what is happening underneath the wrapping (I have in mind the corrosion question). The fabric will become damp and in many cases wet when the ship is in flight; therefore, there will be an alternate process of wetting and drying of the fabric which must be detrimental to the metal underneath.

I am fully aware that to remedy the faults complained of is in the nature of a large undertaking and it may be necessary to remove the bags from the ship. Until this matter is seriously taken in hand and remedied I cannot recommend to you the extension of the present "Permit to Fly" or the issue of any further permit or certificate.

3.7.30

F. McWADE
Inspector-in-Charge, AID
at RAW Cardington, Bedford

Colonel Outram, on receiving Mr McWade's letter at the Air Ministry next day, sent a minute to Wing Commander Colmore stating that he would have to submit the document to Sir John Higgins, the Member of the Air Council under whom such questions would be dealt with, but that before doing so he wished to have Wing Commander Colmore's comments. The reply from Wing Commander Colmore was as follows:

DAI

I feel sure you will agree that we cannot accept, as a matter of principle, that the gasbags in an airship should be clear of all girders. Also I expect you will agree that we can accept padding as being a satisfactory method of preventing holes forming in gasbags from this cause.

As far as we can trace at present there have been remarkably few nips in the gasbags of R.101 and that the holes which have occurred are due to the bags fouling girders. We have little doubt that padding will be a permanent remedy and, if this is accepted, then it is certainly not a large undertaking to put the matter right. In fact, we hope to complete the necessary padding in R.101 by the end of the present week or, at any rate, some time next week.

We do not think any objection can be taken to wrapping padding round obstructions of this nature.

The above covers our views but I should be very glad to discuss the matter with you when you are next at Cardington.

RAW
8.7.30

R. B. B. COLMORE,
DAD

Colonel Outram explained to the Court at the Inquiry that, in view of Wing Commander Colmore's opinion, and after making other enquiries, he was convinced that the matter was not so serious as he had at first supposed, and that he, therefore, came to the conclusion that it was not necessary to submit Mr McWade's report to Sir John Higgins. He stated that even if he had known of Colonel Richmond's minute of July 2nd he would still have thought it unnecessary to do so. The result, therefore, was that neither the Secretary of State nor any member of the Air Council learned anything about it.

A fair inference from the facts is, that in view of the very special knowledge and experience possessed by the high officials at Cardington in every detail of airship construction, the remedy for what was no doubt regarded as a serious matter was left to their judgment, and it was considered that, notwithstanding the anxieties that had been expressed, adequate steps could and would be taken at Cardington to put the matter right. It has always to be remembered that the officers and experts specially acquainted with every detail of airship construction were concentrated at Cardington, just outside Bedford, and that the officials at the Air Ministry in London, who were technically their superiors, though accepting and discharging their proper responsibilities at Headquarters, were, almost without exception, men whose training and experience had been gained in the course of service with aeroplanes as distinguished from airships.

When, therefore, questions arose at Cardington (such as the proper way of dealing with the escape of gas), which are peculiar to airships, there was a natural tendency at the Air Ministry to rely upon the advice and judgment of the airship experts who were congregated there. No doubt this situation sometimes resulted in the determining voice, in dealing with difficulties reported to the Air Ministry as arising out of the construction or flying of the R.101, being that of the very people who were engaged in designing or flying the ship. There was less opportunity for securing an outside opinion or taking effective instructions from Headquarters than would be the case if the science of airships was more advanced or more widely studied. Thus, officials at the Air Ministry, whose special experience and technical knowledge were based on the construction and flying of aeroplanes, inevitably looked to Cardington, to a very large extent, to solve its own problems.

It is proper to add that Colonel Richmond, in a memorandum drawn up in the following September, expresses himself as satisfied that adequate padding proved a satisfactory cure. The incident was closed, so far as Mr McWade was concerned, by a minute from Colonel Outram of July 11th communicating the joint view of himself and Wing Commander Colmore. The minute includes the following paragraph:

> Of course I fully realise the necessity of avoiding the contact of these
> damaging points to the gasbags. I have taken the matter up with DAD (i.e.
> Wing Commander Colmore), who is in agreement, but as you yourself

realise, it is impossible to alter the hull structure of the ship at this stage. The only expedient at the moment is to pad, and it is your duty to see that every point which may lead to damage is padded in a proper manner.

PROGRAMME FOR INSERTION OF NEW BAY

The R.101, having been got back into her shed at dawn on June 29th (the day after her Display at Hendon), was now available for the insertion of an additional middle section which would increase her overall length from 732 feet to 777 feet, and which was calculated to enlarge her "useful lift" by some 9 tons. The girder work, all most carefully designed, had been ordered from Messrs Boulton & Paul earlier in the year and was ready to be assembled in the ship when she was cut in two. The additional gasbag (the largest of the whole series) had been manufactured at Cardington, and it only remained to decide when the ship should be parted. The division was to take place at Frame 8 and there was to be inserted a new Frame called 8a between Frames 8 and 9. There was, however, one consideration which might have postponed the operation. The R.100, which had successfully performed an "endurance flight" of 53 hours early in the year, had undergone some modification in construction and had still to go through a further continuous flight of 24 hours before she attempted the journey to Canada. If she failed to perform this further flight satisfactorily, she might be unable to enter upon the Canadian voyage, and Sir John Higgins raised with the Secretary of State the question whether, in that event, the R.101 might not have to be commissioned to take her place and undertake the crossing of the Atlantic. If, therefore, the R.101 was to be available as a substitute, it was necessary to postpone the cutting of her open until the result of the R.100's further trial was known.

Sir John Higgins' minute, sent to the Secretary of State on July 14th, was as follows:

> DAD (i.e. Colmore) has now applied for authority to commence work on parting the airship tomorrow. Until, however, R.100 has completed her next trial flight and shown that the modifications to the cover, etc. are satisfactory, a possibility still remains that the R.101 may be required for the Canadian flight. In the circumstances I do not think R.101 should be put out of action for the present, even at the risk of delaying the Indian flight. I propose, therefore, if you agree, to hold up work on R.101 for a week in the hope that R.100's flight will be completed by then. In the meantime DAD will press on with such work as is not dependent on opening up the airship.

Lord Thomson replied to Sir John Higgins' minute on the same day, as follows:

> So long as R.101 is ready to go to India by the last week in September this further delay in getting her altered may pass.

I must insist on the programme for the Indian flight being adhered to, as I have made my plans accordingly.

Sir John Higgins informed Wing Commander Colmore of Lord Thomson's view, and on July 17th Wing Commander Colmore replied to Sir John Higgins in the following minute:

> Every effort is continuing to be made to complete R.101 to enable the flight to India to take place at the end of September. Work on girders and parts is very well forward and a reliable estimate can be made of the time required to complete these parts and to assemble the frame.
>
> It is in the parting of the ship and the insertion of the new bay, however, that delays may occur which cannot be foreseen, and, in our opinion, if we are to work to this programme it is absolutely essential that work on parting the ship should commence immediately.
>
> In the event of further trouble with R.100 during her re-trial flight I am afraid the only alternatives would be either to abandon the Canadian flight until these troubles have been overcome or to carry out the flight with R.101 and postpone the Indian flight until November.

Sir John Higgins was thus faced with the difficulty that the Secretary of State was only prepared to authorise delay in opening up the R.101 and inserting the new bay if this postponement would not prevent the Indian flight being undertaken at the date then contemplated, which was the end of September. On the other hand, Wing Commander Colmore was pointing out that the immediate cutting open of the R.101 might result in no ship being available to undertake the projected Canadian flight, and was suggesting that, as an alternative, the Indian flight might be postponed until November. Sir John Higgins felt it necessary to see Lord Thomson again on the subject, and what passed at the interview (on July 21st) may be gathered from Sir John Higgins' minute to the Secretary of State made later on that day, and from Lord Thomson's reply.

These important documents run as follows:

Sir John Higgins to Lord Thomson

S. of S.

1. I understand from our conversation this morning that you do not approve of the proposal that R.101 should be kept as a standby for the Canadian flight, and that if the modifications which have been made to R.100 do not prove satisfactory, the flight to Canada will have to be put off until satisfactory modifications are completed on this ship.

2. I propose, therefore, to issue instructions to DAD to part R.101 immediately so as to give the best chance of its being ready according to the programme date which is being worked to.

3. Every endeavour is being, and will be, made to keep to this
   programme date but, as stated in my loose minute of the 30th June,
   this date does not leave any margin for unforeseen circumstances.
21.7.30.   A.M.S.R.

(The minute of June 30th here referred to had stated that, according to the
programme to which Colmore was working, the R.101 should be completed with the new bay by September 22nd. It continued "One trial flight
will be necessary before the airship leaves for India, so the end of September
is the earliest date on which the flight can commence. This leaves no margin for eventualities and assumes that the trial flight will be completely
successful.")

Lord Thomson to Sir John Higgins

A.M.S.R.
The first paragraph of your minute states the position correctly.
   I note and approve course of action proposed in paragraph 2.
   As regards paragraph 3, I am sure everything possible will be done and
am not unduly pessimistic.
22.7.30   T.

Decision to install reversible engines

Accordingly, the insertion of the new bay was at once begun. The vessel was
cut in two before the end of July and the work of enlargement, with a vast
range of consequential adjustments, was carried forward at full pressure
without intermission. But there was another circumstance which threatened
to postpone the projected date of completion. The original plan of providing the R.101 with four engines which worked only ahead and a fifth which
worked only astern had been modified. Instead of this, all engines were to
be capable of working forward; as ultimately fitted, two of them would also
work astern. There was delay in supplying these reversing engines and their air-
screws, and by the end of August it was calculated that, with day and night
work on these items, it might just be possible to complete the installation of
the reversing engine by September 22nd. Early in September it was feared that,
owing to delay in delivering the starting gear, it would be impossible to adhere
to this date. In fact, reconstruction was complete by September 25th but,
owing to weather, the R.101 was only able to leave her shed on October 1st.

INVESTIGATION OF AIRWORTHINESS OF R.101 AS MODIFIED

Every effort, therefore, to save time in carrying out the alterations to the
R.101 and in getting her out of the shed, was undoubtedly made; but there

is no reason to infer that the work was not properly done because of any pressure in its execution.

Another indication of the urgency with which matters were being carried through at the last stage is supplied by the way in which the two independent consultants, Professor Bairstow and Professor Pippard, had to act as compared with their more deliberate procedure with reference to the original designs in 1929.

This contrast must be explained further in detail. In 1929, before the R.101 left the shed for the first time, these two gentlemen, who are distinguished scientists and experts in airship construction, were employed to examine a complete set of calculations prepared by Colonel Richmond and his Department and called "Design Memoranda" Nos. 1 to 32, for the purpose of making a Report as to the airworthiness of the new ship. They drew up an elaborate Report, based on their examination both of these Design Memoranda and of diagrams and other data supplied by the Royal Airship Works. In this document (dated November 5th, 1929) they commented on any departure from the criteria of the report of the Airworthiness of Airships Panel, and they stated:

> We do not see any such danger as would render the airship unairworthy for trial flights; during these flights, experience will be gained on which the grant of a Certificate for overseas use can be decided.

The various trial flights were authorised by temporary "permits to fly" based on the views expressed in this document, and on the results of inspection from time to time by the Inspection Department of the Air Ministry.

After making their Report of November 5th, 1929, however, these two independent consultants had no further official connection with the R.101 until the summer of 1930. In June, 1930, they were invited by the Air Council to undertake an investigation of the airworthiness of the R.101 when modified by the insertion of the new bay. The Air Council stated that it would be guided by the terms of the consultants' Report in deciding whether the modified airship should be granted a "Certificate of Airworthiness", without which the Indian flight could not be sanctioned.

Four more "Design Memoranda" were accordingly put before them, on which Professor Bairstow raised a number of queries in the course of September. These queries were dealt with by Colonel Richmond. Matters were now urgent, for a further temporary "Permit to Fly" was needed before the reconstructed R.101 could undertake its final trial on October 1st and, apart from this, a Certificate of Airworthiness would be necessary before she could start for India. Accordingly, on September 26th, Professor Bairstow's sanction to the issue of a "Permit to Fly" was obtained by telephone; his full Report was to be furnished in time for the issue of the Certificate of Airworthiness. On October 1st, Professor Bairstow sent to the Air Ministry the following letter, from which it will be observed that he and his colleague had not yet had time to prepare their final Report:

The Secretary,
Air Ministry,
Adastral House,
Kingsway, WC2

October 1st, 1930

Dear Sir,

Airworthiness of R.101 with additional bay

In accordance with instructions, we have examined the new information supplied to us by the Royal Airship Works, and have satisfied ourselves that R.101 as now existing with its additional bay complies with the specified requirements of the Airworthiness of Airships Panel.

The difference between the conditions of loading of R.101 now submitted and those of the original design on which our previous report was based, surprised us by their magnitude; the differences are not primarily a consequence of the addition of the new bay.

A good deal of general thinking and comparison on limited information has been required in reaching our conclusion and we have not had time since receiving essential information from the RAW to prepare a sufficiently considered written report. We are proceeding to put our first draft into final form.

L. BAIRSTOW

P.S. The substance of this letter was agreed with Professor Pippard last evening.

ISSUE OF CERTIFICATE OF AIRWORTHINESS

It is manifest that Professor Bairstow was working under severe limitation of time. Enough had been secured to justify the "Permit to Fly", and the final report was to be expected later. In fact, no further report from these two gentlemen was ever received, and at the Inquiry Professor Bairstow explained that he was actually engaged in drafting it when he heard of the disaster. The Certificate of Airworthiness issued by the Air Ministry was dated October 2nd, and was handed over to the ship just before the flight to India started, as soon as the Inspection Department of the Ministry was satisfied.

It is evident, therefore, that the Air Ministry's intention, as expressed in June, had been to get a final report from the two Professors before granting the Certificate of Airworthiness, and to be guided by the terms of this Report in deciding whether to grant it. But, owing to want of time, the actual course of events was that the Airworthiness Certificate was granted and handed over, and the flight to India begun, before this Report had been received or even completely written.

PROFESSOR BAIRSTOW'S UNFINISHED REPORT

The draft of the Report, so far as it had gone when its authors heard of the disaster, was produced by Professor Bairstow at the Inquiry, and the following extracts are material:

> The most important considerations before us—although due in part to the addition of a new bay—arise chiefly from the difference between the fixed weights of R.101 as completed and flown and the weights assumed in design. This point is referred to in Design Memorandum No. 38 as follows:
>
>> Owing largely to increase in the weight of power cars, passenger accommodation structure and bow and tail structure, the final fixed weight of the ship as completed considerably exceeded that used in design and its disposition was such as to produce, in the light condition of the ship, an excessive tail moment.
>
> A table prepared from the memoranda submitted to us shows in greater detail the variations of weight between "R.101 designed" and "R.101 modified". One of the effects of the heavier structure, etc. is a marked reduction in the differences between the "heavy" and "extreme light" cases of loading.
>
> The considerable differences in weight between the designed and realised condition have corresponding consequences in the forces and moments which the airship has to resist. The bending moments for R.101 and its new bay are everywhere greater for corresponding states than for R.101 as designed. The same generalisation is not possible for shearing forces, there being a short section near the centre of the airship where the modifications have produced a reduction in the magnitude of the shearing force.
>
> We have not been provided with calculations relating to R.101 as completed and before the addition of the new bay but sufficient information is available to show that much of the change found is not consequential on the added bay. We have in fact found our task one of difficulty owing to the lack of tables of forces and moments comparable with those for "R.101 designed" as given in Design Memorandum No. 3. Instead of some 200 pages of tables dealing with different states of loading we have Design Memorandum No. 35 and seven sheets of loadings and an additional note prepared at our request dealing with aerodynamic loadings in the vertical plane. We have necessarily had to change our procedure and decide the question of airworthiness on general considerations and not on specific

calculations. It is our opinion that the newness of the venture would have justified complete recalculation of the stresses in R.101 when the magnitude of the changes in fixed weights had been realised. Such recalculation was at one time proposed.

It would not be fair or reasonable to deduce from the uncompleted draft of this Report that its authors were proposing to reach a pronouncement adverse to the airworthy qualities of the R.101 as reconstructed. On the contrary, though sounding a note of criticism and warning in connection with some of the calculations put before them, the general conclusion undoubtedly was that the R.101 was fit to fly. Indeed, as already stated, the temporary "Permit to Fly" under which she took her last trial flight on October 1st was issued with Professor Bairstow's approval.

But the draft report does undoubtedly show that there was not sufficient time to spare for the re-examination of aerodynamic calculations by the two independent referees to be anything like as complete as their earlier investigations. It is right to add that Professor Bairstow, after the disaster and in connection with the Inquiry, made, at the request of the Court, a very full and elaborate set of calculations from the data and dimensions of the reconstructed ship, and established that, from the theoretic point of view, her airworthy properties were adequate. Indeed, from some points of view, the lengthening of the ship had the effect of reducing rather than increasing the stresses imposed upon her.

It is convenient to close this part of the present Report at this point, and to postpone a description of the R.101's last trial flight to the part which follows. For the circumstances of this last flight are so closely connected with the decision that the start for India should be made on October 4th that it is better to deal with the trial itself in that connection.

DECISION TO START INDIAN FLIGHT

It is now necessary to put together the material which will show how the conception that the R.101 should undertake the flight to India came to be developed, and in what circumstances her actual date of departure (October 4th, 1930) came to be fixed.

The project of an Indian flight was really implicit in the experimental programme adopted in 1924 provided that the course of research and investigation then set on foot was found ultimately to justify it. Originally, as has been stated above, it was intended that both the R.100 and R.101 should be fitted with engines burning a fuel which could be safely carried and used in the tropics. But, when it was decided that the R.100 should have petrol-burning engines, the task of undertaking the flight to India necessarily fell upon the R.101. In 1926 work was begun in connection with the erection of mooring masts at Ismailia and Karachi and the building of a shed big enough to contain the R.101 at the latter terminus. The date at first contemplated for the Indian flight was unavoidably postponed because, as originally constructed, her useful lift was too small to allow of so prolonged and critical an undertaking. Reference had already been made to the communication of this change of time-table to the Government of India, and, when the R.101 was taken into her shed at the end of June, 1930, for the insertion of a new bay, official communications from the Air Council showed that it was contemplated that the Indian flight "should now take place in September next".

Wing Commander Colmore, who was the officer at Cardington responsible for carrying through the revised programme, drew up a Progress Report on the work then in hand, dated July 11th, in which he stated that it was impossible to give a firm estimate of the time required for joining up the new bay in the ship, but that he aimed at completing the ship by September 22nd. He added:

every effort will be made to complete the ship as quickly as possible, but we have no allowance in our programme to cover unforeseen delays.

It is this Progress Report which is referred to in Sir John Higgins' minute of July 14th, and which led to Lord Thomson's comment:

I must insist on the programme for the Indian Flight being adhered to as I have made my plans accordingly.

The Secretary of State was here referring to the above programme that the reconstructed R.101 should be completed by September 22nd and that the Indian flight should take place at the end of September. Indeed, in a minute of July 2nd, Lord Thomson had already written:

I should like to be able to count definitely on starting for India during the week-end September 26–28th. I ought to be back by October 16th.

This general programme was so well understood that on August 13th, the Government of India telegraphed to inquire what would be the exact date of arrival of the R.101 at Karachi. Before a reply was sent, Wing Commander Colmore was consulted, and as a result, Mr Reynolds, Lord Thomson's private secretary, put before the Secretary of State the following Memorandum dated August 26th:

1. The date of the departure of R.101 for India now depends on five separate factors:
    (i) the completion of the work on inserting the extra bay;
    (ii) the completion and installation of a reversing Tornado engine to enable the airship to have five engines going ahead;
    (iii) the completion of a reversible airscrew suitable for the engine;
    (iv) suitable weather for getting the airship out of the shed when ready for flight; and
    (v) the carrying out of a satisfactory trial flight of not less than 24 hours between being taken out of the shed and starting on the flight to India.

2. The position with regard to the above five factors is as follows:
    (i) the work on the airship at RAW should be completed by September 22nd;
    (ii) the reversing engine should be delivered to RAW by the 4th September but without the starting gear;
    (iii) airscrews have been ordered to two different designs and are due for delivery between 16th and 28th September.

3. If the dates given above are worked to, it will just be possible to have the reverse engine installed with airscrew by the 22nd September. Day and night work is going on on all these items.

4. There would therefore be six days available for getting the airship out of the shed and carrying out the trial flight. It is clear that this leaves no margin, but may just be possible.

It is plain, of course, that the programme of starting for India at the end of September could only be provisional, for at this time the work of reconstruction was not complete, and even if no further delay occurred in its execution there still remained the necessity for a further trial or trials and the consideration of what those trials showed.

Time-table influenced by Imperial Conference

At a Conference with the Secretary of State which Wing Commander Colmore attended on August 29th, the latter stated that owing to delay in delivery of the starting gear for a reversing engine, he could not get the R.101 ready to leave the shed by September 22nd as he had hoped, and Lord Thomson is recorded as replying "that he could probably arrange for the Air business of the Imperial Conference to be put off until about October 20th if necessary". Colmore was to do his utmost to start the flight on October 4th so as to arrive at Karachi about five days later, and the plan was to leave Karachi about October 13th or 14th and so get back to England about October 18th or 19th.

It is quite clear from the documents that the Secretary of State felt confident that he could thus count upon being back in this country in time to undertake his part in the Imperial Conference on October 20th.

It was therefore decided to send a reply to the Government of India stating that the present intention of the Air Council was that the R.101's flight to India should start "at the end of September or during the first week of October".

THE FINAL TRIAL

Preparations were now rapidly pushed forward. Early in September, a detailed, though still provisional, time-table for the double journey was drawn up and a list of probable passengers was settled. It was decided that when the R.101 came out of her shed she should undertake a trial flight under a temporary "Permit to Fly", but that she must have a final and official "Certificate of Airworthiness" before she started for India. The rather hurried circumstances in which this "Permit to Fly" was secured have been described above. The remaining work of reconstruction, including the fixing of a new outer cover between frames 3 and 12, proceeded so well that on September 11th, Wing Commander Colmore reported that he hoped, after all, to complete the ship by September 22nd, in which case she could be handled to the tower on the next favourable opportunity. But a few days later, in order to increase the engine power astern, it was decided to

	As first completed: 5th Oct., 1929 (tons)	After minor modifications: 26th June, 1930 (tons)	After new bay: 27th Sept., 1930 (tons)
Gross Lift	148.6	152.0	167.2
Fixed Weights	113.6	111.3	117.9
Useful Lift	35.0	40.7	49.3

install a second reversing Tornado engine which had just arrived from Messrs Beardmore, although this would delay the completion of the airship to September 25th.

She was "gassed up" so as to become air-borne in the shed on September 26th, and her lift and trim were ascertained next day. It will be convenient here to set out in a table the comparison of these figures with those which were ascertained when the R.101 was first completed, and also when (before putting in the new bay) her gas bags were enlarged.

Though the R.101 was ready to leave her shed on September 27th, she had to wait for a spell of very calm weather such as would enable her to be brought out with safety and handled to the tower. The opportunity did not arise until the morning of October 1st, and she started her final trial flight at 4.30 p.m. on the same day.

This flight had been intended to have a duration of 24 hours. Indeed, at an earlier stage, Sir John Higgins had contemplated that before the R.101 got a Certificate of Airworthiness she would have to do 48 hours' endurance flight. It was a condition of the contract under which the R.100 was built that she should satisfy a corresponding test, and she in fact flew on one of her trials for 53 consecutive hours. In the case of the R.101, however, this final trial was ended after a lapse of 16 hours 51 minutes, and the circumstances in which it was abbreviated need to be considered.

Reason for reducing duration of final trial

On the evening of September 30th (which was a Tuesday), the day before the R.101 came out of her shed, Wing Commander Colmore communicated with the Air Ministry, enquiring whether the Air Member for Supply and Research would agree to the duration of the impending trial flight being reduced to less than 24 hours if the ship behaved well, and if Major Scott was satisfied. The Air Member was no longer Sir John Higgins, for he had been succeeded in that position at the beginning of the month by Air Vice-Marshal Dowding. It is due to both these distinguished officers to explain that their training and experience had been with aeroplanes, and they necessarily looked to the officials at Cardington, not only for advice, but for guidance on technical matters especially connected with airships. Air Vice-Marshal Dowding told the Court that he enquired of Wing Commander Colmore what was the reason why the duration of the flight should be cut down, and that Colmore answered: "So that we may have a chance, if all goes well, of starting on Friday evening. We shall thus have all Thursday to work on the ship, as well as Friday." The Friday, it will be observed, was October 3rd, and the circumstances in which it became necessary to postpone the start to Saturday will be explained later.

Air Vice-Marshal Dowding agreed to the request, and at 4.30 p.m., on October 1st, the eleventh and last trial flight began. Air Vice-Marshal Dowding was on board.

Behaviour of R.101 on final trial

At the Inquiry, no written report was forthcoming of the behaviour of the ship on this flight (except as to the working of the wireless installation). If any such report was ever made it must have been kept on the R.101, and has been destroyed with the ship. The absence of a report would be in marked contrast with the course followed on some earlier occasions. Major Scott, Colonel Richmond, Wing Commander Colmore, Flight-Lieutenant Irwin (the Captain), and Lieutenant-Commander Atherstone (the 1st Officer), all took part in this trial flight, and were of course narrowly observing the behaviour of the reconstructed ship. But as they all perished in the disaster four days later, the only witnesses who could give evidence on the matter at the Inquiry were Air Vice-Marshal Dowding (who had never been in an airship before), Mr Raisbeck (Chief Examiner of the Inspection Department at Cardington), who made a few notes, and half a dozen others, who were members of the crew, attending to particular branches of duty. Living airship officers of experience, like Squadron Leader Booth and Captain Meager, did not happen to be on board during this trial flight and can say nothing at first hand of the ship's behaviour on this occasion. There are, however, two documents in existence which throw some light on this important matter: one is Colonel Richmond's diary, and the other a very detailed private journal kept by Lieutenant-Commander Atherstone.

Colonel Richmond's record runs as follows:

> *1st October (Wednesday).* R.101 brought out of shed at approximately 6.30 a.m.
> *Wednesday to Thursday.* Trial flight. Impossible to carry out full speed test owing to the early failure of the oil cooler in the forward starboard engine. Flying conditions were very perfect, and under these conditions, all other items in the ship behaved admirably.

The relevant portion of Lieut.-Commander Atherstone's journal is as follows:

> *Wednesday, 1st October.* This morning at 0630 hours R.101 was at last taken out of the shed in a very light N.Ely. wind and put on to the tower. . . .

During the morning orders were given to have everything ready for flight by 1600 hours. At 1530 the passengers came on board and the ship slipped from the tower shortly after 1600 hours. The ship flew over London and then down the Thames and over Southend. The night was spent off the East coast and in the morning we came in just north of Yarmouth and straight back to Cardington. The trial was very successful except for a burst oil cooler in the starboard forward engine car which put that engine and the Beverly out of action for the rest of the flight. The ship appeared to be much better in the air than before and the cover was really good.

Notwithstanding the absence of any written report, the general conclusion which must have been drawn by the responsible officers on board at the termination of this final trial flight may be safely assumed. The vessel had been exposed to no very strenuous experience, for there was very little wind, and Colonel Richmond has recorded that "Flying conditions were very perfect." It was not possible to have any full speed trial owing to the breakdown of the oil cooler of one engine. This breakdown, however, was not in itself a serious matter, and was repaired after the ship returned to Cardington. The officers were undoubtedly well satisfied with the performance of the ship.

Air Vice-Marshal Dowding told the Court that he had consulted his predecessor, Sir John Higgins, as to the attitude of mind of Wing Commander Colmore and the rest of the Cardington Staff, and that Sir John Higgins, speaking from a long experience, had said "that they were very enthusiastic over the airship but that he did not think that any advice that they would give would err on the side of rashness at any time; in fact, when it came actually to making a decision their advice would rather be on the cautious side".

Longer trial to be preferred

At the same time it cannot be doubted that if time had permitted, these officers would have preferred a longer test, if not a whole series of further flights. Squadron Leader Booth gave definite evidence on this point, based on conversations he had had with Flight-Lieutenant Irwin in Lieutenant-Commander Atherstone's presence. The following questions and answers appear to be important:

Q.4076. After the insertion of the new bay did you have a conversation with Flight-Lieut. Irwin and others with regard to the ship?—Yes.

Q.4077. As to what was to be done about trials and so on?—He mentioned some time before the ship actually left the shed, in conversation with me and Lieut.-Commander Atherstone, that he hoped they would fly 36 or 48 hours at a reasonable cruising speed in bad weather in order to thoroughly test out the ship.

Q.4082. Now we know that in fact she only did some 16 hours and 51 minutes flight. Do you know, as a result of anything that you have been told by Flight-Lieut. Irwin or anybody else on the ship, whether or not the officers were satisfied with that and satisfied with the behaviour of the ship?—I think that after this flight they were satisfied generally with the way that she handled under those conditions.

Q.4083. The weather as we know was almost ideal for flying?—Yes.

Q.4084. In your view would the insertion of the new bay make any difference to the handling of the ship in fair weather?—No, I do not think it would make any difference at all.

Q.4085. In fair weather?—In fair weather.

Q.4094. You told us a very important thing. You told us that Flight-Lieut. Irwin had expressed to you his hope that there would be a 36 or 48 hours trial, at a reasonable cruising speed in bad weather, in order thoroughly to test the ship?—Yes.

Q.4095. Then you told us that after the trial of some 16 hours in very calm weather, the officers (including Flight-Lieut. Irwin, I suppose) were satisfied with the way in which she handled in that calm weather?—Yes.

Q.4096. Have you any reason to think that, after finding that she handled well in calm weather for 16 hours, Flight-Lieut. Irwin changed his previous view that more elaborate trials in bad weather would be expedient?—No, I have no reason to think that he changed his mind.

It is really quite beyond dispute that the reason why this final trial flight was shortened was because the intention to start on October 3rd or 4th left so little time for preparation after it was over. Even though the trial were to disclose no defects to be remedied, there were many things to be done before the Indian journey could begin, and the Captain wanted every hour for a last look round. Indeed, this must be the reason why no report on the condition of the gasbags after the flight of October 1st–2nd appears to have been made. This is, however, a very different thing from supposing that so important a matter was not closely attended to. The situation was that, in view of the intention to start for India before the end of the week, the important matter was not to prepare elaborate documents, but to use the time in making a thorough examination of every part of the ship and repairing any defect that was found. Enthusiastic and confident as the officers of the R.101 were, they were the last people to leave anything to chance if it could be avoided. It is also to be remembered that when the ship was taken to her tower on October 1st she was handed over by the Building and Inspecting Staff at Cardington to the Captain and crew, so that after this date it is not the authorities at Cardington, but the officers of the R.101 who would ascertain the results of the final trial flight and arrange for any necessary repairs.

Importance of prolonged trial test

But while there is no reason to suppose that the R.101 did not start for India until after any defects ascertained during her last trial had been remedied (and the officers in charge of her would certainly have refused to start if this had not been so), it is impossible to overlook the fact that the trials of the reconstructed ship were cut down to a degree that would never have been thought proper if it had not been for exigencies of time. Squadron Leader Booth, speaking with an obvious sense of responsibility and with the experience he had gained from being Captain of the R.100, placed the matter in its true light in the following impressive answers:

> Q.4098. You will agree with me that the fact that the ship behaved well, as she seems to have done, in quite calm weather, would not seem to be quite the same thing as trying her out in bad weather?—I agree.
>
> Q.4099. Is that your view?—Yes.
>
> Q.4100. Do you regard a trial of 36 or 48 hours as useful from the practical point of view solely to discover consumption of fuel, or do you think that it is of value for the purpose of seeing how the ship behaves hour after hour under varying conditions?—I think that it is of great value for training the crew, and finding out fuel consumption, and also finding out if any defects occur after long periods of flight. In R.100 we did a 50 hours' flight, and certain defects, and very important defects occurred after flying about 45 hours, which would have seriously hampered the ship if they had occurred over the middle of the Atlantic.
>
> Q.4101. In your view, if you had been responsible, do you think that the trial of the modified R.101, before she started to India, was adequate?—I think that the officers concerned who had more experience of that ship than I have (and, of course, Major Scott, who had more experience of airships than anyone) were quite satisfied with the ship. They were confident in the ship and in their crew, but, at the same time, I feel that their decision to leave, or their agreement to leave, at that time was biased by the fact of the Imperial Conference coming off, and the psychological moment in airships when they could carry the Secretary of State to India, and bring him back to time. It biased their judgment in agreeing to fly. If that Imperial Conference had not been coming off, I feel confident that they would have insisted upon more trials, as was done in the case of R.100 before she left for Canada.

That this would be the view of an experienced and cautious airship officer who was planning trials without any regard to such considerations as are referred to by Squadron Leader Booth, is further made plain by another document which was produced at the Inquiry. It was a scheme of suggested trial flights drawn up at a much earlier stage by Flight-Lieutenant Irwin himself. After providing for flights by day and by night under good weather conditions, he had proposed a flight of 24 hours' duration under reasonably adverse weather conditions to be followed by "a flight of 48 hours' duration under adverse weather conditions to windward of base. Ship to be flown for at least 6 hours continuous full-speed through bumpy conditions and the rest of the flight at cruising speed. Ship to be berthed in shed as soon after landing to mast as possible, and a complete bow to stern inspection carried out." When it is remembered that the only trial of the R.101 after the new bay was inserted lasted for under 17 hours, and that under "perfect flying conditions", after which she started for India without ever returning to her shed for further inspection at all, it is impossible to avoid agreeing with the view of Squadron Leader Booth expressed in the final answer quoted above.

POSTPONEMENT OF START TO OCTOBER 4TH

It remains to describe how the decision was reached to start on Saturday, October 4th, instead of the previous day. On Thursday evening, October 2nd, Wing Commander Colmore came up to London and attended a conference with Lord Thomson. He reported that the trial flight was quite satisfactory except for the breakdown in the oil-cooler, and this was due to a defect of material which ought to be quickly remedied. Lord Thomson asked whether the start could not be made on Friday evening, to which Wing Commander Colmore replied that this would not leave time for the crew to have the necessary rest before undertaking so long a journey. The Secretary of State at once acquiesced and suggested starting on Saturday morning. Wing Commander Colmore pointed out that a morning start would bring them to Ismailia at the wrong time of day, since the estimated period for this first stage was 48 hours and it was important, for meteorological reasons, not to reach Ismailia before dusk. Wing Commander Colmore therefore suggested that the start might be made on the Saturday evening. Lord Thomson accepted this suggestion, but added an observation which shows quite clearly that he was relying, as he was entitled to do, on the advice of his experts and had no desire to over-rule their better judgment. Air Vice-Marshal Dowding, who was present at the interview, told the Court that the Secretary of State's words were something to this effect: "You must not allow my natural impatience or anxiety to start to influence you in any way. You must use your considered judgment." An abbreviated note made at the time by Mr Reynolds, Lord Thomson's Private Secretary, conveys the same idea in very few words:

> Colmore: "Leave Saturday 5 or 6 o'clock."
> Thomson: "No rush on my account."

Absence of full-power test

Before the conference broke up, Air Vice-Marshal Dowding pointed out that the R.101 had never done full-power trials, and a conclusion was reached, according to Mr Reynold's note, that the ship "ought to do full-power test near home", i.e. after leaving Cardington for India. The written instructions given to the ship before she left contained no such direction. It would seem obvious that there is a distinction between carrying out full-speed trials as a test to discover whether the vessel is efficient, and putting this extra strain on the ship when she is endeavouring to accomplish a flight of exceptional duration and difficulty. At any rate, when the ship started for India she did not waste fuel in full-power tests but continued on her way (as her wireless messages show) at normal cruising speed.

Confidence in carrying out time-table

The actual hour of the start on the Saturday evening was left to be fixed at Cardington in consultation with Major Scott. Colonel Richmond's diary shows that at midday on Friday it was decided the ship should leave between 6 and 8 p.m. the following day. Air Vice-Marshal Dowding told the Court that just before the conference at the Air Ministry broke up Lord Thomson observed:"Well that is all settled; I can make certain of being back on the 20th." It is manifest that the Secretary of State was entirely confident, and that he derived this confidence from the views of the officers who were advising him. It was realised, however, that though the R.101 got safely out to India, circumstances might arise which would delay her immediate return, as the return journey would be more difficult to accomplish owing to weather conditions and fuel requirements, especially on the Karachi to Ismailia stage. Plans had in fact been tentatively made for the Secretary of State to return from Karachi, if need be, by aeroplane.

What is so impressive, on studying the details of these last hours before the R.101 started for India, is the high courage and genuine confidence of all concerned. For four years they had been preparing for this moment and, notwithstanding that the date of the Imperial Conference tended to condition the hour of their start, they believed themselves to be prepared for it. The last entry in Lieutenant-Commander Atherstone's private diary is as follows:

> *Friday 3rd October.* It was decided this morning that the flight to India would not commence until 1800 hours tomorrow as it would be too much of a rush to get everything ready by this evening. We really did need all yesterday and today to get everything on the top line. A reserve lubricating oil tank was put in today to hold 112 galls. lubricating oil and a spare oil cooler is also to be carried. One of the emergency ballast bags was found to be defective and had to be renewed and all the others carefully examined. Also

the gasbags with low purities were purged through, and altogether the ship was given a proper look over. The weather conditions appear to be pretty good, with not much wind about. I think we should be able to get away with about 28 tons of fuel on board, which should give us nearly 100 per cent reserve. Everybody is rather keyed up now, as we all feel that the future of airships very largely depends on what sort of a show we put up. There are very many unknown factors, and I feel that that thing called "Luck" will figure rather conspicuously in our flight. Let's hope for good luck and do our best.

THE FINAL JOURNEY

The R.101 started on her flight for India on Saturday evening, October 4th, 1930. She was slipped from the mooring-tower at Cardington at 6.36 p.m., GMT (7.36 summer time: the clock was put back that night). It was, of course, already dark. There was as yet no rain, but the wind was blowing in gusts and its force was rising. The barometer had been dropping during the day.

There had been organised at Cardington a Meteorological Department, in charge of an able scientist, the late Mr Giblett, who perished in the disaster. The Department was under the general direction of Dr G. C. Simpson, FRS, Director of the Meteorological Office of the Air Ministry, who greatly assisted the Court by his evidence at the Inquiry. Here it will be sufficient to say that a chart prepared by the Meteorological Department at Cardington showed that at 1 p.m. on October 4th there was a centre of low pressure south of Iceland and of high pressure in Northern Spain. A corresponding chart five hours later showed that the centre of the depression was moving eastwards, and that the barometric gradient was getting steeper, i.e. there was an increase in wind velocity, and still higher wind was to be expected.

The weather conditions, therefore, at the time when the R.101 started were far from ideal, and evidence was given at the Inquiry that Major Scott came off the ship an hour before she was due to leave and said that he was going to get all the passengers on board early, as he wished if possible to get away before the original starting time, as the barometer was falling.

FUEL, BALLAST AND NUMBERS ON BOARD

The ship carried about 25 tons of fuel oil. Ten tons of this would be in tanks from which the contents could be jettisoned in an emergency. Under

The final journey of R.101, October 4th, 1930

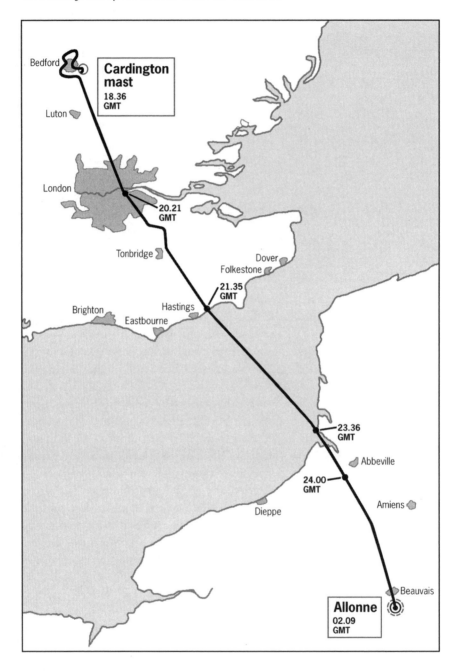

favourable conditions, two-thirds of the total quantity carried, or even less, might have been sufficient to reach Ismailia. Even if circumstances were adverse, the fuel provision was fully adequate—a fact which should be remembered when considering whether the Captain, when finding himself in difficulties before the crash, would seek to lighten his ship by dropping oil.

In preparing to start, the R.101 took on board 9¼ tons of water ballast, but 4 tons of this were got rid of before, or at the moment of, leaving, to compensate for the weight of passengers, crew, etc., and to help in the initial rise. It is worth noting that the dropping of so much water ballast at the start meant that if during flight more water ballast had to be dropped forward of the control car, this could only be done by sending a man forward to perform the operation.

So far as can be ascertained, the lift and load of the R.101 when she started approximated to those prevailing when her trial flight began on October 1st, the greater weight of oil being compensated for by a smaller quantity of water ballast and by other adjustments.

There were 54 people on board, six of them passengers, while another six were officials from the Cardington Airship Works. The officers and crew of the ship, therefore, amounted to 42. A list of those on board, also indicating those who escaped from the disaster with their lives, is given in an Appendix.

Available sources of information

The materials available for a description of the experiences of the R.101 after leaving Cardington down to the moment of the disaster are of three kinds: wireless messages sent from the ship and received at Cardington or other receiving stations; the statements of the six survivors; and observations from the ground of various people, mostly in France, who watched the vessel as she passed. The Court is most grateful to the French Authorities for assisting to make these witnesses available. Most of them were private citizens, living in Beauvais or its vicinity, who had no special experience of airships or aeroplanes, and no means of judging accurately on such a night how high the vessel was from the ground, since they did not know anything of her actual dimensions. One witness, however, was the resident in charge of the Poix Aerodrome north-west of Beauvais (M. Maillet), who was accustomed to make observations of aeroplanes, and another witness (M. Rabouille), who worked in a button factory in the daytime, but happened to be out rabbit-snaring that night very close to the place where the R.101 fell, gave a remarkably clear account of her movements just before she struck the ground. Putting together the material drawn from the three sources named above, it is possible, notwithstanding the loss of all the officers responsible for her navigation, to present some account of the last journey of the R.101 as follows.

FROM START TO THE COAST OF FRANCE

The R.101 got away from the tower in trim, i.e. with her nose and tail in the same horizontal line. Squadron Leader Booth, who saw her off, estimated that she was at the time approximately half a ton light, so that apart from the use of elevator combined with engine-power she would have risen steadily until reaching her pressure height. There had been a little difficulty in getting the new starting-engine of one of the forward power-cars to function, and this had somewhat delayed the departure, but, as far as is known, once the start was made all the engines worked as they should for some time. After circling Bedford the vessel set her course for London, by which time rain had begun to fall. She mounted gradually to her pressure height (about 1,000 feet) and thereafter rose further to 1,500 feet, which would mean that she spilled about 3 tons of gas. Mr Leech, who had been in the ship on several of her trials, noted that she was pitching and rolling more than before, and recalled speaking to Squadron-Leader Rope about it. This was when the vessel was over Hitchin. Squadron-Leader Rope had noticed the movement but did not appear worried about it.

A wireless message sent off from the ship at 8.21 p.m. runs:

> Over London. All well. Moderate rain. Base of low clouds 1,500 feet. Wind 240 degrees [i.e. about West-South-west]. 25 m.p.h. Course now set for Paris. Intend to proceed via Paris, Tours, Toulouse and Narbonne.

An hour later the R.101 was requesting the Meteorological Office at Cardington to wireless a forecast of the weather to be expected from Paris to Marseilles "with special reference to wind and cloud" and at 9.47 the following message shows that she was just reaching the Channel:

> At 2135 GMT crossing coast in vicinity of Hastings. It is raining hard and there is a strong South-westerly wind. Cloud base is at 1,500 feet. After a good get-away from the Mooring Tower at 1830 hours ship circled Bedford before setting course. Course was set for London at 1854. Engines running well at cruising speed giving 54.2 knots. Reached London at 2000 hours and then set course for Paris. Gradually increasing height so as to avoid high land. Ship is behaving well generally and we have already begun to recover water ballast.★

The crossing of the Channel took two hours, for at 11.36 p.m. the vessel in her next wireless message reported:

★ This reference to recovering water ballast has a special interest. The R.101 was fitted, on the top of its envelope, with catchment arrangements by which, when rain fell, water could be catapulted to increase ballast and so compensate for loss of weight arising from consumption of fuel. There is no reason to suppose that any considerable addition to the ballast was thus obtained, but the incident is significant because it shows that at the time the R.101 did not consider herself too heavy.

Crossing French coast at Pointe de St Quentin. Wind 245 true 35 m.p.h.

The Point of St Quentin is at the mouth of the Somme and its distance from Hastings is nearly 60 miles. The vessel was on a proper route
from London to Paris, and it was a route well known to Squadron Leader
Johnston, who had often navigated aeroplanes between the two capitals. It
will be noted that, according to the two telegrams last quoted, the wind
velocity was increasing. But it must be borne in mind that, to those in an
airship, the force and direction of the wind can only be ascertained by
observation of drift over the ground, since an airship (apart from gusts or
lulls), has no sensation of movement with the moving air, but only of passage through the wind-stream, whatever it is. In fact, the wind observations
reported by wireless from the R.101 do not appear to have been quite
accurate, for, unless the wind which she encountered from time to time
was stronger than she reported, her engines working at cruising speed (even
allowing for the temporary breakdown of one engine referred to in the
next paragraph), would have carried her a good deal further in the time.

In the meantime there had been trouble with the engine in the after-
car. Two of the survivors, Mr Binks and Mr Bell, were the engineers in
charge of this engine and their evidence has enabled the facts to be accurately ascertained. Before reaching London the main oil pressure connected
with this engine failed, and it required the attention, not only of the two
engineers who were in charge of the after-car, but of Mr Gent (the Chief
Engineer) and Mr Leech (Foreman Engineer from Cardington). The engine
was not got working again until about 11 o'clock, shortly before the ship
crossed the French coast. This incident partly accounts for the length of time
occupied in crossing the Channel. But it has no further significance, for the
evidence of survivors and other indications make it certain that the engines
of the ship were working satisfactorily till orders were given just before the
crash.

Height across the Channel

Evidence was given at the Inquiry as to the height at which the R.101 was
flying when crossing the Channel. Mr Leech, who was assisting to get rid of
the oil-pressure trouble in the after-engine, mentioned that when going over
the Channel he estimated that the R.101 was flying at a height of 700 or
800 feet, and that he came to this conclusion because of the distinctness with
which he saw the white caps of the waves, and from previous flying experience over the sea. Mr Cook, who was an engineer in charge of the port
mid-ship engine, testified that when the R.101 was flying over the Channel
he looked out of his engine-car several times, and could distinctly see the
waves of the sea being lashed up. He considered that the R.101 was
extremely low over the water, and he noticed that she several times got lower
and then climbed again. Mr Disley, the electrician, had occasion to go and

speak to the wireless operator in the wireless cabin adjoining the control room, where he remained for about ten minutes. This happened at about 10 p.m., and while he was in the wireless cabin he heard a conversation between Lieut.-Commander Atherstone, the first officer, and the height-coxswain who was at the elevator wheel. Lieut.-Commander Atherstone took over the elevator wheel from the height-coxswain, the altimeter at that moment reading 900 feet, and himself pulled the ship up to 1,000 feet. On handing back the wheel to the coxswain he remarked "Do not let her go below 1,000 feet."

Mr Disley then left the wireless cabin. He explained that at this time Squadron Leader Johnston was dropping calcium flares into the sea for the purpose of ascertaining the drift of the ship. It may be, therefore, that the vessel had been allowed to come down to about 1,000 feet in order to permit of the drift of the R.101 being thus ascertained without intervening cloud. Squadron Leader Booth, when asked for his observations with regard to the incident of Lieut.-Commander Atherstone taking over the elevator wheel, said that he thought it tended to show that the height-coxswain was perhaps rather careless in maintaining the flying height of 1,000 feet over the Channel, and that he might have let the ship sink below that height several times until at last Lieut.-Commander Atherstone took the wheel himself (as he was a very experienced man on the elevators from his previous training), just to show the height-coxswain how he wanted the ship flown. He did not think that Lieut.-Commander Atherstone would have taken the wheel from the man and operated it himself until he became strongly impressed with the importance of bringing the ship up to 1,000 feet.

11 p.m. to 2 a.m. watch

At 11 p.m. the watch on the R.101 was changed, and men who came on duty at this hour remained on watch until 2 o'clock next morning. It is clearly established that the disaster occurred between 2.05 and 2.10 a.m., and it is therefore of extreme importance to ascertain whether anything occurred during the preceding watch of three hours which indicated impending trouble or put the officers of the ship specially on their guard. Nothing whatever in the evidence or documents which were before the Court lends any support to such a conclusion. On the contrary, there are the strongest reasons for believing that nothing abnormal occurred until after the watch was changed at 2 a.m., or, at all events, that any earlier incident was of a sort which would escape observation.

A wireless message was received at Cardington from the R.101 at 0018 a.m., giving the ship's midnight position. The message was as follows:

> To Cardington from R.101.
> 2400 GMT. 15 miles SW of Abbeville. Average speed 33 knots. Wind 243 degrees (i.e. WSW), 35 miles per hour. Altimeter height 1,500 feet. Air tem-

perature 51° Fahrenheit. Weather—intermittent rain. Cloud nimbus at 500 feet.

 After an excellent supper our distinguished passengers smoked a final cigar, and having sighted the French coast have now gone to bed to rest after the excitement of their leave-taking. All essential services are functioning satisfactorily. The crew have settled down to watch-keeping routine.

This was the latest message as to the position of the ship and the course of her voyage sent by the R.101 to Cardington. But the ship continued at intervals to send out calls for the purpose of checking her position by Directional Wireless, or for testing the strength of her signals. Her last wireless signal addressed to Cardington was sent at 1.28 a.m. As regards Directional Wireless, she had made use of the Croydon Station while crossing the Channel, and after reaching France got corresponding help from the station at Le Bourget, just north of Paris. Not only so, but at a quarter-to-two her signals enabled a cross-bearing to be worked out by lines of intersection from Valenciennes (80 miles to the north-east), and Le Bourget (40 miles to the south). The resulting position—one kilometre north of the landing-ground at Beauvais—was sent to the ship by Le Bourget at 1.51 a.m., and its receipt was acknowledged by the R.101 at 1.52 a.m. This is the last message or signal of any kind that the ship ever sent off.

While the Captain of the R.101 would not be likely to use his wireless communication to report unimportant or temporary difficulties (no report was made of the trouble with the after-engine) it seems impossible to suppose that any serious mishap could have occurred until after the watch was changed at 2 a.m., and this inference is greatly strengthened by the fact that the watch *was* changed in the ordinary course. For if the Captain had been conscious at that moment of any serious trouble he would certainly not have allowed the men who were going off duty to turn in, but would have ordered them to stand by. The evidence of the survivors, and in particular of the surviving engineers, is conclusive on this point, for had any such order been given the men going on duty would have heard of it.

Two other pieces of evidence relating to the period before 2 a.m. remain to be recounted. Mr Leech told the Court that at about 1 a.m. Flight Lieutenant Irwin came into the smoke-room and spoke to him and the Chief Engineer, Mr Gent. The Captain made no remark about the behaviour of the ship except that the after-engine was continuing to run satisfactorily, and when the Captain left the smoke-room Mr Gent turned in and Mr Leech again went round all the engine-cars. He found that all engines were running well and came back to the smoke-room where he was sitting alone when the disaster occurred. His evidence as to the movement of the ship in the last few minutes, which will be recounted in the following paragraphs, is of the greatest importance.

The other piece of evidence which falls within the period before 2 a.m. is the observation of M. Maillet at the Poix aerodrome. Poix is half-way between Abbeville and Beauvais, and the R.101 passed this point at about one o'clock. M. Maillet told the Court that the airship passed to the west of the aerodrome; he saw white lights in a line, but it was too dark or cloudy to see the outline of her shape. This witness gave an estimate of her distance from the aerodrome and of her height in the sky, but, since it was too far off for him to see her red side-light, and since so enormous an object might well appear to be nearer than she really was, it would be dangerous to rely on this. M. Maillet said that he had an impression that she was struggling very hard against the wind.

THE LAST INCIDENTS OF THE FLIGHT

The ship reached Beauvais at about 2 a.m. and passed somewhat to the east of the town. A number of Beauvais citizens gave evidence at the Inquiry and recounted what they observed. In most cases they had been woken out of their sleep by the noise from the approaching engines and went out-of-doors to see the sight. Estimates of the height of the vessel in the air, made in such circumstances, are necessarily unreliable, but there is no doubt that it was the impression of these witnesses that the R.101 was labouring heavily in very gusty weather. There was a storm of rain and wind at the time. A curious feature of the testimony of more than one of the Beauvais witnesses is that the row of lights along the side of the ship became temporarily obscured; no amount of rolling would explain this and it seems probable that the explanation is to be found in an intervening cloud.

For the events which happened on the R.101 after 2 a.m. the Court has to rely on the evidence of six witnesses who survived—four of them engineers responsible for working the after-engine (Binks and Bell), the starboard midship engine (Savory), and the port midship engine (Cook). One of the remaining witnesses was the electrician (Disley), and the other a foreman engineer on the staff at Cardington (Leech). There is also a significant statement on one point taken from a rigger named Church before he died from his injuries.

These witnesses give a remarkably clear and consistent account of what occurred. Before summarising the evidence of each of them more in detail, it is desirable to state the general effect of their testimony, which the Court unhesitatingly accepts.

At a few minutes after two the vessel got into a long and rather steep dive—sufficiently steep to throw the engineers attending to the engines off their balance, and to cause furniture in the smoke-room to slide down to the forward bulkhead. This first dive may have lasted for half-a-minute, and would bring the ship many hundreds of feet nearer the earth. At length the ship was brought out of this first dive (doubtless by the height-coxswain putting his elevator hard up), and she returned for a very short time to an approximately even keel. But this was immediately followed by a second dive of shorter duration which brought her, nose first, to the ground, when she immediately burst into flames. It is clearly established that, before she crashed, orders were given from the control car by engine-room telegraph to reduce the speed of the engines, if not to stop them. Orders to this effect would take some seconds to transmit, since each engine car has a separate telegraph, but the significant thing is that the bells were heard ringing and, (in at any rate one case), the orders were received and acted upon before the vessel passed into her second dive. At about the same time that the bells were heard ringing, Chief Coxswain Hunt passed aft from the control car to the quarters where Mr Disley the electrician, and the crew, were sleeping, and warned them, saying "We're down, lads." The inference, therefore, that those responsible at that moment for navigating the vessel realised that she was bound to come to earth, and were making preparations for it, is over-whelming. The blow with which the nose of the ship struck the ground seems to have been less severe than might have been expected. One witness described it as a "crunch". After first striking the earth, the wrecked ship moved forward about another 60 feet before finally coming to rest.

EVIDENCE OF SURVIVORS

It is now necessary to set out the most material portions of this evidence in more detail.

Dealing first with the after-engine car, Binks was due to relieve Bell at 2 o'clock. He proceeded from the crew's quarters along the keel, passing through Frames 8, 8a, 9, and 10, into Frame 11—approximately 140 or 150 feet. (If, therefore, the ship had already taken up a steep angle, he must have observed it.) He descended into his engine-car, and the time, according to him, was then 3 minutes past 2 o'clock. (Bell thinks it was 2.05.) At any rate, Bell, who was waiting to be relieved, drew his attention to the fact that he was late: it was owing to this circumstance that Bell's life was saved. Bell was still standing in the position where the engineer on duty has control. Just after Binks arrived, the ship put her nose down and started the first dive which would be "not much more than possibly 30 seconds". (Binks and Bell agree as to this.) She then returned to a more even keel for a few seconds ("not more than 10" according to Binks; "not more than 5" according to Bell), and then got into another dive, the length of which Binks estimates at 10 seconds, and Bell at 20. Just as the ship was passing into her second dive the telegraph rang to "slow". Bell immediately obeyed the order, and it had been carried out before the car hit the ground. The crash was followed immediately by explosion and fire, but Binks stated that his car did not strike the ground heavily, but bumped along the ground so that the bottom caved in.

As regards the port midship engine, Cook relieved Blake at 2 o'clock. Blake, on handing over, reported that everything was all right. About 5 minutes after Cook entered the car, and after Blake had left it, the ship took up a "slight diving attitude". He could not estimate the length of that dive because, as the ship took up a diving attitude, his engine telegraph rang for the engine speed to be reduced to "slow". He carried out that order, and as he did so the ship took a steep diving attitude. The second dive, in his opinion, was quite considerably steeper than the first. After he had slowed his engine, he looked out of the doorway of the engine car, as he inferred that something serious was happening by reason that he had received an order for "slow" after his engines had been running at cruising speed for such a long period. As he looked out, the main body of the ship struck the ground. He succeeded in stopping his engines and a second crash came, followed by an explosion. Between the first and second striking of the ground was a matter of seconds, and he thought that an explosion took place simultaneously with the second bump.

Savory, who was in the starboard midship car, states that he took over this engine from his mate Hastings at 2 o'clock. He does not seem to have observed the first dive followed by a straightening out, and he speaks only of the final plunge. He says that the ship gave a dip which was just sharp enough to throw him against the starting engine. He was standing with his back to the starting engine looking aft. After that, all he recollects is, that he heard "rumbling and crashing and things breaking", but he does not know whether that was due to his car hitting the ground. His engines were still running at cruising speed, for he had noticed no signal on his engine telegraph. It should be appreciated that the noise in the engine car is so great as to drown the sound of the telegraph bell: any change of orders on the indicator must be observed with the eye. Savory also stated that he heard no explosion at all. The only thing he seems to have remembered was that a vivid flash entered the open door of his engine car, which scorched his face, and practically blinded and dazed him.

Disley, the electrician, was asleep in his bunk near the switchboard, which was in his charge. He was lying with his head in the direction in which the ship was proceeding, and was actually awakened by the first of the two dives. While still in his bunk he felt the ship starting to come out of this dive, and his own impression was that she not only got for a short time on an even keel, but actually became nose up. At that moment the Chief Coxswain, Mr G. W. Hunt, came to where he was lying and passed on in the direction of the crew's space, saying "We're down, lads." The moment after Hunt had passed, a number of things happened at once. He heard the telegraph bells ringing, and the ship took up a final dive. The switchboard was close to his left hand; he started to get out of his bunk and to cut off the electric current. There were two field switches; he remembers "tripping" one of them. He did this because he knew that in any aircraft crash there might be a chance of fire. But, unfortunately, the pulling out of one switch would not cut off all the current of the ship, as there were two generators running and he had no time to "trip" the second field switch. Disley stated that when the ship hit the ground the lights went out. This seems to show that down to that moment the circuit in the forepart of the ship was still unbroken—a very probable cause of fire when the crash came. The impact, he believes, was not sufficiently severe to throw him down. As, however, he and the other survivors a moment later were all struggling for their lives out of a burning mass of wreckage, and all sustained injuries as well as having to pass through a horrible experience, recollection of such details must be uncertain.

Leech was alone in the smoke-room, which was in the interior of the vessel, amidships. The ship, he says, took up a steep angle, the effect of which was to upset a siphon and some glasses which were on a table, and throw them on to the floor. The motion caused him to slide along a settee up to and against the forward bulkhead. He at first estimated that this dive lasted for 45 seconds, but on reconsideration thought it might be only 15 or 20 seconds before the ship began to straighten out again. He then picked up the siphon and glasses from the floor and replaced them on the table, which had also slid down against the bulkhead. Just after doing this, he felt the nose of the ship go down again, and he heard the engine-room telegraphs ring. He himself thought that the angle of the second dive was slightly less than that of the first. A few seconds later, the vessel struck the ground. There was no very violent jar; the striking was more of a "crunch". At the moment of impact the lights in the smoke-room went out, and within a second there was a flash of flame. The effect of the impact was that the ceiling of the room shut down on the top of the settee, and this prevented him from rising more than 4 feet. He ultimately got out of the room and escaped into the open by tearing away the partition with his hands.

Finally, there is the statement of a rigger named Church, who died three days after the crash. The condition of this man when his statement was taken was such that it was very difficult to obtain any information from him. He was probably the rigger on watch in the forward part of the ship, and his account ran as follows:

> I would consider the flight rather bumpy, but not exceptionally so. The second watch had just come on and I was walking back when the ship took up a steep diving attitude. At this moment I received an order to release an emergency forward water ballast ($\frac{1}{2}$ ton) but before I could get to it the crash came.

The water ballast referred to was in the nose of the ship. Unlike most of the emergency ballast, it could not be released from the control car, but had to be jettisoned locally.

THE ORIGIN OF THE FIRE

The only direct evidence as to the part of the ship in which the fire started is the statement of Rabouille, the rabbit-catcher, who was approximately 250 metres away from where the ship fell. He heard three explosions, and at that moment the ship lit up, the flames seeming to come from the fore part of the vessel. This conclusion is indirectly confirmed by several considerations. No one (except Church) escaped alive who was in the fore part of the vessel. The indications on the ground show that the ship must have struck with the underside of her bow: the marks on the earth indicate that the propellor of the starboard forward engine was still revolving and this engine car was twisted completely round by the impact. A careful diagram was prepared and put before the Court based on the marks on the ground and the condition of the wreckage which established that the angle of final descent was between 15 and 25 degrees.

Though the R.101 had been specially fitted with heavy-oil engines in order to reduce the risk of fire, she was carrying petrol for use with her starting engines in four of the engine cars. In the event of a crash this was an undoubted source of danger. But if a spark caused by the broken electric circuit reached a mixture of hydrogen-gas and air it would instantly set the mixture on fire, though the force of the immediate explosion would vary with the proportions of the mixture. This seems, therefore, to be the most probable cause of the fire. It started immediately the ship came to rest on the ground and spread with immense rapidity. The flames must have swept almost instantaneously along her length. They died down, however, before completely consuming the after end, and fabric still remained on the underside of the port elevator. This last fact is of very great importance in determining the final manœuvres of the vessel.

CONDITION OF THE SHIP AFTER THE CRASH

The R.101 came to rest with her forepart in a wood of small trees and her afterpart in a meadow. It is not to be expected that those who escaped from this burning mass of wreckage could make close examination of the condition of the ship at the time, but after getting away Disley and Cook did notice two facts of importance. Disley remembered that though the cover was burning on some parts of the ship, there appeared to be no cover left on top of the ship at all; it seemed to be a skeleton aft of frame 10 and 11. Cook, who had escaped from the port midship-engine car, on getting away from it, walked a few yards through the wood and looked back toward the tail of the ship. The only part of the ship on which he saw any fabric left was on the under-side of the elevator, which was upright. He saw the position of the elevator quite clearly in the light of the flames. The height-coxswain, therefore, had put up the elevator in an effort to raise the nose of the ship. The number of turns of wire on the drum of the elevator wheel in the control car, and on the auxiliary drum, definitely confirms this conclusion.

Immediately after the disaster, a Committee of Investigation, of which Air Commodore Holt was Chairman, went over to France to hold an Inquiry. The Committee consisted of Major J. C. P. Cooper (Inspector of Accidents); Professor Bairstow; Squadron Leader Booth; Messrs T. S. D. Collins, A. E. Gerrish and E. F. Randle (Technical Staff Royal Airship Works); Mr F. M. McWade (Inspector of the Aeronautical

Inspection Department); and Messieurs P. Jougland and H. Bournat (French Aviation Department). The Committee finished their investigations on October 10th, and later made a report. In the course of their report and when dealing with the controls the Committee stated:

> In the final closed-circuit of cable operating the elevators a fracture had occurred on the side which would be pulled to raise the elevators, and this fracture was close to one spliced end of the short length of cable inside the tensioning spring. The spring itself was extended to several times its normal length but was not broken. This cable was jammed under the pulley wheel on the horizontal girder but this was obviously due to recoil following fracture of the cable.
>
> On the evidence available we have been unable to arrive at a definite conclusion as to the cause of the fracture of this particular cable, and we consider that the broken pieces which, together with the principal parts of the auxiliary control mechanism have been preserved, should be the subject of laboratory examination.

Major Cooper had all the parts of this control gear brought back to the Royal Aircraft Establishment at Farnborough, and kept in close touch with the laboratory examination which was subsequently carried out there. In his opinion the further examination established beyond doubt that the control cable broke after, and not before, it became heated.

The Court had further tests of this cable made at the Engineering Laboratory at Cambridge. The two broken ends each had been exposed to intense heat for a distance of about half an inch, and the presumption that this heat had been applied before the cable parted was therefore strong. Mr W. E. Woodward, who conducted the further experiments, came to the conclusion that the cable certainly did not break before the conflagration. The Court unhesitatingly accepts this conclusion. The break could not have been the cause of the accident as it only happened either during or after the fire.

The Committee of Investigation formulated the following conclusions based on the evidence afforded by the wreckage:

(a) That no part of the main structure of the airship broke in the air.
(b) That impact with the ground occurred when the airship was inclined nose-downwards at an angle of between 15 and 25 degrees from the horizontal.
(c) That the elevator control wheel was set for full "Up elevator", while the rudder was practically straight at the time of the crash.
(d) That a violent explosion occurred immediately or very shortly after the ship struck.

The possible causes of the accident are dealt with in the following section of the Report.

DISCUSSION OF CAUSE OF DISASTER

In discussing the cause of the accident, one starts with a series of definitely ascertained facts. It is then possible to exclude, by a process of reasoning which appears conclusive, certain suggested explanations which need to be examined before they can be rejected. In the result, the analysis indicates, with some degree of confidence, the general nature of the true cause, though precise detail can never be attained, since no one who was in the control-car has survived.

THE ESTABLISHED FACTS

The following facts may be regarded as definitely established:

When the watch was changed at 2 a.m., there was no cause for immediate alarm known to those in charge of the navigation of the ship. The vessel must have been at least 1,000 feet above the ground. The ground itself at this point is 200–300 feet above sea level.

At 2 a.m. the elevator wheel would be handed over to another height-coxswain. (The difficulty of the new hand at once getting the "feel" of the ship is dealt with below.)

The weather was exceedingly bad. A strong wind was blowing from the SW; at that elevation its velocity might attain to 40 or 50 miles per hour. Moreover, the wind was not steady but was blowing in fierce gusts which would cause the nose of the vessel to move through a considerable angle above and below her horizontal line of flight. The height-coxswain would seek to limit or counteract this movement by use of the elevator.

The ship in her trials had lost gas at an abnormal rate, certainly by the wearing of holes in the gasbags, and perhaps through her valves when she rolled.

On the Indian journey she had rolled more than ever before, and had failed to keep height as the officer of the watch intended at an earlier period.

If she was becoming increasingly heavy, this could be counteracted by suitable use of the elevator, but in very bumpy weather it would be more difficult to detect the rate and extent of the change.

All her engines had been running satisfactorily at cruising speed for a considerable time right down to 2 a.m. This ought to give a speed through the air of a little over 50 knots. The course of the vessel was not directly in the teeth of the wind, and her speed over the ground might be expected to be 15 to 20 miles per hour.

In these circumstances, at about five minutes past two, her nose dropped and she continued in this position for about 30 seconds, descending rapidly during that period of time. Her pitch downwards was sufficiently severe to wake up a man who was asleep in his bunk, and to cause things to slide to the lower end of the smoke-room.

The height-coxswain, by putting his elevator up, succeeded at length in bringing the ship again to about an even keel, but she remained in this position only for a few seconds.

At about the time when it appeared that she was not further responding to up-elevator so as to recover height, the officer of the watch gave orders through the engine-room telegraph to reduce speed.

About this moment the vessel got into a second steep dive, which lasted for only a few seconds before she struck the earth. The impact was not severe.

The slowing down of the engines combined with the warning given by Chief Coxswain Hunt to Disley and the crew, is only consistent with the view having been taken that the vessel could not recover.

Apart from reducing speed, the only other action that could be instantly taken to lighten the impact would be to drop such ballast as could be released from the control car. Releasing ballast in the nose of the ship which could not be automatically controlled was a further and slower operation, and yet orders were given to Church to do this.

The fire did not break out till after the ship struck the ground.

POSSIBLE EXPLANATIONS

Structural weakness

First among the explanations of the accident which may be definitely rejected is any idea that the vessel, from internal weakness, broke up in the air. This had happened with some previous airships—with the *Shenandoah* for example, and the R.38. But in the present instance such an explanation is entirely inadmissible. The elaborate care with which the ship had been designed and constructed is set out earlier in this Report. All the evidence of her behaviour at the critical moment goes to show that she came down intact. Rabouille, who watched her fall, was quite clear that she did not break up at all before she struck the ground. The preliminary Committee of Investigation came to the same conclusion. When the remains of the ship lying on the ground were examined, it was found that in spite of the blow she had received she had only crumpled up to a small extent, with a reduction in total length of 88 feet. This was chiefly due to the buckling of the base members of the triangular transverse frames which encircled the vessel. The conclusion, therefore, is that the R.101, so far as her metal structure was concerned, was abundantly strong, and that her designers had provided adequately for withstanding the aerodynamic forces which she might encounter in flight.

Control gear

Next, the explanation may be set aside that there was any failure in the control gear. If the break in the wire controlling the elevators had occurred in mid air, very serious results might have followed therefrom. But this is quite inconsistent with the position in which the elevator was found after the crash, and, it is conclusively established that the break in this control wire occurred in the course of, or in consequence of, the subsequent fire, and not, therefore, before the accident.

Weather conditions

Next, the weather conditions have to be considered as a possible explanation of what occurred.

The R.101 started from Cardington after receiving weather reports that she might expect to meet at 2,000 feet wind of the speed of 20 to 30 miles per hour in Northern France, and the period in respect of which this forecast was made ran from 5 p.m. on October 4th, to 5 a.m. on October 5th. These forecasts seriously underestimated the wind she actually met with, and indeed after she had started she received a further forecast from the Meteorological Office at Cardington indicating that at 2,000 feet she might expect to meet in Northern France wind of 40 to 50 miles per hour. Consequently the wind conditions she actually had to face were much more severe than had been anticipated when she started.

Squadron Leader Booth expressed the view to the Court that at the time of the accident "the weather, from an airship point of view, over land was extraordinarily bad, or extremely bad". "During the war," he added, "and since the war, ships have flown in worse weather as regards the strength of the wind, but on practically every occasion it has been bad weather over the sea, where you do not get turbulent effects or violent gustiness such as may be experienced over land." This view may be accepted, and it amounts to saying that the weather conditions constituted a predisposing cause in the presence of which it would be much more difficult to surmount a sudden crisis otherwise occasioned.

But the evidence as a whole does not justify the conclusion that the accident was simply due to the weather. (If it were otherwise, such a conclusion would be extremely damaging to any argument in favour of airship travel, for, bad though the weather was, it was not worse than must occasionally be experienced in the course of a long journey.) Dr G. C. Simpson gave to the Court an elaborate and most instructive account of the circumstances in which very sudden and severe vertical currents are sometimes met with in the air. But the result of his evidence was to establish that the meteorological conditions in the neighbourhood of Beauvais at the time were not such as to permit of vertical currents of very high velocity being present. The wind was blowing with pronounced gusts, and this would aggravate a characteristic of the ship which had been noted on some of her trial flights, viz., her tendency when on a horizontal path alternately to drop and raise her nose through a considerable angle. The height–coxswain, of course, would attempt to control this variation in pitch by the use of the elevator. Squadron Leader Booth, dealing with this sort of movement, told the Court:

> Normally you should keep within 250 to 300 feet on either side of your flying height; that is under normal bumpy conditions. That might be extended possibly to 400 or 500 feet under bad conditions. I think that is an absolute maximum.

Dr Eckener, the distinguished President of the Zeppelin Company, who was good enough to come over to this country to assist the Court with his views, said that under gusty conditions he had experienced an angle of pitch up to 18° or 19°.

On this part of the case, therefore, the Court reaches the conclusion that the accident could not be explained solely by reference to abnormal weather conditions. Some other cause, combined with these admittedly bad conditions of weather, must be sought. The right view seems to be that the weather was a predisposing cause in the sense that if the weather conditions had been good the ship would have had a much better chance of escaping disaster. In particular, it must not be assumed that the path of the gusts moving over undulating country, with the Beauvais ridge only five miles away to the south, would be uniformly horizontal.

Competence of officers and crew

Next, it is necessary to review the probabilities of an error in navigation causing the accident. One of the consequences of the R.101 starting for India without first having gone through a more complete set of trials is, as Squadron Leader Booth pointed out, that the officers and crew had had less training in flying the ship than might have been desirable. Moreover, the opportunity of practical experience in other airships was necessarily limited. Yet Major Scott had probably had more practical experience than anyone in the service. Wing Commander Colmore, Squadron Leader Johnston and Flying Officer Steff had all, like Scott, flown with the R.100 to Canada and back. During the war, Flight Lieutenant Irwin had been Captain of all types of non-rigid airships. In 1921 he was given command of the R.36; in 1924 he was selected to be Captain of the R.33. Squadron Leader Booth, who had served under him as First Officer, expressed to the Court the highest opinion of his capacity, saying that he was exceptionally good in handling a ship in the air and was distinguished by thoroughness and carefulness in the carrying out of his work. The other officers also had records of much distinction and the Court would entirely reject, as an explanation of the disaster, any failure in skill on the part of any of them. It seems clear that the vessel passed in a few moments from a condition which appeared to be safe into a condition of extreme insecurity, but there is no reason to doubt that the officers in charge dealt with the crisis to the best of their ability.

The actual movements of the elevator would be under the control of one or other of the height-coxswains. Three (in addition to Chief Coxswain Hunt) were carried on the Indian voyage and it is impossible to determine which of them took over the wheel at 2 a.m. Nor is it material to enquire. They were all trained men and the coxswain on duty would be under the immediate observation and control of the officer of the watch. There is, therefore, equally little ground for suspecting any deficiency on the coxswain's part.

Evidence was given to the Court that at a change of watch, when the new hand comes on duty, it is difficult, especially in bumpy weather, for him at once to get the "feel" of the ship. Dr Eckener stated that it was his own experience when in a Zeppelin that after a change of watch the coxswain had to "feel his way" into the prevailing flying condition of the ship and that until he did so, increased motion was noticeable. He took the view that if the vessel, shortly after a new coxswain had taken over, was exposed to a strong gust above her nose at a time when she happened to be pitched downwards it would be very difficult for the man to judge the extent of the elevator action which would be needed to counteract the dive.

The conclusion, therefore, is that there is no reason to attribute the accident to any failure in the competence of officers or crew, but that in view of the recent change of watch and of the prevailing weather it may well have been impossible to bring the ship rapidly back to a horizontal position if her nose was forced down in the way suggested.

Longitudinal movement of gasbags

A suggestion put forward from various quarters to the effect that the R.101 might develop instability owing to longitudinal movements of the gasbags has received most careful attention.

Owing to the fact that the novel gasbag wiring of the R.101 provided bulkheads of a "slack" variety, longitudinal surging of the gasbags to a limited extent is a possibility.

It would appear, however, from drawings and information supplied from Cardington, that, under extreme conditions, the longitudinal movement of the centre of gravity of a gasbag could hardly exceed 3 feet, and even if a considerable number of the gasbags were sufficiently deflated to enable them to participate in this movement, the reduction in fore-and-aft stability would be relatively insignificant. The depth of the centre of gravity of the ship below its centre of buoyancy was 29 feet, and the pendulum action consequent on this depth would limit the range of instability to 3 or 4 degrees on either side of the horizontal, even in the case where the ship was merely ballooning with engines stopped.

Officers who had flown in both the R.100 and the R.101 formed the opinion that the latter ship was comparatively sluggish in answering to her elevator controls, and this may quite possibly be due to a certain measure of instability occasioned by longitudinal gasbag movement. This movement, however, is so limited in extent that by itself it is quite insufficient to account for a serious loss of control, even in the tempestuous conditions which prevailed at the time of the accident.

Loss of gas

The experts (both theoretical and practical), who gave evidence to the Court believe that the explanation of the disaster must be associated with a substantial loss of gas. In this connection certain subsidiary questions arise:

(1) Was the loss of gas general throughout the length of the ship, or was it chiefly concentrated in the fore part?
(2) Was the loss of gas a gradual process in consequence of which the ship became steadily heavier, or is it to be explained by a sudden catastrophe which would empty the contents of one or more of the forward gasbags immediately before the final dive? or
(3) Is the explanation a gradual loss of gas spread over a considerable interval, culminating in a further and catastrophic loss?

On the subject of the possibility of a gradual loss of gas, extremely important evidence was given to the Court by Professor Bairstow. In the interval which occurred between the two periods when the Court sat, he worked out calculations which he subsequently explained to show that if the ship steadily lost gas, her increasing heaviness would nevertheless not call for more than a very slight adjustment of the elevator until she approached a critical condition. As she put her nose further up to counteract this increasing heaviness, her speed forward through the air would drop owing to increased "drag". A critical condition, beyond which steady flight ceases to be possible, would be reached if she ever became $13\frac{1}{2}$ tons generally heavy, and earlier if the heaviness was due to deflation in the forward part of the ship. Yet Professor Bairstow's calculations went to show that a very considerable loss of gas might take place before any large movement of the elevator would be required, and that in certain circumstances the loss of the last 2 or 3 tons of dynamic lift would produce an exceedingly rapid change in the available pitching moment.

The importance of this evidence is of course that it suggests the possibility of some such gradual deterioration having gone on through the wearing of holes in the gasbags or through gas escaping through the valves when the ship was rolling, without the full extent of the loss being promptly appreciated in the control car. On the other hand, the practical experts were disposed to think that, in any event, there was superimposed upon any slow change of condition such as these calculations seem to make possible, a more definite and sudden further loss of gas from a forward gasbag or gasbags within a very short time of the disaster.

The chief difficulty in the way of supposing a prolonged and substantial leakage of gas is that such a condition of affairs would make itself known to the officer of the watch by the increasing angle of pitch needed to regain height. If serious leakage were suspected, one would expect that men going off duty would be told to stand by. The fact that no survivor knows anything of the men whose watch was ended being kept on duty militates against the hypothesis of prolonged leakage, at any rate if it were so pronounced as to be observed.

DR ECKENER'S CONCLUSIONS

After Professor Bairstow had explained the result of his calculations, Dr Eckener gave evidence. His view was to the following effect:

> The extremely interesting and clear statements given yesterday by Professor
> Bairstow based on the experiments made in the wind tunnel clearly show
> that by assuming certain losses of gas it would be impossible to prevent an
> airship of the R.101 type from stranding in a trimmed and loaded condition,
> as was the case with the R.101 immediately prior to stranding (unless there
> be, for instance, sufficient time to retrim the ballast). Professor Bairstow, in
> my opinion, has dealt in a most convincing manner with all factors
> determining the pitching moment. I particularly agree with him that the
> elevator is rendered ineffective when the ship comes into certain out-of-
> horizontal positions, and also that a heaviness of 13 to 15 tons is the
> maximum which can be carried dynamically.

Dr Eckener then went on to contrast the pitching moment of the Graf Zeppelin with that worked out for the R.101 by Professor Bairstow, pointing out that the larger figure in the latter case was due to the greater effectiveness of the elevator. He then proceeded to discuss what must have been the course of events to produce the disaster and said:

> In forming my opinion I commence with the fact that the ship made a sudden very steep dive, and that in spite of the probable dropping of ballast she could no longer be kept on a level keel, although she had been able up to that moment to hold her altitude. It lies very near at hand to connect the sudden occurrence of head-heaviness with the particularly steep dive, because the steep dive itself can hardly be explained by the sudden loss of gas, because the effect of a rent in one of the fore gasbags would not show itself so suddenly. The whole happening no doubt was as follows: At 2 o'clock the new watch came on to take over control of the elevator. He (the coxswain) would have to feel his way into the condition of the ship. This is an old experience. The weather was bumpy and the ship probably not only heavy, three to four tons, but a little heavy by the nose owing to the loss of gas in one of the forward gasbags—in the same gasbag which later sustained a large rent. It is very difficult at once to feel the head-heaviness of a ship, when the ship is heavy as a whole and at the same time head-heavy. It may now have happened that in a slight gust of wind the ship made a movement downward which the new coxswain of the elevator did not immediately and correctly counteract, because he could not be quite clear about the condition of the ship. The movement became steep because the ship now received a current of air from above on her nose, thus accentuating the effect of the head-heaviness. The gas between the gasbags and the outer cover escaped to the tail of the ship, thus increasing the pitching moment still further. Owing to this unusual violent movement of the ship the already damaged gasbag sustained a larger rent from which the gas now quickly escaped. Thus it took some time (perhaps fully 30 seconds) to bring the ship back on a level keel. This would be done by putting up the elevator and by dropping fuel; otherwise it would not have been possible, in my opinion. This oil would fall under the ship, owing to the fact that the vessel, owing to her reduced speed in the strong wind, was making very slight way over the ground, which I estimate as 4 to 5 miles per hour. The ship having righted, through the throwing out of ballast, was unable to maintain her horizontal position, by reason of the fact that the gas continued to escape quickly and because the ship had no longer the pitching moment upwards. The people in the control-car would know that they were going down, and they therefore stopped the engines, and thus, with the second dive, the stranding occurred.

Concurrence of other officers

Before Dr Eckener had given evidence, Squadron Leader Booth had given a written statement of his opinion as to the cause of the accident. He agreed generally with Dr Eckener's view.

He considered that the ship was flying more or less normally at 1,500 feet just prior to the accident. At any rate, at 2 a.m. he thought that everything on the ship must have been normal because, otherwise, the watch would not have been changed. His view was that the ship might have been 4 tons heavy at that time. He arrived at this figure by taking into consideration the expenditure of fuel, the amount of gas expended, and the rain that had been encountered. Before he heard Dr Eckener's evidence he thought that some accident had happened to the ship when flying at 1,500 feet, but having heard that evidence he was inclined to think that Dr Eckener's suggestion that the steep dive which the ship took after 2 a.m., when the watch was changed, may itself have led to damage to a gasbag. Those on the ship, by using full elevator, would pull the ship out of the dive, but if gas continued to escape and the ship continued to get heavy forward, she might have got into a second dive in spite of the fact that ballast had during these incidents been dropped. After that, the officer in charge in the control-car would slow his engines to reduce the force of the impact.

Squadron Leader Booth thought that in an emergency of this kind it would take the officer of the watch some seconds to realise what was happening. He had been in the ship flying over France for three hours, during which time undoubtedly the ship had been pitching up and down 5, 6, and possibly 10 degrees, so that during the first 10 degrees of the dive he may have considered that it was merely a normal dive occasioned by the weather conditions. Until the officer realised that he had to take action, the ship would be getting into a more unmanageable position, and thus time would be wasted. He did not think that it could be assumed that the moment the ship started putting her nose down in the first dive, action would be taken to correct it. Speaking of the position of a man in the control-car he said that, normally speaking, when coming out of a steep dive in which considerable height had been lost, the ship would be pulled out of the dive by the use of a large angle of elevator, and that angle of elevator would be kept on so that the ship would get an equally steep climb in order to regain height. The height-coxswain would see from his instruments that he was a long way below his correct height, and would pull the ship up sharply and keep her at that angle in order to return to, and possibly to exceed, his flying height. If the height-coxswain then saw, in spite of his excessive use of the elevator, that the ship appeared to be coming only slowly out of the dive and did not appear to be continuing her upward path, notwithstanding the dropping of ballast, he would immediately know that his position was hopeless, because he had 15 or 20 degrees of up-elevator and yet the ship would not be recovering. All that he could do then would be to report to the officer of the watch, who probably would have noticed the position for himself. If the ballast had gone and the elevator was hard up, and yet the ship was still horizontal, they must have realised that there was nothing more they could do except to send a man forward as a last chance to release the ballast in the nose. After that, if the nose again fell, those in the control-car could only slow down the engines and attempt to decrease the force of the impact. They might possibly turn the head of the ship to the wind if they had time, but he did not think in this particular case that there would be time to do so.

Captain Meager was in agreement with Dr Eckener's view as to the cause of the accident, but thought that the rent in the gasbag was caused by the first dive. He could think of no way of explaining the course of events spoken of by the witnesses without assuming some substantial loss of gas.

Squadron Leader Wann said that, having examined many theories, the only one that he could really get to fit the facts of the accident was a large gasbag failure forward in the ship, though he could not judge whether the failure took place immediately prior to the dive, or whether it was during the first dive.

Having examined alternative explanations in detail, and excluded, for the reasons given, all but the theory of a substantial loss of gas, the Court would in any case be led to adopt this last named explanation as the inference to be deduced from rejecting other conceivable causes. But when this conclusion is confirmed by the unanimous opinion of the experts, both British and foreign, who, after giving close attention to the evidence assisted the Court with their views, the conclusion suggested by the absence of any other explanation is confirmed and ratified by the judgment of practical men, and acquires a positive validity. For reasons which will be developed in the following paragraphs, the Court has reached the conclusion, that whatever the pre-disposing circumstances may have been, the immediate cause of the disaster was leakage culminating in a substantial loss of gas from one or more of the bags in the fore part of the ship. It will, of course, always be impossible to re-establish every detail, but in the light of the evidence of survivors and experts this general deduction may be regarded as solidly founded.

The definite conclusions at which the Court arrives, and the course of reasoning which leads to their adoption, are set out below.

Was there want of manœuvring space?

Before explaining the theory of the accident which the Court adopts, it is convenient to mention one more possible, though not probable, alternative which has been considered and rejected. It is clearly established that, whatever may have been the cause of the first long dive, the vessel lost much height before she was brought into a horizontal position. Is it possible to assume that the reason why she did not rise again was that she had no more room to manœuvre, and that the navigating officer knew or feared that if her nose was forced up too quickly her tail would strike the ground? To prevent this, the elevators would have to be eased off, or even put down. On this assumption, another downward gust hitting her bow at that moment, when her angular velocity had been checked, might have started a second and final dive.

The circumstance which justifies the rejection of this conjecture is the fact that the cable on the drums showed that the elevators were hard up at the instant when the ship struck the ground, and there could hardly have been time to get them into this position a second time if they had been eased off or even put down a few seconds previously. The elevators must have been put hard up before the end of the first dive, and the probability is that they remained in this position to the end. If this state of affairs is accepted as established, the fact that this elevator action did not succeed in bringing the ship's nose up, proves almost conclusively that it was not want of manœuvring space, but a serious loss of buoyancy, which explains the ultimate disaster.

CONCLUSION AS TO CAUSE

The conclusion reached as to the cause of the disaster is as follows:

THE THREE PHASES

The clearest way in which to explain the theory of the accident which the Court adopts, is to regard the final movements of the R.101 as consisting of three phases. In the first phase she drops her nose and descends, at a noticeably steep angle, for half a minute or thereabouts before, by use of up-elevator, she is brought back to an approximately horizontal position. The second phase then begins and continues for a short time during which, in spite of her utmost efforts, she does not succeed in getting her nose appreciably up but continues horizontal until she suddenly passes into a third phase, when she dives again and strikes the ground almost at once at an angle of at least 15 degrees.

In seeking the explanation of these successive movements, it is best first to direct attention to the second phase. Notwithstanding that the vessel had lost much height during the first phase, if she had been in a normal condition there seems no reason why she should not have pointed her nose up again and regained altitude. From the fact that she failed to do so, it may be argued most conclusively that she was by then crippled beyond recovery, and the inference is that, though momentarily on an even keel, she was descending rapidly to earth. The action of Chief Coxswain Hunt in leaving the control room to warn the crew indicates that, in spite of his great experience, his assistance there was no longer of any use and that those in charge knew there was nothing they could do which would prevent the ship from stranding. And the explanation of this would be provided if she had lost sufficient gas in the fore part of the ship. All that remained was to minimise the impact, and accordingly orders were given to stop the engines and release ballast. If this was the course of events the ship would proceed to put her nose down again, enter upon her second dive and crash.

Now, working back to the first phase, the question is what was the course of events which brought the ship down from say, 1,200 feet, into this first long dive? Inasmuch as the reasoning above set out suggests, and, indeed, practically requires, that at the end of the first dive the vessel had lost a quantity of gas forward, it is natural to assume that this loss of gas had begun before the first phase was entered upon, though it became greater as the vessel descended. If the fore part of the cover had become torn and wind entered the envelope, serious damage to gasbags would be most likely to occur with startling suddenness. The reconstruction of the first phase would therefore be somewhat as follows:

Assume that the vessel had become somewhat heavy and was being buffeted in the wind so that her nose was sometimes above and sometimes below the line of horizontal flight. If she had been raised by a buffet, the elevator would be put down by the coxswain who had just come on duty to check and counteract this movement. The coxswain, not yet having got the "feel" of the ship thoroughly, might put his elevator rather more down than was necessary, or keep it down longer than was exactly right. The vessel's nose would drop. If when her nose is inclined downwards she gets a strong buffet of wind above her nose it will push her nose further down. If she was already heavy from loss of gas—especially if a rent had occurred in a gasbag which involved progressively rapid deflation—the descent is emphasised. The ship is now on her downward track in the first phase. The coxswain will begin to put his elevator up, and in order to get the ship out of her first dive has to put it up harder. None the less, she does not come out of her first dive as rapidly as she should because she is losing more gas all the time. The slowness of her recovery would give significant warning of the crisis.

This gives the explanation of the course of events which is most consistent with the evidence, and at certain points is the only explanation which readily presents itself in accordance with the facts. At other points it is no doubt possible to assume certain variations in the data. For example, the final dive might have been assisted by another buffet of wind, and the exact relation between the angle of the elevator and the amount of gas lost can never be ascertained by any process of reconstruction.

How the vessel began to lose gas can never be definitely ascertained. The weather was exceptionally bad; the gasbags were hard up against padded projections, some of which may have begun to wear the fabric; the bumpiness of the wind and the pitching of the ship would intensify the strain; and earlier flights had indicated the possibility of leakage through chafing, or, if the vessel rolled through an unusually large angle, through intermittent opening of the gas valves. But it seems very probable that the more serious and sudden loss of gas which followed was connected with a specific misfortune such as the ripping of the fore part of the envelope. Something of this sort had happened on a previous occasion [see p. 182] and no amount of care could secure that it would never happen again. If a rip had begun in the fore part of the envelope it would tend to develop into a larger tear which would both check the speed of the R.101 through the air and expose the gasbags to additional strain. This seems the most probable explanation of a further loss of gas in increasing quantity and suddenness. But whatever the precise circumstances may have been, the explanation that the disaster was caused by a substantial loss of gas in very bumpy weather holds the field. This is the unanimous view of all the three members of the Court of Inquiry.

SUBSEQUENT CALCULATIONS BY THE NATIONAL PHYSICAL LABORATORY

After the public sittings of the Court of Inquiry were closed, the National Physical Laboratory was asked to make a series of calculations for the purpose of ascertaining what would be the theoretic movement of the R.101 on various assumptions as to loss of gas, angle of elevator, increasing pressure due to buffets of wind, and so forth. These calculations were assisted by experiments made with a model, some 4 feet long, which precisely reproduced the external form of the R.101, and by measuring the effect upon this model of currents of air of ascertained velocity when the model was put in various positions in a wind-tunnel. The use of models for the working out of theoretical calculations cannot be regarded as taking the place of full-scale experiments or as reproducing in due proportion all the factors in actual operation. Nevertheless, if it could have been said that, on the assumptions which the Court was prepared to make, the track followed by the R.101 immediately before she crashed could not have been such as it in fact was, this would have given ground for mistrusting the conclusions at which the Court was prepared to arrive. These calculations are of great complexity for they involve, in each case, assumptions on a large number of points, and these assumptions may be varied in many ways. The Court is greatly indebted to the officials of the National Physical Laboratory for the investigation which they have carried through, and understands that the full results are likely to be published hereafter, as a contribution to aeronautical science, by the Aeronautical Research Committee. If the factors are not suitably chosen, it appears that the R.101 would be more likely to come to the ground tail first, which it is quite certain she did not do. But by varying the assumptions these calculations indicate that she might follow a course through the air in her last moments which closely approximates to what actually occurred.

Produced for our benefit were diagrams, worked out by the scientists at the National Physical Laboratory, showing what would be the motion of the R.101 under conditions there assumed. On inspection of one of these diagrams, it will be apparent that the plotted course of the ship most closely agrees with the actual sequence of events. It must be clearly understood that each diagram furnished by the National Physical Laboratory has been worked out in accordance with certain assumptions. The National Physical Laboratory is in no respect responsible for the assumptions made; its diagrams merely represent what, according to theoretical calculations, would be the track of the airship if a given set of assumptions were fulfilled. But the significant thing is that on the assumptions indicated above it is demonstrated by the calculation that the R.101 would, in fact, go through a series of movements which closely approximate to those which are proved actually to have occurred.

The conclusion as to the cause of the accident which is above set out is, therefore, not merely the conclusion recommended to the Court by the body of expert evidence which was presented before it, and the conclusion which by its own course of reasoning the Court is prepared to affirm, but it is a conclusion which is shown by the calculations of the National Physical Laboratory to be consistent with the facts and to correspond to assumptions which may reasonably be made.

Before bringing this Report to a close my colleagues and I desire to add certain general observations.

It is clear that if those responsible had been entirely free to choose the time and the weather in which the R.101 should start for the first flight ever undertaken by any airship to India, and if the only considerations governing their choice were considerations of meteorology and of preparation for the voyage, the R.101 would not have started when she did. She was undertaking a novel task in weather conditions worse than any to which she had ever been exposed in flight, and with the prospect of more unfavourable weather after she started. She had never gone through trials which proved by their length and conditions that she was well able to cope with a continuance of unfavourable circumstances. The programme of trials drawn up by her Captain had never been carried through, and the intended length of her last trial was avowedly cut down in order to provide a little more time for preparation before the date which was contemplated for her to start for India. No adequate speed trials had ever been carried through, and indeed this fact was so clearly realised that an official of the Air Ministry urged that she should conduct such speed trials on her voyage to India.

It is impossible to avoid the conclusion that the R.101 would not have started for India on the evening of October 4th if it had not been that reasons of public policy were considered as making it highly desirable for her to do so if she could.

But this is not to say that the authorities, political and technical, who were responsible for, or acquiesced in, this decision, would ever have done so if they had considered that the risk that was being taken was unjustified. The Secretary of State expressly stated that he relied on his experts, and it must never be forgotten that he was entitled to do so. Granted that it must always have been difficult for the distinguished officers at Cardington who sailed in the R.101 to resist the strongly expressed urging of the Secretary of State that a start should be made in time for him to be a passenger and to return for the Imperial Conference, we do not for a moment believe that Colmore or Scott would have accepted, without the strongest protest, the carrying out of a course which would in their judgment expose the whole enterprise to ruin, and risk the lives of men under their orders as well as those of distinguished passengers, to say nothing of threatening to make havoc of future airship policy. Wing-Commander Colmore's conversation with the Secretary of State, of which Mr Reynold's notes are convincing evidence, proves this. The real situation can only be reconstructed by resolutely excluding from the mind the sombre impression produced after the event by the disaster.

We think the atmosphere in which the decision to start was taken must be regarded as made up of several elements.

There was the knowledge possessed by all concerned that the carrying out of this first flight to India was in any case an experiment involving a first experience of conditions which could never be defined and allowed for by theoretic calculations, but must be faced sooner or later by resolute men who believed whole-heartedly in the policy to which it would give expression.

There was the influence exerted upon them by a long period, continually extended by intervening difficulties and disappointments, during which they had been waiting for the day when the flight could be undertaken—a period much greater than had been first anticipated or calculated.

There was the knowledge that further developments in airship policy which might involve expenditure of more public money, the building of more mooring towers, and the construction of a yet bigger airship, the design of which had been already authorised, could not be proceeded with until the existing outlay was seen to be justified by results.

There was the stimulus arising from the fact that the R.100, notwithstanding considerable gas-leakage and a very alarming experience when over the St Lawrence River, had made its journey to Canada and back without serious mishap.

There was the fact, which never should be overlooked by those who now criticise, that more careful calculations had been made with regard to every part of the R.101 than of any previous airship.

And there was the personality of the Secretary of State, whose enthusiastic backing of this part of British air policy must have been from first to last a most comforting support to the Cardington experts, and whose resolution to travel himself in the ship, provided it started at a date which made this possible, gave the cachet of Government support in the most striking way to the enterprise which completely filled the minds and hopes of the officers who perished.

Airship travel is still in its experimental stage. It is for others to determine whether the experiment should be further pursued. Our task has been limited to ascertaining, as far as is possible, the course and cause of a specific event. That event brought to a close, in a few moments of tragedy, an enterprise upon which years of concentrated effort had been directed by the pioneers who perished. The circumstances of their death can only add to the admiration evoked by their skill, courage, and devotion.

JOHN SIMON

J. T. C. MOORE-BRABAZON

C. E. INGLIS

APPENDIX: LIST OF THOSE ON BOARD ON INDIAN FLIGHT

The names of survivors are in italics.

Passengers (6)

Brig.-General The Rt. Hon. Lord Thomson, PC, CBE, DSO (His Majesty's Secretary of State for Air).
Sir W. Sefton Brancker, KCB, AFC (Director of Civil Aviation).
Major P. Bishop, OBE (Chief Inspector, AID).
Squadron Leader W. Palstra (Representing Australian Government).
Squadron Leader O'Neill (Deputy Director of Civil Aviation, India, Representing Indian Government).
Mr James Buck (Valet to Secretary of State for Air).

Officials from the Royal Airship Works (6)

Wing Commander R. B. B. Colmore, OBE (Director of Airship Development).
Major G. H. Scott, CBE, AFC (Assistant Director (Flying) Officer in Charge of Flight).
Lt.-Colonel V. C. Richmond, OBE (Assistant Director (Technical)).
Squadron Leader F. M. Rope (Assistant to Assistant Director (Technical)).
Mr A. Bushfield (Aeronautical Inspection Directorate).
Mr H. J. Leech (Foreman Engineer).

R.101 officers (5)

Flight Lieutenant H. Carmichael Irwin, AFC (Captain).
Squadron Leader E. L. Johnston, OBE, AFC (Navigator).

Lieut. Commander N. G. Atherstone, AFC (1st Officer).
Flying Officer M. H. Steff (2nd Officer).
Mr M. A. Giblett, MSc (Meteorological Officer).

R.101 crew (37)

Chief Coxswain	G. W. Hunt
Asst Coxswains	Flight-Sgt. W. A. Potter
	L. F. Oughton
	C. H. Mason
Riggers	E. G. Rudd
	M. G. Rampton
	H. E. Ford
	C. E. Taylor
	A. W. J. Norcott
	A. J. Richardson
	P. A. Foster
	W. G. Radcliffe
	(died at Beauvais, 6.10.30)
	S. Church
	(died at Beauvais Hospital, 8.10.30)
1st Engineer	W. R. Gent
Charge-hand Engineers	G. W. Short
	S. E. Scott
	T. Key
Engineers	R. Blake
	C. A. Burton
	C. J. Fergusson
	A. C. Hasting
	W. H. King
	M. F. Littlekit
	W. Moule
	A. H. Watkins
	A. V. Bell
	J. H. Binks
	A. J. Cook
	V. Savory
Chief Wireless Operator	S. T. Keeley
Wireless Operators	G. H. Atkins
	F. Elliott
	A. Disley
Chief Steward	A. H. Savidge
Stewards	F. Hodnett
	E. A. Graham
Galley Boy	J. W. Megginson

Total on board, 54.

THE MUNICH AIR CRASH, 1958

THREE REPORTS RELATING TO THE ACCIDENT TO ELIZABETHAN AIRCRAFT G-ALZU AT MUNICH AIRPORT ON 6TH FEBRUARY 1958

∞∞∞∞∞

CONTENTS

On the 6th February 1958, the Manchester United football team were on their way home from Belgrade, having just drawn 3–3 with Red Star to secure a place in the semi-finals of the European Cup. The plane had to make an intermediate landing at Munich airport to refuel, during the course of which the weather deteriorated. Twice the BEA Elizabethan aircraft attempted to take off, only to fail. Shortly after 4 pm, a third attempt was made. But the plane never became airborne; it overshot the runway and smashed into a house, killing 21 people instantly.

This book is the story of the three inquiries which were held subsequently in an attempt to find the causes of the crash, and to determine whether the captain was in any way to blame.

Aircraft accident at Munich Airport, 6 February 1958

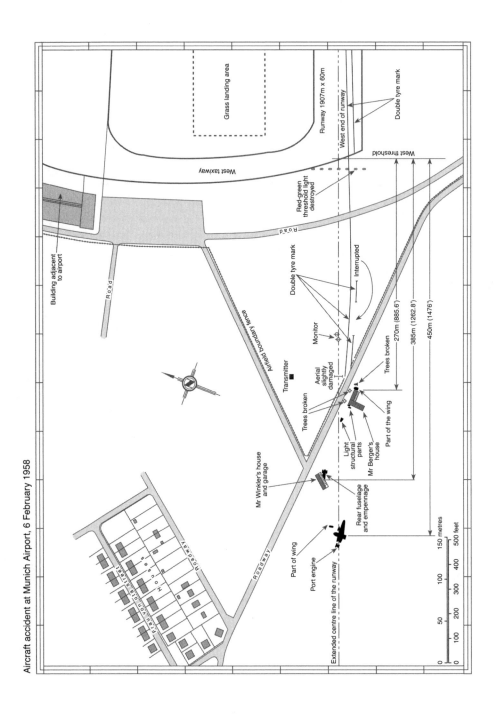

PART I

∘∘⚬◯◯⚬∘∘

GERMAN INQUIRY INTO THE ACCIDENT

CIRCUMSTANCES OF THE ACCIDENT IN BRIEF

The aircraft had carried out a special flight on 3rd February, 1958, from England to Belgrade, making an intermediate landing at Munich-Riem for refuelling purposes. On 6th February it flew back from Belgrade, bound for Manchester. As planned, it again made an intermediate landing at Munich to refuel, landing there at 1417 h. The take-off, at 1603 h, was normal at the outset, but the aircraft did not become airborne. It overshot the boundary of the manoeuvring area and, when outside this area, struck a house and a wooden hut and was severely damaged by the fire which followed. Of the 44 occupants on board, 21 were killed instantly. The others received injuries of a more or less serious nature. Two died later in hospital as a result of their injuries. The house which was struck by the aircraft was badly damaged by fire. The hut was destroyed by fire.

INFORMATION REGARDING THE ACCIDENT

GENERAL

Aircraft

Airspeed AS 57 Ambassador, Works No. 5217. Year of construction: 1952.

Owner and operator: British European Airways Corporation (BEA), Keyline House, South Ruislip, Middlesex.

Maker: Airspeed Ltd./de Havilland.

The Certificate of Registration and Certificate of Airworthiness, issued by the Ministry of Transport and Civil Aviation were valid on the day of the accident.

Crew

THAIN, James, person-in-command, born 7th February, 1921—slightly injured.
Holder of British Airline Transport Pilot's Licence No. 24, 827, which was valid on the day of the accident.

Experience
1941–1946 Royal Air Force.
From October 1946: BEA, as First Officer, and from 1951 as Captain. On 23rd March, 1955, he completed a conversion course on Elizabethan aircraft, since which he had flown 1,722 h on this type of aircraft. His last flight

check was on 14th October, 1957. His total flight time amounted to 7,337 h up to the day of the accident. In the 30 days prior to 2nd February, 1958, he had flown about 26 hours and during the last three days prior to the accident, 7 h.

RAYMENT, Kenneth Gordon, First Officer,* born 11th March, 1921—died in hospital from injuries on 15th March, 1958.
Holder of British Airline Transport Pilot's Licence No. 21,951, which was valid on the day of the accident.

Experience
Began his flying training in 1940 in the Royal Air Force. In 1944 he was seconded to British Overseas Airways Corporation and joined BEA in March, 1946. In March, 1953, he completed a conversion course on Elizabethan aircraft and since then had flown 3,143 h in this type of aircraft. His total flight time up to the day of the accident amounted to 8,463 h. During the 30 days prior to 2nd February, 1958, he had flown barely 6 h and during the last three days prior to the accident, 7 h.

RODGERS, George William, Radio Officer, born 14th September, 1922—slightly injured.

Cabin personnel

CABLE, William Thomas, steward, born 13th February, 1917—killed.
BELLIS, Margaret Ursula, stewardess, born 27th July, 1922—slightly injured.
CHEVERTON, E. Rosemary, stewardess, born 31st May, 1932—slightly injured.

Passengers

38 — including the Manchester United football team and journalists.

Weather conditions

The Munich-Riem meteorological office of the German Meteorological Service issued the following report:

> Time 1504 h—surface wind 300°/8 kt—surface visibility 1.6 NM slight snowfall—8/8 stratus at 600 ft (precipitation ceiling)—QNH 1004.0 mb/29.65 inches—QFE 942.7 mb/27.84 inches—temperature 0°C. Dew point −1.6°C.

On 6th February the following observations (QNY) were made:
> Snow + rain (mixed)   from 0420 to 0650 h

---

* "First Officer": this appears to be an error in the German text. Rayment's rank was Captain and on this flight he was performing the duties of pilot-in-charge.

Rain only	0650 to 1120 h
Snow + rain (mixed)	1120 to 1150 h
Moderate snowfall	1150 to 1550 h
Slight snowfall	1550 to 1850 h
Moderate snowfall	1850 h

The following screen temperatures (height 2 m above ground level) and relative humidities were measured:

At 1400 h	+ 0.1°C	95%
1500 h	0.0°C	96%
1600 h	− 0.2°C	91%
1700 h	− 0.8°C	89%
1800 h	− 0.9°C	91%

Munich–Riem Airport

Geographical location:	48°07′54″ N.
	11°41′57″ E.
Elevation:	528 m = 1732 ft
Density altitude	884 m = 2900 ft
Runway (QFU) 249°	
Length	1908 m, concrete
Width	60 m

Stopway available at end of concrete runway: 250 m (grass surface).

ACCIDENT DETAILS

The aircraft, which landed at Munich at 1417 h, made three attempts, from 1519 h onwards, to continue the flight to England. The crew twice abandoned take-off. The third attempted take-off resulted in the accident. The following is a chronological record of R/T communication between the aircraft and Munich Aerodrome Control, taken from the tape-recording:

h.m.s.

1519:00   Aircraft requested clearance to taxi to runway. This was given immediately, together with the meteorological information required for take-off, in the following words: "Wind 290/8 knots—cleared to Runway 25—QNH 1004".

1521:30   Taxi clearance was repeated with the words: "Cleared to line up and hold". Instructions for the flight (clearance) were then given.

1530:10   Aircraft reported: "I am ready to take-off". Clearance to take-off was given immediately, surface wind being repeated—290/10 knots.

1530:40   Aircraft reported: "Rolling", and at—

| 1531:20 | "We are abandoning the take-off".
| | This message regarding abandoning of take-off was repeated by the aircraft at the request of Air Traffic Control, and permission to taxi back along the runway to the initial position was requested. Permission was given and the aircraft taxied back to the beginning of the runway.
| 1534:40 | The aircraft again reported "Rolling", and at —
| 1535:20 | reported abandoning of second take-off with the words: "We're abandoning this take-off as well". The aircraft continued its run to the end of the runway and then taxied to the terminal building.
| 1559:30 | On request, the aircraft again received clearance to taxi to the runway and was given the surface wind.
| 1602:40 | Aircraft reported that it was ready to take-off and immediately received clearance to take-off.
| 1603:06 | Aircraft again reported: "Rolling".
| 1604:00 | Aircraft called up, but the message was interrupted after the first identification letters had been given.

The following detailed picture is provided by Captain Thain's oral and written reports and by the witnesses' statements, which are thus far in agreement.

On the flight from England to Belgrade the aircraft was flown by Captain Thain. It was agreed that on the return flight Captain Rayment should act as pilot-in-charge. For this reason, Captain Rayment was sitting in the left-hand seat. Captain Thain was sitting on the right. In the aircraft documents, however, Captain Thain was shown as person-in-command for the return flight as well.

Captain Rayment abandoned the first take-off, which had been preceded by an engine run-up. The reason for abandoning take-off was that the boost-pressure readings of both engines showed upward variations, rising 2 or 3 inches above the usual reading of 57.5 inches. The second attempt at take-off followed immediately after the aircraft had taxied back to the beginning of the runway. The engine run-up was not repeated. Captain Thain abandoned the second take-off because the boost-pressure reading (this time on the port engine only) again rose beyond the normal maximum value to 60 inches.

In each case the take-off was abandoned approximately half-way down the runway. After the second attempt the aircraft continued rolling as far as the end of the runway and from there proceeded to the terminal building. The passengers disembarked. The two pilots remained on the flight deck. Mr Black, the BEA Station Engineer, went on board to find out why the aircraft had returned. He then pointed out to the two pilots that the variations in boost pressure were connected with the elevation of Munich Airport. After a short discussion, the pilots decided to make a third attempt at take-off and the passengers were told to board the aircraft again.

Before the fresh attempt to take off, a further engine run-up was carried out. After take-off had begun, the boost-pressure reading of the port engine again fluctuated somewhat, but this ceased after Captain Thain had throttled back slightly for a short time. After he had opened up the throttle fully again, no further fluctuations were observed.

The aircraft never became airborne in the course of the third attempt at take-off. It travelled on over the whole length of the runway and the adjoining grass-covered stopway (250 m). At the end of the stopway it crashed through a wooden fence which marked the aerodrome boundary, cleared a secondary road and struck a house standing on the other side of the road. The left wing was torn off outboard of the engine mounting. Parts of the tail unit were also torn off here. The house caught fire. The aircraft then crashed into a wooden hut standing on a concrete base about 100 m further on, striking it with the right side of the rear section of the fuselage. The fuselage was torn away on a level with the trailing edge of the wing. The hut and the part of the fuselage which was torn away caught fire. The remainder of the aircraft wreckage slid on for a further 70 m.

The Luftfahrt-Bundesamt representative charged with carrying out the preliminary investigation arrived at Munich by air at 2200 h on the day of the accident. The scene of the accident presented the following appearance:

The scene of the accident was guarded by police. All the fires had been extinguished and the fire-fighting vehicles had departed. There was continuous snowfall at a temperature of $-3°C$. The main wreckage had been pulled apart in order to extricate the victims and extinguish the fire. The fuselage lay in a normal attitude, pointing to the right in relation to the direction of flight. On the port side the fuselage had been torn open throughout almost its entire length and towards the rear was increasingly compressed in the vertical plane. The port engine was torn away from its mounting and lay on the ground in a normal attitude, only a few metres from the remains of the wing. It had not somersaulted, and its accessories and their mountings appeared to be still intact. The nose of the aircraft (flight deck) was stove in on the left side. The deformation and the pieces of bark found showed that this indentation was caused by a tree standing beside the house which caught fire. As a result of this indentation the pilot in the left-hand seat had been trapped in his seat.

The right wing was only slightly damaged and the engine attached to it appeared to be completely undamaged. The blades of the two propellers were only slightly deformed. The main undercarriage was down at the time of the impact. It was torn off.

The landing flaps (split flaps) on both sides showed an equal angle of deflection, about $10°$. They were locked in this position. The flight deck was only slightly damaged; but nothing definite could be determined from the position of the switches and levers, since during the extrication of the trapped pilot extensive changes had obviously been effected.

The whole wreckage was covered with a layer of snow about 8 cm thick.

Underneath this there was a rough layer of ice. Details concerning the deposit of snow and ice are dealt with later.

Traces of the powder from the fire-extinguishers showed that minor fires had broken out in the immediate vicinity of the forward fuselage section. There were no discernible effects of fire on the aircraft here.

Next to the house which the aircraft had struck first there were trees which had been snapped off at a height of 3 m or knocked down. From the point at which the aircraft had broken through the fence its tracks could clearly be discerned, extending back to the runway. The double track of the right side of the undercarriage could be followed back to the runway without difficulty. The left-hand wheel-track was interrupted in places. Nowhere was there any nosewheel track to be seen.

From the end of the runway to the fence, in the direction of take-off, the wheel-tracks showed a slight swing to the right. Two days after the accident, when the snow had melted, the tracks were particularly clearly visible. On the runway, about 50 m short of the end, a skid-mark began. It was clearly visible on the concrete and from the strewn sand which the wheels had pushed aside (see plan). This mark showed that at this point all four wheels of the main undercarriage were locked. This skid-mark continued for approximately a further 30 m beyond the end of the runway. It then stopped and there remained the impression of the free-running wheels on the grass surface. The track of the right-hand twin wheels was strongly marked; that of the left-hand wheels was fainter and at times interrupted. The track of the right-hand wheels was uniformly clear throughout the whole length (250 m) of the stopway as far as the point at which the aircraft crashed through the fence. The left-hand wheels had at times left the ground. The skid-mark and wheel-marks were still clearly visible at the time of the survey of the scene of the accident by the Commission of Inquiry on 30th April, 1958.

CAUSES OF THE ACCIDENT

The Commission, with the agreement of all parties to the proceedings, was able to *exclude* at the outset a number of points which might have been taken into account as possible causes of the accident, viz.:

(a) There were no indications that the airport services, the air navigation services (Flugsicherung) or the German Meteorological Service had contributed to the accident through any defects in installations or functioning.

(b) The presence of the house, 9.50 m high, outside the aerodrome, beyond the runway, and of the hut, 3 m high, did not contravene either the German regulations or the Standards and Recommended Practices of the International Civil Aviation Organisation (ICAO). The Commission arrived at this conclusion in agreement with the expert on aerodrome construction, Dr-Ing. Gerlach of Stuttgart.

(c) The members of the crew held valid licences. There were no manifest reasons for doubting their proficiency.

(d) The *aircraft documents* were valid and in order.

(e) It was not possible to establish that there had been any defects in the *technical installations* of the aircraft.

   According to Captain Thain's statement, the engines were working satisfactorily. The fact that take-off had been abandoned twice previously does not give cause for any conclusion to the contrary. The variations in boost pressure which, according to the credible depositions of Captain Thain and of Mr Black, the aircraft engineer, led to the abandoning of the two first take-offs, were occurrences which commonly arise at aerodromes at elevations such as that of Munich, without implying engine trouble. The two engines, which were only slightly damaged, have been subjected to a test run by the manufacturer. The Commission has had before it a test report submitted by BEA. According to this, both engines showed the prescribed take-off power during the test run. No defects were found which could have been a contributory cause of the accident. The Commission saw no reason to doubt the accuracy of the test report.

In addition, there were no indications of defects in the other technical installations.

(f) The loading of the aircraft lay within the permissible limits.

(g) No objection could be raised with regard to the condition of the fuel with which the aircraft had been replenished. Samples of the fuel found in the aircraft after the accident have been tested in England at the instigation of BEA. BEA has notified the Commission of the result of the test. According to this, the chemical composition of the fuel corresponded to the relevant specifications. There are no reasons to doubt the accuracy of this statement.

Since none of these factors comes into consideration as a cause of the accident, and since, on the other hand:

- it had snowed during the afternoon of 6th February, 1958,
- the aerodrome was covered with slush at the time of the accident, and
- the investigations in the evening showed a layer of ice on the wings of the aircraft,

the Commission considered itself primarily concerned with the question of whether the following explained the occurrence of the accident:

(a) Rolling friction caused by snow on the runway,
(b) The effect of slush on the free-running of the wheels, and
(c) Alteration in aerodynamic efficiency caused by wing icing.

The following views were arrived at after detailed investigations and consultations:

Rolling friction caused by slush on the runway

It is obvious that snow or slush on the runway can increase the rolling friction to such an extent that a take-off is impeded or even becomes impossible. The Commission has had before it numerous reports on experiences and accident reports concerning cases where slush has led to difficulties. Twenty-one reports from the collection of the German Institute for Air Traffic Statistics, the ICAO collection, publications of the Flight Safety Foundation, New York, and reports of Trans-Canada Airlines were utilised for purposes of comparison. In addition, BEA submitted, *inter alia*, a number of reports for the study of incidents of this kind. These reports may be summarised to the effect that the extent to which take-off is impeded depends on the thickness of the slush and the type of aircraft. Aircraft with nosewheels are affected to a greater extent than aircraft of tailwheel design, because, in slush, the nosewheel causes an increasing nose-heavy moment as the rolling speed increases and this must be overcome by the pilot by means of considerable force on the elevator control. All experience goes to show, however, that it may be assumed that take-offs can be made with nosewheel aircraft without danger up to a slush-depth of at least 5 cm.

At Munich-Riem on the afternoon of 6th February, 1958, the runway was first of all wet but free of snow and slush. From 1120 h onwards, mixed snow and rainfall set in, at 1150 h moderate snowfall and from 1550 h slight snowfall, temperatures being initially above zero but from 1500 h onwards dropping to 0° and later below 0°. Snowfall continued after the time of the accident. On the basis of the records of the aerodrome meteorological office, Dr H.K. Müller, head of that office and serving on the Commission as meteorological expert, showed convincingly that on the basis of data concerning snowfall and temperature, established from the records, by 1600 h a total of 4–5 cm of snow must have fallen, which, on the runway, would have subsided to form a layer of slush approximately 0.75–1 cm thick. This estimate tallies with the observations of the witness Bartz. As Traffic Manager of the Flughafen München-Riem G.m.b.H. (Munich-Riem Airport Co. Ltd.), he had driven down the runway by motor vehicle during the period of the first two take-off attempts. In order to check upon the conditions on the runway, he had left the vehicle several times to determine the depth of the slush as accurately as possible by inspection. He transmitted the following report on the state of the runway to the air traffic control tower by R/T: "Runway covered with thin layer of slush". In the course of his statements to the Commission he reported, *inter alia*, as follows:

> We stopped in front of the position at which aircraft hold before they are cleared to the runway and there watched the first two attempts by the Elizabethan to take off. After these two attempts we received permission from the control tower to drive on to the runway. We always carry an R/T set with us for this purpose. We then drove on to the runway, left the vehicle and inspected the conditions. We found that the entire runway was covered with slush approximately 0.5–0.75 cm deep. None of it was snow, but it was a jellified, watery mass covering the entire runway. We began from the east and drove off the runway at the west end. We did not merely stop, but got out and established the fact that the tracks left by the aircraft consisted purely of water.

As against this, Captain Wright, who landed at Munich at 1558 h on 6th February, 1958, with the BEA Viscount 802, states that he estimated the slush–depth as 1–1.5 inches in places, but that in parts the runway was merely wet and was free of slush. This estimate must, however, be regarded as unreliable, since, as Captain Wright was judging during the process of landing and was looking from the pilot's seat, he could not have obtained a precise impression of the deposit of slush. Moreover, his report to the control tower on the state of the runway was "Braking action fair". All the other aircraft landing and taking off on scheduled services at the time made the same or similar reports.

According to the reliable statements of the personnel responsible for inspecting the runway, the deposit of slush on the runway cannot have amounted, on an average, to more than 1 cm at the most.

The Commission is convinced that the rolling friction caused by so thin a layer of slush cannot have been a cause of the accident. This would be contradictory to the experiences quoted above. No case is known in which this has caused take-off to be abandoned on concrete runways, let alone caused an accident. The expert, Prof. Dr Schlichting, moreover, has put forward the view that, assuming a rolling-friction coefficient of $\mu = 0.06$, the rolling distance required for a normal take-off may be increased by approximately 110 m at the most. In actual fact, on 6th February, 1958, all scheduled operations at Munich-Riem were conducted without any hitch whatever, before and after the accident—and this is in spite of further snowfall. Sixteen aircraft landed and took off in the course of the afternoon. From the runway-condition reports given by the persons-in-command of these aircraft it may be seen that none of them mentioned any impediment worthy of serious consideration. In addition, Captain Thain, person-in-command of the aircraft involved in the accident, had already pointed out in his first statement on 8th February, 1958, that he was satisfied with the condition of the runway. He attached special importance to this statement and its inclusion in the report. He also expressly stated at the time that he would otherwise not have made a third attempt at take-off. From all this the Commission is convinced that the layer of slush on the runway did not increase the rolling friction to such an extent that the accident could be attributed to this.

Icing of the undercarriage

Nor, in the opinion of the Commission, did the slush have such an effect on the free-running of the wheels as to be a cause of the accident.

The Commission considers that locking of the wheels owing to slush during the process of take-off is entirely ruled out. The wheel-tracks on the runway did indeed show that, at the end of the runway, both sides of the main undercarriage were locked at times. There must, however, have been other reasons for this, as will be explained later. At the V1 speed of 117 knots (= 216 km/h), which was attained and, at times, exceeded, the wheels (tyre diameter 38″ = 96.5 cm) were rotating at about 1200 rpm. Added to this is the fact that, at the narrowest point between the tyres, the twin wheels are 28 cm apart. Given such a considerable gap and such a high speed of rotation and corresponding force, there can be no question of the wheels having become locked owing to the watery slush on the runway accumulating either between the wheels or in the region of the oleo legs [shock absorbers].

From the outset, the possibility that the snow could have become caught up and accumulated in the undercarriage of the aircraft during the take-off run to such an extent that the wheels would have been braked to a considerable degree also appeared to the Commission extremely remote, since not a single indication of this came to light. The Commission nevertheless went into this question with special care, since Captain Thain did not consider it out of the question that this might provide an explanation of the accident. He too, however, was unable to put forward any actual facts which might have indicated any such braking action on the undercarriage in the case of the accident at Munich. He merely quoted parallel instances. The Commission has studied occurrences of this kind. In addition, Captain Key, in person, gave evidence before the Commission regarding an incident of this nature which took place on 14th January, 1955, at Cologne-Wahn. He made, in particular, the following statements:

> We taxied out in darkness in order to take off for Berlin. We had been informed that the runway was in a serviceable condition. It had snowed practically all night, but the snow had turned to rain and the ground was rather slushy. We began the take-off and after a few seconds it was evident that the aircraft was not accelerating to the extent that it should have done. The engine readings were normal, but before I reached V1 I decided to abandon take-off. A few hundred yards short of the end of the runway we came to a stop, and the runway is, as you know, exceptionally long.
>
> During the take-off run I had to apply extraordinarily high engine power in order to keep the aircraft rolling. During inspection after disembarking I found that the undercarriage was tightly packed with frozen snow which was effectively braking both the main wheels and the nosewheel.
>
> I myself have no doubt that had we continued take-off until reaching V1 we would never have become airborne, even if both engines had continued to function normally. Nor would we have come to a standstill while still on the runway.
>
> I further recall that Captain Brown had a similar experience in Düsseldorf the same day. In his case, take-off was continued and the aircraft left the ground at a very late stage. I believe that owing to the quantity of snow which had collected in the wheel-well the nosewheel did not retract properly.

Even if it is now no longer possible to clarify all the circumstances of this special case, the possibility, at any rate, cannot be excluded that, with the Elizabethan, in exceptional circumstances, snow and ice may pack the undercarriage and impair the smoothness of take-off when the manoeuvring area is covered with wet snow and temperatures around 0°C prevail. There can be no doubt, however, that many very unusual factors would have to coincide in order to produce such an effect. All the time and all over the world aircraft are taking off and landing with the same or a similar type of undercarriage in snow and meteorological conditions such as prevailed at Munich on 6th February, 1958, without the occurrence of difficulties such as Captain Key describes. All the facts established argue against the Munich incident's presenting a parallel case. The BEA Viscount 802 which landed from Vienna on the same day at 1558 h and took off again at 1721 h (i.e. after the accident to the Elizabethan), under still more unfavourable conditions, had an undercarriage similar to that of the aircraft involved in the accident. The smaller gap between the twin wheels would make this undercarriage, if anything, appear still more vulnerable to becoming clogged with snow than the undercarriage of the Elizabethan. The take-off nevertheless took place without any difficulties whatever. In the Cologne incident Captain Key noticed at an early stage that the aircraft failed to accelerate—possibly because snow which had previously collected while the aircraft was temporarily stationary had frozen. Captain Thain, on the other hand, stated expressly that until just before the end of the runway he had had the impression of a normal take-off. The aircraft did indeed attain V1 without difficulty (as will be shown in greater detail below). In Cologne, dry snow assumed a damp condition owing to rising temperatures, so that probably a relatively firm "sticky" snow was present. At Munich, on the other hand, rain had turned to snow and the snow was still so wet that a watery track remained where the wheels of the aircraft had travelled. The witness Bartz stated this categorically. Such a liquid slush would by no means have had the necessary density and adhesiveness to pack the undercarriage to such an extent as Captain Key describes. Braking of the undercarriage main wheels by ice would probably have left traces in the rubber. On the only tyre still available, however, which has been examined by the makers and which the Commission inspected during the proceedings in Munich, no trace whatever of such damage was discernible. Finally, prior to the beginning of the third attempted take-off, the accumulation of slush or ice in the undercarriage must have been somehow visible. Captain Key, describing the Cologne incident, states that his undercarriage was packed with a wide "apron" of snow and ice up to the wings. In the case in point, at Munich, the aircraft had already made two attempts to take off. It had covered the distance from the terminal building to the runway and back and had twice travelled over the greater part of the runway. There was no basic change in the runway conditions between the first, second and third attempted take-offs. Nevertheless there was nothing discernible on the undercarriage prior to the third take-off. Even if none of the other witnesses saw anything of it, Mr Black, the Station Engineer, who, according to his own statement, walked round the aircraft again, shortly before the third take-off, looking for possible defects, would at any rate have been bound to have noticed anything. But, as he stated in reply to express questioning, he had noticed nothing. A photograph placed at the disposal of the Commission, taken before the third attempted take-off, clearly showed that there were no traces whatever of any ice or snow packing. Thus, besides general experience and probability, so many important points argue against the assumption that the undercarriage was braked by slush that, in the opinion of the Commission, this cannot have constituted the cause of the accident.

Wing icing

It remained for the Commission to investigate whether there was a deposit of ice on the wings of the aircraft at the time of the attempted take-off and whether such a deposit led to the inability of the aircraft to take off within the take-off area available and constituted the cause of the accident.

At the outset, the fact that there was indeed a deposit of ice on the wings of the aircraft at the time of the attempted take-off did not appear to have been established with sufficient certainty, because exact observations concerning ice accretion were not made until 2200 h on the day of the accident, i.e. not until six hours after the accident, and because snow had continued to fall steadily after the accident until 2200 h. The Commission, however, came to the conclusion that the wings were iced up at the time of the attempted take-off.

At 2200 h on 6th February, the scene of the accident presented the following picture:

The wrecked aircraft, which lay 70 m from the centre of the fire and to windward of the latter, was covered with a layer of snow 8 cm deep. This was powdery snow which could be pushed or blown off from the surface of the wings without difficulty. Underneath there was a very rough layer of ice. This had not blended with the snow lying on top. Its thickness amounted to about 5 mm. From numerous spot-checks it must be concluded that the entire surface was covered with this layer of ice and that it was interrupted only in the region of the two engines over the width of the propeller slipstream. These facts are based on the reports of the Chief Inspector of Accidents of the Luftfahrt-Bundesamt, charged with the preliminary investigation, and the statements of the witnesses Graf zu Castell and Dipl.-Ing. Goetz, which are in agreement. These two witnesses proceeded at once to the scene of the accident with the Chief Inspector, after he had landed at Munich at 2200 h, and all arrived at the same results after investigations undertaken independently of one another. Their reports were not contradicted by the BEA representative who made a partial inspection of the crashed aircraft on the same evening.

Purely on the basis of calculation, this deposit of ice, the thickness of which was established as 5 mm, could have formed from the wet snow which had fallen in Munich during the period between the landing of the aircraft and the accident. Dr H.K. Müller, the meteorological expert, on the basis of the records of the aerodrome meteorological office, stated that at 1400 h in Munich there was a thin layer of snow not yet of measurable dimensions, but that a further 4–5 cm of snow fell prior to the time of the accident. In his opinion it is, moreover, not possible to say exactly what thickness will remain when a layer of snow has turned into ice. We may, however, regard it as possible that the thickness of the ice in such a case amounts to about one-seventh to one-tenth of the layer of snow from which it has formed. Thus we may at any rate proceed from the assumption that the observations regarding the ice deposit at 2200 h, on the one hand, and regarding the snowfall between 1400 and 1600 h, on the other, are not contradictory.

In point of fact, the amount of precipitation which, by calculation, corresponds to the ice deposit noted had collected on the wing of the crashed aircraft prior to take-off. This is borne out by the fact that during the stay in Munich the deposit had not been cleared from the wings of the aircraft, in spite of the snowfall, and that the snow must consequently have remained lying there. The snow which fell directly after the aircraft landed may, indeed, partly have run off the wings at first, as observed by the witnesses Wiggers and Black during refuelling. Snow which had fallen on the wings and perhaps melted at the outset must, however, very soon have begun to cling.

The aircraft flew from Belgrade to Munich at altitudes of 21,000–25,000 ft at an air temperature of −21°C to −25°C. From this it must be concluded that the outer skin of the wings was thus severely supercooled. The observation of the witness Wiggers indicates that snow began to cling at an early stage; during refuelling he had already noticed, from the wing tips, the building-up of a layer of snow. Consequently, it is to be assumed that well before the first attempted take-off at 1519 h the wings were already covered with snow and that later the layer which led to icing had formed, owing to the further snowfall. In the case of all the other aircraft which took off that afternoon snow had, in fact, collected on the wings and in each case it had been removed by personnel of the air transport undertakings. These *a posteriori* conclusions were clearly confirmed by the witnesses Schombel and Wöllner, who were twice heard by the Commission in order to give BEA the opportunity to put forward any protests. When the aircraft taxied out to the third attempted take-off both these witnesses had been watching it for some time from rooms fairly high up in the terminal building and at a distance which permitted making reliable observations. The witnesses stated that they saw the wings, outboard of the engines, covered with a thick, unbroken layer of wet snow. In reply to the suggestion that they might have been deceived on account of the colour of the wing, they stated definitely that they were quite certain about the layer of snow. There is no reason at all to doubt the credibility of their statements. The Commission held the witness Schombel to be a particularly valuable and reliable witness as regards the observation concerned, because he had been employed at Hamburg-Fuhlsbüttel Airport for some time and had been engaged on the removal of ice from aircraft. His observations are therefore based on knowledge of a highly expert nature. The Commission is therefore convinced that complete confidence can be placed in his depositions and that of the witness Wöllner, which is in agreement with them.

The depositions of Captain Thain and Station Engineer Black regarding this question do not detract from the conclusive nature of the evidence given by these witnesses. Captain Thain did indeed declare that he had observed no layer of snow on the wings but saw only melted snow running off the trailing edge of the wings. He was also in agreement with Captain Rayment that nothing need be done about the snow. The pilots, however, as must be inferred from the evidence of Captain Thain, had at no time such a view over the wing as would have permitted them to judge the condition of the upper surfaces of the wings reliably. Prior to re-embarkation they went direct from the terminal building to the aircraft and then never left it until the accident occurred. The upper surfaces of the wings, however, were not visible, either from that part of the apron over which they walked or from the flight deck, as the aircraft is a high-wing monoplane. From the pilot's seat, only the forward curve of the wing profile is visible. From outside the aircraft the wing surfaces cannot be seen at all from the front unless one stands in a raised position and from the rear they can be seen only from quite a distance. It is therefore entirely possible that the crew, on their way to the aircraft, saw nothing of the layer of snow. Mr Black can therefore also have seen nothing when he walked round the aircraft again and inspected it thoroughly before it taxied away to make the third attempted take-off. Captain Thain's observation about melted snow running off the trailing edges of the wings is explained simply by the fact that engine gases are exhausted through two openings over the wing; the wing surfaces became heated at this point and it was there that the snow melted. Thus, from this angle, also, no doubts arise concerning the reliability of the statement that a considerable layer of snow had indeed formed on the wings of the aircraft during its stop at Munich. The question as to the time when this layer of snow turned into ice is not a decisive factor, since Prof. Dr Schlichting, the expert, when questioned, emphasised more than once that this is of no noteworthy importance to the aerodynamic assessment of the take-off and flying qualities of the aircraft. The freezing-up of the layer of slush by the time of the accident can, however, be explained. It is true that in the case of the first attempted take-off at 1519 h, at a temperature of approximately 0°, the humidity of the air still amounted to 96%. Cooling by evaporation will thus still have been slight at this juncture. Only a film of ice will have formed on the cooled wing, under the layer of snow observed. When the last attempted take-off was initiated, however, the air temperature was already −0.2°C and the humidity of the air was 91%. Thus there existed conditions which point to the fact that by the time the aircraft taxied out for the third attempted take-off and during the first phase of take-off, the cooling by evaporation had become so highly effective that the wet snowy mixture turned into the rough sheet of ice which was observed in the late evening of the same day.

Thus, even if all circumstances indicate that the ice accretion observed at 2200 h did indeed arise from the layer of slush on the wing observed by the witnesses, the Commission had nevertheless still to consider the question of (a) whether it might not have originated wholly or partly from the precipitation which fell after the accident and, for this reason, (b) whether it had indeed been fully established that icing was a cause of the accident. It is true that the snow falling after the accident at temperatures of −0.2° (1600 h) to −3°C

(2200 h) was dry. Thus it could not have turned directly into ice. The question to be investigated, however, was whether, as a result of the fires caused by the accident, the snow (dry, in itself) had melted whilst still in the air or on falling on wings possibly heated by the fires to above 0° and had only solidified into ice when the fires were extinguished.

The idea that the wings were perhaps warmed by the heat still remaining from the engines or by the fuel in the wing tanks was suggested during the proceedings. These and similar theories regarding subsequent ice formation all fail, however, to stand up to closer investigation. Arguing against the theory of subsequent ice formation is the fact that with such a process of melting and refreezing the snow would probably have become more firmly blended with the ice-layer proper in the transitional zone. According to the report of the Inspector making the investigation and the statements (agreeing with this report) of the witnesses Graf zu Castell and Goetz, the lack of cohesion between the ice layer and the powdery snow on top was, however, extraordinarily marked. The snow could be "blown away", whereupon a sheet of ice immediately came to light. The fires which occurred would not have been sufficient to melt the snow in the air or on the wings. The minor outbreaks of fire in the immediate vicinity of the aircraft were soon extinguished and do not come into consideration as sources of heat. The hut, on the other hand, burned for a longer time, viz., to about 1700 h, according to the report of the Munich Airport Administration. This centre of fire, which was certainly considerable, was situated, however, 70 m from the wreckage. Added to this is the fact that the wind was blowing away from the wreckage, in the opposite direction. In these circumstances it is extremely improbable that the radiant heat from any of the fires breaking out in the region of the aircraft wreckage had any effect on the snow. The remaining engine heat cannot have affected the entire wing to such an extent; it cannot have radiated thus far. Finally, it also appears out of the question that the fuel with which the aircraft had been replenished could have warmed up the whole wing again after the accident. Since it is established without a doubt from the statements by the witnesses Schombel and Wöllner that the fuel failed to cause the snow which fell prior to the accident to melt on the wings, it is quite out of the question that this should have happened after a further drop in outside temperatures and one-and-a-half hours after refuelling. Furthermore, the fuel remaining in the aircraft prior to refuelling, after a flight at high altitudes, must have had a very low temperature. According to information from the firm which supplied the fuel, the temperature of the fuel taken on was not above about 0°C, because the tanker was parked in the open.

Even if all these points are not considered to be finally convincing, however, there nevertheless remains as a decisive argument against any theories regarding subsequent ice formation the fact that, on the parts of the wing above the two engine nacelles,* there was no ice deposit on the evening of

* Nacelles are external structures on an aeroplane, used to contain objects such as engines and fuel tanks.

the accident and no layer of snow before the accident, whereas elsewhere the wing upper surfaces were covered with snow or ice before and after the accident. Thus to this extent the observations of the state of the wings before and after the accident are in agreement. The parts of the wing above the engines would, however, have been iced up in the same way as the other parts of the upper surfaces had the ice actually originated from the precipitation which fell after 1600 h, for there is no way of explaining why a subsequent snow-fall over the engine nacelles should have been different from that on the other parts of the wing. Engine heat continuing to exert an effect on the wing upper surfaces for a while after the accident could at any rate not entirely have prevented subsequent ice formation at these points. With the drop in temperature after 1600 h, the engine heat would not have lasted as long as would be necessary for the formation of an ice layer 5 mm thick. Above all, during the accident the port engine broke away from its mounting as a single unit and lay 5 m away from the wrecked aircraft, so that on this side there was no longer any heat-conserving element. Thus, in the case of subsequent ice formation the remains of the port wing ought, in any case, to have been uniformly iced up throughout, outboard and inboard of the engine. But this was not the case. Consequently, the engine zones on both sides could only have been cleared by the engine heat, by the exhaust gases led over the upper wing surface and by the propeller slipstream before the accident. Hence the deposit of ice cannot have originated as a result of precipitation which did not fall until after the accident.

The Commission is convinced that the deposit of ice on the wings which, on the basis of all the foregoing, was undoubtedly present during attempted take-off, prevented the aircraft from becoming airborne at any time. The fact that, under certain circumstances, wing icing can render an aircraft unable to fly, or at any rate considerably impair its take-off qualities, is well known in aviation. Although this would scarcely have required special proof, the Commission asked Dr-Ing. Pleines, the expert on air traffic statistics, to put forward a number of parallel cases. These do not, indeed, prove that such must have been the case at Munich on 6th February, 1958, but they do clearly illustrate the dangers of wing icing in principle. Other reports on similar incidents have also been referred to. In particular, the reports by the Flight Safety Foundation, New York (Safety Suggestions), Trans-Canada Airlines, and the Department of National Defence, Ottawa, relating to ice accretion on aircraft on the ground, provide appropriate comparisons. Finally, the Commission of Inquiry has had before it a number of instructions providing for de-icing in cases where the wings of aircraft on the ground are covered by snow, ice or hoar frost (see p. 277). These would, without doubt, not have been issued (and, in particular, would not have been so emphatic) had it not been established that any accretion on the wings entails a risk of considerably impairing the flying characteristics of any aircraft.

In order to check the general principle (founded on experience) that wing icing is highly detrimental to the flying qualities of aircraft, the

Commission arranged for a scientific investigation relating to the crashed aircraft to be conducted. Prof. Dr Schlichting, the Director of the Institute of Flow Mechanics at the Technical University, Brunswick, was commissioned to undertake this investigation. Prof. Dr Schlichting is well known to the Commission as a recognised authority on aerodynamics. In compiling his report he has taken into account all available scientific material. The BEA representatives, assisted by an aerodynamics expert employed by the manufacturer, de Havilland, were afforded the opportunity of submitting to Prof. Dr Schlichting the material which they considered necessary for compiling the report, as well as the technical and aerodynamic data relating to the crashed aircraft, and of having a discussion with him at a joint meeting on 20th May, 1958, in Brunswick. The Commission also made available to Prof. Dr Schlichting the aerodynamic calculations put forward orally by a BEA representative on 1st May, 1958, when the Professor was absent. All the BEA material referred to was taken into consideration when the report was being compiled.

On the basis of the report the Commission arrived at the following conclusions:

As the main starting point it takes, on the one hand, the fact that, even assuming an extremely high rolling-friction coefficient (due to slush) of $\mu = 0.10$, the aircraft would have been bound to become airborne after a rolling-distance of 1,080 m at the latest. On the other hand, given this intensity of rolling friction, the expert's calculations show that with wing icing of about 5 mm (the presence of which has been established) and a roughness height (based on this) of about 3 mm, the aircraft could not have attained the lift coefficient required for unsticking within a rolling distance of less than about 2,270 m (i.e. at a point outside the aerodrome). There is, however, much to suggest that the rolling-friction coefficient was lower. Even if we proceed from the relatively low rolling-friction coefficient of $\mu = 0.06$, however, the iced-up aircraft could still not have left the ground within a rolling distance of 1,900 m (i.e. not before the end of the runway).

There may be some uncertainty in the exact determination of the thickness and roughness of the ice and in the determination of the rolling-friction coefficient. The Commission has been assured by the Inspector making the investigation, however, that a conservative estimate of ice thickness and roughness has intentionally been given. The rolling-friction coefficient had to be set higher rather than lower. Consequently, everything suggests that owing to icing there was no question of the aircraft's unsticking before the end of the runway, even had it still been accelerating unhindered at this juncture. At this juncture, however, for other reasons (of which more will be said below), the aircraft was no longer accelerating. General flying experience and aerodynamic calculations are thus in agreement about the fact that an aircraft with such a degree of ice accretion as the aircraft involved in the accident would not, in the conditions obtaining at Munich on 6th February, be capable of taking off and flying within the take-off area available.

The increase, owing to icing, in the required take-off distance is due to two factors: the decrease in the maximum lift coefficient, as a result of which the necessary unstick speed was increased, and the rise in profile drag which reduced acceleration. The expert calculates the reduction in acceleration thus: the V1 speed of 117 knots was attained at about 1,680 m, given a rolling-friction coefficient of 0.10, or at about 1,400 m, given a rolling-friction coefficient of 0.06, assuming a roughness of 3 mm. This theoretical calculation corresponds approximately with the facts actually established, for in his description of the process of take-off Captain Thain stated that the aircraft had accelerated normally. He could not indicate either the point along the runway at which he had made his observation regarding the decrease in the speed reading or the point at which V1 was attained. Judging from the sequence of his whole account, however, the drop in speed can only have set in towards the end of the runway. Captain Thain stated that during the process of take-off he at first only watched the instruments and did not look out of the aircraft. Only when he perceived a drop in speed did he look out. He then saw that they were in alarming proximity to the aerodrome boundary. Captain Rayment's exclamation, made at about the same moment, "We won't make it", would naturally only have been made when they were already in a zone of the runway where catastrophe was seen to be unavoidable. There is therefore much to suggest that the drop in speed occurred approximately at or beyond the 1,800 m mark.

According to Captain Thain's account, the aircraft first attained V1, maintained, for a while, the speed it had reached, and only then lost speed appreciably. A certain interval must therefore have elapsed between the attaining of V1 and the drop in speed. At 117 knots a rolling distance of about 400 m is covered in 6.5 seconds and a rolling distance of about 200 m in 3.2 seconds. The interval during which V1 was maintained would probably have lain within these values. If we proceed from this, and assuming that the drop in speed occurred within the zone beyond the 1800 m mark, then it is highly probable that V1 was indeed attained between 1400 m and 1600 m, as the expert has calculated. Captain Thain's statements thus provide a certain confirmation of the expert's calculations, as far as there can be any question of precise confirmation, considering the element of uncertainty in Captain Thain's reconstruction of what happened. Under these circumstances the Commission considers it amply certain that V1 was attained between 1400 m and 1600 m and was maintained or exceeded at any rate to within the region of the 1800 m mark.

Nevertheless, although the nose was pulled up and the emergency tail bumper was at times on the ground, the aircraft could not be raised off the ground. For this, however, there is no explanation other than that given by the expert, viz., that owing to icing and the resultant decrease in lift coefficient, an unstick speed considerably higher than the normal one was required, and the fact that V1 was not attained until a rolling distance of about 1400 m had been covered could be attributed only to the increase in profile drag, which, likewise, could be accounted for only by icing. Thus icing was a cause of the accident.

In spite of the foregoing facts, the Commission feels unable to declare with complete certainty that icing was the sole cause of the accident, owing to the fact that Captain Thain's observation regarding the drop in speed towards the end of the runway can neither be refuted nor be explained with complete certainty. There may indeed be some uncertainty about the objective accuracy of the observation itself, since it is a generally acknowledged fact, based on experience, that, for subjective reasons, statements by witnesses are subject to error precisely when it is a question of giving an account of what happened in an unnerving catastrophe. On the other hand, it is entirely possible that the drop in speed of which Captain Thain spoke so definitely did indeed occur. There is then the further doubt as to where it occurred and why it happened. There is much to suggest that the aircraft slowed down at the point on the runway at which the tracks of the locked wheels were visible after the accident. The loss of speed reported by Captain Thain would then have the perfectly natural explanation that, in the final section of the runway, Captain Rayment saw disaster approaching and braked the landing wheels sharply. All four landing wheels were locked, as could still clearly be seen during the Commission's inspection in Munich. A simultaneous locking of all the wheels, however, can hardly have occurred except as a result of braking. But if this were the case it is not out of the question that a misunderstanding between the two pilots played a part at this juncture, for, whereas Captain Rayment (probably) applied the brakes, Captain Thain, in the hope of averting the catastrophe at the last moment, did exactly the opposite, viz. (as he stated during interrogation), pushed the throttle lever forward as far as possible. Thus the measures taken by the crew to avert the accident or make it less serious cancelled each other out. Whether it would have made any difference to the accident or the severity thereof if either the brakes had been applied and the throttle closed or the brakes had not been applied and the aircraft had rolled on beyond the end of the aerodrome at full throttle cannot be stated with certainty. It is neither entirely out of the question that, if the aircraft had progressed unimpeded it would, before reaching the scene of the accident, have come within the limits of the required unstick speed (increased by icing), nor is it a sheer improbability that braking and closing of the throttle would have lessened the impact of the aircraft with the house and hut and could have made the results of the accident less serious. If the pilots did act in opposition in the manner outlined above, the Commission would regard this less as a pilot error (pardonable in these circumstances) than as faulty division of responsibility between pilot-in-charge and second pilot.

As stated, it is not certain what actually happened at the point where the skid-mark was made on the runway. Even if we do not doubt that the brakes were applied, there remains the question of whether the drop in speed and the formation of the skid-mark really occurred at one and the same spot or whether the speed decreased just before, for other reasons. Captain Thain's statement (the only source of information that can be considered) did not clarify this, because he noticed no braking. Aerodynamic explanations for such a loss of speed have been discussed with the experts. It is not out of the question that the pilot, after attaining V1, increased the angle of attack of the aircraft in order to initiate the unstick, with the result that the flow conditions over the iced-up wing changed and drag consequently increased. This, however, could not be proved by calculation. It is also possible that one of the pilots lowered the flaps just before the end of the runway; for, according to Captain Thain's definite statement, the aircraft was taking off without flaps (as prescribed by BEA for Munich-Riem Airport). On the other hand, at the scene of the accident the flaps on both sides were found to be at take-off setting. Their design does not preclude the possibility that, when the accident occurred, the flaps fell out of their own accord to an equal angle on either side, but this is not very probable. Flap-deflection, however, would also fail to account with sufficient certainty for a drop in speed of more than 10 knots. No indication of any other influences could be found.

After all this there still remains an element of uncertainty in the reconstruction of the course of the accident. This makes it appear not entirely out of the question that towards the end of the fatal take-off there arose, in addition to wing icing, a further circumstance which was a contributory cause of the accident. But this does not rule out icing as the cause of the accident, for, even if a further circumstance affected the course of the accident in some way within a zone of the runway lying beyond about the 1800 m mark, this does not alter the fact that the aircraft would normally have become airborne long before this and that the accident would not have occurred if the aircraft had not been iced up.

SUMMARY

The results of the Inquiry into the accident may thus be summarised as follows:

During the stop of almost two hours at Munich, a rough layer of ice formed on the upper surface of the wings as a result of snowfall. This layer of ice considerably impaired the aerodynamic efficiency of the aircraft, had a detrimental effect on the acceleration of the aircraft during the take-off process and increased the required unstick-speed. Thus, under the conditions obtaining at the time of take-off, the aircraft was not able to attain this speed within the rolling distance available.

The decisive cause of the accident lay in this.

It is not out of the question that, in the final phase of the take-off process, further causes may also have had an effect on the accident.

Brunswick   STIMPEL

31st January, 1959   REICHEL

BOCK

UTTER

STATEMENT BY CAPTAIN J. THAIN

On the 6th February, I was in command of Elizabethan aircraft G-ALZU which was chartered to fly from Belgrade to Manchester via Munich, and after landing at Munich, the engines were switched off at 13.11Z.

I proceeded to the Met. Office with Captain Rayment and Radio Officer Rodgers. It was snowing and the tarmac was covered with puddles of water and slush to a depth of about one inch. After the Met. briefing Captain Rayment and I completed the Flight Plan and extracted from the Operations Manual the V1 and V2 speeds for the flight. We left the Met. Office and I walked to the Air Traffic Control Office to file a Flight Plan. Captain Rayment did not accompany me, I believe he went to the BEA Office. Outside the Air Traffic Control Office I was met by Captain Rayment, and after taking the Operations Manual from me we discussed the snow which had fallen on the wings of the aircraft. He told me that he had looked at the wings of the aircraft and in his opinion it was not necessary to have them swept. I agreed with him and then left to sign the ship's papers in the BEA Office whilst he walked to the aircraft. After signing the papers I departed for the aircraft, and upon approaching it, studied the snowfall on the starboard wing. A thin film had formed but was not easily identified because it had thawed where it had fallen on the ribs of the aircraft wing, and I saw the thawed snow running off the trailing edge of the wing.

After the passengers had boarded the aircraft, the doors were closed, engines started, and the chocks were removed at 14.19Z.

Captain Rayment was occupying the left-hand seat and manipulating the flying controls, and I was sitting in the right-hand seat performing the duties of co-pilot—as we had done on the previous sector from Belgrade.

When all the cockpit checks had been completed and we had received clearance to take off, Captain Rayment opened the throttles and we started to roll down the runway. I followed the advancing throttles with my left hand, and when they reached the maximum position I lightly tapped his hand which he removed and then I held my hand behind the levers. Captain Rayment called "Full Power" and I confirmed saying "Full Power" then, monitoring the temperatures and pressures and warning lights, called "Temperatures and pressures OK, Warning Lights out". We continued to accelerate down the runway and when we achieved 90 knots I called "90", and then "100" when we reached 100 knots. At this point I heard an uneven note in the engine noise and glancing at the boost pressures I was just able to see both indicators fluctuating before Captain Rayment retarded the throttle levers. He called "Abandon take-off" and I immediately gripped the control column and assisted him in holding it fully forward whilst he applied the brakes. We slowed down and obtained permission to back-track in order to make another attempt to take off. Before we reached the take-off point Captain Rayment said he wished to open the throttles a little before releasing the brakes and from that point he would open the throttles more slowly than he had done on the first attempt. We had both recognised that there had been boost surging which might have occurred through too fast a movement of the throttle levers. A power check was not considered necessary and after positioning the aircraft for the take-off, clearance was obtained to take off.

Captain Rayment opened the throttles to about 28″ of boost, released the brakes and we started to roll forward. He continued to open the throttles slowly but positively, and, with my left hand behind the levers I followed this movement until the levers were in the fully open position. I then tapped his hand which he removed. The starboard engine boost pressure was steady at $57\frac{1}{2}$″, but the port pressure rapidly increased beyond the maximum figure of 60″. I believe I said "The port is off the clock" and then pulled both throttle levers back to the closed position. We continued to roll towards the end of the runway and I decided to return to the tarmac to consult the engineer. Whilst we were taxi-ing down the runway I completed the cockpit checks and when we were clear of the runway Captain Rayment asked me to take over the taxi-ing whilst he informed the passengers on the public address system the reasons for our return to the tarmac. I agreed and took over the controls. I recall that I could not see any other tyre marks in the snow and also that it was not possible to identify the edge of the perimeter track in between the markers. Captain Rayment then took over again and we parked the aircraft on the tarmac.

Engineer Black boarded the aircraft and inquired the reason for our return. I told him that we had abandoned two take-offs because of boost surging and he reminded us of the fact that surging had been a frequent occurrence at Munich in the past due to the height of the airfield. He continued that the technique adopted was to control the surge by manipulating the throttle lever. I acknowledged this and said that whilst I was aware of this remedy, if the movement of the throttle lever became out of synchronisation with the surge to any extent, it could develop into a snaking movement of the aircraft which with snow on the runway was undesirable. This aspect was discussed with Captain Rayment and recalling that we had found the landing run and nosewheel steering satisfactory on landing from Belgrade I decided to make a third attempt. Captain Rayment then asked Mr Black if there was anything that could be checked and he said nothing apart from a complete re-tune of the engines. I confirmed my intention to depart and at that point learnt that the passengers had been off-loaded. I asked the engineer to tell the Traffic Officer to board the passengers as quickly as possible. Whilst we were waiting for this to be done I talked to Captain Rayment about the snow. We looked at the wings and agreed that we had lost the thin film which we had observed before our initial departure and again considered that there was no necessity to have the wings swept. By this time the passengers had boarded the aircraft but one was missing and after about five minutes he was found and then we departed.

The visibility had improved and there was less snow falling. We carried out a complete power check at the take-off point, and when the cockpit checks were completed I told Captain Rayment that I would control the throttles if surging was experienced on this run. Clearance was given to take off and Captain Rayment opened the throttles to about 28″ with the brakes on. The readings were quite steady, he released the brakes and we started to roll forward. He continued to open the throttles and with my left hand I followed this movement until the levers were in the fully open position. I tapped his hand which he removed and then Captain Rayment called "Full power" and having checked the instrument readings I replied "Full power". I checked the temperatures, pressures and warning lights and then called "Temperatures and pressures OK, warning lights out". At about 85 knots the port boost started to surge, I called "Port surging slightly" and pulled the port throttle lever back until the surging was arrested (the reading was about 54″) and then advanced the lever again until it was fully open and indicating $57\frac{1}{2}″$. The starboard indication had remained at $57\frac{1}{2}″$ throughout. I called "Full power again" and glanced at the temperatures and pressures. I then looked at the Air Speed Indicator, the speed was 105 knots and I called "105". The boost remained constant at $57\frac{1}{2}″$. The needle of the ASI was flickering slightly and when it indicated 117 knots I called "V1" and waited for a positive indication of more speed. Captain Rayment was adjusting the trim of the aircraft. (Up to this point, whilst I had not looked out of the cockpit, I had not experienced any feeling that the acceleration had been other than normal under the circumstances.) The needle hovered at 117 knots and then dropped 4 or 5 knots. I was conscious of a lack of acceleration: the needle dropped further to about 105 knots and hovered at this reading. Suddenly, Captain Rayment called out "Christ, we won't make it!" I looked up for the first time and saw a house and a tree. All this time my left hand had been behind the throttle levers; I raised it and banged the throttles but they were fully forward. I believe Captain Rayment was pulling the control column back—he called hurriedly, "Undercarriage up" and I selected up and then gripped the ledge in front with both hands and looked forward. The aircraft's passage was very smooth as if we had become airborne and it looked as if we were very slowly turning to starboard; I remember thinking that we couldn't possibly get between the house and the tree. I lowered my head and then the aircraft collided.

After the impact I glanced up and through the snow which had fallen on the windscreen I saw a vivid glow which appeared to extend round the nose of the aircraft. From this point we were subjected to many violent movements and the sound of the aircraft breaking up filled the air. I next looked up when we came to rest—we didn't appear to be on fire—I gave the order to evacuate the aircraft and at the same time released my safety belt. Captain Rayment made an effort to leave his seat but called out that he couldn't move because his foot was jammed. I remember saying "Come on man, get out" but he could not move. I told him to hang on whilst I had a look at the outside, expecting fire to break out at any moment and then left the cockpit. Outside I ordered the crew to run away from the wreck because of the fire hazard, the Radio Officer remained and we quickly identified five or six small fires. Two were inboard of the starboard engine underneath the wing which was almost intact, and the others were at the end of what was left of the port wing. I returned to the cockpit and collected the two fire extinguishers pausing to tell Captain Rayment that it was necessary to put the fires out before I could assist him. We were unable to extinguish all the fires but the airport firemen were quickly on the scene and they eventually put the remaining fires out. The rescue work continued.

6th March, 1958   J. THAIN
Captain
Elizabethan Flight, BEA

APPENDIX TO THE STATEMENT BY CAPTAIN J. THAIN

In view of the preliminary reports made by the German authorities in which they have stated that the accident is associated with ice formation on the aircraft wings, I am most anxious to ensure that all aspects of the accident are brought to the attention of the Court and thoroughly investigated.

In particular, from the evidence submitted two main facts have emerged, firstly, the aircraft speed did not exceed V1, secondly, the loss of speed could not have been caused by ice on the wings. From these facts therefore, it would appear that the cause of the accident had no connection whatsoever with ice accretion on the wings. Furthermore, the indications are that the cause is directly connected with a loss of speed which could only manifest itself by restricting the free rotation of the aircraft wheels.

6th March, 1958   J. THAIN
Captain
Elizabethan Flight, BEA

ADDENDUM TO THE APPENDIX OF THE STATEMENT OF CAPTAIN J. THAIN

As I am given to understand that the Variable Decision Take-off Technique as practised by BEA is not necessarily the same as that used by other operators, I should like to take this opportunity of explaining it in detail for the purposes of clarity.

Within BEA the use of the variable decision speed (V1), selected to give the optimum benefits on take-off performance, is one of the basic principles used in calculating permitted take-off weights for Viscount and Elizabethan aircraft.

Group A standards to which these aircraft operate require the take-off weight to be so limited that should an engine fail at the decision speed (V1), the aircraft shall be capable of either:

(a) continuing the take-off with one engine inoperative, reaching a height of 50 feet within the take-off distance available, and thereafter clearing all obstructions by a prescribed margin, or,

(b) being brought to a standstill within the emergency distance available.

It will be seen from the above that V1 (decision speed) actually represents a distance, but in the absence of a suitable way in which to measure the distance during a take-off run, the distance has been associated with a speed calculated for a hard dry runway. No figures are available for wet or snow-covered runways. The V1 speed then, represents a point beyond which the take-off cannot be abandoned with safety.

V2 speed

A second speed is used in this method which is known as the take-off safety speed or V2. This takes into account the aircraft's gradient of climb with one engine inoperative, and also the difficulty of keeping the machine straight at slow speeds in the asymmetric state.

The pilot is instructed not to attempt to fly the aeroplane off until the V2 is reached in order to ensure that (1), the machine will have the required gradient of climb to clear an obstruction in the net flight path, and (2), that he will have sufficient rudder control to check the natural swing resulting from engine failure.

Operating procedure

During the take-off, the pilot monitoring the instruments calls "V1" when that speed is attained. The pilot manipulating the flying controls then knows that he is committed to continue the take-off. The pilot monitoring the instruments then calls "V2" when that speed is reached and the plane is flown off.

Conclusions

From the foregoing, the pilot's actions immediately prior to the accident may be more easily explained.

When our V1 speed of 117 knots was reached I called "V1". Captain Rayment then knew we were committed to the take-off. However, the aircraft failed to accelerate to the V2 speed for which he was waiting. He would have been wrong in attempting to fly under these conditions, and indeed, the fact that the tail bumper did not touch the ground, indicates that the aircraft was never at a sufficient angle of attack to fly.

CAPTAIN J. THAIN

THE EFFECT OF HOAR FROST, SNOW AND ICE ON TAKE-OFF

Notice to Licensed Aircraft Engineers and to Owners of Civil Aircraft
14th March, 1947

(1) As a result of a recent accident, it is necessary to draw the attention of all concerned to the dangers of the adherence of hoar frost, snow or ice to aerofoil surfaces, and to stress the vital importance of removing such deposits immediately prior to take-off.

(2) When an aircraft has been standing in the open overnight or even for a period during the day at low temperatures, a deposit of hoar frost may be formed. This deposit will affect the aerodynamic characteristics of the aircraft to such an extent as to increase the drag and stalling speed, and decrease the rate of climb.

(3) It is not sufficient to remove any snow which may have fallen because any hoar frost underneath will still remain. Snow will also adhere to hoar frost and will not be completely blown off when the aircraft commences to take off.

(4) Glaze ice is caused by supercooled rain falling on aircraft surfaces which are at a temperature below freezing point. It is not easily visible at a distance and may have the same effect as hoar frost.

(5) The de-icing of control surfaces alone is insufficient as the presence of hoar frost or glaze ice on the main planes will be sufficient to affect the take-off to a dangerous degree.

By order of the Board,
R. E. HARDINGHAM
for Secretary
Brettenham House, Strand, London, WC2

PART II

∞∞◐◐◐◐∞∞

REPORT OF THE REVIEWING BODY APPOINTED TO
CONSIDER AND REPORT UPON THE ACCIDENT

INTRODUCTION

On the afternoon of the 6th February 1958 the British European Airways aircraft G-ALZU crashed while taking off from the airport at Munich. A Commission of Inquiry appointed by the Federal Republic of Germany duly inquired into the causes of the accident and issued a report dated 31st January 1959. As will amply appear hereinafter, both the captain of the aircraft, Captain James Thain, and the British Airline Pilots' Association (BALPA) disagreed with certain of the findings of the German Commission of Inquiry, and your predecessor, the then Minister of Transport and Civil Aviation, on 10th June 1959 appointed us to be an independent reviewing body with the following terms of reference:

> To consider the representations made by and on behalf of Captain Thain with regard to the accident to BEA Elizabethan G-ALZU at Munich on 6th February, 1958: and, having regard to those representations and to the Report of the German Commission of Inquiry on the said accident, to report to the Minister whether or not in their opinion Captain Thain took sufficient steps:
>
> (a) to satisfy himself that the wings of the aircraft were free from ice and snow;
> (b) to ascertain whether or not in the conditions prevailing at the time the runway was fit for use; and
> (c) to ascertain the cause of the difficulties encountered on the first two attempts to take off before making a third attempt.

THE FACTS IN OUTLINE

The aircraft G-ALZU was an Airspeed Ambassador, a type assigned the class name of "Elizabethan" by British European Airways. It had been constructed in 1952. The Elizabethan is a high-winged monoplane powered by two Bristol Centaurus 661 engines; it has a tricycle undercarriage. Since no question arises as to any defect in the aircraft, no further details need be given save to mention that the port engine was fitted with a Peravia Recorder; this is a power-driven roll of waxed paper used to record, against a time base, data as to altitude, engine speed, and manifold pressure. The Peravia recording was recovered after the crash and throws some light on the course of events.

The aircraft was on the return stage of a charter flight between Manchester and Belgrade, carrying the Manchester United football team and journalists and others, the total number of occupants, including the crew, being 44. It landed at Munich in order to refuel. The captain in charge of the aircraft was Captain Thain and his First Officer was Captain K. G. Rayment, who was fatally injured in the crash. On the outward journey to Belgrade Captain Thain had flown the aircraft; on the return, including the attempted take-offs from Munich, Captain Rayment flew the aircraft and Captain Thain acted as co-pilot. In fact, Captain Rayment was senior to Captain Thain, he came to be serving under him owing to the fact that a First Officer originally rostered to accompany Captain Thain on the flight had dropped out and Captain Rayment came in as his substitute.

Captain Thain had in the past flown with Captain Rayment but on those occasions Captain Thain's rank was that of First Officer and he had flown under Captain Rayment's command. The aircraft had flown from Belgrade at a height of between 14,500 and 16,500 ft at temperatures in the region of −21° to −25°C. During the descent to Munich through cloud, the wing de-icing equipment was operated: this comprises a petrol-burning heater used to supply hot air to the interior of the leading edge of the wing, and is fitted with a device which automatically cuts out operation at about 90 knots and thus comes into operation on landing.

The aircraft arrived at 1417 h, i.e. 2.17 p.m., local time. (In this report all times given are local time, which was one hour in advance of GMT.) It was snowing at the time, and snow and slush were lying on the ground, including the runway; the screen temperature was in the vicinity of freezing point. The aircraft made a normal landing and after arrival at the apron Captain Thain went first to the Met. Office for briefing on the next leg of the flight, and next to the Air Traffic Control Office; Captain Rayment reported to the BEA office. Meanwhile, refuelling commenced at 1425 h; the aircraft's wing tanks had a capacity of 1,000 gallons and they were filled, 726 gallons being taken on in the process. Mr W. N. Black, the BEA Station Engineer, assisted in the refuelling, which finished at 1438 h. The wings were not swept or de-iced; Captain Thain's decision in this respect will be examined in detail later.

At 1519 h, the aircraft obtained clearance to taxi to the runway, and at 1530 it commenced its first attempted take-off. The aircraft accelerated to approximately 105 knots when Captain Rayment abandoned take-off because the boost on both engines was fluctuating. Brakes were applied and the aircraft came to rest approximately 450 yards from the far end of the runway. It received permission to back-track, returned to the starting point, and at 1534 h commenced its second run. On this occasion, the throttles were opened more slowly and the starboard engine boost was steady, but at about 85 knots the port boost gauge "fluctuated quite a lot" (Captain Thain's phrase) and went above the permitted maximum of 60 inches. Captain Thain thereupon ordered the take-off to be abandoned and decided to return to the apron for consultation with the Station Engineer. The aircraft rolled to the far end of the runway and taxied back to the Terminal Building, arriving at 1539 h. Captain Thain took over the controls while taxi-ing.

Mr Black knew that boost surging was not an uncommon phenomenon on Elizabethan aircraft at Munich, owing to the airfield's height of 1732 ft above sea-level. He so informed the pilots, and advised that the normal way of dealing with it was to inch the throttles back to maintain the required 57.5 inches of boost. The pilots thereupon decided to make one further attempt at take-off. The passengers had been off-loaded; they were recalled and the aircraft again cleared to taxi to the runway at 1556 h. Neither pilot had left the cockpit during the aircraft's 20-minute wait on the apron.

The aircraft reported "rolling" on its third and last attempted take-off, by R/T at 1603.06 h. It never became airborne. Fifty-four seconds later, the radio operator called Munich control but before he had had time to complete his identification, the transmission was cut short. The aircraft had traversed the entire runway and the continuation stopway, broken through the boundary fence and struck a house, after which it broke up. The last R/T message ended with the loud noises associated with the collision with the house.

THE GERMAN REPORT

The German Commission of Inquiry was able to narrow down its search for the causes of the accident to a detailed investigation of three possible factors, viz.:

(a) rolling friction caused by snow on the runway;
(b) the effect of slush on the free running of the wheels;
(c) alteration in aerodynamic efficiency caused by wing icing.

On the first factor, snow on the runway, the Commission found that the snow had subsided into a layer of slush not more than 1 cm thick and that this slush on the runway did not increase rolling friction to such an extent that the accident could be attributed to it.

On the second factor, the Commission found that there could have been no packing of the twin wheels with ice such as to exert a braking effect, basing themselves on the facts that nothing of the kind had been detected after the first two abortive take-offs, that no mark attributable to such a condition had afterwards been found on the one surviving tyre, and that other aircraft with similar undercarriages had taken off without difficulty from the airport that afternoon.

On the third factor, the Commission decided that the wings of the aircraft had, at the material time, acquired a layer of rough ice some 5 mm thick, with a roughness height of 3 mm, and that this prevented the aircraft from attaining the lift coefficient required for unsticking within the length of the runway. This they therefore found was the decisive cause of the accident.

EVENTS SUBSEQUENT TO THE GERMAN REPORT

The finding that the aircraft attempted to take off with its aerodynamic efficiency impaired by the formation of ice on its wings, constituted a serious criticism of the commander of the aircraft and pointed to a breach of article 17(2) of the Air Navigation Order, 1954, which provides:

> Before the aircraft flies or attempts to fly the person in command shall satisfy himself ... (vi) ... that the wings and control surfaces are free from ice and hoar-frost.

Neither Captain Thain nor BALPA accepted the above-mentioned finding. Among other moves, the Association, on Captain Thain's behalf, submitted certain arguments and fresh evidence to the German Commission and requested that it reopen the Inquiry. The gist of the submission was that the evidence did not establish the presence of ice on the wings and that the behaviour of the aircraft could and should be accounted for by the retarding effect of slush on the runway, and did not point to icing. The fresh evidence consisted of statements (a) by three persons who took part in rescue operations and stated that they saw no ice on the wings when, immediately after the accident, they took part in extricating Captain Rayment from the wreckage, and (b) by two air traffic controllers, Erich Laas and Kurt Gentzsch, who watched the last take-off from the control tower. The latter both spoke of the aircraft making a normal run for the first half of the runway, the nosewheel then left the ground but after some distance it touched down again, leaving the ground, according to Laas, once more before the end of the runway. (Gentzsch did not speak of the nosewheel again leaving the ground, but thought the aircraft rolled to the end of the runway and then unstuck.) This was submitted as consistent *inter alia* with a nose-heavy pitching moment caused by running into deeper slush or by frozen slush retarding the free running of the wheels.

The German Commission on 14th March 1960 issued a written decision that the facts, evidence and other points to which their attention had been drawn, did not justify the reopening of the proceedings. To this was appended a detailed statement of their reasons, a translation of which was before us. We conceive this document, although subsequent in date to our Terms of Reference, to form part of the report of the German Commission to which we ought to have regard and we accordingly now refer to its contents.

The Commission first dealt with the fresh evidence of the rescuers; they pointed out that none of the three spoke of the part of the wings outboard of the engines since they were concerned with the part adjacent to the fuselage and their evidence did not conflict with the finding of the Court. They also dealt with an argument advanced by Captain Thain that the fire-extinguishing powders used after the crash would have lowered the freezing point of water and would account for the absence of ice on the slipstream portion of the wings when examined six hours later. This point, as developed before us, will be examined later; the Commission rejected the argument in the following passage:

> These considerations put forward by Captain Thain are based on the assumption that the wings, at least in the region of the engines, were so heavily sprayed with extinguishing agents as to make it possible for the melting-point of the snow to drop to $-3°C$ at this spot. All available reports regarding the fires and the activities of the fire-fighting services, however, show that these parts of the wreckage lay outside the main centres of fire. In the vicinity of the aircraft only a few minor fires *on the ground* broke out and were fought with extinguishing agents. There is no indication that on the upper surfaces of the wings (particularly in the region of the engines) any extinguishing measures were necessary or extinguishing agents deposited.

They next dealt with a submission that slush or water might have collected on the outer edges of the runway on account of its camber and, as the aircraft's course was not down the centre of the runway, might account for increased retardation at some point. They said:

> The fact that the runway has a slight camber is not new to the Commission. The effect of this camber is that any possible melted snow can drain off better from the runway. On one side of the runway the manoeuvring area shows a natural fall-away. On the other side special drainage has been constructed. Provision is thus made on both sides for the further draining-off of the water. Since the amount of precipitation which fell prior to the accident was by no means great, it appears out of the question that any quantities of water or melted snow worth mentioning should have collected anywhere. What is more, the witness Bartz stated that on the day of the accident he not only checked the condition of the centre of the runway but also made spot checks on both outer edges of it. He was therefore able to say with certainty that he did not find any slush or water collected there.

The Commission reported that the statements of Laas and Gentzsch had been before them from the outset and their observations from a considerable distance had been considered, together with the evidence as to tracks on the runway and the evidence of Captain Thain. BALPA, however, had submitted in writing the argument that the evidence of Laas and Gentzsch showed that the angle of attack necessary for unsticking, and the necessary speed for this, were never simultaneously attained throughout the entire take-off process, and that wing icing could not therefore have caused the accident; and that these witnesses' statements suggested rather inability to unstick owing to restriction of free running of the wheels. With regard to this submission, the Commission expressed the following views and reasoning:

(a) They had concluded, on the evidence of Captain Thain and others, that speed V1 was attained between 1400 and 1600 m and maintained or exceeded to 1800 m. The question to be considered was therefore whether between 1400 and 1800 m the aircraft attained the necessary angle of attack for unsticking with clean wings.

(b) It was highly improbable that, so near the end of the runway, Captain Rayment would not have attempted to unstick.

(c) A witness named Meyer, whose statement was appended, observed the track of the emergency tailwheel up to about 100 to 150 m short of the end of the runway—he had walked back about 40 m along the runway and could not see the beginning of the tailwheel track, and:

> It is thus confirmed that before the 1800 m mark (i.e. over the rolling distance on which V1 was exceeded) the aircraft had the angle of attack otherwise necessary for unsticking, for a period not precisely ascertainable but at any rate ample.

(d) The evidence of Laas did not conflict with the above as he saw the unsticking of the nosewheel towards the end of the runway; Gentzsch was clearly wrong in thinking the aircraft unstuck, and if his statement negated the unsticking of the nosewheel before the end of the runway, the track of the tailwheel showed him to be wrong. Of the statement that the nosewheel unstuck for a short time in the middle of the runway, they said:

> If we assume that this observation is correct (and the overall impression made by the statement as well as the witness's experience suggest this), then we must ask ourselves whether his statement really differs decisively from those of most of the other witnesses. According to the Commission's former and present opinion, this is not the case, for when this witness speaks of unsticking in the middle of the runway, it does appear that the nosewheel first left the ground for a short time at about 900 m and very soon afterwards (Gentzsch says 60–100 m) touched the ground again. Laas could not say exactly where the nosewheel afterwards left the ground again, but he stated that it occurred, at any rate, before the end of the runway was reached and that he had the impression that it was primarily only a

question of putting the nose down in order to gain speed. This indicates that the second part of his statement tallies with the observations of the other witnesses and that they merely disregarded the first brief unsticking of the nosewheel at 900–1000 m. In other words, Laas and all the other witnesses are agreed in principle that the nosewheel unstuck within the second half of the runway, towards the end of the runway. All the statements, however, including that of Laas, are vague, inexact and mutually at variance concerning precisely for how long, on what section of the runway and at what angle of attack this occurred. The reason for this uncertainty would lie, on the one hand, in the fact that the aircraft was already at a considerable distance from the witnesses and, on the other hand, that in assessing all these statements it must be remembered that when watching the take-off the eye-witnesses did not yet know that it would culminate in an accident and they consequently did not pay conscious attention to every detail of the take-off process. If these points are taken into consideration, the statements of all the eye-witnesses can easily be brought into line with the conclusion in (b) and (c), viz. that the pilot tried to unstick the aircraft between 1400 and 1800 m.

(e)   The Commission therefore concluded that the assessment of the witnesses' statements failed to show that the pilot did not try to unstick although between 1400 and 1800 m V1 was exceeded and V2 almost attained.

The Commission further dealt with the evidence of Laas and Gentzsch as to the earlier unsticking of the nosewheel in the following passage. This is a matter to which we attach importance and the Commission's observations are given in full:

> The statements of the witnesses Laas and Gentzsch also fail to justify the further opinion advanced that restriction of the free rotation of the undercarriage wheels (whether due to slush or other causes) might have been a contributory cause of the accident. The observation that the nosewheel left the ground for a short time at about 900 m but soon afterwards touched down again can be explained by the fact that V1 had not yet been attained and Captain Rayment was possibly reducing, for a while, an angle of attack which perhaps appeared to him somewhat excessive. Captain Thain's remark that a "nose-heavy pitching moment" might have come into play here, can, it is true, be accepted in theory. This is contradicted in practice, however, by the fact that any braking action which could have put the nose down against Captain Rayment's will must have occurred abruptly and Captain Thain would have been bound to have become aware of it physically, or, at any rate, from the speed reading. His statement, however, makes no mention of it. Another point telling against this is the fact that the aircraft *afterwards* gained speed normally, exceeded V1 and almost attained V2, as Captain Thain mentions in his statement. It is out of the question that the sinking of the nosewheel observed by Laas and Gentzsch at about 1000 m should be identical with the drop in speed from 117 kt to 105 kt observed by Captain Thain, since from the sequence of events in *his* statement it

can be seen that this drop in speed can only have occurred just short of the end of the runway.

The Commission finally dealt with a further submission by BALPA that, in the prevailing conditions, 5 mm of ice could not have been produced on the wings by the snow which fell during the time the aircraft was at Munich. They said it was not relevant to inquire whether the snow and slush had turned completely to ice, as the aerodynamic assessment of the aircraft's performance did not depend on whether the layer was wholly, or only partially, ice. Moreover, the wings were supercooled by high-altitude flight when the sleet fell upon them.

SUBMISSIONS AND EVIDENCE: OUTLINE

At the public inquiry it was submitted on behalf of Captain Thain that we should give an affirmative answer to each of the three questions posed in our terms of reference. Of these, the first (whether Captain Thain took sufficient steps to satisfy himself that the wings of the aircraft were free from ice and snow) occupied the greater part of the time spent in the hearing. Captain Thain's counsel accepted that if in fact ice had been present on the wings during the third and fatal take-off attempt, it would be difficult for us to say "yes" to this question, and he led evidence and submitted arguments with a view to establishing that no ice was or could have been present on the wings at that time. This involved inviting us to say that the findings of the German Commission were wrong in this respect. We refer later to the question of the extent to which we feel our terms of reference enable us to disagree with those findings, but we say at once that this was clearly a relevant submission and was one properly put in the forefront of Captain Thain's case.

Counsel also appreciated that a finding by us of no ice would not conclude the first point in his favour, because theoretically circumstances might be such that although no ice formed, the prevailing conditions should have led a prudent pilot to take steps towards satisfying himself which might not have been taken. His submissions here were that Captain Thain had done all that a reasonable captain could have been expected to do in the material circumstances.

A similar submission was made with regard to the second question (whether Captain Thain took sufficient steps to ascertain whether or not in the conditions prevailing at the time the runway was fit for use). If the German Report was correct in finding that the slight depth of slush on the runway had so little retarding effect as not materially to have affected the take-off run, we would be unlikely to reach an adverse finding on this question, but the answer became much more debatable since it was submitted that both the state of the runway and the effect of that state were different from that found by the German Commission. This was, in part, derived from the cardinal submission that there was no wing icing, because that submission had necessarily to be accompanied by the argument that the unusual behaviour of the aircraft must be attributed to a cause or causes other than icing, and the cause suggested was the drag effect of slush on the runway. If this submission were correct, the state of the runway was an effective cause of the accident and the submission made on the second question was that at the relevant date little was known about slush hazards and that in the then prevailing state of knowledge Captain Thain had acted reasonably in the steps he took as regards the runway, although they led him to the belief (erroneous if his case were accepted) that it was safe to use. The submission, previously made, that ice had had a braking effect on the aircraft's wheels was not pursued before us, and we think it clear from the evidence of wheel-marks (see below) that this suggestion could not be supported: we refer particularly to the evidence that all the main wheels, after being locked, commenced to run freely at the same point, a fact consistent with brakes being released but quite inconsistent with retardation by ice packing the undercarriage.

On the third question (whether Captain Thain took sufficient steps to ascertain the cause of the difficulties encountered on the first two attempts to take off before making a third attempt) we were presented with evidence as to the course of events, and it was submitted that Captain Thain had correctly diagnosed the trouble and acted reasonably in deciding upon a third attempt. The witnesses called before us were the following:

Captain E. R. Wright, captain of the BEA Viscount which landed at Munich five minutes before the Elizabethan's final run.
Mr W. N. Black, the BEA station engineer at Munich.
Captain R. T. Merrifield, who gave evidence both as Chairman of BALPA and as captain of a BEA Viscount which visited Munich two days after the accident.
Dr H. L. Penman, PhD, MSc, F Inst P, head of the Physics Department of Rothamsted Experimental Station, as to ice formation.
Mr R. F. Jones, a Principal Scientific Officer at the Meteorological Office, Air Ministry, who attended the German Inquiry as meteorological adviser to the British accredited representative.
Mr J. R. D. Kenward, Superintendent of Performance and Analysis, Engineering Department, BEA.
Mr G. M. Kelly, a Senior Inspector, Accidents Investigation Branch, the British accredited representative at the German Inquiry.
Mrs R. V. Thain, BSc, as to the effect of fire extinguishing powder on the freezing point of water.
Captain James Thain.

In addition we were furnished with a large number of documents, including statements of some of the witnesses before the German Inquiry and including two papers, one prepared by Captain Thain and one by BALPA setting out reasoned submissions on matters at issue. We now turn to a detailed consideration of the relevant facts, as a necessary preliminary to answering the three questions.

WING ICING

Meteorological conditions at Munich

Two reports of the Airport Meteorological Office at Munich, as furnished to
the German Commission, are supplied. On comparison of these with the
times of the aircraft's stay at Munich, it will be seen that snow is recorded as
falling continuously from arrival to last attempted departure, the fall being
described as "moderate" up to 1550 h, 13 minutes before the last run started,
and as "slight" thereafter. The witnesses spoke of the snowfall as having practically ceased at the time of the third run. The screen temperature, it will be
noted, fell from + 0.1°C just before the aircraft's arrival to −0.2°C at 1600 h,
just before its final run; and was recorded as precisely zero at 1500 h, or 19
minutes before clearance for take-off was first obtained. The snow was lying
on the ground but melting. Its condition on the runway will be considered
later; at the apron it was slushy and footprints became filled with water.

Mr Jones informed us that radio sonde observations made at 1300 h
showed that at approximately 500 ft altitude above the airfield the temperature was −0.2°C and at approximately 2000 ft was −3.2°C; at that time the
screen temperature (2 m above the ground) was +0.2°C. It followed therefore that falling snow would not, at the material time, have encountered an
ambient temperature above zero and commenced to melt until at or very
near the ground. The German observers had described the snow at about the
time of the accident as "wet snow, with big flakes" but Mr Jones thought it
unlikely that there was any water content in the snow, saying "it is quite
common to refer to big flake snow as being wet. It is also easy to imagine it
as such, because it frequently falls on a surface which is itself just above
nought and it melts on impact."

The amount of snow falling during the aircraft's stay can be judged from the fact that in the seven hours ending at 2114 h the recorded precipitation was 5 mm (the measurement is of the water equivalent). This seven-hour period embraced four hours of "moderate snow" and three hours of "slight snow" and during the Elizabethan's stay of under two hours, most of it in "moderate snow", Mr Jones thought that probably not more than 2 mm of precipitation could have fallen. We agree with his assessment, as regards the precipitation at the meteorological enclosure, which was 100 to 200 yards from the apron. Snowfall may vary in density within relatively small distances, and this assessment may not hold good for the runway, some 1000 yards away from the apron. It is also important to note that temperatures may vary within short distances. Dr Penman said "temperatures at the same level above ground can vary by several tenths of a degree quite easily … so that a temperature of 0°C in the screen might be appreciably more or even appreciably less on the apron."

Factors affecting the temperature of the aircraft wings

The Elizabethan had flown from Belgrade at temperatures below −20°C and had the wings not been artificially heated they would have been substantially below zero on arrival. We accept Captain Thain's evidence that the wing heaters had been used on the descent to Munich, and indeed it would have been surprising if in the prevailing conditions they had not. During operation of the heaters the leading edges of the wings would have been well above zero, and probably substantial areas of the wing surface as well. The heaters cut out during landing and thereafter any residual heat would diffuse through the wings. We think it unnecessary to attempt further evaluation of the effect of the wing heaters in view of what we now have to say about the effect of refuelling.

The wing tanks of the Elizabethan are of integral construction. Shortly after arrival 3,300 litres of fuel were uplifted; this is 726 gallons, and the tank capacity is approximately 1000 gallons. Since, as we were informed, the aircraft was refuelled to full tanks, the balance of some 274 gallons had arrived with the aircraft and its temperature had been influenced by the super-cooling at high altitude and by the use of the wing heaters. This temperature is problematical, but the temperature of the 726 gallons uplifted can be assessed. The fresh petrol came from bowsers which had been standing in the open, and the German Commission had information from the fuel suppliers that its temperature was "not above about 0.0°C". The greater part of the volume of the wings consisted of petrol, in direct contact with the metallic structure of the wing, and of that petrol nearly three-quarters was at approximately the same temperature as the ambient air. Whatever the effect of super-cooling at altitude, and of the wing heaters, the temperature of the wings soon after refuelling can have differed only fractionally from the prevailing air temperature.

The refuelling commenced at 1425 h and finished at 1438 h. It was at 1500 h that the screen temperature was recorded as precisely zero. It appears to us that in these circumstances the temperature of the upper surface of the wings must have then been in the vicinity of freezing point. Owing to the possibility of a fractional difference between air temperature at the screen and at the apron, and to the impossibility of assessing the exact temperature of the uplifted fuel, it is not possible to be precise to a tenth of a degree, but we do not think the wing can have differed from the screen temperature by more than half a degree.

The state of the wings: direct evidence

Two of the witnesses at our inquiry, Mr Black and Captain Thain, gave evidence relating to the state of the wings. We were furnished with the written statements made to the German Inquiry by five further witnesses on this matter. A photograph of the aircraft taken from a window in the Terminal Building at 1550 h was supplied to us; it was taken from above and shows the starboard wing surface. This body of evidence falls into two groups, dealing respectively with the two periods when the aircraft was standing on the apron.

As to the first period from 1417 to 1519 h, Mr Black said that his duties in connection with refuelling took him on to the mainplane surfaces from shortly after arrival for about 25 minutes, during which he walked out as far as the wing lettering (registration letters on the starboard wing and corporation letters on the port wing) to check the ailerons.* It was snowing lightly and the wings were wet with melted snow, but there was no trace of snow adherence at any point: "When I was up on the wing, the wing was quite clean and as the snow was contacting the wing the snow was melting immediately on contact." Captain Thain, on leaving the control office, met Captain Rayment and afterwards walked towards the aircraft and, in his own words, "studied the snowfall on the starboard wing." His evidence continued:

> I had to wait till I got fairly close before I could really identify any snow, and when I got close to the leading edge or to the wing, I saw a thin film of partially melted snow on the wing. It had thawed in places, and I could see the water from the melted snow running off the trailing edge right the way along. I continued walking towards the door, and found that two airport hands were trying to pump some water into the aircraft, but they had not got a suitable connection for the water hosepipe, and the chap could not stand up because of the slush on the ground. I stood there assisting him, and at the same time, with my face towards the direction of the trailing edge of the starboard wing. I suppose I stood there for about three minutes or perhaps four minutes.

* Ailerons are small hinged sections on the outboard section of the wing.

His position at that time, he added, was between the fuselage and the starboard engine nacelle, and during the three or four minutes he watched the thawed snow running off the trailing edge of the wing. Refuelling had then ceased. The third witness on this part of the matter was Robert Wiggers, a refueller employed by the fuel company, whose written statement to the German Commission said "Refuelling took place in driving snow. I noticed that the inner section of the wings was clear of snow, whereas there was snow lying on the outer sections."

During the second period when the Elizabethan was stationary on the apron (1539 to 1556 h) it was observed from the second floor of the terminal building by three, perhaps four, persons attending the Air Navigation Services School at the airport. The three were Siegfried Schombel, Hubertus Wollner and Johannes Bogen; the fourth was Heinz Tismer, whose statement does not indicate his position. All four made statements that they observed the starboard wing from about 50 yards distance and saw snow lying on it. The German Commission attached particular weight to the statements of Schombel and Wollner, who gave oral evidence before them. Schombel's written statement includes this observation "after the mechanic had given the 'all clear' signal for taxi-ing, the snow remained lying on the wings, in spite of the slipstream. It was sticky wet snow." Wollner stated "I can testify with absolute certainty that there was wet snow on the outer section of the right wing, I cannot remember if there was any snow on the centre section." The photograph mentioned above was taken by another student at the Air Navigation Services School and the print, which we examined, is consistent with the above statements. The wing surface is of unpainted metal, with the exception of the lettering and of a narrow band of anti-corrosive paint behind the engine exhaust. The photograph shows a distinct change in the colour of the wing surface at the edge of the propeller slipstream, the outboard portion showing white while that behind the propeller is darker; moreover the registration letters do not appear in the print, either from some photographic effect of refracted light or because they were covered by snow. There were three ice indicator marks on the starboard wing, narrow black lines painted on the fore part of the wing, outboard of the propeller slipstream, and extending some distance back from the leading edge. These are visible in the photograph, plainly so at the leading edge but becoming less distinct as the eye proceeds across the wing surface.

Mr Black did not examine the wing surface at this period. He walked round the aircraft but the wing surface was above his eye level. (As the German report accurately stated, "from outside the aircraft the wing surfaces cannot be seen at all from the front unless one stands in a raised position, and from the rear they can be seen only from quite a distance.") When the aircraft taxied away and reached a sufficient distance for the wing surface to be seen Mr Black observed, according to his recollection, that the mainplane was clear of snow except for the wing tips. He told us he could not explain why there should be snow on the wing tips and not on the rest of the wing.

Captain Thain did not leave the cockpit during this second visit. Speaking of Captain Rayment and himself, he said "We both looked out of our respective windows and studied our respective wings and we found that we had lost that very thin film of partially melted snow which I had observed walking out to the aircraft, and from my seat the wing appeared quite clean." The engine nacelle interrupted his view of the inboard portion of the wing, but he could see the ice indicator marks and further outboard, his eye level was below the wing level, but he could see the leading edge, and, because of the curvature of the wing, he could also see the upper surface for the first tenth or twelfth part of its width. He emphasised that of the part of the wing within his vision he could see the metal with no snow on it.

The state of the wings: indirect evidence

It may be possible to deduce the presence or absence of wing icing immediately prior to the accident from observed facts as to (a) the performance of the aircraft on its final run, or (b) the condition of the wings after the accident. We deal later with the first of these sets of facts but can say at once that no useful conclusion as to icing can in our view be drawn from them. The second however is of prime importance: the German Commission attached considerable importance to deductions from what was ascertained after the crash, and a large portion of our Inquiry was taken up in submissions and evidence designed to show that the German conclusions were in this respect erroneous.

The inspection of the wreckage by Captain Reichel, the West German Chief Inspector of Accidents, and his two assistants was made by the light of arc lamps six hours after the accident, and of the intervening period slight snowfall was recorded in the first $1\frac{1}{2}$ hours and moderate snowfall thereafter. The temperature at 2200 h was $-3.0°C$. We were told by Mr Jones and Mr Kelly that the evidence of the German investigators was that they brushed powdery snow off the wings in places and exposed a layer of ice underneath. We inquired how the depth of that ice, stated as 5 mm, was measured, and we were informed that it was not measured. According to Mr Kelly's evidence

> Captain Reichel ... described how he had swept the snow off with his hand and found a rough layer of ice. That was all he said to begin with. Later on ... he was asked to give some estimate of the depth or thickness of the ice and he said 5 mm ... I understood Goetz to say he examined the wing at one or two places simply by pushing his hand underneath the snow and feeling about with his fingers and he said at certain parts of the wing there was a rough layer of ice under the snow.

Mr Kelly had seen a news film, which chanced to have been taken at the time of the inspection, showing Captain Reichel brushing powdery snow off the trailing edge of the wing; he said:

it would be possible to state that there was a layer of rough ice there, but I should not think you could make any accurate assessment of its depth without taking some such action as digging a pin in it or scraping it off and measuring it, and I have not heard that that was done at all.

No evidence was proffered to us to controvert the German finding that the ice layer had not blended at all with the superimposed snow. As to the finding that there was no ice under the snow in the place behind the engines, the only criticism offered was that the whole wing was not examined but that the findings were based on "spot checks" made, according to counsel, in seven different places, and that these might be insufficient for the formation of a true picture.

We think that the primary facts as found by the German Commission must be accepted, save that the depth of the rough ice layer is not established as 5 mm and may have been substantially less. These findings of course relate to a time at or after 2200 h. We also had the evidence, in written statements, of the three individuals who took part in rescue operations and whose testimony had been furnished to the German Commission after their report. Karl-Heinz Seffer, aircraft mechanic of the German Air Force, in the process of freeing Captain Rayment from the cockpit, climbed first on to the fuselage and then on to the starboard wing between fuselage and engine: he crossed this wing to its trailing edge, near the fuselage, where he got down. He said:

> Whilst I was doing this I did not notice any deposit of ice on the fuselage or on this part of the wing. I was wearing rubber boots. I am particularly inclined to assume that there was no deposit of ice, because if there had been I would probably have slipped. I cannot say whether there was any ice on the wings outboard of the engines, nor did I notice any snow on the wings.

His father Otto Seffer, employed in the airport traffic service, stood on the upper surface of the fuselage: "There was no ice to be seen, if only because everything was smashed up." Gerd Skwirblies, PAA aircraft engineer, opened the port side of the fuselage, near the pilot's seat, with an axe:

> At the spot at which I opened up the fuselage, there was, for certain, no ice. My companions were wearing rubber boots and were moving about on top of the fuselage, near the cockpit, without slipping. From this I conclude that there was no ice on the top of the fuselage either. Whether there was ice or snow on the wings, I cannot say. I was not looking for that. But I seem to remember that the leading edge of the wing was free of ice.

These statements tend to establish that there was no ice behind or inboard of the engines immediately after the crash, which is not in conflict with the findings of the investigation at 2200 h.

We now turn to the deductions from the above facts, all of which were debated before us. It is an important preliminary to this matter to recall that a snowflake falling in a temperature below freezing point is "dry"; it is pure ice and contains no water; but that if it falls into an ambient temperature above freezing point its minute strands of crystalline ice begin to melt so that the snowflake then contains water and is "wet". Likewise if it falls on to an object itself above freezing point it commences to melt. If a dry snowflake falls on an object itself below zero it does not adhere to the object, but if a wet snowflake falls on such an object its free water refreezes and causes it to adhere to the object. The binding element in wing icing is freezing water. Now the air temperature at Munich airport fell steadily from the $-0.2°C$ recorded four minutes before the last run to the $-30°C$ recorded at the time when the inspection commenced. Unless therefore there was an abnormal variation between the temperature at the airport screen and that at the point where the wings came to rest, perhaps 1,500 yards distant, the snow falling at all times between the accident and the investigation must have been dry. Such snow falling on an aircraft wing coated with ice and *ex hypothesi* below zero would not adhere to the ice because there would be no free water present to bind the two together by freezing. The finding, therefore, of a layer of ice outboard of the engines covered with powdery snow which had not blended with the ice is consistent with that part of the wing being ice-covered at the time of the crash. Is it also consistent with its being free from ice at that time? If the wing were then clean, the ice can only have been formed by the melting of the snow that fell thereafter, and its subsequent refreezing as the temperature dropped.

There are two objections to this hypothesis. Firstly there is the question whether the wing temperature was at that time high enough to melt the falling snow (which was only "slight snowfall" until 1850 h), bearing in mind not only the recorded temperatures but also the fact that the physical change from solid ice to liquid water or vice versa involves a heat transfer of 80 calories per gramme (cu.cm) of water. If snow is melted by falling on a wing of a temperature above zero, the act of melting itself thus extracts heat from the wing and lowers its temperature, so accelerating the cooling which was taking place during the time in question. The second objection is that, according to the evidence, the melting and refreezing process would not produce two disparate layers, one of clear ice and one above it of powdery snow, but would produce a blending between the upper ice and the lower snow, or as Dr Penman put it, "some degree of adhesion" between the two. That witness said "as it is described to me now" (marked lack of cohesion between ice layer and superimposed snow) "there is obviously a discontinuity in the physical system and one feels there must be discontinuity in the history of the formation."

As to the first objection, we were not invited to consider the point, dealt with in the German report, that the fires which broke out in parts of the wreckage raised the temperature either of the air or of the wing surface sufficiently to melt falling snow. Instead it was suggested to us, as it had been to the German Commission when the reopening of their Inquiry was sought, that the use of fire extinguishing powder on the wing surfaces had the effect of lowering the freezing point of water. The powder, according to this submission, would lie more heavily in the area behind the engines and the difference in quantity, and its consequent effect on the freezing point, accounted for the difference in the conditions found behind the engines and elsewhere on the wings.

In support of this contention Mrs Thain gave evidence of experiments with a sample of the fire extinguishing powder used at Munich airport. The powder contained sodium bicarbonate and although it also contained a water repellent to prevent caking, she found that it went readily into solution in water, even when merely dusted on to a water surface, and that the freezing points of different concentrations of solution were as follows:

Solution 1 in 1000, freezing point	$-0.4°$ C
1 in 100	$-3.0°$ C
1 in 10	below $-3.0°$ C

In addition, Mrs Thain thought that the ice produced by the subsequent re-freezing would be thicker than that produced by the freezing of rainwater. Her reason was that different constituents in the powder would crystallize out of solution at different points, providing, as the temperature dropped, a combination of solid and liquid matter which would be more viscous than the slush of water in the process of freezing and would stand on a slightly sloping wing to a greater depth than would water. However she had made no comparative tests of the viscosity of the solution while in process of freezing compared with that of water at a similar stage. Of what may have happened, she said:

> I visualise that this snow could be intermittent or not heavy continuous snow, and that the snowflakes would fall, and where they came in contact with the powder they would melt. I do not think they would melt sufficiently quickly to enable the snow to run off, to enable the solution to run off the aircraft, and as the temperature fell you would reach a point (because you do not need a very high concentration to lower the freezing point) and somewhere between $0°$ and $-1°$C the majority of the ice would form and the thickness would depend on how much snow you actually trapped in your solution. I do not think you can be specific on exactly how much snow would fall on how much fire extinguisher powder.

When it was suggested that her evidence did not account for the absence of ice beneath the dry snow behind the engines, she said:

> As I read the Report I visualised that Captain Reichel brushed it away from the engine and found there was no ice, and I think one could mistake snow on top of a thick body of slush as complete snow, and that if one did that one would

automatically dismiss the lot as snow, whereas in fact it could have been possibly slush in contact with the engine which he brushed off.

In this connection Mr Jones had suggested that the area behind the engines must have been hot at the time of the crash, so that snow alighting there would melt, that the finding of snow lying here at 2200 h showed that it had in the intervening time passed below freezing point, and that at the moment of freezing the melted snow lying on it must have turned to ice. He could not understand why there was not at least a film of ice behind the engines under the snow.

Captain Thain said that the fire extinguishing powder was projected from a portable apparatus. The apparatus delivered a powerful jet of powder and he saw it used to extinguish a fire under the starboard wing. The fireman started to move away to a house which was burning, but Captain Thain called him back as the fire under the starboard wing had reignited. "I stood there while the fireman put out the fire for the second time ... there is no doubt that he gave the starboard engine a jolly good dousing." He saw him hold the nozzle 6 to 10 feet from the starboard engine, round which he concentrated. He did not see him applying powder to any other part of the starboard side, nor sprinkling the starboard wing as a precautionary measure.

We accept Mrs Thain's evidence as to the lowering of the freezing point of a solution containing the powder, and if there had been any evidence of a distribution of powder over the whole of both wings, this factor would explain some melting and refreezing despite the prevailing temperature. But in our view it does not explain the discontinuity between the rough ice and the superimposed snow, nor does it explain the absence of ice behind the engines. The last-named finding is a puzzling feature in any view of the matter. If any substantial part of the wing was heated by the engines, either this must have cooled very rapidly at a time when no snow was falling, or there was inaccurate or insufficient observation. It is here that we encounter a difficulty inherent in the nature of our inquiry. Our function is to consider Captain Thain's representations and the German report. As already mentioned, Captain Thain's representatives furnished us with a great deal of the material which was before the German Commission, but they were not of course in a position to call Captain Reichel or his assistants, whose evidence is the foundation of this part of the case. This evidence was accepted by the German Commission, of which Captain Reichel was a member, and it would be improper for us to speculate as to whether, for example, the number of spot checks taken was sufficient or whether the investigators had mistaken dense slush for dry snow. We feel at liberty to criticise the reasoning of deductions set out in the German report, where such criticism is relevant, but it is out of the question to criticise evidence of witnesses we have not seen or to speculate on what answers they would have given to questions on details of their observations. These considerations lead us to say that we have insufficient information to enable us to decide whether or not, by reason of the prevailing temperatures, the ice found at 2200 h could not have formed after the accident.

It was further submitted to us that 5 mm must in any event be an over-estimate since the snow equivalent of a maximum depth of only 2 mm of water had fallen during the aircraft's stay at Munich and if the whole of this froze on the wing it could produce an ice layer only fractionally deeper than 2 mm. Furthermore some of the precipitation had been seen running off the wing by witnesses. This is in our view a convincing point: we discuss below how far pre-take-off conditions can have permitted ice formation, and we think it true to say that if the post-accident ice was 5 mm thick it could not have been formed from pre-accident precipitation, and that if it was formed from pre-accident precipitation it could not have been 5 mm thick.

The effect of spray

It emerged during the evidence that during its last run the Elizabethan threw up clouds of spray. Mr Black said "the aircraft went along the runway as if it were a snowplough" and later said "It just looked as though a flying-boat was taking off." He added that the unusually low fuselage of this type of aircraft seemed to be deflecting the spray. If this happened during the last run it would appear that it must have happened on the first two runs. Now, as we shall see, what was lying on the runway was melting snow, slush, or water, and *if* any of this spray landed on the wings and *if* those wings were at the appropriate temperature the wet spray would freeze and adhere. This point does not seem to have emerged until our Inquiry, and there are no experimental or other data to show the trajectory of spray thrown up by the wheels at the relevant speeds, but it seems not impossible that it should reach the wings, except perhaps in the propeller slipstream since the blades might intercept and scatter it. In considering the origin of the ice found at 2200 h therefore there is a possible source other than natural precipitation which in our view merits investigation. It was not investigated before us because Captain Thain through his counsel did not wish to make a point of it.

The effect of the evidence

Having assembled the facts and supporting evidence, we have to see whether they lead, as was submitted, to the conclusion that at the time of the last attempted take-off the wings were free of ice. We see no reason to doubt the eye-witnesses who saw melted snow running off the wings at or shortly after the time of refuelling. This points to the wings at that time being appreciably above zero centigrade. The last person to note this was Captain Thain and no one speaks of this happening after he had embarked, a fact consistent with our view that the wings were then at about zero. The time of Captain Thain's observation is not known but assuming it to be 1500 h, there elapsed an hour between it and the final run, during which 20 minutes was spent in taxi-ing, holding, making two abortive runs, and returning. During that hour the wings could have been at any temperature between say +0.5°C and −0.5°C according to what local variations from screen temperature existed. It is impossible to assert that they must have been thawing or must have been freezing at this time. In one of the documents before us, Mr Jones, starting with the assumption that the wing had cooled from +10°C on arrival to zero in 30 minutes or less, proceeded as follows:

> If the ambient temperature is 0°C and the relative humidity very high (i.e. wet bulb temperature also very close to 0°C) the wing when cooled to 0°C in about half an hour will remain at 0°C and there will be no further melting of snow as it falls and the freezing process, if any, will be very slow indeed. The wing will remain wet with a maximum of 0.5 mm of water depth on it (from the half hour's melting although, of course, some water must have run off) and the subsequent snow will accumulate on the wing, i.e. snow equivalent to about 1 mm of water, corresponding to the snow falling between 1447 h (half an hour after landing) and 1550 h. At 1550 h the snowfall became very light and at 1600 h the temperature in the meteorological enclosure was −0.2°C and the relative humidity had fallen to 91 per cent. Slow freezing was then inevitable *provided the air temperature in the meteorological screen was typical of the air over the whole aerodrome.* When dealing with temperatures to one tenth of a degree C no meteorologist could state positively that this was so. The small margin of temperature therefore makes it impossible to say with certainty that freezing was proceeding. All that seems reasonably certain is that there was snow on the wings and that beneath the snow there was a thin layer of water or ice. Freezing of the water film ... would cause some of the snow above to be held and would lead to a rough surface to the ice. It could be argued, and no one I think could positively contradict it, that the freezing of the wet film containing embedded snow occurred after the accident since the temperature continued to fall after the accident.

That analysis demonstrates both the theoretical uncertainties of the situation and how crucial the prevailing meteorological conditions were to the aircraft's safety. Do the observations of the eye-witnesses during the second visit to the apron help to resolve the uncertainties? We accept, without attaching great importance to, Captain Thain's observation of the small portion of wing he could see from the cockpit. We think the witnesses who looked down from the terminal building, corroborated by the photograph, establish that snow was lying on the wing and not melting; whether there was ice under the snow they could not tell. It was submitted that the above-mentioned photograph showed some water lying under the starboard wing at 1550 h and that this water must have dropped from the wing. We agree that the darkness on the ground, contrasting with the white track-marked snow elsewhere on the ground, is probably water; it lies beneath the inboard section of the wing, largely in the vicinity of the engine, where melting of any falling snow would certainly take place. Whether this water came from this aircraft or from another aircraft which, as the tracks show, had previously stood there, and whether it fell from the trailing edge of the wing or from the vicinity of the engine and ran into the position seen in the photograph, it is quite impossible to determine. We do not think the photograph helps us in this respect. Whether or not there was ice under the snow on the wing, and whether or not, if so, the snow was freezing to it and thickening the layer, depends upon a temperature variation within so small a compass that, in the light of the evidence of Dr Penman and Mr Jones, we are unable to find that the presence of ice is conclusively established, although on balance of probability we think it not unlikely that there was at least a thin film of ice present under the snow.

The German report is in substantial accord with our reasoning as regards the position up to 1500 h. It says "It is true that in the case of the first take-off at 1519 h, at a temperature of approximately 0°, the humidity of the air still amounted to 96%. Cooling by evaporation will thus still have been slight at this juncture. Only a film of ice will have formed on the cooled wing, under the layer of snow observed." However it goes on to say:

> When the last take-off was initiated, however, the air temperature was already
> $-0.2°C$ and the humidity of the air was 91%. Thus there existed conditions which
> point to the fact that by the time the aircraft taxied out for the third take-off and
> during the first phase of take-off, the cooling by evaporation had become so highly
> effective that the wet snowy mixture turned into the rough sheet of ice which was
> observed in the late evening of the same day.

We were pressed to say that the reasoning in the latter passage was erroneous, and Dr Penman was called expressly to deal with cooling by evaporation. We need not however comment upon his calculations since we differ from the view of the German Commission as to what happened after 1500 h because we cannot accept the proposition, underlying their reasoning, that the air temperature at the wing was exactly the same as that at the screen. Moreover we think that factors other than evaporative cooling, such as the temperature of the uplifted petrol, could be at least as powerful in influencing the temperature of the wing.

Steps taken by Captain Thain

It is well known to pilots that ice may form in critical meteorological conditions such as those outlined above, and it is common practice for precautions to be taken in such conditions. See for example Civil Aviation Information Circular No. 150 of 1954, *The Effect of Frost, Ice and Snow on Aircraft Performance. Precautions before Take-off,* which states that snow

> will also be liable to freeze to the surface if the temperature has fallen from just
> above freezing point during the snow. It is never safe to assume that snow, though
> apparently of the dry variety, will be blown off during take-off . . . Particular care is
> necessary when the temperature is in the neighbourhood of freezing point and delay
> occurs between the removal of the snow and take-off.

An example of the steps taken in the prevailing conditions is afforded by the evidence of Captain Wright. On arrival he inspected the wings of his Viscount. Asked whether this was a routine check he agreed but added "in those circumstances of temperature I would say a specific and special check". He climbed on a stand in order to inspect his wings: he found a little water and melted snow and if he had departed then he would not have de-iced the wings. (He had had his de-icing equipment switched on while descending through cloud but thought it had been switched off before landing). When about an hour later he was ready to embark his passengers he inspected again; heavier snow was falling and he found it freezing to the wings. He therefore had the aircraft de-iced. The Viscount took off at 1720 h. Asked why he regarded his first check as special, he said "because of the temperature and the fact of the temperature dropping slowly with the length of time on the ground, getting dark, and temperatures obviously falling, and as a matter of interest with a slight precipitation forming of any frozen kind I would always do that." He had ascertained the temperature from the Meteorological Office. His evidence continued:

Q. Would you regard the temperature being at or about zero as being important in your consideration of de-icing?

A. Yes, obviously so. In relation to my first check on the wings, the amount of pre-cipitation, melted snow, water, was the first consideration. If there had been more present at that temperature then I would have had it de-iced, but there was so little ... it was so very little as to be negligible.

The German Commission had evidence that similar precautionary action was taken by those responsible for the other aircraft taking off from Munich that afternoon. "In the case of all the other aircraft which took off that afternoon snow had, in fact, collected on the wings and in each case it had been removed by personnel of the air transport undertakings." This refers to four aircraft other than the Elizabethan and the Viscount, namely a DC-3 departing at 1408 h, a DC-7C at 1433 h, a Convair at 1544 h and a DC-6B at 1554 h. (The German report appears to be inaccurate in stating that 16 aircraft landed and took off in the course of the afternoon. We were supplied with a memorandum from the Station Superintendent, Munich, showing that after 1300 h (midday GMT) eight aircraft landed and the six mentioned above departed.)

Captain Thain described his action in detail when giving evidence to us. On alighting at the apron he found the ground covered with watery slush and pools of water about an inch deep. Fifteen or twenty minutes later, after completing the flight plan, he met Captain Rayment and discussed the snowfall on the wings: "He told me that he had looked at the wings and in his opinion they did not need sweeping." He agreed with him. Asked why he agreed, he said "I could not think of a better authority than Captain Rayment, a senior captain in BEA. He had gone out and looked at the wing and he came back and told me he had done so." This conversation took place outside the Air Traffic Control Office, in view of the aircraft. Captain Rayment did not say how he had looked at the wings, nor did Captain Thain ask him, but Mr Black was then on top of the wing and there would be a ladder in position for his use. Captain Thain said "I think there is every likelihood that Captain Rayment would have used that ladder."

After the conversation Captain Thain visited the BEA office, signed the ship's papers, and returned to the aircraft, at this stage making the observations of water running from the wing already detailed above. Before he embarked he was approached by the Station Engineer, Mr Black, who asked him if he required the aircraft to be de-iced. Captain Thain did not remember this conversation but accepted Mr Black's evidence which was that in reply to the question Captain Thain said that he did not consider that the aircraft required de-icing at all. After embarking for the first attempted take-off, Captain Thain made no further observation of the wings from the cockpit. He said he had by then satisfied himself of the position. The following are his answers in this respect to his counsel:

Q.   Did you consider at that stage, just before the first take-off, that there was any need whatever to sweep snow off the wings?

A.   It is always a possibility when you have got snow falling.

Q.   But did you consider it necessary to do so?

A.   No, there was insufficient; you have got to have snow to sweep off.

Q.   And you had addressed your mind to it?

A.   Absolutely, and I decided that, with the very very small quantity that was there, it was not necessary to sweep it off.

Q.   And it was actually snowing at the time, was it?

A.   Very lightly.

Later, before the final attempted take-off, Captain Thain again considered the question of snow on the wings. His observations from the cockpit window have been given above. He said he discussed the matter with Captain Rayment, who reported seeing the same conditions on the port wing, and formed the view that there was no necessity for the wings to be either swept or de-iced. By this time, he said, there was virtually no snow falling, only "a flake here or there."

Captain Thain was asked by us whether he had ascertained the ground (screen) temperature. He could not recall having been told this before landing, nor making inquiries about it when visiting the Meteorological Office. His evidence continued:

Q.   Did you think it important to make any inquiries about the temperature?

A.   I think I was aware of the fact that the temperature was approximately zero.

Q.   But in connection with any ice on your aircraft, that was the most critical temperature in the whole thermometer, was it not?

A. Yes, but at the same time I was aware of the fact that the temperature when I arrived at Munich was certainly not below zero, but was above it.

Q. What made you think that?

A. Perhaps by experience ... There was snow falling at the time when we arrived there, and the snow which was falling was wet snow.

Q. You are saying it was wet snow, and therefore you thought the thermometer was above zero?

A. Yes ...

Q. Did you change that view at any time up to the accident?

A. No ...

Q. Did you give any thought to the possibility that it might be going below zero?

A. I did not think it would be going below zero.

Q. Why not?

A. At that particular time it was not far advanced in the afternoon. There was complete cloud cover ... I did not expect the temperature to fall below zero, or to zero.

Captain Thain said he was well aware of the dangers of icing. He was familiar with Circular 150 of 1954 and with a BEA instruction that "Captains should ... make absolutely certain immediately before take-off that the lift and control surfaces of their aircraft are clear of snow." He said that if he had thought that his wings had a temperature below freezing he would have had them de-iced. He agreed that on his second visit to the apron he took no steps to satisfy himself about wing conditions except to observe from the cockpit window, and that inside the cockpit he was not in a position to check the outside temperature (except by radio, which was not used). As to his decision before the last run, he was asked:

Q. Is it fair to say you were going on general impression and general feeling rather than on any observation or any concrete information about temperature?

A. My opinion was based on what I had seen of the snow melting on the wing, and the general feeling that I had.

Q. Yes, of course that was some considerable time earlier, was it not?

A. It was earlier. .... (He said it was about 40 minutes earlier)

Q. You did not think it right, in view of that lapse of time, to ask for specific information about temperatures, or have a look at your wings a bit closer to?

A. No, I was satisfied when I saw that the snow that had been on that wing had been blown away, the aircraft did not have any snow on it.

Shown the photograph referred to above, Captain Thain agreed that it gave the impression of a wing covered with snow outboard of the propeller slipstream but free of snow behind propeller and engine. He agreed that the alteration in colour at the edge of the slipstream could not be accounted for by the band of anti-corrosive paint. Asked what could account for the change, other than the edge of a covering of snow, he could offer no explanation.

Upon the evidence it was submitted on Captain Thain's behalf that he had acted correctly; that every indication which he had pointed to a thaw; and that a captain could not be expected to have moment-to-moment reports of temperature changes. It was further urged upon us that the amount of ice which could have formed between the first and last departures was infinitesimal, and that we must consider the position of a captain with a great deal on his mind. Our opinion on this part of the matter is given later.

RUNWAY CONDITIONS

The runway: direct evidence

The runway at Munich has been lengthened since the accident. It was then 1908 m long (2087 yards). It is 200 feet wide and lies at a compass bearing of 249°. At the material time aircraft were landing and taking off from E-N-E to W-S-W. At its nearest point (about two-thirds of its length, starting from the east) it was approximately 950 m from the terminal building. The surface was concrete, slightly cambered.

The only witness, so far as we are aware, who examined the runway from the ground at the time in question was Herr Bartz. Direct evidence at our Inquiry was given by three pilots, Captain Wright, Captain Merrifield and Captain Thain.

Captain Wright landed his BEA Viscount five minutes before the Elizabethan's last run; in fact the latter was holding at the end of the runway when the Viscount landed. Captain Wright, looking down from an eye-level height about 10 feet from the ground, observed the ruts made by aircraft wheels in the snow or slush covering the first two-thirds of the runway and from them estimated that the depth of cover was one to one and a half inches. The last third was covered in slush with large pools of water. He saw distinct banks at the edge of the runway, as though the snow had been swept earlier. The snow or slush on which he landed had a retarding effect, so that instead of having to brake, as he would have had to do on bare concrete in calm conditions, he had slowed to taxi-ing speed by about the mid-point in the runway and thereafter applied power. While taxi-ing he was asked by control to report on braking action; he applied his brakes and found that "a fair amount of braking could be applied without causing any sliding." When taking off again for London at 1720 h the Viscount again experienced retardation attributable to the slush: it was the practice to time the run with a stopwatch; in ordinary conditions, with the aircraft lightly loaded as this was, the elapsed time to V2 of 106 or 107 knots would be about 23 seconds, but to the best of Captain Wright's recollection it was on this occasion nearer 30 seconds and the aircraft used about two-thirds of the runway before unsticking.

On arrival at London Airport it was found that the nosewheel of the Viscount had on the take-off accumulated a great deal of slush which had turned to ice: the back of the oleo and the steering jacks were covered with a thick coating of ice, estimated as varying between 2 and 5 inches in thickness the steering jacks had disappeared in a ball of ice.

Captain Merrifield had landed another BEA Viscount at Munich two days later, on the 8th February 1958. By then a thaw had set in and from the air the runway appeared clear although the grass areas of the airfield were still snow-covered. About half-way down the runway this witness found a large pool of water 200 to 300 yards long on the northern side of the concrete and extending to the half-way mark. He landed on the south side to avoid the pool.

That part of Captain Thain's evidence which dealt with the runway was as follows:

> When we first touched down the aircraft was inclined to slide on what I thought to be some packed snow, it was slippery. When we got further down the runway we found that the precipitation or snow on the runway was rather different: it was watery, there were some bare patches and the braking effect was quite satisfactory. I reported this to the control tower.

He did not recollect whether a special braking test was carried out, as in Captain Wright's case, but thought they would have braked in the normal way. It was Captain Rayment who operated the brakes. He did not remember his aircraft being retarded by slush as the Viscount had been. He recalled nothing special about the state of the runway. On the first abortive take-off the aircraft stopped and turned approximately 400 m from the end of the runway, and on the second it taxied to the end in order to return to the terminal by the perimeter path. He did not see the banks of snow on either side of the runway spoken of by Captain Wright, nor anything unusual in the state of the runway. When taxi-ing back after the second run he had difficulty in identifying the edge of the perimeter path owing to the snow: there were no tracks of other aircraft to be seen on this path, so far as he recalled.

We may summarise the direct evidence by saying that while Herr Bartz, who examined the runway at about 1535 h both from a vehicle and on foot, gives a picture of a runway covered with slush of a uniform depth and consistency ("a jellified water mass" "approximately 0.5 to 0.75 cm deep"), the two pilots noted a difference in condition between the easterly two-thirds and the westerly one-third, and one of them gave an estimate of the depth of the first part as five times greater than did Herr Bartz (one inch =

2.540 cm). None of these witnesses observed any significant change in the depth of the cover nor did the pilots experience any increased drag at any particular part of the runway. With these considerations in mind we proceed to see what light can be thrown on the matter by the behaviour of the aircraft on its third and final run.

The final run: evidence

In evidence Captain Thain was asked what happened when the needle of the ASI reached 117 knots and answered:

> The needle hovered at that speed; it was flickering. I waited for an increase in speed, but it did not come forward, and after a few seconds at that speed the indication fell off about four or five knots. It was flickering quite a lot. It paused at about 112 knots, and then it fell off again to 105, flickering quite a lot. I thought I felt at that time — well, I certainly felt a lack of acceleration, but the thought passed through my mind about the accuracy of the instrument. I could not make up my mind. The next thing that happened was a cry of alarm from Captain Rayment.

He had no idea how much runway they had used when V1 was attained; he said the needle stayed at 117 knots for "several seconds" and at 112 knots for one or two seconds. While the speed was at 117 knots Captain Rayment was operating the elevator trimmer. He did not look up from the instruments until Captain Rayment's ejaculation: "When he uttered his cry of alarm, things happened very quickly indeed. I looked up, banged the throttles, and almost at the same time he called 'undercarriage up.' " He was "pretty sure" they had not then reached the end of the concrete. It was afterwards ascertained that the nosewheel retracted but the main wheels did not. He was not conscious of the nosewheel retracting, but "I was aware of a strange feeling of believing that I was airborne. We had at that time reached a very smooth passage." At this stage the nose of the aircraft was up, but he had no knowledge of the aircraft's attitude up to the time of his colleague's cry. He himself did not close the throttles.

Further evidence of this attempted take-off is provided by the observations of the two Air Traffic Controllers, Laas and Gentzsch, and by the tracks of the aircraft's wheels. The evidence of the tracks was given in the German report as follows:

> From the point at which the aircraft had broken through the fence its tracks could clearly be discerned, extending back to the runway. The double track of the right side of the undercarriage could be followed back to the runway without difficulty. The left-hand wheel track was interrupted in places. Nowhere was there any nosewheel track to be seen.
>
> From the end of the runway to the fence, in the direction of take-off, the wheel-tracks showed a slight swing to the right. Two days after the accident, when the snow

had melted, the tracks were particularly clearly visible. On the runway, about 50 m short of the end, a skidmark began. It was clearly visible on the concrete and from the strewn sand which the wheels had pushed aside ... This mark showed that at this point all four wheels of the main undercarriage were locked. This skidmark continued for approximately a further 30 m beyond the end of the runway. It then stopped and there remained the impression of the free-running wheels on the grass surface. The track of the right-hand twin wheels was strongly marked; that of the left-hand wheels was fainter and at times interrupted. The track of the right-hand wheels was uniformly clear throughout the whole length (250 m) of the stopway as far as the point at which the aircraft crashed through the fence. The left-hand wheels had at times left the ground. The skidmark and wheel-marks were still clearly visible at the time of the survey of the scene of the accident by the Commission of Inquiry on 30th April, 1958.

The track of the rear wheel was also visible in the snow at the end of the runway: see the earlier statement of the witness Meyer, mentioned above.

The time taken by the run can be gauged with accuracy from the transcript of the tape recording of R/T communication between the aircraft and control, in conjunction with the written statement of Mr G. W. Rodgers, the radio operator of the Elizabethan. He reported "rolling" as the aircraft began to move, this being recorded at 1603.06 h. He heard Captain Rayment call "undercarriage up" and immediately called control but "before I could do more than give the call sign the aircraft crashed." The tape records this message as commencing at 1604.00 h.

Relevant data are also furnished by the Peravia recording of the port engine performance referred to above. On the recording the time scale is 2 minutes to about $\frac{1}{8}$ inch, so that precision as to seconds cannot be obtained, but Mr Kenward, who interpreted it in evidence, thought he could certainly read it accurately to within 5 seconds. Two traces were recorded on the wax cylinder, one showing boost pressure, the other rpm. The boost pressure trace shows that from the opening of the throttle power was applied for approximately 50 seconds. After 20 to 25 seconds the recording fell from about 59 inches to about 54, presumably from throttling back, but after 10 to 15 seconds it returned to 59, staying at this pressure for a further 15 seconds approximately, after which it fell abruptly below static pressure, indicating that the engine was throttled right back, remaining there until it reverted to static pressure, as it would when the engine stopped.

The importance of the record lies in its corroborating Captain Thain's evidence about throttling back during the run, and in its demonstrating that the throttles were cut an appreciable time before the crash. Owing to the coarseness of the scale it is impossible to be precise about the length of this time or to say at what point on or after the runway it occurred, but Mr Kenward thought it clearly corresponded to a point either near the end of the runway or on the overrun area. This, it will be recalled, is the vicinity where the skid-marks appeared, and as Captain Thain neither closed the throttles nor braked, it is not unlikely that the beginning of the skid-mark represents the point where Captain Rayment cut power as well as braked.

The outstanding feature of Captain Thain's evidence is his firm recollection of the airspeed dropping from 117 to 112 and then to 105 knots. The German Commission rightly pointed out that "for subjective reasons, statements by witnesses are subject to error precisely when it is a question of giving an account of what happened in an unnerving catastrophe." Memory plays strange tricks with the victims of shock. We do not doubt, nor did the German Commission, that Captain Thain was giving his honest recollection, but in the circumstances it may not be an accurate recollection. It is certainly a consistent recollection: Captain Thain mentioned the drop in speed when interrogated by Captain Reichel two days after the accident, according to the transcript of the interview furnished to us.

The final run: inferences

It was submitted on Captain Thain's behalf that, accepting his evidence as accurate, the remarkable deceleration of which he spoke, could only be attributed to an increase in either the depth or the density of the slush or both. The German report reconciled the evidence with their view of what happened by attributing the drop in speed to the applying of the brakes by Captain Rayment and by stating that the sequence of Captain Thain's account showed that the deceleration took place towards the end of the runway. We find it difficult to follow this reasoning. Captain Thain's statement appended to the German report does not, as it seems to us, necessarily indicate that there was little lapse of time between the deceleration and the witness looking up and seeing the house in front of him. Moreover, Captain Rayment's cry "Christ, we won't make it" can only indicate that up to then he had been trying to make it, and if that is so he cannot have applied the brakes until at any rate the moment of the cry. Yet this was after the deceleration first to 112 knots and secondly to 105 knots, according to the statement. If Captain Thain's recollection has transposed the order of events, it is unreliable and must be rejected. On the other hand it is honestly and consistently given and is entitled to consideration. If it is correct, we cannot accept braking as the cause of deceleration and must look elsewhere. Moreover even if Captain Thain's recollection has transposed the order of events we do not think braking can have caused the deceleration of which he spoke. The wheels were locked for 90 yards, which at 117 knots would be covered in $1\frac{1}{2}$ seconds. A deceleration of 12 knots in this time is nearly $\frac{1}{2}g$; this would be impossible in the conditions obtaining even if the wings were not lifting at all. Since the aircraft was at full incidence, such a deceleration is doubly impossible as a result of braking alone; the probable loss in the conditions obtaining would be 1 to 2 knots at the most.

The deceleration must have been caused by either a diminution of power or an increase of drag. There has never been any question of the former and the cause of the deceleration must have been drag increase. We have considered possible causes and can find none save an increase in the depth or density of the slush. According to Captain Wright as well as Captain Thain the slush changed in character two-thirds of the way down the runway from being predominantly snow to being predominantly water, i.e. its density increased. This, if the depth remains constant, must increase its drag, and if the increased drag is applied to the main wheels, the nosewheel then being clear of the ground, the resultant pitching moment may return the nose-wheel to the ground. Once that happens, drag increases further since it is applied to six wheels instead of four. It is in this connection that the evidence of Laas assumes significance. Laas's statement says:

> The aircraft gradually built up speed, the nose wheel leaving the ground approxi-mately half-way along the runway, but the aircraft did not become airborne within a period which could be considered as normal. I then observed that the pilot pressed the nose of the aircraft down again, until the nose wheel touched the ground, as if he wanted to gain extra "play" in order to pull the aircraft off the runway, but I could not make out with the naked eye whether the aircraft actually became airborne.

This clearly accords with the possibility outlined above. It is also consistent with Captain Thain's evidence that when the acceleration was checked at 117 knots Captain Rayment was operating the elevator trimmer. The question arises whether it is also consistent with scientific knowledge of the drag effects of slush of varying density.

At the time of the accident very little was known about slush drag, and Dr Schlichting was driven to employ the assumption that this drag could be expressed as an increase in the coefficient of rolling friction, taking arbitrar-ily double or alternatively treble this coefficient for his calculations. Since that time, however, and partly because of this accident, more has become known on this subject, and it is now believed that slush drag increases with speed (as indeed Dr Schlichting suggested) whereas rolling friction decreases with speed as the weight is taken on the wings. One of our number, Professor Collar, has prepared a paper giving tentative conclusions based on data now available. This paper gives an interpretation of Captain Thain's account of the aircraft's run in the light of these tentative conclusions.

This paper shows that there is nothing improbable in Captain Thain's account, particularly of the deceleration. If it is correct, it leads to the con-clusion that, just as Captain Rayment was about to lift his aircraft off the runway his nosewheel came down and by the time he had lifted it off by elevator trim he had lost the minimum speed (110 knots) at which, with a clean wing, he could fly off. This interpretation explains the accident with-out postulating wing icing, although of course it does not disprove icing, and it is because we think this is a feasible explanation of the events that we have already stated that no firm conclusion as to ice can be drawn from the per-formance of the aircraft. But we are far from saying that this is what must have occurred. We are not required to ascertain the causes of the accident,

and if we were so required we should be unable to do so for lack of sufficient evidence. The reconstruction conflicts with the evidence of a number
of persons whom we have not seen, for example Gentzsch, whose statement
about the run is:

> It began rolling normally and built up speed until it was about half-way along the
> runway: the nose wheel left the ground, but touched down again after about 60–
> 100 m. The aircraft continued to roll as far as the very end of the runway …

Also Schombel, whose evidence on wing icing is referred to above, watched
the run, and gave this account:

> During the take-off it struck me that, approximately from half-way along the run-
> way, the pilot was trying, with all his might, to get the aircraft off the ground, and I
> noticed the particularly large angle of attack. The nose wheel was high in the air; the
> emergency tail wheel, according to my observation, was on the ground. This attitude
> became slightly modified during the take-off process. The nose wheel remained off
> the ground.

Bartz's evidence likewise, as to the uniformity of the slush, cannot be reconciled with this reconstruction. We have already indicated that it would be
wrong to criticize persons who have not given oral evidence before us, it
would be equally indefensible to pick out statements favourable to a theory
and reject others. The German Commission saw the witnesses, or such of
them as they wished to see, and rejected the view canvassed above. We have
neither the material nor the wish to say they were wrong. What we can say,
however, is that their conclusion is not reconcilable with Captain Thain's
evidence. We have already given our views on the suggestion that the deceleration was caused by braking: a further point is that the German
Commission's reconstruction of the run takes the aircraft to 117 knots at
between 1400 and 1600 m, whereas the deceleration by braking, as shown
by the skid-mark, commenced at 1850 m. If the aircraft reached 117 knots
by 1600 m it should have reached a higher speed by 1850 m unless indeed
the slush drag was such as to render 117 knots the maximum obtainable
speed. Professor Schlichting's curve 6 in his technical report [not given here]
shows the aircraft reaching 117 knots at 1550 m, 120 knots at 1650 m, and
123 knots at 1800 m.

We may leave this part of the case by saying that the only evidence of
deceleration during the run (apart from the braking at the end of the runway) is that of Captain Thain. We have no reason to reject it, and it is not
inconsistent with much of the other evidence, including the time factor. It
is however inconsistent with some of the evidence, as mentioned above,
and if it is unreliable, its unreliability is accounted for, without the slightest
criticism of Captain Thain, by the effect of shock. If one discards this evidence, the aircraft attained V2 but failed to unstick owing to icing, or the
slush was of sufficient depth to prevent V2 being attained, or of course

there may be a combination of the two factors. Therefore having considered fully Captain Thain's representations concerning the final run we are unable to make any useful deduction as to either the presence of ice or the degree of slush drag.

Steps taken by Captain Thain

Captain Thain's description of the runway conditions has been recorded. He did not regard it as in any way unusual or unfit for use. However, he had had no great experience of such conditions in the past; asked whether he had encountered similar conditions before, he said "I suppose I have at one time or another ... My particular experience was probably less than average because I have been, since joining BEA, on flights operated down to the Mediterranean." Before the outward journey to Belgrade he had not been to Munich for "five years, maybe three." Prior to the final run, the Elizabethan had twice that afternoon taxied over the western end of the runway, once on landing and once after the second run, and after the first run it had passed the half-way mark. We asked Captain Thain some questions regarding his observations on these occasions:

Q. Did it occur to you on any of those three occasions when you were at the western end of the runway that in the conditions it was a matter of some importance to know what the runway was like throughout the whole of its length?

A. Yes.

Q. Did that lead you to take any special precautions by way of looking or gauging what the position was?

A. Well, I was not concerned at all by the deposit of slush on the runway.

Q. Why not?

A. It did not present a problem.

Q. Would you like to expand that answer?

A. Well, it just did not present a problem.

Q. You felt just as happy with it as you would have with a dry concrete runway?

A. I did not say that, but it did not strike me as a problem for taking off.

Q. Did it occur to you there might be differences in the depth of the snow or water on it?

A. No, it did not.

After Captain Thain had said that a captain accepted responsibility for the safety of his aircraft, the evidence continued:

Q. Including considering the problem of whether the runway surface is not safe enough to take off on?

A. I think that, including that, yes.

Q. You accept that as something which, in appropriate circumstances, he should address his mind to?

A. Yes.

Q. Have you yourself ever gone out on foot or in a vehicle to inspect a runway surface before taking off over it?

A. I cannot recollect having done that, no.

Q. Have you heard of it being done by other captains?

A. In isolated circumstances, yes.

Q. Does it come to you as a surprising statement that other captains may do that in some circumstances?

A. I think you would have to be awfully concerned about the state of the runway.

Q. Before you go and look at it yourself?

A. Yes, for this reason, that there must be a group of airport staff whose job it is to service and look after the airfield, and they cannot just sit back and do nothing about it; one expects it to be up to a certain standard.

Captain Thain said that he did discuss with Captain Rayment before the last run one aspect of taking off on slush, namely whether if throttling back to deal with boost surging produced a swing, it could be corrected by steering the nosewheel without slipping. No other aspect of runway conditions was discussed, and he was quite satisfied. He did not think the slush would retard the aircraft "to any large extent", nor did Captain Rayment mention such retardation. He had not noticed the retardation on landing, as Captain Wright had; he thought that although he was not at the controls he would have noticed it if it had happened.

There was no evidence that the captain of any other aircraft departing from Munich that afternoon had experienced any difficulty with the runway or had thought it right to make a personal inspection of its surface or to take any other special steps. Captain Wright said that the conditions, though not unprecedented, were not often encountered and with his lightly loaded Viscount he did not consider it necessary to inspect the runway, as he had done on some occasions.

THE FIRST TWO ATTEMPTS TO TAKE OFF

There is little that we need add to the recital of the facts already set out above, as a preliminary to considering the third question put to us. The Peravia record shows that at the first attempt power was applied to the port engine for about 32 seconds and that it took about 14 seconds to reach full power. On the second attempt it took about 25 seconds to reach full power, corroborating Captain Thain's statement that the throttles were opened more slowly; power was applied for about 32 seconds. On both these occasions the boost is recorded as reaching somewhere between 59 and 60 inches. Mr Black was so familiar with boost surging at Munich that on seeing the aircraft returning to the tarmac, he felt sure it had been encountered.

THE THREE QUESTIONS

Having set out the relevant facts, and our views on Captain Thain's representations upon disputed questions of fact, we are now in a position to deal with the three questions upon which we are required to give our opinion. The first is whether the captain took sufficient steps to satisfy himself that the wings of the aircraft were free from ice and snow. In forming our views on this question, we have to bear in mind that our task is to consider the steps which Captain Thain took up to the third and last attempted take-off. Had the relevant time been that of the first take-off the considerations would have been different. The aircraft first asked for taxi clearance at 1519 h, and at that time Captain Thain had had recent experience of conditions outside the cockpit. He had not ascertained the recorded temperature, nor himself inspected the upper surface of the wings, but he had had the report, made some 40 minutes earlier, from Captain Rayment, and he himself had seen the water running from the trailing edge. It may be that at that stage his decision not to have the wings swept or de-iced was correct, the decision accorded with Mr Black's views, and Mr Black had had the best opportunity to judge, having been upon the wings throughout refuelling. But the time we have to consider is not 1519 hours but 1556 hours, when the Elizabethan reported ready to taxi for the last time. It was then at least 40 minutes and probably longer since Captain Thain had watched the thawed snow falling from the wing, and 78 minutes since refuelling had ceased and anyone had inspected the whole upper surface of the wings. It was also 56 minutes since the screen temperature had reached zero and within 4 minutes of the time when the reading was taken as $-0.2°C$. Since the previous decision the aircraft had taxied to one end of the runway, made two runs, and taxied back from the other end and, experiencing whatever temperature variations there might be in its path and having any evaporative cooling accelerated by the forced draught generated by its speed.

In these circumstances we have no doubt that Captain Thain ought to have made a personal inspection of the wings before reaffirming the decision neither to sweep nor to de-ice. Inspection means obtaining a ladder or stand and examining the top of the wings, not looking at the small portion visible from the cockpit. It is clear from the answers reproduced above that Captain Thain's omission to take this or any other positive step originated in his ignorance of the ambient temperature, and his failure to acquaint himself with the available information on this subject was, in our view, a serious error. We find that he departed with some snow on the wings, in breach of the BEA instructions; the factors making it impossible for us to say, positively, on the evidence before us whether there was ice under the snow, are factors emphasising the necessity for practical examination at the time. Captain Thain had then far less information than we have, and the greater the doubt the greater the necessity for precautions. The fact that he was unfamiliar with Munich, and had had no great experience of weather of the kind in question should also have led him to act with caution. We think it true to say that he had a great deal on his mind, in that he had been unexpectedly confronted with the boost surging; this is a matter which may help to explain his actions, but it cannot affect our finding that to the first question we must return a negative answer.

In approaching the second question, namely whether Captain Thain took sufficient steps to ascertain whether or not in the conditions prevailing at the time the runway was fit for use, we recognise that for a captain to make a personal inspection of a runway is an extreme and infrequent action. Captain Thain found the runway being used without comment by arriving and departing aircraft, and regarded as safe by the airport authorities; these matters, as he accepts, did not absolve him from responsibility, but he was entitled to have regard to them. The duty upon him was perhaps higher than in the case of captains of some other aircraft using the runway that afternoon because of his long take-off run, lengthened by the necessity to correct the boost fluctuation; but, as he said in evidence, Munich was not a marginal airport, and he would have had no reason to suspect that he had not enough runway unless he had possessed a knowledge of the drag effects of slush which was not then available. Furthermore, had he made an inspection and found the conditions to be as described by Bartz he would have rightly accepted the runway as safe, whereas had he noted from the ground, as he had from his cockpit, a change in the character of the slush at the two-thirds point along the runway, he could not be expected, in the then prevailing state of knowledge of slush-effects, to have appreciated its significance. We find therefore that he did take sufficient steps to ascertain whether in the prevailing conditions the runway was fit for use.

The third question is whether Captain Thain took sufficient steps to ascertain the cause of the difficulties encountered on the first two attempts to take off before making a third attempt. This question presents no difficulty. We have no doubt that Captain Thain acted correctly in consulting with the Station Engineer and that the trouble was correctly diagnosed. We think he acted properly in deciding to make the third attempt.

CONCLUSION

In conclusion we think it right to emphasise that while we are unable, for the reasons given, to reach a firm finding upon Captain Thain's representations that there was no ice on the wings during the final run and that the accident was due solely to slush drag, this uncertainty does not affect our answers to the questions posed in our terms of reference. Had Captain Thain established that there was no wing icing, our answer to the first question would still have been "no", and had he established slush drag as the sole cause of the aircraft's behaviour, our answer to the second question would still have been "yes".

We therefore have to report that we have given full consideration to the representations made to us by and on behalf of Captain Thain with regard to the accident to the Elizabethan aircraft G-ALZU at Munich on 6th February 1958, that we have had regard to the report of the German Commission of Inquiry into the said accident, including that Commission's reasons for refusing to reopen their inquiry, and that in our opinion Captain Thain did not take sufficient steps to satisfy himself that the wings of the aircraft were free from ice and snow, but that in our opinion he did take sufficient steps to ascertain whether or not in the conditions prevailing at the time the runway was fit for use and did take sufficient steps to ascertain the cause of the difficulties encountered on the first two attempts to take off before making a third attempt.

E. S. FAY
R. P. WIGLEY
A. R. COLLAR
18 August 1960

PART III

∞∞QQ∞∞

EXTRACT FROM THE REPORT OF THE SECOND REVIEW TO CONSIDER WHETHER BLAME IS TO BE IMPUTED TO CAPTAIN THAIN

INTRODUCTION

On 8th April 1968 we were appointed by the President of the Board of Trade to conduct an Inquiry in private with the following terms of reference:

> To consider in private such evidence as may be presented with regard to the accident to BEA Elizabethan G-ALZU at Munich on 6th February 1958, being evidence which was not considered by them when they reported to the Minister of Aviation on 18th August 1960 and having regard to such evidence, to the matters considered by them in that Report, to the Report of the German Federal Office of Aviation relating to the re-opened Inquiry into the said accident and to the Memorandum of the Royal Aircraft Establishment at Farnborough on the Application of the Results of Slush Drag Tests, to report to the Board of Trade whether, in their opinion, blame for the accident is to be imputed to Captain Thain.

THE QUESTION OF BLAME

We are required to report whether in our opinion blame for the accident is to be imputed to Captain Thain. Blame implies fault plus causation. In the material respects we have to consider whether Captain Thain was at fault and if so whether that fault caused or contributed to the accident. We have examined his behaviour as commander in permitting Captain Rayment to fly the aircraft and during the final run. We have found fault in his breach of the BEA seating rule, and we have criticised his inaction when monitoring the Air Speed Indicator. We find affirmatively that the former did not adversely affect the flying of the aircraft and had no connection with the accident. We find that no causal connection is established between the latter and the accident. In these respects therefore no blame attaches to Captain Thain for the accident.

There remain the questions of wing icing and runway slush. Whether Captain Thain was at fault in these respects formed two of the three specific questions that were the subject of our 1960 Inquiry. We then found him to be at fault in regard to icing and not at fault as regards slush. We dealt at length with the steps taken by Captain Thain as regards wing icing in our 1960 report. We similarly dealt with his actions as regards the runway. At our present Inquiry no further evidence was given as regards Captain Thain's consideration of runway slush and no suggestion was made that our previous findings needed re-examination. On the other hand his action as to wing icing was reconsidered in evidence and Mr May submitted that we should revise our view in this matter.

Responsibility for wing icing

We can summarise the relevant evidence as follows:

1.   Article 17(2) of the Air Navigation Order 1954 (in force at the date of the accident) provided: "Before the aircraft flies or attempts to fly the person in command of the aircraft shall satisfy himself . . . (vi) . . . that the wings and control surfaces are free from ice and hoar frost." Vol. 5 of BEA's Flying Staff Standing Instructions required that captains should make absolutely certain immediately before take-off that the lift and control surfaces of their aircraft were clear of snow. A Ministry circular (No. 150/1954), *The Effect of Frost, Ice and Snow on Aircraft Performance, Precautions before Take-off* reminded those concerned that snow

> will also be liable to freeze to the surface if the temperature has fallen from just above freezing point during the snow. It is, therefore, never safe to assume that snow, though apparently of the dry variety, will be blown off during take-off. Snow should therefore be completely removed before taxi-ing out to take-off, and a careful inspection made to ensure that no underlying deposit of ice remains. Such under-lying deposits will necessitate the use of de-icing fluid. Particular care is necessary when the temperature is in the neighbourhood of freezing point and delay occurs between the removal of the snow and take-off. It is important in such conditions to remove any fresh snow which has fallen since the previous removal.

Captain Thain was familiar with these provisions.

2.   Before the first departure from the apron at 1519 h Captain Thain from his own observations and in conjunction with Captain Rayment and the Station Engineer, Mr Black, assessed the situation and decided not to have the wings swept or de-iced.

3.   Before the second and last departure at 1556 h Captain Thain's only additional action was to study the small portion of the wing surface which he could see from the flight deck and to discuss what he saw with Captain Rayment.

4.   The information upon which Captain Thain acted was (i) his observation from the ground of water running from the wing and of the wings bearing "a thin film of partially melted snow"; (ii) information from Mr Black, who had found the wings clean when he had been upon them for refuelling up to about 1440 h; (iii) information from Captain Rayment, who told him that he had looked at the wings and that in his opinion they did not need sweeping; (iv) his observation of the snowfall, which he said had virtually ceased by the time of the second departure; and (v) his opinion that the temperature was above zero. His evidence on temperature is given in the 1960 report. He had assessed the temperature by observation and experience and could not recall having ascertained the ground temperature although he had visited the Met. Office.

The screen temperature had been zero at 1500 h and −0.2°C at 1600 h. The aircraft had landed at 1417 h, cleared to taxi on the first departure at

1519 h, returned to the apron at 1539 h and made its final departure at
1556 h. It had been standing and taxi-ing in falling snow and had made
two abortive runs in slush. We thought in 1960 that in these circumstances
there was a clear duty on the captain to make sure that the wings were free
of both ice and snow and that he had not done so.

At the present Inquiry Captain Kelly, who had been an Ambassador pilot
when with BEA, expressed the view that he would not himself have had the
wings swept or de-iced. He thought that if the captain were satisfied at the
time of the first departure, no further investigation of the situation was
needed in the circumstances before the second departure. He would know
from the temperature gauge in the cockpit that there had been no sudden
fall in temperature. He said that if the gauge "was still at the same temperature as it was in the first place, and there was no obvious change of
circumstances outside, there was no reason to reverse the decision made 40
minutes earlier." Freezing at or fractionally below zero would be an
extremely slow process.

The air temperature gauge is not regarded as a particularly accurate
instrument. Indeed Captain Thain did not rely on it: he was asked (in 1960)
"Were you in a position inside the cockpit to check the outside temperature?" and answered "Not accurately, no." Captain Kelly did not support
Captain Thain's action in assessing temperature by observation of the melting snow, but we understood him to be saying that if Captain Thain had had
reasonably accurate temperature information it should have made no difference to his action.

We are unable to accept this as an accurate interpretation of the duty of
a captain in command either under the Air Navigation Orders and BEA's
rules, or in common sense. Once the temperature approaches zero a captain
must assume that it may drop below zero. Indeed he ought to assume that it
may already be below zero at parts of the taxiway and runway: local variation
in temperature of several tenths of a degree are not uncommon. We remain
of the view that Captain Thain ought to have appreciated the critical nature
of the prevailing air temperature and ought to have made, or caused to be
made, an inspection of the whole of the wing surfaces followed by any necessary action to deal with what was found. At the end of the day we cannot
say whether ice would have been found nor whether the deposit which we
are satisfied would have been found would have frozen to the wing during
taxi-ing and the take-off run. These uncertainties emphasise the imperative
nature of the duty to inspect and take action. These are safety precautions
and, as with all safety precautions, a margin for error must be allowed.

Fault therefore we reaffirm. Was there blame? We have said that ice may
possibly have contributed to the accident but that we think it unlikely to
have done so. In these circumstances we cannot and do not find blame. It
would of course be wrong to assert that blame exists unless its existence is
proved. Our finding that icing was unlikely to have been a contributory
cause of the accident means that as a consequence we find that the fault with

regard to inspection is unlikely to have been a cause of the accident. We therefore do not find that blame in this respect for the accident is to be imputed to Captain Thain.

Responsibility for runway slush

Captain Thain had not noticed any retardation during the landing by Captain Rayment, nor had it occurred to him that the slush on the runway presented any problem. He did not think it would retard the aircraft to any large extent. He accepted that his responsibility for the safety of his aircraft involved considering, in appropriate circumstances, whether the runway surface was safe for take-off. He had never himself, so far as he could recollect, made a personal inspection of a runway on foot or in a vehicle, but he knew that pilots had done this on isolated occasions. Before he took such a step, he said, he "would have to be awfully concerned about the state of the runway . . . for this reason, that there must be a group of airport staff whose job it is to service and look after the airfield   one expects it to be up to a certain standard."

Captain Thain did in fact address his mind to one aspect of taking off in slush. This was the question whether, if throttling back to deal with boost surging produced a swing, it would be corrected by steering the nosewheel without slipping. Should he have thought of excessive retardation, or uneven retardation? We must bear in mind the date of the accident. In 1958 no experimental investigation of the effect of slush drag had been conducted and the theoretical calculations of drag then accepted were found in the light of subsequently gathered experimental data to be incorrect. Our present extensive knowledge of these matters is derived almost wholly from subsequent tests—tests partly occasioned by this accident. But in 1958 there was no general appreciation by pilots of the magnitude of the drag due to slush of the depths with which we are concerned in this case.

Captain Thain was entitled to have regard to the fact that the runway was being used without comment by other aircraft and appeared to be regarded as safe by the airport authorities. Captain Wright, who told us in 1960 that he had sometimes inspected runways before take-off, did not think inspection necessary at Munich at 1720 h, although he had experienced retardation on landing at 1555 h. Captain Thain faced a longer take-off run than Captain Wright with his lightly loaded Viscount but, as the former said, Munich was not a marginal airport. We reaffirm the view we reached in 1960 that Captain Thain would have had no reason to suspect that he had not enough runway unless he had possessed a knowledge of the drag effects of slush which was not then available. We do not think he was at fault in failing to investigate the runway personally or in failing in any other way to recognise and deal with the problem which we now know was presented by the presence of slush on the runway.

CONCLUSION

We can summarise our conclusions as follows:

1   The cause of the accident was slush on the runway.
2   It is possible but unlikely that wing icing was a contributory cause.
3   Captain Thain was not at fault with regard to runway slush.
4   Captain Thain was at fault with regard to wing icing, but because wing icing is unlikely to have been a contributory cause of the accident, blame for the accident cannot in this respect be imputed to him.
5   Captain Thain was at fault in permitting Captain Rayment to occupy the Captain's seat, but this played no part in causing the accident.

In accordance with our terms of reference we therefore report that in our opinion blame for the accident is not to be imputed to Captain Thain.

S. WIGNALL *Secretary*   E. S. FAY
18th March 1969   A. R. COLLAR
                                                          J. R. JEFFREY

APPENDIX: LIST OF THOSE WHO DIED IN THE CRASH OR LATER IN HOSPITAL

Crew of the aircraft

Captain K. G. Rayment   co-pilot
W. T. Cable   steward

Manchester United football players

Geoff Bent   reserve left back
Roger Byrne   captain and left back
Eddie Colman   right half
Duncan Edwards   left half
Mark Jones   centre half
David Pegg   outside left
Tommy Taylor   centre forward
Billy Wheland   inside right

Manchester United officials

Walter Crickmer   secretary
Tom Curry   trainer
Bert Whalley   team coach

Journalists

Alf Clarke   *Manchester Evening Chronicle*
Don Davies   *Manchester Guardian*
George Follows   *Daily Herald*
Tom Jackson   *Manchester Evening News*
Archie Ledbrooke   *Daily Mirror*
Henry Rose   *Daily Express*
Frank Swift   *News of the World*
Eric Thompson   *Daily Mail*

Other passengers

B. P. Miklos   Yugoslav travel agent
Willie Santinoff   United supporter

INDEX

The Loss of the Titanic, 1912

Scott, F., greaser 56, 115
searchlights 9–10, 88, 98, 110
second class passengers 11, 18, 38–9, 94
  decks and accommodation 21, 22, 23,
    24, 26
  into boats 66
  saved 68, 104, 105
Ship's Rules 40
ship's side doors 29
Smith, Edward Charles, Master 38, 62,
    67, 96
  action that should have been taken
    about the ice by 49–50
  received ice message 44, 46, 48
speed 9, 10, 48–9, 50, 52, 97, 98
  recommendations on 109, 110
  of steamers 88
stewards 24, 25, 27, 61, 62
Stewart, G.F., chief officer of *Californian*
    74, 112, 124, 126
Stone, H., second officer of *Californian*
    72–5, 112, 124, 129, 131, 133, 134,
    135, 136
structure of ship 27–30; *see also* design
    and construction
sub-division *see* watertight sub-division
submarine signalling 19, 34–5
super-refraction theory 131
Symons, look-out 48

telephones 19, 34
third class passengers 11, 18, 38–9, 94
  decks and accommodation 21, 22, 23,
    24, 26
  foreigners 39, 66, 105
  into boats 66–7
  saved 69, 104, 105
time of foundering 11, 106, 123
time of year 9, 40, 41, 43, 96
tracks (lane routes), across Atlantic 9, 40,
    41–2, 49, 79, 88, 96, 97

"turning point" 41, 42

"United States Pilot (East Coast)" 42

Victualling Department 25, 38, 94
  saved 69, 105
Virginian 67, 74, 101, 102, 103

water ballast 28, 32, 58
watertight bulkheads 12, 15–17, 23, 26,
    27–8, 92–3
  Board of Trade Rules 78, 85, 87, 90,
    91, 92–3
  flooded 53, 55–6, 57
  recommendations 107–8
watertight compartments 17–19, 24, 27,
    28, 55–6
  Board of Trade Rules 78–9, 82, 83,
    85, 92
  recommendations 108
watertight decks 57–8
watertight doors 16–17, 26, 28–9, 35
  after collision 50, 53, 54, 57, 58–9, 99
  drill 109
watertight sub-division 28, 56, 57–9,
    92–3, 107–8
weather conditions (calm) 47, 49, 101
White Star Line 13–14, 40, 123
Wilde, H.F., Chief Officer 38, 46, 62
wireless telegraphy 9, 19, 34, 79–80, 83,
    85, 95–6
  on the *Californian* 121
  operators 9, 95, 109
  recommendations 109, 110
  rooms 19
women 38
  into boats 61, 62, 63, 64, 65, 101
  saved 68–9
wreckage 68, 74, 124–5

Ypiranga 100, 102

INDEX

R.101: the Airship Disaster, 1930

The Munich Air Crash, 1958